VIOLENCE GOES TO COLLEGE

VIOLENCE GOES TO COLLEGE

The Authoritative Guide to Prevention and Intervention

By

JOHN NICOLETTI, Ph.D.

Nicoletti-Flater Associates
Lakewood, Colorado

SALLY SPENCER-THOMAS, Psy.D.

Health Psychologist, Regis University
Denver, Colorado

CHRISTOPHER BOLLINGER, M.S.

Director of Residence Life, Heidelberg College
Tiffin, Ohio

With a Foreword by
Special Agent Elizabeth Prial, FBI

Charles C Thomas
P U B L I S H E R • L T D.
SPRINGFIELD • ILLINOIS • U.S.A.

Published and Distributed Throughout the World by

CHARLES C THOMAS • PUBLISHER, LTD.
2600 South First Street
Springfield, Illinois 62794-9265

ISBN 0-398-07190-X (hard)
ISBN 0-398-07191-8 (paper)

Library of Congress Catalog Card Number: 2001027140

With THOMAS BOOKS *careful attention is given to all details of manufacturing
and design. It is the Publisher's desire to present books that are satisfactory as to their
physical qualities and artistic possibilities and appropriate for their particular use.*
THOMAS BOOKS *will be true to those laws of quality that assure a good name
and good will.*

Printed in the United States of America
SM-R-3

Library of Congress Cataloging-in-Publication Data

Nicoletti, John.
 Violence goes to college : the authoritative guide to prevention / by
John Nicoletti, Sally Spencer-Thomas, Christopher Bollinger ; with a fore-
word by Elizabeth Prial.
  p.   cm.
 Includes bibliographical references (p. 247) and index.
 ISBN 0-398-07190-X -- ISBN 0-398-07191-8 (pbk.)
 1. Campus violence--United States--Prevention--Handbooks, manuals,
etc. 2. Universities and colleges--United States-- Safety measures--
Handbooks, manuals,etc. 3. Universities and colleges--Security measures-
-United States--Handbooks, manuals, etc. 4. Conflict management--United
States--Handbooks, manuals,etc. I. Spencer-Thomas, Sally. II. Bollinger,
Christopher. III. Title.

LB2345 .N53 2001
378.1'9782--dc21   2001027140

This book is dedicated to
Tanner Johnson Thomas
Nicholas Rex Thomas
Theresa Tafoya
Richard Tafoya
May they someday have violence-free college experiences.

FOREWORD

VIOLENCE GOES TO COLLEGE is an invaluable resource for understanding, preventing, and providing solutions to the growing problem of violence on college campuses. This timely work provides a comprehensive approach to addressing the ever-increasing problem facing our youth today. The authors combine their expertise in violence prevention and law enforcement techniques to create a how-to manual equally applicable to both professional and lay readers.

The conceptualization of violence as a virus with various causes, strains, and manifestations lends itself to effective analogies to demonstrate our vulnerabilities as well as our ability to fight the disease that is reaching near-epidemic proportions. Examples are fact-based, contemporaneous, and illustrative of the wide range of violence that routinely takes place on college campuses. From mass murders, hate crimes, riots, and date rape to hazing among both fraternities and athletes, this book demonstrates the need for different approaches and responses for the various types of violence in terms of prevention, intervention, and dealing with the aftermath.

The researchers provide a background for understanding the origins and causes of violence, as well as catalysts such as alcohol, peer acceptance, and individual versus group motivations. The book additionally addresses barriers to intervention such as secrecy and lack of reporting both at the student and administrative levels.

This prevention and solution-oriented guide offers realistic answers for all those concerned with the effective resolution to violence on college campuses. "Action beats reaction" is a common phrase among law enforcement professionals that is fittingly applied here. The authors detail specific strategies beginning with physical environmental factors, promotion of alternatives to violence, implementation and composition of a Threat and Violence Assessment Team (TVAT), and compilation of a crime report database. The book further emphasizes policy development complete with sample policy statements and reporting forms specific to different strains of violence. In addition, the authors describe enforcing consequences appropriate to the infraction and managing the aftermath to maximize healing on an individual and community basis.

While *Violence Goes to College* is theory-based and research-driven, it presents real answers to real issues. The authors avoid hype and sensationalism as they address urban legends and debunk faulty advice to potential victims. This compelling book demonstrates that although college campuses are not immune to violence, awareness and planning are the antibody.

ELIZABETH M. PRIAL, PSY.D.
Special Agent
Federal Bureau of Investigation

PREFACE

OVER THE COURSE of the last few decades, violence has infected new areas of society such as the workplace, schools, and religious sanctuaries. As violence prevention experts, we have been observing and intervening as the violence spreads to new locations. College campuses are not immune.

- According to a *Chronicle of Education* survey, universities reported 951 arrests for weapons-law violations in 1997, a 4.4 percent increase from the previous year (August 1999, *Student Affairs Today*).
- In August 1999, Florida A&M University cancelled classes after a homemade bomb exploded in a bathroom on campus. The speculated motive was racial hatred.
- In 1999, The Harvard Injury Research and Control Center reported that 3.5 percent of 15,000 college students surveyed across the country said they had a gun at school; this figure rose to 7 percent among students who "binge drank." Binge drinking is defined as five or more drinks in one sitting. Even more disturbing, this figure rose to over 12 percent of students who said they needed a drink "first thing in the morning."
- In March 1999, a riot broke out in East Lansing, Michigan, after Michigan State University's basketball team lost to Duke University. During the outbreak, students and others burned police cars and caused more than a half million dollars in damage.
- According to the National Center for Victims of Crime in Virginia and the American Medical Association, one in every four women is raped or sexually assaulted during their collegiate experience.

When violence occurs on a college or university campus, the entire community is impacted. The ripple effects of one rape, one hate crime, or one riot spread rapidly and significantly contaminate the learning environment. Concentration and creative thought are stifled when fear is overwhelming. In order to deal with violence, campuses must not only treat the symptoms of the virus but they must also inoculate and prevent further infection.

Violence Goes to College is the first violence prevention and intervention guide for college communities designed to prepare concerned individuals with up-to-date information and strategies to address campus violence. This user-friendly resource will provide busy college personnel, students, and parents with directed, well-researched strategies to prepare for the possibility of tragedy *before* it strikes. Collectively, we bring decades of experience in both higher education and violence prevention to the task of developing these effective tactics. In addition to authoring three books on violence prevention, our violence experience includes consulting with the FBI and serving on national prevention panels. *Violence Goes to College* offers hope that somewhere between Pollyanna and paranoia, campuses can find a healthy balance between reasonable protection and personal freedom.

The book is organized into three sections: The first addresses broad campus violence concerns and violence conceptualization. The second explores general prevention strategies. The third looks more in depth at particular forms of campus violence including sexual assault, rioting, hate crimes, hazing, homicide, non-sexual assault, arson and bombing.

ACKNOWLEDGMENTS

OUR THANKS TO Anna Reishus for her help in organizing the bibliography; Regis University's Dayton Memorial Library for their research assistance; Susan Richardson and Jerene Anderson for their mentoring and support; Diane Cooper for her helpful feedback and encouragement; Clark Newman, Alice Reich, Frank Lavrisha, Rebecca Flintoft, and David McInally for their review of the manuscript; NASPA Task Force on Violence for their insights; the BACCHUS & GAMMA Peer Education Network for shared aims; the Clery Family and Security on Campus, Inc. for their assistance in the research process, their relentless commitment to preventing campus violence, and their permission to share the story of their daughter Jeanne; Eileen Stevens and Hank Nuwer for their review of the manuscript and permission to share the story of Chuck; Darlene and Robert Krueger and their lawyer Brad Henry for their suggestions and permission to share the story of Scott; and Randy Thomas and Lottie Flater, for their patience and love.

NOTE TO THE READER

ALL THE INFORMATION provided herein is general in nature and designed to serve as a guide to understanding. These materials are not to be construed as the rendering of legal or management advice. If the reader has a specific need or problem, the services of a competent professional should be sought to address the particular situation.

The foreword is the opinion of Dr. Prial and does not constitute an endorsement by the FBI.

For more information or consultation, contact Nicoletti-Flater Associates at:

Nicoletti-Flater Associates
3900 South Wadsworth Boulevard, Suite 480
Lakewood, CO 80433
303-989-1617
www.n-fa.com

CONTENTS

Part II

**DEVELOPING ANTIBODIES: GENERAL PREVENTION
STRATEGIES FOR THE COLLEGE COMMUNITY**

VIOLENCE GOES TO COLLEGE

Part I

LEAVING "IT-WILL-NEVER-HAPPEN-HERE": HELPING COLLEGE COMMUNITIES ACKNOWLEDGE VIOLENCE POTENTIAL WITHOUT CREATING PANIC

Chapter 1

SEEING VIOLENCE AS A VIRUS

"INEVER THOUGHT it would happen here." We hear this statement repeatedly in the aftermath of tragic incidents. Most people want to believe that they are immune from harm, and that their learning and working environments are safe havens. When violence occurs, they often feel blindsided, but in retrospect they can usually identify subtle and sometimes not-so-subtle warning signs.

In order to understand the current state of campus violence, one must look to two sources of information–the factual and the theoretical. We must start by taking a look at what we know. This can be accomplished both by looking at our history and by looking at what current research is telling us. When we examine the impact high-profile cases have had on the campus culture over the past several decades, we can learn a great deal. While these cases may have only directly impacted a small number of individuals, their legacy continues to influence how many colleges think about violence. So, the first step is to look at our history to understand where we are today. Then we can appraise what credible sources are telling us about the prevalence and trends of violence on our campuses.

The second step is to develop a conceptualization that is relevant and useful to college campuses. We have found that a particularly effective conceptualization is achieved by thinking about violence as a virus. By using this analogy, we can examine the many different "strains" of violence hosted on college campuses.

WHAT CAN WE LEARN FROM CAMPUS VIOLENCE HISTORY?

The following list of high-profile cases of college violence is not intended to be an exhaustive account of all devastating tragedies college communities have faced. Rather, certain cases were selected to illustrate how various forms of violence can forever change campus culture.

High-Profile Cases: History and Impact

- **July 13-14, 1966: Chicago Massacre South Chicago Community Hospital–residences for student nurses in training Chicago, Illinois**

On this July night, Richard Speck brutally murdered–stabbed, strangled and sexually assaulted—eight nursing students in their Chicago townhouse. The 24-year-old sailor broke into the townhouse through a mesh screen door armed with a pistol and a knife. Initially he stated that his motive was robbery, but after taking his victims' money, he proceeded to tie up the women. Over the next several hours he murdered each victim, except one who hid terrified under a bed. She would later be a crucial witness, leading to his eventual capture and conviction. This "crime of the century" is not usually thought of as a campus crime per say, but it was. From this tragedy of mass murder involving college women sprang a new genre of horror—a story that would be repeated in multiple novels, films, and reality in the upcoming decades.

• August 1, 1966: The Texas Sniper University of Texas Austin, Texas

Charles Joseph Whitman, a former Eagle Scout and Marine Lance Corporal, was a student at the University of Texas. In the early morning hours of August 1, 1966, Whitman stabbed his mother and wife to death in their homes. Later that same morning he bought ammunition and a shotgun. When he arrived on campus, he had an arsenal of weapons and knives that he brought to the top of the Tower, a University landmark that overlooks most of the campus grounds. On his way up he killed the receptionist and two other people who were touring the Tower. From an elevation of two hundred thirty-one feet, Whitman shot at people crossing the campus.

The siege lasted ninety-two minutes, an eternity for this type of crime. Finally, Whitman was shot to death by two Austin police officers. In the end, seventeen people were killed including Whitman and an unborn child, and thirty-one were wounded. An autopsy of Whitman's body indicated that he had a brain tumor, but experts remain unclear as to the extent to which this tumor affected his behavior.

In September 1999, the University of Texas moved to reclaim this landmark by reopening the Tower. All visitors to the observation deck must pass through a metal detector and are prohibited from bringing any packages with them. Thus, the legacy of this one terrible act of violence still haunts the University of Texas today. With two major massacres impacting college campuses during this violent one-month period in the summer of 1966, the image of college campuses as ivory tower sanctuaries sheltered from violence was shattered.

• May 4, 1970: Kent State Riots Kent State University Kent, Ohio

In late April 1970 the United States invaded Cambodia, escalating the Vietnam War. Shortly after, protests emerged on college campuses across the country. At Kent State University, anti-war gatherings became increasingly intense. Students began by peacefully burying a copy of the Constitution, then built bonfires in the streets of Kent, and eventually clashed with police. Because of this escalation, the mayor declared a state of emergency and called in the Ohio National Guard. On May 2, the ROTC building was set ablaze in the presence of over 1,000 demonstrators. By Sunday, May 3, the campus looked like a war zone and most of the campus assumed that the university was in a state of martial law.

On the morning of Monday, May 4, 3,000 people began to gather in the Commons area for an anti-war rally scheduled for noon. Initially the rally was peaceful, and the accounts of the following events are still subject to debate. Just before the rally was about to commence, officials made the decision to disperse the demonstrators. What ensued was an escalating confrontation between demonstrators and enforcement, and in the end twenty-eight guardsmen fired over sixty shots, wounding nine and killing four Kent State students. This event is critical to appreciating campus violence history for two reasons. First, the politically driven campus protests of that era can be compared and contrasted to rioting that many campuses are experiencing today. In understanding potential rioting triggers and diffusion tactics, we need to ask, "What are the similarities and differences in the campus culture now and then?" Second, the community response in the aftermath of the tragedy can serve as a model for other schools facing such violence. At Kent State at that time and for years to come, students, faculty, and staff all participated in the recovery and the future direction of the campus.

- **January 14, 1978: The Chi Omega Murders**
  Florida State University
  Tallahassee, Florida

Ted Bundy is probably the most notorious serial killer in American history. His modus operandi: preying on young women and luring them in with his charm and perception of vulnerability. On the night of the Chi Omega murders, Bundy apparently walked right in the front door of the sorority, leaving it wide open after he entered. He then attacked the sorority sisters in their rooms while they slept. He beat them, raped them, bit them, and strangled them. Two victims died and two survived. Like Richard Speck's attack on the nurses a decade earlier, this event magnified the vulnerability of women living on campus and perpetuated a perception of college women as accessible sexual prey.

- **February 24, 1978: Chuck Stenzel**
  Alfred University
  Alfred, New York

Hank Nuwer, hazing expert, describes the

following tragedy in his books *Broken Pledges* and *Wrongs of Passage*. February 24, 1978 was Tapping Night at Alfred University's Klan Alpine fraternity. Chuck Stenzel had recently re-enrolled at Alfred. His mother thought, in hindsight, that he probably chose to join the fraternity to increase his chances for making the lacrosse team (several brothers played the sport) or to get closer to his existing friends. The "Klan" had a reputation of being an "animal house," and ironically, the theme for this particular Tapping Night was, "Don't Stop 'til You Drop." Sometime after

Figure 1. February 28, 1978. Chuck Stenzel was a sophomore at Alfred University when his brothers at the Klan Alpine Fraternity locked him in the trunk of a car after giving him a pint of bourbon, a fifth of wine and a six pack of beer, with orders to consume all before he would be released. He died of acute alcohol poisoning and exposure to the cold. Chuck's mother, Eileen Stevens formed C.H.U.C.K. (Committee to Halt Useless College Killings) in August of 1978 and has become a leading anti-hazing activist.

7:00 P.M., a fraternity brother came to Chuck's room to congratulate him on his acceptance with a pint of Jack Daniel's whiskey. The brother then led Chuck to the car where he was to ride in the trunk. The temperature outside was below freezing. There were two other pledges in the trunk with Chuck who later testified that he chugged not only his pint, but also most of another pledge's pint of Scotch.

Chuck arrived at the fraternity house at some point before 9:30 P.M. at which point he drank more beer and wine in festive celebration and drinking games. One of the goals of the night was to fill a trashcan up to a marked line with vomit. Chuck was given a shower at some point and when he began to pass out, he was placed on his side on an uncovered mattress. Chuck and another unconscious pledge were left in the room unattended until 11:30 P.M. when a fraternity brother came in to check on them and noted that Chuck's fingernails had turned blue. None of the three sober brothers on site knew CPR, and the rest of the brothers were too drunk to be of any assistance. By the time an emergency medical crew arrived, Chuck was dead. Chuck's blood alcohol content at the time of death was .46, a four-fold increase from the legal definition of intoxication. Two other pledges, one of whom the ambulance crew found in a locked closet, were close to death and were rushed to the hospital. They survived.

From that night on, Chuck's mother Eileen Stevens bravely chose to speak out against the dangers of hazing. She founded C.H.U.C.K. (Committee to Halt Useless College Killings), a national anti-hazing organization. She speaks to groups on this issue sharing her personal experience as a mother of a hazing victim. Alfred University is now leading the cause to prevent hazing. In 1999, Alfred helped orchestrate an NCAA study that exposed significant hazing activity in college athletics.

• **April 5, 1986: Jeanne Clery**
  Lehigh University
  Bethlehem, Pennsylvania

Just a few days after her parents dropped her off at Lehigh University following her spring break, Jeanne Clery was asleep in her unlocked room when she was brutally raped, beaten, and murdered by a fellow student. Josoph Henry had easily gained entrance to the dormitory because the door had been propped open with empty pizza boxes. After the murder he boasted about his attack to his friends. In 1987, he was sentenced to

Figure 2. April 5, 1986, Jeanne Clery was found dead in her residence hall room. She had been raped, sodomized, beaten and strangled. Her attacker, Josoph Henry bit her face and breasts, to make sure she was dead. The night of the murder, Josoph Henry walked through three security doors. In the months prior to the murder, students had lodged complaints about his behavior and threats to female students to administrators. Since this tragedy, the Clery family has developed a non-profit organization called "Security On Campus" and is largely responsible for the passage of 27 campus safety laws.

the electric chair.

Jeanne's parents thought they had been acting in her best interest when they encouraged her to attend Lehigh because it looked so safe. What they did not know was that Lehigh had experienced thirty-eight violent crimes within a three-year period. The Clerys filed a $25 million civil suit against Lehigh for negligence. The suit was settled out of court, and the Clerys used the settlement and their own money to begin one of the largest campaigns to stop campus violence to date. In 1988 they founded Security on Campus, Inc., and in 1990 lobbied for the successful passing of the federal bill called the "Student Right-To-Know and Campus Safety Act" now known as the "Jeanne Clery Act." They continue to be very vocal and tireless in their pursuit to expose the truth about campus violence and to educate the public on how to prevent future tragedies.

- **August 1990: Gemini Killer University of Florida and Santa Fe Community College Gainesville, Florida**

The college town of Gainesville, Florida, experienced total devastation and panic when five bodies of brutally murdered college students were discovered within forty-eight hours. Three of the students were from the University of Florida and two were from Santa Fe Community College, both schools of Gainesville, Florida. On August 26, 1990, the day before classes were to start at the University of Florida, two freshmen women were found stabbed in their townhouse residence. The killer had raped and mutilated one of these victims; the other appeared to have been stabbed in her sleep. The next day police found another female student naked and decapitated in her residence. On August 28, a maintenance man found two more victims, both college students. The 23-year-old female had been raped and stabbed

in the back, and the 23-year-old male had been stabbed thirty-one times.

In the aftermath of these discoveries, the residents and students of Gainesville were terrified, and the town was in a state of siege. Many students purchased guns, creating a hazard to officers who were knocking on hundreds of doors to follow up on thousands of leads. It took investigators one year to track down and arrest serial killer Danny Rolling for the crimes. Rolling blamed the killings on his alter ego "Gemini," but profilers described him as a sexual predator who preyed upon women. He chose women who would most likely have no interest in him—educated, beautiful, successful college women. In 1994, the jury gave him the death penalty. We believe that it is not a coincidence that four of America's most deadly and notorious serial and spree killers—Speck, Whitman, Bundy, and Rolling—chose college students as their victims.

- **June 3, 1991: *Time* Magazine Headline "Date Rape" College of William and Mary**

In 1991, *Time* magazine put a face to date rape. In that issue, they covered the story of Katie Koestner, a woman who dared to speak out against a silent epidemic. A graduate of the College of William and Mary in Williamsburg, Virginia, Katie testifies to her experience of being sexually assaulted by a fellow student, someone she met during her first week of school. Since then, she has become an activist for the issue, speaking to millions through college keynotes, inspiring an HBO documentary titled, "No Visible Bruises," and making television appearances ranging from "Oprah" to "Larry King Live" to "The NBC Nightly News." According to her audience, her powerful story humanizes a crime that few speak about and empowers both women and men to try to stop it.

- **September 29, 1997: Scott Krueger**
  MIT
  Boston, Massachusetts

Five weeks after the promising freshman Scott Krueger arrived on the prestigious campus of MIT he died from an alcohol overdose. Scott was a pledge at the Phi Gamma Delta house, better known as FIJI. Scott was not a big drinker, but on "Animal House Night" he and the other pledges were expected to drink two cases of beer, Jack Daniels whiskey, and Bacardi rum within a short period of time. He passed out, was carried to a basement room and left alone after which he inhaled his own vomit into his lungs. According to his doctors, the critical point of the night was when his "big broth-

ers" chose to leave him by himself so that they could go back upstairs for another drink. Scott's blood alcohol content was .41.

FIJI had very serious and well-known alcohol problems in the years before Scott's death. Police and emergency medical personnel had been summoned to the FIJI house at least fifteen times in the few years before Scott's death to deal with outrageously large parties, drunken fights, underage drinking, and to assist severely intoxicated students. MIT clearly knew of these problems and more.

Rather than indict the university for manslaughter and hazing, the district attorney indicted the MIT fraternity. A sealed indictment was handed up from the DA's office on September 14, 1998, but was not made public to anyone until September 18, 1998. Interestingly, MIT and FIJI National agreed to disband the local chapter between September 14 and the 18, and no individual showed up at FIJI's arraignment two weeks later. The indictment remains open and if the chapter ever reopens at MIT it could be prosecuted. Despite the lack of closure on this case, the steps taken were groundbreaking in that the threat of a criminal indictment for a university or Greek association in the aftermath of a hazing death became viable.

The Krueger family prepared to file suit against MIT for the university's responsibility in the death of their son. In September 2000, MIT agreed to pay the Kruegers $4.75 million as compensation and $1.25 million for a scholarship established in the memory of Scott. In addition, the MIT president publicly apologized and accepted blame for MIT's role in Scott's death.

Two weeks after the announcement of the MIT settlement, the Krueger family filed suit against the MIT fraternity. The Kruegers' attorney Brad Henry was quoted in the *Boston Globe* (9/27/00) as saying, "They [FIJI] simply can't disband themselves out of accountability." Because of the intense

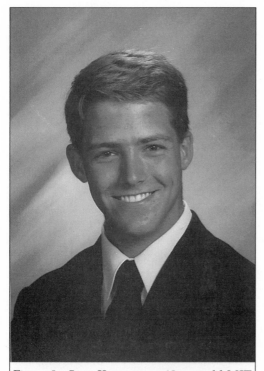

Figure 3. Scott Krueger, an 18-year-old MIT freshman died after lapsing into an alcohol induced coma as a result of a hazing experience at Phi Gamma Delta fraternity.

media coverage in the aftermath of this tragedy, the deadly consequences of college hazing practices as well as binge drinking reached public consciousness.

- **October 6, 1998: Matthew Shepard University of Wyoming Laramie, Wyoming**

During October 1998, Matthew Shepard, an openly gay student at the University of Wyoming, met Aaron McKinney and Russell Henderson, two local roofers at the Fireside Lounge. McKinney and Henderson lured Shepard into their truck by posing as two gay men. The two roofers robbed Shepard, pistol-whipped him repeatedly, and left him tied to a fence. He remained bound and unconscious for eighteen hours in subfreezing temperatures. Shepard died five days later from the injuries. The brutal crime and dramatic trials brought significant media attention, and Shepard became a national symbol for gay rights and the effects of hate crimes. The University of Wyoming and the community of Laramie banded together in mourning by wearing or displaying yellow ribbons in his memory.

Along with a deluge of concern and activism came a backlash of hatred. Shepard's funeral and the ensuing trials brought anti-gay protests. McKinney's "gay panic" defense, claiming he snapped during a methamphetamine-induced fury instigated by memories of a childhood homosexual assault, brought additional media attention.

In addition to learning about effective community response and the impact of campus hate crimes, the Matthew Shepard tragedy taught campuses another lesson: how to handle a media circus. During the ordeal demonstrators representing all sides of the issues implanted themselves on campus in a national spotlight. Campus officials quickly learned that media parameters were necessary to protect the students and to control the dispersion of legitimate information.

- **March 27-28, 1999: Michigan State University Riots Michigan State University East Lansing, Michigan**

In stark contrast to the politically motivated riots of earlier days, the riots of the late 1990s have been dubbed "The Right to Party" movement. As colleges began to crack down on underage drinking and public drunkenness, students revolted in violent ways. The most notorious of these riots were a series of riots at Michigan State University in East Lansing. After school administrators put a ban on alcohol at a popular tailgate site, an estimated 10,000 students and townspeople torched cars, hurled bottles at police, set more than sixty fires, and caused up to $1 million in damage. While this particular riot at MSU created a great deal of media interest, it was not the first riot MSU faced.

Since September 1997, there have been four alcohol-related riots at MSU. These incidents have negatively impacted the tenuous community relationship where the 43,000 MSU students significantly outnumber the 25,000 year-round residents of East Lansing. The university has spent a great deal of time trying to determine the underlying cause of the riots, to no avail. It seems to some that rioting has become trendy and fun; as one student commented, "It was a blast in all senses of the word. We came together as a school, burned some things, showed some skin and that's fine. It was Spartan pride." Interestingly, police are dismantling the anonymity that rioting brings by posting pictures of the rioters on the Internet.

- **October 2, 1999: University of Vermont Hockey Team Hazing University of Vermont Montpelier, Vermont**

On October 2, the University of Vermont (UVM) hockey team held its initiation party.

A freshman goalie, Corey LaTulippe, had warned university officials in September about the hazing party before it happened. Despite warnings from the Athletic Department, the party took place. Shortly after the initiation party, LaTulippe was cut from the team and subsequently filed a lawsuit against the university alleging assault and battery, invasion of privacy, and violation of his civil rights. Rookie players were ordered to arrive at the party with their pubic hair shaved, wearing thong underwear. Then they were forced to perform push-ups while dipping their genitals in cups of beer. Depending on the number they were able to perform, each athlete then had to drink his own glass or that of another rookie. During the evening they were also instructed to walk around holding each other's genitals.

During a deposition, the issue of Corey's consent was broached. Corey stated, "I didn't feel I had a choice (to decline the invitation to the initiation party) . . . this is what you had to do."

An initial UVM investigation concluded in disciplinary action against several players for their roles; however, LaTulippe's lawsuit renewed investigation by the university and the Attorney General. The Attorney General's conclusion was that the allegations were essentially true, and the entire team had lied to UVM investigators. In January 2000, the UVM president made a bold move by cancelling the remaining games of the team's Division I hockey season.

The University of Vermont ended up settling the lawsuit for a payment of $80,000. One of the team's captains pleaded no contest to a charge of providing beer to a minor. He agreed to pay fines and court costs and is ordered to perform fifty hours of community service. He was also given a suspended thirty-day jail sentence.

This case demonstrated what recent research has been telling us: hazing happens

to athletes. The stance the UVM president took was unprecedented. Whether or not it will serve as a standard for future hazing violations remains to be seen.

Fads and Trends of Violence

College campuses are generally viewed as safe places for individuals to go to develop critical thinking skills, learn about the world, develop social skills, and have fun. Recently, violence on campus has generated significant attention in the media. High-profile rioting and rape incidents have made national news and have caused increasing concern around the country.

Many wonder if these events are isolated situations hyped by the media or if they truly represent a trend in our society. Fads in American culture are very commonplace. They gain much attention in a short period and fade out just as quickly. Violence fads are often created by urban myths. For example, during the mid-nineties many people thought they would be shot if they flashed their car's headlights at a car that was driving at them with no headlights in the dark. People feared that it was part of some rite of passage for gang members. For a few weeks, this myth circulated the Internet and grapevines. When this pattern of violence did not materialize, the fad dissolved.

In contrast to fads, trends are patterns of violence that alter the norms of our society. Fads can turn into trends because of what has been termed "copycat" behavior. Humans tend to learn from watching other people. When certain individuals see someone achieve a desired goal through violence without consequences, they begin to believe that the ends justify the means.

When threats and acts of violence are consistent over time, individuals adapt their way of living to minimize the impact. Soon, the adjustment becomes second nature and people consider the changes in the behavior to be normal. Current airport security is a consequence of a violence trend. Prior to the 1970s, safety checks were minimal. However as terrorism, hijackings, and bomb threats increased in frequency throughout the early seventies, the airline industry took major counteractive measures. The current security strategies in airports can be quite intrusive and intense. Before this trend in violence, travelers would have thought a security guard rummaging through their bags was a major violation of privacy. Today, airline passengers have adapted to this practice and may even welcome it. If airports discontinued the security measures tomorrow, many people would likely be too afraid to fly.

Another example of a trend in violence involves product tampering. Not too long ago, stores sold over-the-counter medication and food products in relatively easy-to-open packaging. At most, childproofing caps existed. After the Tylenol* tampering incidents and the multiple copycat crimes that followed, products were protected with seals and plastic wrapping. This trend has resulted in an inconvenience and increased product costs, but the public does not seem to mind. In fact, most of us would not buy a bottle of cough syrup if there were not a protective seal wrapped around it. We have adapted to these security measures barely realizing a violent trend has changed the norm of our culture.

Violent mass killings in schools and workplaces are another trend in our society. At first, the instances were rare and isolated. Now it is clear that the trend is increasing in frequency and intensity. The killings are happening more often and there are more casualties. Furthermore, this form of violence is changing workplace and school culture. Schools and businesses are implementing metal detectors, increasing security, and improving identification procedures. Many are developing emergency plans to deal with a siege situation.

When trends are established, profilers can begin to develop psychological and behavioral indicators of common elements found in perpetrators. In essence, a profiler attempts to understand the "why" of the crime to get to the "who." By understanding the motives of the criminal, profilers can attempt to predict future directions of a crime trend.

A significant problem in identifying fads versus trends on college campuses is that our current knowledge base is inadequate. On one hand, there are many secrets hidden in campus life such as a preponderance of unreported acquaintance rape, and on the other hand we are sometimes bombarded with information about overblown single cases of violence hyped by our sensation-driven media.

CONCEPTUALIZING VIOLENCE AS A VIRUS

Violence is like a virus with many different strains. Motives, perpetrator profiles, victims, and outcomes are diverse, and like a virus, these features of violence mutate when exposed to different hosting sites. Understanding violence in terms of its similarities to a virus can help prevention and intervention efforts. Violence is not static, and each time the virus mutates, those who seek to prevent it lag behind.

Too often, different strains of violence are lumped together when people attempt to develop prevention strategies. People assume that violence does not mutate. For instance, in the aftermath of the Columbine High School massacre dozens of national "Violence Summits" emerged to find solutions to school violence. At these meetings hundreds of experts and concerned protectors gathered to discuss a multitude of violence issues including gang violence, bullying, hate crimes, sexual abuse, and more. Frequently, attendees left with increased confusion rather than clarity. Many sought the magical elixir; the one antibody to cure all, and found it did not exist.

One prevention strategy may be effective with a particular type of violence in a particular setting, but that tactic may lose its potency when the strain of violence moves to a different hosting site or to a different population. For example, domestic violence in the home presents a different set of challenges than when domestic violence spills over into the workplace or onto a college campus. For one, there are many more potential victims in a workplace setting or on a college campus. Furthermore, victims are affected differently; varying environmental factors impact how violence develops, and each situation demands tailored interventions.

The Host Site: Violence Impact on a Campus Community

> Violence is threaded through many aspects of American life, but it is perhaps most out of place in an institution devoted to education and development.
>> Mary Roark (1993). *Campus Violence: Kinds, Causes, and Cures,* p. 4.

Unfortunately in our society, we have grown accustomed to seeing violence in our inner cities and poorest neighborhoods. Media attention has made violence in our high schools and workplaces seem increasingly common. However, violence on college campuses is a concept that many people have difficulty reconciling with images of ivy-covered brick and sun-drenched, grassy quadrangles. College campuses are places for intellectual growth and developing civility, not rape, murder, and assault. Much of college violence happens behind closed doors, during the darkest hours of the night, or under sworn secrecy, and thus, many of us can continue to pretend that it is not happening. Or maybe we believe that it is happening on someone else's campus, but not ours. The truth is that all campuses are vulnerable to many forms of violence, an issue explored in greater depth in Chapters 3 and 4. We must be willing to acknowledge that it is happening before we can correct it.

Beyond Treating the Symptoms

While it is beyond the scope of this book to explore all the roots of violence in our society, it is safe to conclude that violence exists because of problems on many levels: personal, familial, social, and cultural. This is not just an issue for police or security to tackle. A reactive stance would tire the most competent enforcement department.

Proactive prevention is critical. All segments of the campus and surrounding communities have a role to play in preventing violence. Admissions, faculty, residence life, athletics, students, parents, alumni, counseling, public relations, student life, community leaders, neighbors, Greek life, human resources, and more need to play an active role. This guide is designed to provide relevant information to all those people committed to preventing violence on college campuses. Specific ways individuals can become involved are explored in Chapter 6.

CLASSIFICATIONS OF CAMPUS VIOLENCE

Violence Typologies

When we begin to think of violence not as a unitary concept, but in the form of multiple typologies, we discover many variations emerge:

Relationship-based	Street/Predatory
Bullying	Terrorist
Assassin	Suicide by Cop
(Suicidal) Avenger	Group-induced
Entrepreneurial	Road Rage

Some of these violence typologies are rarely seen on college campuses. Terrorist attacks, assassinations, and suicide-by-cop (provoking a law enforcement officer to use deadly force), seldom occur at institutions of higher education. Entrepreneurial (committing violence to gain a profit, e.g., robbery), road rage (e.g., aggression from parking shortage frustration), and bullying are common, but outside the scope of this book. Four of these general categories of violence seem to play out in various combinations on college campuses: predatory, avenger, relationship-based, and group-induced.

Predatory

For many violent offenders, the violent act is a means to an end. Violence is used to get something they want. A mugger attacks to get money. A terrorist holds others hostage to achieve a desired outcome. For the predator, the violence is the desired outcome. The thrill is in the kill or assault–the planning, execution, and aftermath. This is the primary goal predators are trying to obtain.

Several subtypes of predators exist classified by their methods of searching for prey and in their attack strategies. In searching methods, predators can be hunters, poach-ers, trollers, or opportunists. The hunter stays within a familiar area or neighborhood to locate prey. The poacher will survey an area away from the home territory. A troller will wander around to areas of vulnerability searching for viable prey. For instance, a troller might make the rounds at several bars looking for intoxicated potential victims. The opportunist builds a sense of trust with potential victims because of a role he or she has managed to obtain. For example, a child molester who works at a day care center is an opportunist.

Predators also vary in their method of attack. The raptor uses the "swoop and scoop" tactic striking potential victims without warning. The stalker will track victims and get to know their habits from afar before attacking. The ambusher will take the Bundy approach of feigning vulnerability and weakness or manipulating victims with charm and seduction in order to lure them into a trap.

Avenger

For the avenger, violence becomes the only possible recourse for perceived grievances. Many of the workplace violence and school violence perpetrators personify this classification of violence. When we examine the pathways to violence in these cases, we find similar sequences. First, there is a string of perceived injustices ending with some form of rejection or discipline. A girlfriend ended a relationship, an authority figure doled out discipline, or peers taunted the perpetrator. Second, the perpetrator initiates a resolution. They may initially attempt to resolve the matter through appropriate channels, but they do not get the results they desire. Rather than drop the issue, the perpetrator becomes obsessed with the issue and moves into the third phase. During the third phase, problem solving narrows and the perpetrator begins to create a violent fantasy of retaliation. This fantasy becomes very satisfying to avengers as they can rework and replay the scene to play out as they wish. The details of these images interest the perpetrator—who is there, how are they responding, where do they go?

When the satisfaction from the fantasies begins to wane, avengers will start to act on their ideas. They may begin with threats or milder forms of violence such as graffiti. Without confrontation, avengers will escalate behavior to more dangerous levels. Avengers usually have particular targets in mind, although they may take down many others in their violent rampage. This often is because they see themselves on a suicide mission and do not think they have anything to lose.

Relationship-Based

This form of violence is unfortunately the most common and frequently the most devastating. Relationship-based violence involves a one-on-one attachment that is exploited. Relationships that have both power differential and privacy are most vulnerable—parent-child, husband-wife, pledge master-pledge. In relationship-based violence, the dominant partner has an "ownership" mentality over the submissive partner. Because the submissive partner is perceived as property rather than a person of equal standing, the dominant partner employs certain strategies to ensure that "the property" is maintained under current control. Often these strategies employ violent tactics.

Group-Induced

Group-induced violence occurs when a group of individuals are swept into a mob mentality. Because the violent act is not the work of one individual, they feel that they are not as accountable. The phenomenon is known as *diffusion of responsibility*. The larger the group, the more anonymous they feel. Group-induced violence can be contagious, in that the excitement of the moment may overpower the better judgment of the onlookers who chose to participate when they would have normally not behaved in such a fashion. Bystanders play a critical role in group-induced violence. Many spectators will watch in fascination as a group begins to engage in violence. By not acting in a way to diffuse the situation, bystanders perpetuate the problem. Others perceive the inaction of bystanders as passive approval of the violent behavior. With more people now involved in perpetuating the violence, the chances for anonymity increases, and more people join in. Group-induced violence is often trigger-driven, that is, ignited by an external event or stimulus.

Strains of Campus Violence

Combinations of the above typologies make up the specific strains of violence in our society. College campuses seem to be particularly susceptible to the strains of violence introduced below. The subsequent chapters will explore these areas in more depth and suggest strategies for prevention and intervention.

Sexual Assault

While stranger rape usually falls under the typology of predatory violence, acquaintance rape is usually a combination of predatory and relationship-based violence. The Higher Education Center reports that between 15 percent and 30 percent of college women have experienced acquaintance rape at some point in their lives. Gang rape is a combination of predatory, relationship, and group-induced violence. Stranger rape and gang rape are more rare, but also occur on college campuses.

Hate Crimes

First Amendment rights are often exercised liberally on college campuses. Sometimes they are abused, as in the case of many hate crimes. Perpetrators of hate crimes intentionally seek victims based on perceived differences in race, ethnicity, gender, sexual orientation, or physical/mental ability. The Anti-Defamation League (ADL) suggests college campuses are fertile grounds for spreading hate. According to *Link, The College Magazine,* there has been a significant increase in hate crimes against Asian-Pacific Americans and the gay and lesbian communities on college campuses in the last couple of years. Another trend fueling the fire of hate is the use of the Internet. Currently the ADL monitors hundreds of hate-filled websites. Hate crime can be considered its own violence typology, but it shares characteristics with group-induced violence and avenger characteristics. Many hate crimes are committed in groups and perpetrators often believe they are "evening the score" for an injustice done to them.

Rioting

In the 1960s, campus riots erupted over civil rights issues and war protests. On today's campuses, riots are erupting over football victories and alcohol restrictions. The damage costs schools and communities hundreds of thousands of dollars. Many times the drunken rioters proudly pose before cameras only to have that evidence used against them in court. While riots often appear spontaneous, sometimes students plan for them by stockpiling bonfire kindling

and by freezing beer cans to throw at windows. In the East Lansing riot of March 1999, T-shirts were even printed days before the riot took place. Anti-riot community coalitions are surfacing in the neighborhoods of schools where riots have happened. Riots are generally group-induced violence with the exception of the group leaders. For them, avenger and predator characteristics also exist.

Hazing

While hazing is usually associated with college students who join a fraternity or sorority, it also occurs in military schools and with athletes. In the past, colleges have often turned a blind eye toward hazing incidents by excusing them as "traditions" and "rites of passage." In the wake of lawsuits and new legislation, schools are taking hazing more seriously. One concern is that most states have recently passed anti-hazing laws. A large-scale NCAA-supported study in 1999 found that hazing of athletes is more common and more severe than many had previously acknowledged. Seventy-nine percent of the over 2,000 survey responders indicated that they were subjected to team initiation behavior that was humiliating, alcohol-related, dangerous, or criminal. Hazing perpetration combines elements of relationship-based violence and group-induced violence.

Non-Sexual Assault, Homicide, and Other Forms of Campus Violence

Campus interpersonal violence includes murder, beating, kicking, punching, slapping, and other violent behaviors combining any number of violence typologies. The most common offenders of simple assault are male athletes and fraternity members, and most of these crimes are closely linked to alcohol abuse. Relationship or dating violence also falls into this category of non-sexual assault; however, the distinctions between this form of violence and sexual assault are often blurry. Avenger violence resulting in homicide also has been experienced on college campuses in the aftermath of perceived academic and social grievances. Other forms of campus violence include bombing and bomb threats, arson, and property damage.

HIDDEN EPIDEMIC OR OVERBLOWN CASE? PROBLEMS WITH CAMPUS STATISTICS

What is the true extent of campus violence? We are just beginning to understand. There are several reasons for our ignorance, some understandable, some inexcusable. The controversy surrounding the issues underlying this uncovering process is heated. On one hand there are violence prevention advocates who declare that the public has a "right to know" what goes on at college and that campus officials are trying to hide the truth. On the other hand, there are college administrators who are tirelessly attempting to ensure statistics are accurately reported while being bombarded with a host of complicating factors.

To some extent the reason that campuses underreport violence is because victims of campus violence frequently do not report their crimes. For some, they fear that they are partly to blame for the violence. As in the case of acquaintance rape and hazing, alcohol is usually involved as is some degree of consent to events leading up to the violence. For instance, rape victims are clearly not responsible for being raped, but many victims are filled with self-blame for putting themselves in risky situations. Others question why they consented to being kissed or fondled before being raped. Victims of hate crimes may experience their own internalized self-hatred and may see themselves as deserving of violence on some level. These issues muddy the waters for the victims deciding whether to act against violence or not.

A second reason victims of campus violence do not step forward is because of fear of retaliation. For many, the perpetrators of violence hold positions of power or are associated with powerful groups—popular students, athletic departments, and Greek leaders. The less powerful victims fear that their accusations may be at best dismissed and at worst punished. They may be cut from an athletic team, blackballed from a fraternity, marginalized, trivialized, or ostracized.

A third reason why victims do not report campus crimes is that they do not believe anything productive will come from stepping forward. They may have heard stories on their campus or on other campuses where violence was either swept under the carpet or dealt with by a mere slapping of wrists. All too often, victims of campus crime will transfer or drop out of school because of the undue pressure of the violence aftermath. This outcome does not seem to justify the months of investigation and public display of their lives that often accompanies our campus and criminal judicial proceedings.

The problems with underreported campus violence statistics, however, do not all rest on the shoulders of the victims. Violence prevention advocates claim that many campuses have fallen into a pattern of "don't ask, don't tell." In 1990, President Bush passed a law to try to change that pattern. The Campus Security Act, now known as the Jeanne Clery Act, requires all colleges and universities to release annual crime statistics to the public. The Clery family, survivors of campus violence victim Jeanne Clery, who pushed for this legislation claim some schools still blatantly cover up reported crimes as a means of protecting public relations. Some schools withhold relevant crime information in the report at the request of families seeking privacy. Other schools do not list all campus crimes because they were not reported to campus security, but rather to offices of residence life or rape crisis centers. The Clerys found that some schools even renamed crime categories to avert reporting. For example, one school renamed "rape" as "advances without sanction." According to the Clerys, another tactic schools have employed is to call land surrounding the campus as "off-campus," thereby legally omitting crimes committed there.

When violence has occurred on a college campus, public statements by university officials are sometimes misleading or overly vague. The public record might state that an athlete "violated the student-athlete code of conduct" rather than calling the behavior "hazing" or "sexual assault." When the behavior is not directly labeled, the perpetrator is not truly held accountable and the public gets a distorted view of what is going on.

In 1997, the Clerys found sixty-three schools who were not in compliance with the reporting law. There were no consequences for these schools. In 1998 Congress passed an amendment to the law tightening up reporting obligations and increasing penalties for noncompliance. These changes went into effect during the summer of 2000, and schools are now receiving fines for noncompliance.

On the other side of the debate, many campus administrators state they are doing their best to comply with the laws and deeply resent the accusations that they are being intentionally misleading. Reporting officials on campuses adamantly state the laws are confusing, constantly under revision, and so detail-oriented they become meaningless. Some claim that so much data is being generated, the purpose of the laws has been lost.

The lack of standardization with other law enforcement reports increases the complications. There are different definitions for crimes like sexual assault and different time frames to calculate the data (e.g., academic year or calendar year). This leads to multiple reports and confused interpreters.

Many campus administrators are highly frustrated with the idea that people who are on Capitol Hill can make sweeping decisions about how campuses will function without understanding how life works from the inside. Much controversy exists on who should report, what information gets reported, and how to maintain privacy of the victims.

Most campus officials agree that having an accurate picture of campus violence is in everyone's best interest. Because there is so much at stake when dealing with such highly charged issues, campuses have learned to partner together to look for solutions. These coalitions will hopefully bring increased consistency and a higher standard for violence prevention.

One controversial solution to the problem of gathering campus violence statistics is to have an objective party look at the data. Campuses are in a bind when they police themselves. On one hand, they have a duty to the institution they are protecting and on the other they have an obligation to uphold federal expectations. Sometimes these demands conflict and objectivity is compromised. Recently, an agency outside of higher education, APBnews, began the task of predicting campus neighborhood crime risk. The system does not track actual crime, but estimates the risk of crime from a high-tech computer model that takes into account past crimes and socioeconomic data. The intent of the crime risk report was to give prospective students and their families comparative information about the rates of violence at various campus communities so that they can make informed decisions about the safety of those campuses. Their first published report in the fall of 1999 caused a great deal of controversy as schools that were poorly rated found APB's statistic gathering faulty and the report misleading. Schools highly ranked for violence potential claimed that the risk of violence in the surrounding neighborhoods did not always reflect the level of violence within the campus. Nevertheless, it was a first attempt at someone outside the system of higher education attempting to report violence patterns in an unbiased fashion.

Because of these problems with our current statistics and reporting, we know we have just begun to scratch the surface of the truth about campus violence. As we begin to gain a clearer picture of what is going on, we will be better able to adapt our prevention and intervention efforts. For the most part, it is in everyone's best interest—institutes of higher education, students, families, and communities—to have a truthful picture of the nature of campus crime. The challenge that remains, however, is finding the best way to gather the pieces of the puzzle.

INSTITUTIONAL RESPONSES TO VIOLENCE: STAGES OF IMPACT

A great deal of research has been conducted on individuals who undergo difficult changes in their lives. Quitting smoking, changing diet, and altering other lifestyle behaviors usually take a great deal of effort and failed attempts are as common as successful outcomes. James Prochaska and Carlo DiClemente have developed a transtheoretical model for understanding individual change that we believe has relevance for institutions as well. They call their model Stages of Change and describe the sequence of spiraling events that occur as an individual moves along a spiraling pathway from precontemplation (no change) to contemplation (thinking about change) to preparation to action to maintenance. The pathway spirals because often people need to repeat previous stages a few times in the process of moving forward.

When we look at stages of change or impact at an institutional level, the model still applies but becomes somewhat more complicated. Because the university or college is not a unified entity, different parts of the institution will move through these stages at different rates. Also, each strain of violence may be a different point along the pathway. For example, a college may have a very well developed strategy for dealing with sexual assault, but nothing in place to address hazing. A final drawback of "stage" models is that they assume everyone must pass through all of the stages. Thankfully, this is not the case. By sharing information and promising prevention strategies, campuses are able to help each other advance by jumping over earlier stages.

Denial or Precontemplation

At this stage, the institution of higher education is truly unaware of the problems of violence occurring. Perhaps, people have not reported the violence or potential reports have been discouraged. No one is assessing or addressing the problem, because it is thought not to exist.

Anger-Defensiveness

When people begin to come forward with information about violence, the initial reaction is often to find fault with the reporter or to otherwise discredit the information. Alleged rape victims are just trying to get back at perpetrators because they have morning-after regrets. Alleged hazing victims have sour grapes because they were not accepted into the group. Alleged hate crime victims are trying to get attention, more privileges, and so on.

Limbo

Limbo is the stage when, due to outside pressure institutions can no longer deny or excuse away violence, but they do not know how to proceed. When increasing numbers of victims come forward, the mental gymnastics required to maintain denial become increasingly strenuous. For instance, when information was emerging about hazing, the initial response from some athletic departments was "that's a Greek thing, not an athletic thing." Then "well maybe it happens at other schools, but it doesn't happen here." Then "well I guess it happens on other teams, but not my players." Soon the evidence becomes overwhelming, and some level of problem contemplation emerges. The problem with the limbo stage is that resistance to acknowledging the violence still remains, so any attempt to address the problem is usually half-hearted. Quick-fix band-aids are applied in haste usually more to show the public that "something is being done" rather than effective, comprehensive prevention. Very often, these attempts are phased out as soon as the public eye blinks.

Catalyst for Change

The catalyst for change is often an event, person, or group of people that show the true colors of the violence in a way that it cannot be ignored. The high-profile cases mentioned earlier provide many examples of catalyst events that forever changed the paths of their institutions of higher education. Fortunately, not every college has to experience a Matthew Shepard or a Corey LaTulippe to fully face issues of hate crimes or hazing. Strong grassroots groups can have similar effects as committed top-down leadership. The factor tipping the balance from inaction or ineffective action to appropriate action is commitment.

Action

When many sectors of a campus community become determined to change, action results. The predatory form of sexual assault is one area that many campuses have committed to addressing. Most people within the campus community accept the fact that sexual assault happens at college. Thus, educational prevention and self-defense programs now abound. Policy and enforcement have improved significantly. Environmental safety strategies are considerable. Action dealing with acquaintance and gang rape is also getting attention, but lags somewhat behind "stranger" rape interventions. Nevertheless, in many ways this form of violence leads the way in the development of a comprehensive prevention plan.

Maintenance

Change can be difficult to maintain, and maintenance is not static. In order for change to continue to be effective, ongoing assessment of the situation must be undertaken and fed back into the system.

Modifications in the strategies must be made accordingly. Again, this usually involves widespread effort and commitment. Sometimes a relapse into old patterns is inevitable, and the pattern of change recycles.

Chapter 2

VIOLENCE 101: UNDERSTANDING THE BASICS

THE PURPOSE OF THIS CHAPTER is to give you a basic understanding of the elements of violence. In the latter chapters we go into detail about how the various types of campus violence differ from each other. Here we draw on the similarities. We begin with some basic definitions of violence and then describe who are the participants in acts of violence. From there we outline a general formula for violence–what are the critical elements necessary for combustion–and we conclude with some ideas to keep in mind when responding to violence.

DEFINING VIOLENCE

Campus violence expert Dr. Mary Roark, former chair of the American College Personnel Association Commission I Task Force on Campus Violence, is an advocate for clear definitions. In the book *Campus Violence: Kinds, Causes, and Cures,* (1993), she states, "once we name something, we can move beyond vagueness to clarity that favors efforts at prevention and control. Words are powerful, and naming gives us an ability to describe, to discuss, to understand, and to eventually make changes" (p. 6). Dr. Roark goes on to make the case that before the terms "acquaintance rape," "sexual harassment," and "dating violence" became recognized terms, people had a difficult time discussing and advocating for the prevention of these problems.

Some violence experts cited in Dr. Roark's writing define violence broadly and include not only physical acts but also verbal, psychological, symbolic, and spiritual attacks. Clearly, violence exists on a continuum and all of these realms are affected; however, clarity is lost with definitions so broad. Other dimensions of violence to consider are (1) is the act of violence one of commission or omission? (2) is the act of violence offensive or defensive? and (3) is the act of violence covert or overt?

We have chosen to endorse Dr. Roark's definition of violence for its simplicity and comprehensiveness: *Violence is behavior that by intent, action, and/or outcome harms another person.*

While violence can be both physical and verbal, we have chosen to focus mostly on the physical aspects of violence in this book. Thus, topics such as sexual harassment and intellectual violence will not be covered here. Violence against property such as vandalism also falls outside the scope of our definition, but may be an important warning sign for impending violence. In addition, many have considered suicide as a form of violence. While suicide is definitely a violent act, harm-to-self falls outside our definition of violence and thus, will also not be discussed here. Threats are another aspect of violence discussed in Chapter 5.

Even though there are many different forms of violence, common dynamics exist among them. By definition, violence has a perpetrator and victim or victims, and most premeditated violence follows predictable steps.

CAST OF CHARACTERS

The "cast of characters" are the people or groups of people usually involved in the act of violence or the response to it. This section is adapted from our previous works *Violence Goes to Work* (1997) and *Violence Goes to School* (1999).

Targets

Targets of violence are the victims. In violence that impacts property, targets can also be buildings or cars. Targets can be intended or by chance; primary, secondary, or tertiary.

- *Victims of Choice:* Victims of choice are chosen by the perpetrator for a reason. The reason may be revenge, easy access, or the victim's likeness to a violent fantasy. Ted Bundy chose women for his victims fitting a particular physical appearance. Avenger perpetrators will often choose the object of their revenge as their targets—professors, supervisors, or judicial officers. Rapists might look for the most impaired woman at the party. All these perpetrators systematically seek a particular victim or victim qualities to carry out their violent behavior.
- *Victims of Opportunity:* Victims of opportunity are often in the wrong place at the wrong time. Rioting usually involves victims of opportunity. The rioters do not have any ill will toward the neigh-

bors and businesses in their path, but the local people often suffer the most damages. Suicidal perpetrators sometimes take out victims of opportunity in their final act of violence believing they have nothing to lose. Sometimes well-meaning individuals who place themselves in the path of the perpetrator in hopes of deterring his or her progress end up being victims of opportunity.
- *Primary Victims:* Primary victims are those individuals who have experienced the violence directly.
- *Secondary Victims:* Secondary victims are the roommates, friends, witnesses, parents, rescue personnel, and others involved but not directly impacted by the violence. These secondary victims are often overlooked in trauma recovery efforts, but many of them may experience a posttraumatic response that is very upsetting.
- *Tertiary Victims:* Tertiary victims are the helpers who also become affected by the violent event. In the aftermath of a violent incident, counselors may be flooded with individuals in crisis, needs for debriefing sessions, and requests for consultation. At the same time these professionals may be dealing with their own reactions to the trauma. They also may be vicariously affected by listening to story after story from the survivors. In some cases counselors may internalize another's pain and become over-

whelmed. As a result they may experience similar nightmares and distressing thoughts as their clients.

Perpetrators

Perpetrators are those who commit the act of violence. Contrary to popular belief, most violence on campus is not perpetrated by outside strangers descending on an otherwise safe environment. In fact, most campus violence experts agree that the overwhelming majority of violent incidents are perpetrated by students.

In the early 1990s, researchers at Pennsylvania State University (cited in Hoffman & Schuh, 1998) asked residence hall staff what type of perpetrators committed the most serious offense in their careers. The RAs responded: 80 percent residents; 6 percent guests; 8 percent unidentified; and 6 percent unknown visitors.

As you will see from ample case examples in this book, the overwhelming number of perpetrators of campus violence are students. But there are definitely cases involving strangers, faculty and staff, and students' loved ones.

Protectors

Protectors are those on campus who do what is in their power to prevent violent incidents from occurring or intervene when violent events are unfolding. All campuses have a security force or a sworn police department providing professional protection. But protectors also include residence life staff, often the first-line responders to campus violence. Coaches, faculty, and others frequently find themselves in situations where they are called upon to intercept violent threats or console victims in the aftermath of violence.

Bystanders

Historically, bystanders have not received a great deal of attention for their role in perpetrating and preventing violence. Regardless of their true feelings about the violent behavior, the silent presence of bystanders has a strong influence in continuing a violent incident. When bystanders do not stand up and confront perpetrators, their silence is interpreted as tacit approval of the actions taking place. The more people the perpetrator thinks support him or her, the more likely the violent act will continue. Most bystanders are fearful of stepping forward and getting involved because they fear they will become the next target of the perpetrator or peers will perceive them as a tattletale.

Bystanders play a critical role in campus rioting. Usually only a handful of instigators are needed to start a riot, but the hordes of curious on-lookers keep it going. The more bystanders present in a riot, the more intense the riot becomes and the more difficult it becomes for law enforcement to intervene. The sheer mass of bystanders becomes a roadblock insulating the violence.

Even though they usually are not physically present during violent acts of sexual assault, bystanders have a role in this crime as well. Bystanders can support attitudes that lead to sexual assault by linking sexual behavior to conquests and talking about potential partners as objects. Violence prevention experts from the Mentors in Violence Prevention (MVP) Program focus on these bystanders in their intervention efforts. They hold all-male workshops, usually through athletic teams, and talk to the men about what they will do if, for example, they hear or see a teammate sexually harass a woman.

FORMULA FOR VIOLENCE

In order for violence to occur, several factors must be present. The perpetrator or perpetrators must believe that access to the target is feasible. The assailant must have either an external catalyst or an internal emotional reaction that triggers the decision to act. Perpetrators must have the physical and mental ability to carry out the act, as well as ample time to complete the violent act. The formula used to assess the possibility of violence is identified by the acronym **TOADS.** This acronym stands for:

TIME
OPPORTUNITY
ABILITY
DESIRE
STIMULUS

(Adapted from *Violence Goes to Work* and *Violence Goes to School*)

Each of these factors can be assessed and impacted by front-line responders (e.g., other students, professors, or security personnel), administration, or the outside professionals who assess the dangerousness of the situation. The components of this acronym are explained as follows:

Time

This refers to the time necessary for perpetrators to complete an act of violence. Violent individuals must have ample time to formulate and design a plan, overcome any inhibitions to engage in violence, gain access to the intended victim or victims, and execute the act. Protectors can remove the time factor from the equation by responding quickly to threats and other lower-level inappropriate behaviors.

Opportunity

Opportunity provides the chance or opening allowing the perpetrator access to the target. Often individuals can disable opportunities through swift intervention. Sometimes they are not even aware that they are doing so. In those instances where an individual can identify a potential perpetrator, security should attempt to control access to the campus. Campus safety officials accomplish this by posting a photograph of the suspect at entryways and, in cases of severe threat, calling for additional outside security.

Ability

The level of threat increases in direct proportion to the perpetrator's ability to commit a violent act. This involves both the requisite physical expertise and mental capability to formulate and execute a plan of action. When assessing a potential perpetrator's ability, one must take into account intelligence, creativity, experience with and access to weaponry, organizational skills, desensitization to violence, and hand-eye coordination.

Desire

The willingness to inflict injury or death on a person, or damage to property, must be present at a serious level in order for violence to occur. The desire usually builds within many violent individuals to the point that they perceive it as overwhelming, and they feel a sense of urgency to act out violently. The timeframe during which this desire builds may be a matter of minutes or years depending on the situation.

For premeditated violence, revenge is a common theme. Like the avenger profile mentioned in Chapter 1 perpetrators who feel powerless often concoct elaborate fantasies of revenge. In these fantasies, they develop the details of the victims, witnesses, times, places, and the actual dynamics of the violent act. This fantasy becomes for them a primary coping mechanism and their ability to problem solve is increasingly narrowed. The satisfaction they receive from these thoughts only goes so far. Many perpetra-

tors eventually act on their revenge fantasies. Threats, vandalism, and cruelty to animals are common before they attack their intended targets. In the end, the desire to act upon their fantasy becomes a mission.

Stimulus

The stimulus is the event, or series of events, which acts as internal or external triggers for the violence. The stimulus precipitates the violence, and can sometimes be anticipated, allowing protectors time to implement a prevention plan.

RESPONDING TO VIOLENCE

Pollyanna versus Paranoia

The thought of violence occurring on a college campus is so distressing that many people respond in one of two extreme ways: Pollyanna or paranoia. *Pollyanna responders* see the world through rose-colored glasses. They believe in the inherent goodness of people and want to instill values of open-mindedness and acceptance. These responders are likely to believe, perhaps subconsciously, that if they do not talk about violence, it will not exist. This approach creates a situation where people naively enter dangerous situations without the awareness or skills to keep themselves safe. By contrast, *paranoid responders* are overly sensitive to the dangers of the world, and would prefer to keep schools in lock-down. Individuals under the guidance of these paranoid types are apt to rebel against the precautions, or become immobilized with fear.

People should be able to talk about violence in a realistic and balanced way. Given today's trend toward increased violence, protectors must consider violence prepara-

tion as important as fire prevention or other disaster preparedness. Most people do not think that disaster preparedness is overreactive or destructive. Each campus community will need to decide for themselves where they fall on the continuum from Pollyanna to paranoia and respond with interventions that best fit their culture.

One-Way Ticket

Responding to violence is a one-way ticket. Once you have implemented an intervention, you cannot go backwards. As mentioned earlier, there are defining events that change the fabric of our culture–airline terrorists, razor blades in apples, product tampering. These events cause "fence posts" or protective action to occur. Once the fence posts go up, they cannot come down. Imagine how people would respond if tomorrow the Federal Aviation Administration declared that security measures were excessive and resources were better spent in other areas. Most people would be extremely concerned about airline safety.

Over time, security measures become safety signals. People see an armed guard at a bank and feel confident that robbers will choose to go elsewhere. Most people feel insecure when driving a car without a seatbelt fastened, even if it is just across a parking lot. Effective security measures provide a barrier between a potential victim and perpetrator, but none guarantee safety. Nevertheless, once a fence post goes up, it stays up.

Overreacting and Underreacting

Sometimes people worry that they are overreacting to a situation. Academically minded individuals tend to value trust and personal freedom. They become concerned about the ramifications of false positives. What if someone were identified as a potential perpetrator and he or she never mean to harm anyone? Would reputations be harmed? Would the wrongly accused sue? What if schools delegate resources to preventing violence, and the efforts are not warranted?

The truth is protectors will never know if they have overreacted, they will only know if they have underreacted. In other words, if protectors take precautions and violence never occurs, they will never know—was prevention effective or was violence never going to occur in the first place? Effective protectors need to take those calculated risks when warning signs are present. They need to feel comfortable with the possibility of false positives.

The only workplace that consistently exercises a zero tolerance for threats of violence is the airline industry. Anyone who is even hinting at possible violence is taken seriously. Thousands of false positives occur everyday. For some it is an inconvenience or a small embarrassment. Most find it reas-

suring that the airline takes these matters so seriously.

Giving Permission

An important part of responding to violence is to give the campus community permission to do what they need to do to keep safe without inflicting further harm. This may seem self-evident but when violence plays out, breaking through these psychological barriers proves to be difficult for many. For instance, when training school children how to respond during a school shooting, students became concerned that leaving the school building would get them in trouble because they had always been taught that as the rule. Generally speaking we are rule-bound creatures. We may think twice in our evacuation efforts before going through an emergency-only door. We may hesitate before breaking a window while trying to escape. Students and campus employees must believe that if they act in good faith while trying to keep themselves or others safe, they will not be held accountable for breaking campus rules.

Planting Trees

Another metaphor useful in understanding violence prevention and intervention is to think of the violent individual as a skier. As perpetrators start down the "hill" of becoming violent, most tend to start slowly and build up speed. Sometimes they start with low-level threats or vandalism to test out how the system will respond. They continue to escalate until they hit a "tree" or barrier in their path.

Trees come in all shapes and sizes. Trees can be *questioning*. Sometimes the investigation process is enough deterrence. *Confronting* trees up the ante. A warning is a confrontation tree. A security system is a confrontation tree. A police barricade is a confrontation tree. The next level of trees consists of implementing *consequences*. A range of consequences exists from probation to community service to suspension or expulsion/termination. Legal consequences are also an option.

Some trees perpetrators can see for quite a distance away and are easily averted. Some trees are easily identified as mirages, nothing real but just a symbol for others to see. Perpetrators sail right through these trees. Other trees are so large that perpetrators know they will not get around them, so perpetrators stop on their own. For those perpetrators determined to get down the hill, protectors must plant many trees to slow down the perpetrator. Most of the chapters of this book give readers ample suggestions on how they can plant effective trees.

Chapter 3

VULNERABLE TO INFECTION:
RISKS TO COLLEGE COMMUNITIES

[Students] come to college in part for freedom and a sense of belonging, and a locked-down campus runs counter to that lifestyle.
—Report from D. Marcus, *U.S. News & World Report,* 2/20/2000.

The dilemma faced by [college campuses] is similar to that faced by inner-city churches. Efforts to insulate the campus from intrusive crime and violence defeat its purpose as an interactive, societal resource.
—John Schuh (1998).
Violence on Campus, p. 19.

CAMPUSES STRIVE TO PROJECT an impression to the community and prospective applicants. Among other things, campuses want to appear friendly, accessible, and community-oriented. Most campuses operate as both a workplace and a home to thousands of people. Sometimes these dual roles can come into conflict when issues of safety are of concern. Because of these and other unique features of the campus environment, values, people and traditions, many colleges are vulnerable to violence. Campus violence experts such as John Schuh of Iowa State University and Mary Roark of State University of New York College at Plattsburgh have written about such vulnerabilities, and we draw from their observations and add our own. We call these factors the setting, the psyche, the society, the substances, and the sacred cows.

THE SETTING

Campuses are often caught in the crossroads between making their campuses welcoming and making their campuses safe. In their effort to make their environments welcoming, certain safety hazards are inevitable.

Access

Most campuses want their facilities and grounds to appear pleasant and friendly to their employees, students, and visitors. Guidebooks frequently feature color photos of people walking in and out of pleasant

30

looking buildings and strolling through open walkways. While access to buildings and campus grounds might not actually be that easy, the pictures are generally accurate.

Who is to say who belongs on campus and who does not? When we consider the number of people who can walk onto the campus grounds with a legitimate reason for being there, the numbers can be staggering. Current students and current staff clearly come and go at will. Prospective students can also drop in at any time. Consider too the number of former students and former staff, friends and family members of all of the above, and the list goes on exponentially. Any number of these individuals can descend upon a campus without any prior warning, at any time. Colleges usually make some facilities like libraries and fitness centers open to the public as a way to build ties with the local community. Thus, the campus doors are more or less open to all who want to enter. These features are fairly unique to the college setting. The permeable boundaries of the campus make predator infiltration all too easy.

Despite residence hall and security attempts to restrict access to buildings, it is an impossible task to monitor the constant ebb and flow of people. Students often rebel against security locks and codes on their residence halls and will frequently prop the doors open with whatever they can find. Propped doors make student life convenient, but they pose challenges for safety.

Permanence of Location

One unique feature of the campus setting is that most campuses cannot relocate. Given the expensive and specialized infrastructure, few would want to purchase campus property for other types of businesses. Furthermore, many campuses build their identity in part from their surroundings. Relocating the campus would most definite-

ly change the climate of the school. The downside of the permanence of campus location is that if the criminal activity in the neighborhoods surrounding the campus increases, the campus is stuck.

At Regis University in Denver, Colorado, houses in adjacent neighborhoods began showing signs of gang activity. Graffiti tags were seen spray painted on walls. Concerned about the safety of the school, campus officials decided to erect a black iron fence around the perimeter of the campus. As an obstacle the fence did possibly deter graffiti from migrating onto campus buildings. As a symbol to the community it set up barriers between the campus and the neighborhood, an indication that the surrounding families were not welcome on the other side of the fence.

Hours of Operation

Colleges operate 24 hours a day, 365 days a year. The day is not over when classes are finished. Sports events, concerts, evening programs, all-night study sessions, and parties keep much of the college community out and about on the campus grounds long after most workplaces are locked down for the night. Even faculty and staff are known to work long hours, often isolated in their offices. Much of the student-related violence occurs during these evening and weekend hours when professional staff such as counselors and administrators may be less accessible.

Predictability

Another environmental vulnerability is that colleges operate on a predictable schedule. Anyone trying to target an individual or group of people would have an easy time anticipating the location. In the Columbine massacre, this predictability factor was a crucial element in the perpetrator's planning. They timed their siege on the high school to correspond to the time when the greatest number of people would be congregating in the cafeteria and library. The movement of college students and staff can be similarly foreseen.

Throughout the year, the activity on college campuses also ebbs and flows in predictable ways. Holidays, summer vacation, and spring breaks usually bring a lull of activity on campuses. Because there is not as much commotion to attend to, people are more likely to let their guards down.

Perhaps the greatest predictable phase of vulnerability for college campuses is the first few weeks of school. During that time, a large group of new faces, mostly young and inexperienced in the world, descend upon unfamiliar territory. A great number of these students are living away from home for the first time; many have not yet learned the social cues for danger; they have not had experiences to figure out how to handle an emergency; and they do not know how to set limits on alcohol consumption. Many parents and school staff hold their breath during this time, in the hopes that the students will successfully negotiate these weeks without incident.

Crowding

Crowded residences make adjustment to college life very difficult for many students. Most are not used to sharing bathrooms with dozens of people and become annoyed over the lack of privacy residence halls offer. Even within the rooms, personal space is limited and irritates those who are used to having their own rooms.

With crowding comes noise. Even with designated "quiet hours," noise is a continuous problem in most campus residences. Students who like their music loud at 2:00 A.M. neglect to consider their neighbors who are studying for their organic chemistry test the next day. Disruption to sleep due to fire alarms in the middle of the night angers this group who tend to be sleep deprived most of the time anyway.

Parking on most campuses can be another trigger for rage. Students tend to outnumber parking spaces and the race to find the space before the 9:00 A.M. exam begins makes blood boil. Mini campus road rage clashes erupt as they cut each other off. When drivers get creative by parking in nondesignated areas the tickets they receive do not do much to quell the anger.

THE PSYCHE

Certain values of an academic institution may place individuals at a greater risk for danger. Colleges tend to foster trust, respect, independence, freedom of expression, and debate. Under certain circumstances these attributes become catalysts for violence. To be clear, these values are assets to campuses, and to discourage their existence would alter campus life for the worse. They do, however, open opportunities for violence that do not exist in institutions where these beliefs are not as widely held.

Unlike other institutions, trust is cultivated on college campuses. Trust is essential when people who have never met each other are forced to share a living space. There is also a general feeling on most campuses of being a community where everyone is expected to treat their neighbors as they would want to be treated. When new faces appear on campus, most witnesses do not think much about it and trust that these people have a legitimate reason for being there.

If someone is questioned about the

whereabouts of another person, they are usually not suspicious of the motive and will give the needed location without thought. When partying together, students trust that fellow students will not hurt them because they are all just out to have a good time. Trust is an asset in most instances on college campuses. Living in such confined quarters would be difficult without it. But when a person decides to become violent, the trust factor works in the perpetrator's favor.

Most schools have a code of conduct for both students and staff that stresses personal integrity and accountability. Campus community members are expected to uphold a standard of behavior that is representative of the mission of the school. They expect to be treated with honor and respect, and when these codes are broken it often comes as a shock to the recipient.

In classrooms and many staff meetings on college campuses differing points of view are encouraged and valued. Diverse perspectives make discussions lively and creative ideas are brought to fruition. Debate and controversy are not suppressed. The First Amendment rights are expressed freely in most cases. Sometimes, however, the topics become too hot and peaceful protests turn angry and violent. Sometimes, First Amendment rights are abused and hate crimes result.

Independence and personal freedom are strongly held values on college campuses. Students experiment widely with personal choices involving appearance, sexual behavior, alcohol and drugs. And when these choices are not harming other people, many faculty and staff are reluctant to step in the way. Even when personal choices run the risk of self-harm, the value of personal freedom is so strong that people who are in a position to make a difference often look the other way. Faculty members are sometimes the greatest upholders of personal freedom. They will see students drag themselves to their 8:00 A.M. class hungover day after day, but they will not confront them because they believe it is not their place to confront this choice of self-abuse.

While security is important, it is not the main mission of most campuses. Therefore, it is understandable why some security measures take a backseat to the above-mentioned values. Nevertheless, the campus community should be aware of the many ways traditional campus values place them at risk for opportunities for violence.

THE SOCIETY

The campus society is comprised of a diverse group of individuals with varying backgrounds and goals. Students, faculty and staff, and community members all contribute to the tapestry of campus life. And each group potentially brings a threat to campus safety.

Students

By far, those most at risk for becoming victims and perpetrators of violence are the traditional age students. According to the Higher Education Center for Alcohol and Drug Prevention, students perpetrate 70 percent of violent incidents on campuses. These individuals face significant developmental challenges during a time when things are changing all around them. For many, they either learn to develop effective coping strategies, or they begin to develop dysfunctional patterns that will impact their future.

Some violence experts have suggested the increase in high school violence, specifically high-profile school shootings, are an additional risk factor to consider on college campuses. In *Schools, Violence and Society* (1996), A. M. Hoffman calls this trend a "rising tide of violence" in America's elementary and secondary schools, and suggests this rising tide may be spilling over onto college campuses. Others argue that there are enough filtering processes in place that weed out these types of violent offenders from ever reaching campus grounds. In any event, the wave of violent shootings in schools across America has emotionally impacted incoming freshmen in a different way than previous classes have had to deal with, and these students are possibly more aware of potential violence than their predecessors.

Developmental Issues

Adolescents often behave as though they are invulnerable. As children, we often take at face value what authorities have told us is dangerous. As adults, we have often experienced enough negative consequences to know how to make better decisions for ourselves. As adolescents, there is a drive for many to test out what we have been told is true and to believe that we will live forever.

Even when tragedy strikes, such as a drunk-driving fatality, many students still believe that it will never happen to them. Too often in the aftermath of an unexpected, violent campus tragedy, a brief period of shock is followed by a gradual slide back into denial. In one case we experienced firsthand, a popular well-liked student had died as a result of alcohol-induced recklessness on a spring break trip. The campus experienced significant grieving. However, the way some students chose to grieve seemed incongruous to the tragedy. A small group of his friends chose to celebrate his life by getting drunk at the local bars.

Freed from the constant supervision of parents, many college students spend a great

deal of time exploring areas that were previously forbidden. Alcohol and sex usually top this list. As students attempt to figure out what role they want alcohol and sex to have in their lives, many struggle with setting limits. The combination of these exploratory pursuits can sometimes have unwanted outcomes resulting in many forms of sexual assault and alcohol-related violence.

College is a stressful time. Much of the stress is because students have large amounts of unstructured time and multiple long-term demands, and they have not learned appropriate time management skills. In addition to time management, many are dealing with financial strains and must juggle one or more jobs on top of their demanding academic schedule. A recent report of the American Freshmen Survey, a collaborative project between the American Council on Education and UCLA's Higher Education Research Institute, found that 30 percent of freshmen are feeling "frequently overwhelmed" at college. These stress levels have almost doubled since the researchers first conducted this survey in 1985. Grades constantly remind students of their status in their goal to obtain their degree. Each unsatisfactory evaluation given reminds them that their dreams may go unfulfilled. The process of chasing this dream can often seem ethereal.

Many students are poor regulators of stress. They switch into "all-or-nothing mode." Rather than find a way to balance their lives, letting their engine idle at a steady pace, students often slam on the accelerator then the brake then the accelerator then the brake. They avoid studying all semester and then stay up for four consecutive nights. They do not drink all week, and then feel they "deserve" to get outrageously intoxicated on the weekend.

Being "on-schedule" versus "off-schedule" can add to feelings of stress and self-doubt. When students progress in college as anticipated, finishing a four-year program in four years, they are considered "on-schedule." This progress is no longer the norm. Students switch majors, take time off to work or travel and experience medical and emotional setbacks that often delay graduation anywhere from one semester to several years. This sense of being "off-schedule" is difficult for many. They become out of sync with their friends, school debts accumulate, and the destination of reaching a degree and prosperous career feels out of reach.

Transitory Population

For the most part college students are a transitory population during their time at school. Most will not stay in one residence for more than one year, and sometimes students relocate several times in one year. Because of their short-term relationship with these residences and to a lesser extent, the college, students provide less consideration for the long-term effects of their behavior on the campus environment.

Rioting and vandalism are prime examples of this lack of consideration. Many get caught up in the excitement and do not think about the effect the destruction will have on those who have longer-term commitments to the institution and surrounding community. East Lansing residents for example spent many years in conflict with Michigan State University students who rioted in the community. Many townspeople criticized the students for their lack of respect for the people who lived there.

Dealing with Diversity

One of the biggest transitions for new students is dealing with diversity. Campuses tend to be diverse places, and differences often bring conflict. Students often come from homogeneous communities with cul-

tures they knew and understood. When they arrive on campus, they are thrown together with students from around the country and the world, who look and act in very different ways. Intolerance for certain groups may have been supported in their home cultures, but is not supported on college campuses. Coming to terms with these differences can be challenging for some students. Some may choose to subvert to hate crimes as their way of dealing with the uncomfortable feelings this process brings them.

Different cultures also have varying norms for acceptable behavior. This includes violent behavior. What may be an innocuous gesture in one culture may offend another. What may seem like strong discipline in one culture is considered violence in another. Raised voices and heated arguments may be common in one culture and a signal for danger in another. These differences make developing a common language about violence difficult.

Many campuses offer special housing options for students. From Greek residences, to substance-free housing, to international students, to families, these residences are designed for the purpose of bringing like-minded individuals together to share common experiences. Sometimes, however, this plan backfires when "in-group, out-group" polarization evolves. This divergence leads to increased misunderstanding and segregation of the groups.

A Word About "Nontraditional" Students

While an explosion of "nontraditional" students has erupted in the last decade, this population still represents a minority of students. According to the book *Violence on Campus* (Palmer, 1998), the "typical" nontraditional student is a woman, over age 30, who is a part-time student and a commuter.

Nontraditional students are less likely to get involved in social activities that revolve around alcohol. In fact, nontraditional students actually spend little time on campus outside of classes due to the many other obligations they juggle. These students tend to be very concerned about family finances and their children.

For these and other reasons nontraditional students are less likely to be either perpetrators or victims of campus violence. Nevertheless, nontraditional students, like faculty and staff, may experience violence at home that will clearly affect their campus life and academics. In some cases violent partners may follow students to school and stalk or attack them there. In addition to being affected by violence in the home and in the general community, nontraditional students are also affected by the violence perpetrated and inflicted upon their traditional-aged peers.

One other issue to consider is the fact that some students have had violent histories, including arrests and jail time, before enrolling in college. In Chapter 7, we discuss legal issues and policy implications in more depth. There we explore the difficult decisions schools have had to face denying or accepting the enrollment of known felons, even murderers. To complicate matters further, individuals who committed violent crimes in their youth often have their records sealed and admissions may not gain access to these important potential violence indicators. Nevertheless, colleges that cater to nontraditional students are finding themselves facing these issues as those who have served jail time attempt to start a new life. Comprehensive databases do not exist giving schools pre-enrollment violence statistics for nontraditional students, so the true extent of the problem remains speculative.

Faculty and Staff

Colleges and universities are workplaces, and like other workplaces they are not immune to workplace violence issues such as the disgruntled employee and the vengeful student. In Chapter 14 on homicide and physical assault, two high-profile cases of workplace violence are described—one involving a professor who murdered his colleagues, and the other a graduate student who murdered his professors. Both perpetrators were "avenger" types; harbored injustices turned to blind rage.

University faculty and staff are not immune from the issues of domestic violence. Employers of many types of workplaces have come to the realization that violence that starts at home can often follow employees to work. In rare, but terrifying cases male perpetrators stalk and sometimes even kill their girlfriends or wives in the workplace. According to the Family Violence Prevention Fund, approximately 13,000 acts of domestic violence against women occur in the workplace each year. When women attempt to protect themselves by moving to a shelter or changing their phone number, their partners still know where to find them eight hours a day.

Universities may have difficulty preventing this type of violence because victims of domestic violence usually do not come forward voluntarily with their concerns. Instead, supervisors can sometimes pick up on cues that domestic violence is occurring from increased absenteeism, clothing worn to conceal bruises, or incessant harassing phone calls from the partner.

Faculty members are especially vulnerable targets on college campuses. They are usually very accessible and predictable, having open office hours and regular class schedules. Faculty members often work in isolated areas and sometimes work late into the night. In contrast to senior leaders of major corporations, faculty are on-site and do not have front-line buffers of administrative staff to work as gatekeepers for their visitors. Faculty members are also common targets of anger as they control major decisions in students' lives. Therefore, grading and exam time can be vulnerable times for faculty safety if there is a particular student who has given them trouble during the year.

Surrounding Community

As mentioned earlier, the campus community involves the larger society in which it resides. Athletic events, concerts, museum exhibits, special lectures, theater performances all bring community members on campus in large groups and as individuals. Outside guests are often invited to campus too as speakers, conference attendees, or for other programs hosted on campus grounds. For the most part, colleges and the towns they live in enjoy a symbiotic relationship—each benefits greatly from the other. But sometimes the outside community can perpetrate extensive violence on campuses and vice versa.

Rioting on campuses is an example of this problem. A large number of individuals engaged in the campus rioting were either from visiting schools or the community. Some of these individuals might even have had feelings of revenge motivating their attacks on campus property. Students from a visiting campus who are present to watch a sporting event might perpetrate violence in the case of an upset or even a victory.

"Pre-frosh" or students who visit during their senior year of high school to become acquainted with the campus are sometimes very vulnerable to violence. In an effort to show them a good time, many college hosts offer these often-inexperienced drinkers large amounts of alcohol. In their naivete, some of the female high school students can find themselves in dangerous acquaintance rape situations while they are totally unfamiliar with the campus and security resources.

THE SUBSTANCES

Because the next chapter is dedicated to the relationship of alcohol abuse and campus violence, we will just underscore the issue briefly here. Alcohol is a prime catalyst to most forms of campus violence. Clearly, there is not a cause-and-effect relationship. Many people get drunk and do not inflict violence, and many people who are not drunk do cause harm to others. Nevertheless, alcohol has biological and social effects on people that increase the probability that violence will occur to individuals under its influence.

Besides alcohol, other drugs can also contribute to campus violence. Much of the relevant literature from the past three decades has been comprehensively reviewed by Robert Parker and Kathleen Auerhahn in their 1998 publication "Alcohol, Drugs, and Violence" and has served as the basis for much of this section. Adapting from one resource cited in this work, there are three ways in which drug use may be causally related to violence:

- **"DRUG" or Psychopharmacological Violence** is related to the actual chemically induced properties of the drug itself. Drugs can cause agitation and paranoia in a perpetrator, and can also cause sedation and memory loss in victims.
- **"SET" or User-Based Violence** en-

compasses internal expectations or needs of the user. One example of this form of violence is economically motivated crimes. Illicit drugs often are expensive, and because of this, users may often engage in other illegal behaviors to obtain the drugs. Others may use drugs to drum up a false sense of courage before committing a violent act.

• **"SETTING" or Culturally Influenced Violence** is violence shaped by expectations or traditions of the social group using the drug separate from the actual effect of the drug. Of these three factors, the setting is often the most powerful predictor of violence. Parker and Auerhahn conclude, "Our review of the literature finds a great deal of evidence that the social environment is a much more powerful contributor to the outcome of violent behavior than are pharmacological factors associated with any of the substances reviewed here" ("Alcohol, Drugs, and Violence," p. 301).

Illicit drugs affect judgment and emotions in different ways. When individuals are under the influence of mind-altering substances, their ability to find alternative ways of coping in social situations can become limited. Some users of drugs rationalize under-the-influence behavior as being acceptable since they were not in their right minds. These cognitive acrobatics reduce personal responsibility and give users a socially acceptable excuse to engage in otherwise prohibited behavior.

The other issue with illicit drugs is that they involve dealing the substances illegally. Students often end up in places that they would not otherwise be to get drugs, and they become easily identified as targets for street violence. Additionally, when students deal drugs out of their on-campus residences, they run the risk of spreading a new virus of violence originating from a different hosting site. In other words, street violence—robbery, gang activity, and other forms of violence usually perpetrated off-campus—can infiltrate the campus boundaries when drug activity is at hand.

The presence of illicit drugs can also influence the climate of the social environment. Social rules of behavior are often discarded when certain drugs are present as the atmosphere becomes increasingly permissive. Because drugs are used in private or semi-private environments, the chances of outside enforcement or social control is slim, and an "anything goes" sentiment can prevail.

According to "Monitoring the Future Study" published by the University of Michigan's Institute for Social Research (Arbor, 1999), the annual prevalence rates for youth drug use for most illicit substances appears to be gradually declining since the mid-1990s. Most notably, inhalant use and crack cocaine use dropped significantly during this time. Ecstasy use seemed to be increasing toward the end of the decade. This research focused on eighth, tenth, and twelfth graders, not college students. Nevertheless, the data can be used to predict incoming trends to college campuses.

Not all illicit drugs that make their way to campus are created equal. Some drugs with a sedating effect minimally impact violence, while others increase violence potential under certain circumstances. Contrary to popular opinion, however, most recent research concludes that it is not the drugs themselves that cause physiological changes leading to violence, but it is the context that drugs are used in that leads to violence. The 1992 Bureau of Justice Statistics indicated that only 5.6 percent of violent perpetrators had positive urinalysis findings of illicit drug use at the time of the offense. Study after study supports the fact that alcohol is overwhelmingly the substance most frequently implicated in most forms of violence.

According to the Higher Education

Center (2000), marijuana is the most frequently used illicit drug in the United States and on college campuses. Data collected by the Core Institute indicates that the annual usage of marijuana has steadily increased since 1990. The specific effects of marijuana depend on the strain of marijuana used, the method of ingestion, the environment in which it is taken, the expectations of the user, and whether or not other drugs are used at the same time. It is generally accepted, however, that the use of marijuana actually suppresses hostility while the user is high.

Heroin is a drug rarely used on college campuses, but one that has recently been making a comeback in the 1990s. A significantly sedating drug, heroin is not usually associated with violence, with one exception. There is some evidence that heroin is associated with economically motivated property crimes. Another comeback drug, LSD, seems to have found its place with some college students. LSD is relatively inexpensive, and does not produce compulsive drug-seeking behavior as more addicting drugs such as nicotine and cocaine. The strength of LSD has declined in the last 30 years, and there is no substantial evidence linking LSD to violence.

"Rave" or "club drugs" have been increasing popular in recent years. Ecstasy and GHB (Gamma hydroxy butyric acid) are two of the most common. Ecstasy acts like a stimulant and a mild hallucinogen, and has been shown to turn off brain cells responsible for memory and sleep. Rave participants usually take the drug to induce a warm sense of well-being accompanied by heightened senses. The drug helps keep them awake during these all-night dance parties. While ecstasy is related to dehydration and may cause long-term brain damage, it is not associated with violence. In fact, one of the stated ideologies behind the raves is called PLUR—peace, love, unity, and respect.

GHB is another story. We explore the effects of GHB and another party drug with potential violent consequences, Rohypnol, in the Sexual Assault chapter of this book (Chapter 10). GHB has been historically used by bodybuilders for its ability to stimulate growth hormone release. Over the Internet individuals can receive kits giving instructions on how to make it in their homes. The actual extent to which GHB and Rohypnol are used in cases of rape is unknown because the necessary urinalysis testing in the immediate aftermath of rape is rare. GHB overdose is another concern when unconsciousness, coma, or even death results as was the case for actor River Phoenix. This consequence usually occurs when individuals take GHB with large amounts of alcohol. Proponents of GHB state that the drug is a less violent alternative to alcohol and may even serve as a helpful sleep aid and nutrient.

There may be a pharmacological link between amphetamines and violence. When use is sustained over long periods of time or when acute doses of speed are extremely heavy, users can experience a "toxic psychosis" that is essentially indistinguishable from schizophrenia. A complicating factor of this research is that users who have shown violent behavior before using amphetamines are more likely to engage in violence after ingestion of amphetamines. Similarly, cocaine use is linked to violent behavior. Because cocaine use can lead to paranoid feelings, some users act out violently to irrational fears while under the influence of this drug.

Methamphetamine is another stimulant popular with the club crowd. It is very inexpensive to make using over-the-counter materials. Abusers usually show signs of agitation and increased physical activity levels. The direct association with meth and violence is unknown and an area for future study. A recent review by the National Institute of Justice (1999) revealed the surprising finding that methamphetamine users were less likely to be charged with a violent offense than other drug arrestees. Nicotine and caffeine while stimulants are not associated with aggression, and may in fact reduce aggressive tendencies by giving agitated people a "time out."

PCP or phencyclidine is often associated with violence, but this assertion is usually based only on single cases. While PCP has not had great popularity on college campuses, its close cousin ketamine has recently been perceived as a recreational drug of choice for some students. "Special K" and PCP are both considered "dissociative anaesthetics" because they diminish the sensation of pain while distorting reality. Despite the reputation these drugs have for causing violence, at least one researcher cited in Parker and Auerhahn's (1998) review believed that emotionally stable people under the influence of these drugs would not tend to act differently than their normal behavior.

Anabolic steroids also have raised concern in relation to violence. Anabolic steroids are related to male sex hormones and promote skeletal muscle development. They are legally available in the United States by prescription. Case studies have called the impact "'roid rage," and have suggested that increased levels of male hormones can lead to homicidal impulses and other forms of violent crime. Others suggest that those who engage in violence while under the influence of steroids are fulfilling an expectation perpetuated by extensive media attention to the issue. Anabolic steroid use by student athletes is currently at its lowest levels since 1985 (NCAA, 1997).

Polysubstance abuse (using several different drugs at the same time) adds increased risk for violence and other negative outcomes for several reasons. First, drugs can have a number of interacting effects with each other when consumed simultaneously. One of these interaction effects is called *synergy* whereby one drug accentuates the effects of another. This problem can be seen with the combination of alcohol and some of the so-called "date rape drugs." The date rape drugs amplify the effect of the alcohol making the victim feel much more intoxicated than they usually would with the same dose of alcohol alone. Second, with increased drug activity and impaired mental state, individuals begin to lose their ability to cope with life stressors effectively. They may begin to resort to antisocial behavior as a means of solving problems and obtaining more drugs.

In summary, alcohol is the only drug whose consumption has been shown to commonly increase aggression. This issue will be comprehensively explored in the next chapter. The data on the other drugs remain inconclusive. Large doses of some drugs including amphetamines, cocaine, and PCP may lead to violent episodes in individuals who are predisposed to psychosis. Illegal drugs are more likely linked to violence through drug marketing and distribution.

THE SACRED COWS

Sacred cows are those groups or individuals that are treated by a different standard than the rest of the campus community. The violent behavior of these people may be excused from consequences due to their perceived importance or influence of powerful stakeholders. Sacred cows can be athletes, or even whole athletic teams, sons or daughters of influential alumni or board of trustees, student body presidents or other campus leaders.

Traditions are also sacred cows. Initiation into college life is an important transition, and initiation practices create bonding and a sense of belonging. Some traditions have existed on campuses for generations and give campus life a sense of history. Lately the values of some of the more dangerous rituals have been thrown into question. Most notably, the recent tragic situation of the collapsed Texas A&M bonfire that killed twelve students challenged the existence of a ninety-year-old ritual. Some claim that the accident was inevitable as each year's students tried to outdo the previous year by building even bigger structures. Campus officials, critics say, turned a blind eye toward the inherent dangers just because the event was a piece of campus history. Supporters claim the tradition was an organized event, scientifically engineered by students and supported by university administration. Even some of those students who lost friends in the tragedy support the continuance of the ritual.

Another tradition at Princeton University was put to an end in recent years. "Nude Olympics" began decades ago with a small group of men doing naked jumping jacks in public areas in the middle of winter. This event evolved to four hundred naked students and organized events such as wheelbarrow races. The university became concerned about the negative image these events were having on the institution as many intoxicated students engaged in these events, some even urinating and having sex in public. In February 2000, in subzero temperatures, Princeton University Nude Olympians were greatly outnumbered by administrators, campus security, emergency medical personnel, and the media. The event was a total flop.

Recently the media has targeted athletes

and fraternity members as the sacred cows in college violence. Some view this scrutiny as unfair stating that athletes and fraternity members are only marked because of their high visibility. Others say the investigation into this issue is long overdue. According to the Higher Education Center 92 percent of documented gang rapes were committed by members of fraternities or intercollegiate athletic teams. The Higher Education Center also reported that male athletes and fraternity members are also overrepresented in non-sexual assault violence such as fistfights.

Jeff Benedict, former director of research at the Center for Study of Sport in Society at Northeastern University suggests that people tend to minimize the seriousness of violence committed by student athletes. According to Benedict's research, athletes comprised only 3.3 percent of the student body but were responsible for 19 percent of the reported sexual assaults. In 1995, he found that no fewer than two hundred twenty college athletes were subject to criminal proceedings, more than half of those crimes were sexual assault or incidents of domestic violence.

The NCAA (National Collegiate Athletic Association) states that scholarships can be revoked if athletes are found to have engaged in serious behavior warranting disciplinary action. Often determining the correct course of action is complicated in these circumstances. Benedict notes that during investigation, a process that can take months to complete, athletes are often allowed to continue playing their sport. He suggests that institutions should immediately remove from play any athlete arrested or otherwise formally charged with a felony or a misdemeanor involving an aggressive act against another student. Furthermore, Benedict recommends that coaches should be careful in choosing who they give scholarships to and avoid rewarding athletes with violent histories.

At the University of Minnesota, independent investigators reviewed forty cases where athletes have been accused of sexual and domestic assaults in order to determine what if any systematic interference occurred to impede a fair judicial process. They determined that only in one instance did an athletic official interfere with the criminal investigation. Nevertheless, investigators did conclude that there was a "pattern of favoritism" among athletic officials toward the accused student athletes, and that many of the alleged victims were treated insensitively.

Others outside of the athletic department have pressured colleges to show leniency to accused student athletes. At Florida State University, President Talbot D'Alemberte suggested that a star football player serve a jail sentence for a $600 shoplifting crime before returning to play. One alumnus wrote, "How dare you treat Athletic Director Hart and Coach Bowden as mere subordinates. I will never give another penny to the university as long as you are president of the institution." In the end, this student worked out a deal to do community service instead of jail time, and he was allowed to return to the football team. The team later went on to win the Sugar Bowl, largely due to this player's performance.

Student athletes are not the only sacred cows of the athletic department. Bob Knight, the fired Indiana University basketball coach made headlines with his history of abusive behavior. He was even caught choking a player. But he was not immediately dismissed from the university. First, he was fined $30,000 and suspended for three games. The university president Myles Brand indicated that the university played a role in allowing this behavior to continue by either ignoring inappropriate behavior or by letting Mr. Knight off with light sanctions. When a local paper polled Indianapolis residents about their views on the matter, 55 percent stated they supported the decision to keep Mr. Knight as coach while 39 percent disagreed. One faculty member stated, "[The decision] sends the message that athletics are more important than academics, that marketing and revenue streams mean more than scholarships" (McKinely, 2000).

Greek life has long been treated as a sacred cow on many campuses. Recently increasing numbers of students have exposed dehumanizing and sometimes life-risking practices they were pressured to endure. Consequently, the Greek system is currently under close scrutiny. Many campuses are asking themselves, "Are the benefits of fraternities and sororities outweighing the consequences?" On a parallel course, many athletic departments are also being closely examined and regulated in attempts to deter hazing rituals.

In conclusion, some areas of campus vulnerability we cannot do much about. Nor do we want to. Most campuses cannot change their location, and will not change the policies and practices that make campus life an open community. However, becoming aware of potential areas of weakness in campus safety can give campuses an awareness that will hopefully lead to early detection of developing violence.

Chapter 4

ALCOHOL: A VIOLENCE CATALYST

Any concerted effort to reduce campus interpersonal violence or crimes
against property must address the use and abuse of psychoactive substances.
—Dr. T. Rivinus and Dr. M. Larimer (1993).
Campus Violence: Kinds, Causes, and Cures, p. 106.

A UNIVERSITY OF CALIFORNIA, Davis senior celebrated his twenty-first birthday by slamming shot after shot for ninety minutes. He mixed tequila with bourbon and whiskey on this rite of passage frequently referred to as "21-for-21." For this tradition, individuals drink one shot for every year of their life. It often amounts to suicide. This student passed out soon after his twenty-first drink. By the time his friends got him to the hospital, his lips were blue. His blood alcohol content was .50, but his official cause of death was choking on his own vomit. Drinking traditions common on college campuses can leave a trail of death and violence in their path.

Georgetown University experienced back-to-back alcohol-related violence and death during the winter of 1999–2000. In December, a Georgetown student vandalized a Jewish menorah while drunk and in February, David Shick, a twenty-year-old junior, died four days after receiving a severe head injury during an alcohol-fueled fistfight. The death was ruled as a homicide by the medical examiner's office. Physical assault is probably the most frequent alcohol-related form of violence; however, the effects of alcohol play a critical role in many sexual assaults, hate crimes, riots, and hazing.

A tradition at the University of Virginia is called "fourth-year fifth"–in which seniors attempt to consume a fifth of alcohol during the last home football game. When asked about this tradition, one student commented, "Come on, all of college is about binge drinking."

Scott Krueger is the person most associated with alcohol-related death on a college campus. As part of an initiation rite into his pledged fraternity Phi Gamma Delta (FIJI), Scott died after consuming a significant amount of alcohol during a short period of time (see Chapter 1 for his story). The case brought national attention because it occurred at a place where alcohol and hazing are not even supposed to be issues. According to MIT, the Institute's high-risk drinking rate is half the national average–23 percent compared to the 44 percent national rate. Yet, Scott's death showed the nation that if a promising student like he could die from alcohol-related hazing, then it could happen anywhere.

In the aftermath of his death, Krueger's

family expressed criticism with the policies and practices of MIT. Among other things, the family felt that the Institute's housing policies played a significant role in Scott's death. To avoid overcrowding its dormitories, MIT required about 60 percent of all freshman males to choose fraternity housing. This factor undoubtedly contributed to Scott's decision to pledge a fraternity, thus placing an unnecessary risk of his subjection to hazing practices. The family was also troubled by the fact that a formal acknowledgment from MIT, and an apology for their role in Scott's death was slow to come, and that no one has yet been held accountable for Scott's death.

To MIT's credit, the school responded to the tragedy in many ways. Enforcement and disciplinary proceedings stepped up, housing provisions improved, and prevention and education increased. ABC's "20/20," A&E's "Investigative Reports," CBS's "48 Hours," and Court TV have all featured special programs on the tragic death of Scott to increase awareness of the dangers of hazing and high-risk drinking. Scott's death and the ensuing media coverage put a human face to the national issue of college alcohol abuse and hazing practices. As one MIT student commented (as quoted in the *Higher Education Center News*):

[Scott Krueger] had become a flash point in the national debate about drinking on campuses, and the handsome face and dimpled smile of his high school yearbook photo had become a symbol of the danger alcohol poses to youthful innocents just sent off to college. . . .

The media attention surrounding Scott's death was soon amplified by additional headlines during the spring of 1998. During this time, the Harvard School of Public Health released a second wave of publications on "binge drinking." This intense media focus on alcohol abuse created an uproar of concern with college administrators and a backlash among many students. Protests and riots after colleges crack down on drinking behavior make some campuses leery of enforcing strict alcohol abuse prevention policies. "Chicken and egg" questions arise: is alcohol leading to violence or are the alcohol abuse prevention measures leading to rioting?

Many college drinking hangouts are losing their fear of student retaliation. On South Padre Island, the violence and social problems associated with alcohol abuse have become so disturbing local residents are trying to lose the 300,000 college tourists they attract each year. Most spring break vacation spots have found that the costs of hosting thousands of drunken college students outweigh the meager dollars they spend while in town. During one spring break season, the South Padre Police Department arrested 530 people, a multifold increase from the normal fifteen to twenty monthly arrest rate. Fort Lauderdale learned this lesson long ago and has changed its marketing strategy from targeting rowdy college students to attracting families, resulting in a huge increase in revenue and decrease in headaches for the area.

HIGH-RISK DRINKING ON COLLEGE CAMPUSES

Alcohol is clearly the drug of choice for most college students. Drinking games have a long history on college campuses. Quarters, chugging races, beer bongs, and many other contests often lead to large quan-

tities of alcohol consumed in a short period of time. With these types of games, drinkers easily lose track of how much alcohol they are consuming, becoming increasingly vulnerable to alcohol poisoning.

What We Know

In the last decade, some researchers investigated the campus phenomenon they labeled *binge drinking*. This catchphrase, used to describe high-risk drinking, is defined by researchers as five drinks or more in a row for men and four or more for women. As Dr. William DeJong, Director for the Higher Education Center for Alcohol and Other Drug Prevention, notes, the problem with this term is that four or five drinks over a several-hour period does not relate to the commonly held image of a drinking binge, especially for college students (DeJong, 2000). Thus, for this book we choose to use the terms "high-risk drinking" or "heavy episodic use" to describe a large amount (e.g., 5+ drinks) of alcohol consumed in a short period of time (e.g., 0–2 hours) or otherwise drinking that exceeds the "injury dose" for a person. Injury dose means the amount of alcohol that typically results in negative consequences for the consumer (e.g., vomiting, severe hangover, fights, falls, blackouts, etc.).

Dr. DeJong also notes that *responsible drinking* is a confusing term as well. Most people, despite where they fall on the drinking continuum, consider their drinking responsible. From our focus groups on campus, we discovered many students believed that responsible drinking meant getting a sober driver to take you home. Dr. DeJong supports this notion and cites research that indicates that even heavy drinkers view their own level of drinking as "responsible." Because of this confusion, we choose to use the term *low-risk drinking* to describe standard guidelines for decreasing consequences related to alcohol use. The 0-1-3 guidelines suggest for some situations no alcohol is appropriate. Zero alcohol consumption is important for those dependent on alcohol, pregnant women, and most high-risk tasks such as driving. Otherwise, for most people one drink per hour with meals, and no more than three in any sitting will usually minimize consequences.

According to research conducted by the Harvard School of Public Health (1998) sponsored by the Robert Wood Johnson Foundation, high-risk drinkers on college campuses tend to be white, live in a fraternity, and have a history of heavy episodic drinking in high school. From this research it appears that frequent heavy episodic drinking is on the increase. In 1993 the rate was 19.8 percent and in 1999 the rate moved up to 22.7 percent. High-risk drinkers such as this group have increased rates of missing class, getting into trouble, and getting hurt.

Recent studies conducted by the Core Institute (cited in Nuwer, 1999) indicate that Greek leaders actually consume more alcohol than lower-level members. Furthermore, as groups, athletes and Greeks drink more than the rest of the college population. According to the National Interfraternity Conference (NIC) (cited in Nuwer, 1999), alcohol is the number one risk-management concern. Alcohol was involved in 95 percent of falls, 94 percent of fights, 93 percent of sexual assaults, and 87 percent of automobile accidents. The NIC also reports that in almost nine out of ten fraternity deaths alcohol played a role.

Hank Nuwer, the national hazing expert, calls one frightening pattern of fraternity response to alcohol poisoning, "Greekthink." In the moment of crisis when an individual has become hurt or is critically impaired by alcohol, there is a devastating pause. At the time when first responders should be racing to get appropriate medical attention, these individuals who are often fairly impaired themselves think, "oh shit." They pause because they are concerned about getting in trouble, about covering up evidence, and about taking care of the problem themselves. This pause often leads to lifesaving minutes lost.

A secondary analysis of the Harvard study presented for the American Public Health Association looked at multidrug users. The subjects of this study were students who drank heavily and consumed two or more illicit drugs. Researchers found that multidrug users were at an even greater risk for alcohol-related accidents, for engaging in unprotected sex, and for getting in trouble with the law than either the binge drinkers (who did not use drugs) or the exclusive substance users (e.g., people who only used marijuana). Another trend these researchers discovered was that close to 60 percent of the multidrug users were regular heavy drinkers in high school, about a twofold increase than among any other drug use subgroups.

Unfortunately, despite the level of consequences and duration of these problematic behaviors, very few high-risk drinkers consider their behavior an issue. Even when they do consider their behavior a problem, very few consider getting help. Evidence from the Harvard Study indicated that only one in five students who recognized they had a drug or drinking problem had ever sought counseling for it.

On the opposite end of the continuum the Harvard Study reports another trend: the percentage of nondrinkers is also on the rise. In 1993 this rate was 15.4 percent and in 1999 the rate rose to 19.2 percent. Low-risk drinkers tended to be black or Asian, over twenty-four years old, and married. This trend actually reflects a larger trend in America towards decreased consumption of alcohol and an increased number of abstainers.

The "Right to Party" Protests

As colleges become more aggressive in their attempt to curb high-risk drinking, the student backlash is gaining momentum. In a later chapter we will discuss the rise of rioting on college campuses as a result of this "Right to Party" agenda. In essence, students are expressing outrage of tighter policies and tougher consequences for underage drinking and drunkenness by wreaking havoc on their campuses. The thought is that if enough damage is done, campus officials will regret their enforcement decisions and become more liberal with their policies. According to Nuwer's interviewees, the students report feeling empowered by gathering together and demonstrating (Nuwer, 1999). They state that their efforts show that campus administrators are very "out of touch" with the student body. If anything, the way this "Right to Party" protest is currently going, the opposite effect is taking place. Many colleges do not want to be bullied by violence and are holding to or increasing the strictness of their policies.

Many agree that the issues of freedoms and responsibility underlying this outrage are valid, but believe the methods of protest are counterproductive. In many countries, drinking alcohol is a symbolic claim to independence and rebellion against authority. These cultural beliefs can be powerful motivators to challenge established rules. A former sorority national president paraphrased in Nuwer's book *The Wrongs of Passage,* states, ". . . in a democracy, students who felt strongly that the state drinking laws were passed in error could take their case to legislators and to the press for an amendment. Those committed to protecting the rights of students must give a little too and consider the rights of their fellow citizens. . ." (p. 78).

Institutional Denial

In his book *Wrongs of Passage,* Hank Nuwer indicates many colleges are in a state of denial when it comes to admitting their institutional drinking problem, very much like an alcoholic. He calls these colleges "addictive organizations" and lists many "enabling" behaviors colleges engage in to allow the students' out-of-control drinking to continue without consequences. *Enabling,* an addictions term, occurs when one person or group of people minimizes the short-term consequences for an addicted person without addressing the long-term problems. For example, between individuals enabling occurs when a friend or spouse calls into work for someone who is incapacitated by a hangover.

Nuwer suggests that on an institutional level enabling is happening when colleges require their Greek houses to hold "dry rushes." Nationals and school administrators will require the undergraduate officers to sign off on contracts stating they will not serve alcohol to minors, but no one ensures these contracts are enforced, and they are often perceived as a joke. When campus authorities conduct house inspections with Greeks, they often announce their visits well enough in advance for members to hide any incriminating evidence. When investigations are conducted, they usually meet the legal requirements, but are not comprehensive enough to uncover what is really going on. Similar practices occur on athletic teams for initiation and recruit hosting practices.

For the general population of college students, there sometimes exists a mentality of "boys will be boys" that can lead to relaxed standards of accountability. According to many alcohol experts cited in *Campus Violence,* this process of thinking often relocates the origin of the problem not with the intoxicated individual, but the substance itself: "The beer made me do it." Those who buy into this line of thinking often excuse otherwise inexcusable behavior with the "drunkenness defense," and thereby promote the continuance of violence.

The mere belief that drunkenness can be used to excuse violent behavior is perhaps the most

straightforward sociocultural risk factor affecting intoxicated violence. . . ."

–Kai Pernanen (1998). *Contemporary Drug Problems,* 25 (3), pp. 477–509.

College alcohol use expert, Henry Wechsler and others wrote an article for *The Chronicle of Higher Education* (1995) on this topic as well. They discuss the tendency of parents and school officials sometimes have of turning the other cheek because they too engaged in alcohol abuse during their college years. The difference is that today lethal sexually transmitted diseases, easy availability of guns, and overcrowded highways make the consequences of alcohol abuse more deadly. The authors sum up this issue with this quote:

Those in denial act as if they believe that this deep-seated American problem can be changed by someone, able and dedicated, working part time in a basement office at the student-health service.

–Wechsler, H., Deutsch, & Dowdall (1995). Too many colleges are still in denial about alcohol abuse. *The Chronicle of Higher Education.* Opinion & Arts Section.

Alcohol and Advertising–A Blessed Curse for College Communities

More universities are giving up big-time revenue from alcohol advertising and sales in an effort to separate themselves from the public relations problems high-risk drinking is causing. Athletic events can bring in significant revenue from the alcohol industry– scholarships, apparel, radio programs, scoreboard ads, as well as consumption of their product. As alcohol-induced unruly student behavior becomes increasingly frowned upon in the public eye, many schools are faced with a dilemma. What, if any, relationship with the alcohol industry is appropriate for a college campus?

Jean Kilbourne, social commentator on advertising practices in the United States, makes convincing arguments in her video *Calling the Shots* (1991)on how the advertising industry targets young adults in the college-age range, and promotes heavy consumption of their product. In particular, she describes several media campaigns linking alcohol with sexual behavior and the objectification of women. She considers these practices highly irresponsible given the significant co-occurrence of sexual assault and alcohol impairment.

In his book *Beer Blast* (1998), alcohol-advertising insider Philip Van Munching, former advertising director for Heineken, gives several examples of beer advertising imagery designed to appeal to young drinkers. The most infamous example, of course is Spuds MacKenzie, the "Party Animal" and Bud Light spokesdog. During his reign, Spuds was frequently shown skate-boarding and dancing and helped increase Bud Light sales 21 percent. The fact that Spuds was also very attractive for children caused an uproar among parents across the nation.

On the other side of the argument, many believe that it is in the alcohol industry's best interest to lower the risk to their consumers for improved public relations and longevity of their market (you cannot buy their product if you die from an alcohol overdose). As Trish Bonnell, an educational director for Anheuser-Busch commented, "The problem isn't alcohol, but rather alcohol abuse." Anheuser-Busch funded a $2.7 million grant for alcohol abuse prevention programs on college campuses. Anheuser-Busch sponsors "T.I.P.S." training for servers of alcohol to reduce underage and problematic drinking and an educational program for high schools featuring a "Flight-for-Life" nurse who talks about the grizzly details of drunk-driving accidents.

Likewise, other beer companies have made efforts to enforce underage drinking laws and to increase education about responsible serving of alcohol. For example, Coors launched a campaign designed to encourage underage individuals to wait until they were of legal age before drinking. Many companies now add tag lines to their advertising spots encouraging "responsible drinking" and discouraging impaired driving. Again, the term *responsible drinking* remains problematic, but the message is a step in the right direction. The Century Council, a national prevention task force funded by America's leading distillers, created "Alcohol 101" an interactive CD-Rom educational tool designed to teach college students about the consequences of high-risk drinking.

Nevertheless, with so many colleges working hard to discourage alcohol abuse, many feel the alcohol advertising on their campuses sends a mixed message to students. Many have banned alcohol advertising or sales from athletic events, school newspapers, and campus celebrations. Other campuses take advantage of the beer industry's educational and prevention opportunities but control the dissemination of the sponsorship. For example, the National Collegiate Alcohol Awareness Week Awards are offered every year to colleges demonstrating outstanding substance abuse prevention strategies. Award applications are under the direction of Fort Hays University, but a little known fact is that the thousands of dollars in prize money is actually funded by Coors. Clearly, the issue of alcohol advertising and sponsorship on college campuses remains controversial and unresolved for many campuses at this time.

HOW ALCOHOL LINKS TO VIOLENCE

There are clear links between alcohol and violence. Consider the statistics:

- Criminal violence and homicide are associated with intoxication by the aggressor and victim in 60–70 percent of documented cases (cited in *Campus Violence*, p. 86). (Rivinus & Larimer 1993)
- The Core Institute reports that almost half of all college students experience violence on campus and alcohol is almost always involved.
- Gun possession at college is significantly more likely among students who drink five or more drinks in one sitting (Harvard Study published in *The Journal of American College Health*, 1999).
- Studies of sexual violence on college campuses estimate that 75 percent of victims and perpetrators had been using alcohol at the time of the crime (cited in *Campus Violence*, p. 86). (Rivinus & Larimer 1993)
- A 1998 study published in the *American Journal of Health Studies* found that alcohol was involved in almost 60 percent of non-sexual assaults perpetrated on college students.
- One study indicated that 27 percent of women had experienced rape or attempted rape after being given alcohol or other drugs by the perpetrator (cited in *Campus Violence*, p. 94). (Rivinus & Larimer 1993)
- According to research published by the Alcohol Related Injuries and Violence Project 35–63 percent of all firearms victims had alcohol in their blood, as well as 18–65 percent of suicide victims (cited in *HECNews*, 2000).

Dr. Timothy Rivinus, a Harvard researcher summarizes some of what we currently know about the relationship between alcohol and violence in the edited book entitled *Campus Violence* (1993). We know that alcohol decreases pain sensitivity, anxiety about future consequences, and frustration tolerance. Flexible problem-solving ability decreases with intoxication. We also know that witnessing or engaging in prior alcohol-related violence plays a major role in the connection between alcohol and violence. Finally, alcohol abuse has a built-in denial mechanism: blacking out. Two studies have shown that alcohol abusers who committed violent acts have little or no memory of their behavior.

We also know that alcohol directly effects the brain. All parts of the brain are eventually impacted with excessive consumption of alcohol, but it is the frontal lobe that plays a critical role in judgment and behavior inhibition. The frontal lobe is one of the first areas of the brain to be affected by alcohol, and thus, appears to lead to increased impulsivity and "acting out" behavior. The frontal lobe is also responsible for long-range planning, and when it becomes impaired, short-term objectives become more pronounced. Thus, in the case of sexual violence, the immediate gratification of forced sex may supercede any fear of long-term legal, emotional, or health consequences.

With violence, not all alcohol is created equal. Research conducted by the Alcohol Related Injuries and Violence (ARIV) project, funded by the Robert Wood Johnson Foundation (cited in Join Together Online, 2000), has shown that beer is overwhelmingly associated with violence. According to these findings, 80 percent of beer is consumed in a hazardous way as compared to 16 percent of liquor and 4 percent of wine. This may be due to the fact that beer is relatively cheaper and is perceived as less harmful than other types of alcohol beverages.

Percent of College Students Drunk in the Last Month and Suffering Alcohol Consequences in the Last Three Months

	Males		Females	
	Low Anger	High Anger	Low Anger	High Anger
Broke something	3%	30%	4%	17%
Felt like hurting others	16%	57%	2%	16%
Felt like hurting self	7%	9%	2%	13%
Vomited	22%	50%	18%	37%

Source: Adapted from an unpublished manuscript (2000). Used with the permission of J. Deffenbacher.

Anger expert Dr. Jerry Deffenbacher suggests that alcohol and anger have a synergistic effect in that anger and alcohol each individually lead to negative consequences, but together in high doses the problems are exponential. In his research, Deffenbacher differentiated low and high trait anger individuals by Speilberger's Trait Anger Scale and then analyzed any differences in their experienced consequences. As reported in the table above, angry individuals were much more likely to experience negative consequences from alcohol than were their non-angry peers.

When thinking about the relationship of alcohol and violence, some wonder again about chicken and eggs. Which comes first? Some argue that decreased inhibitions of the drinker can lead normally nonviolent individuals to act on aggressive impulses. Clearly, alcohol affects judgment. People are much more likely to say and do things when intoxicated that they normally would not say or do when sober. Intoxicated people also distort what they hear other people saying. Thus, alcohol impairment can lead to social misunderstandings or an overreaction to a perceived threat, and can evolve into anger.

On the other side of the argument, some state that alcohol increases risk-taking in those already prone to anger, and becomes their excuse to act violently. We know that alcohol consumption tends to promote aggression because people expect it to. A person who intends to engage in a premeditated violent act may get intoxicated to create the "liquid courage" to act out.

RECOMMENDATIONS

Despite heightened awareness of the dangers of alcohol abuse, some college administrators are still somewhat hesitant to create and enforce effective policies that restrict alcohol access and discourage overindulgence. Some hesitate because they fear student backlash against their decisions. After passing an alcohol ban on their Greek organizations, Michigan State University (MSU) and Southern Illinois State University at Carbondale (SIUC) both succumbed to student pressure to reverse the decision. The students argued that morale and recruitment at the Greek houses had dropped significantly since the ban and that some organizations were consequently suffering financial problems. Campus officials conceded to reverse the original decision when the Greek organizations promised to uphold strict alcohol policies stating that they had learned from their mistakes and could prove to be responsible. Time will tell how the decisions to re-

Student Support for Tougher Policies

Policy	Nondrinkers	Drinkers/ Nonbingers	Occasional Bingers	Frequent Bingers
Prohibit kegs on campus	86.4%	67.7%	48.6%	34.6%
Enforce rules strictly	93.2%	75.0%	54.2%	35.2%
Crack down on Greeks	90.1%	69.5%	47.1%	28.2%
Hold hosts responsible	81.1%	59.9%	45.3%	33.3%
Crack down on underage drinkers	93.5%	76.9%	56.6%	37.1%

Source: Wechsler, H., Nelson, T., & Weitzman, E. 2000. From knowledge to action: How Harvard's College Alcohol Study can help your campus design a campaign against student alcohol use. *Change: The Magazine of Higher Learning.* January/February 2000.

allow alcohol in the fraternities will play out. We are not particularly optimistic, knowing that Greek members tend to be the heaviest drinkers of all. According to Dr. Henry Wechsler, 81.1 percent of those living in fraternity or sorority houses binge drink as compared to the national 44 percent rate.

It is true that there is a subpopulation of college drinkers that are very committed to defending their "right to party," but as Dr. Henry Wechsler of Harvard points out, it really depends on who is asked. More than four out of five nondrinkers support the prohibition of kegs on campus, the strict enforcement of the rules, and the crackdown on underage drinkers and abusive Greek drinkers. The majority of low-risk drinkers and many occasional high-risk drinkers also agree to these measures, as well as the idea of holding party hosts responsible for their guests.

Gather Accurate Information

In order to be able to address the problems of alcohol abuse, each campus must assess where the problems are. This can be accomplished by several needs assessment strategies. Student focus groups give small groups a chance to answer structured questions about the who, when, and where of alcohol misuse. Focus groups give rich qualitative data, especially groups that represent diverse aspects of campus, but responses can be biased because of a lack of anonymity. Surveys can free students to state the truth without fear that their answers will be traced back to them, but sometimes the statistics generated from surveys raise more questions than they answer. Colleges seeking to understand the prevalence of these behaviors often use standardized questionnaires such as the Core Instrument, but surveys such as these do not address the issues of change and motivation. Clearly, a combination of strategies will give colleges the most accurate picture.

When alcohol-related violence occurs, some experts suggest taking Blood Alcohol Content (BAC) levels from both victims and perpetrators. This information can help determine issues of consent in cases of sexual assault. When a sexual assault victim appears impaired, but the BAC is low, medical providers can be alerted to screen for date rape drugs such as Rohypnol. When we have better evidence linking alcohol to campus violence, we have better leverage to impose appropriate restrictions on the access to alcohol and have better information from which to offer relevant prevention tactics.

Community-based Approach

Because a problem such as substance abuse is so entrenched in the campus community, a comprehensive strategy for change is appropriate. Such a strategy must involve a committed cross-section of campus representatives who are up to the task of challenging these behavioral and attitudinal norms. Many campuses have created a task force representative of the following groups of individuals for the purposes of generating effective change strategies.

Presidents

Top-down support is critical to the success of a prevention program requiring a community-wide embrace. The Director of the Higher Education Center for Alcohol and Other Drug Prevention, Dr. William DeJong states, ". . . college and university presidents must address problems related to student drinking. . . . Many of the things college presidents worry about–student death and injury, weak academic performance, property damage and vandalism, strained town-gown relations, negative publicity–are linked to student alcohol use."

In 1999, The Presidents Leadership Group sponsored by the Robert Wood Johnson Foundation urged college presidents to "Be Vocal, Be Visible, Be Visionary" in their response to alcohol and other drug problems on campus. The report suggests that colleges do not need to return to prohibition, but do need to determine the appropriate role of alcohol in a learning community.

One direct way college presidents can demonstrate their commitment to alcohol abuse prevention is to allocate a budget and staff reflective of such a communitywide problem.

Faculty

Because of their highly respected status and contact with students, faculty members have substantial potential for impacting student attitudes and behavior toward alcohol and its relationship to violence.

Faculty can play many roles in dealing with this issue. They often witness the effects of post-partying consequences as students come to class hungover with a laundry list of excuses why their work is not done on time. They are in an excellent position to confront and refer students who are in trouble. Classrooms provide captive audiences for discussion and lecture on this topic that so many fear to face head-on.

In the mid-1990s, *curriculum infusion* became a big prevention buzzword. The movement made attempts to get alcohol issues and other drug topics integrated into almost every syllabus. Several schools found that curriculum infusion had a ripple effect in alcohol abuse prevention. From the process, faculty became more invested and informed about what students were doing. Students seemed more open to the topic when it was presented as an "academic topic" rather than through the assumption that they were all problem drinkers. Issues gained importance to the community at large when funneled through the minds of the most elite thinkers around.

Student Life Staff

Personal counseling services, health services, residence life offices, student activities, security officers, judicial officers, and other administrators all have vital roles in alcohol abuse prevention and intervention. Many of their roles are discussed in other sections of this chapter and throughout this book. Another excellent sourcebook *Promising*

Practices, (Anderson & Milgram, 1996) compiled by David Anderson and colleagues provides additional information for professional student life staff.

Parents

A sensitive discussion of drugs and alcohol use can be even more difficult when discussed in the context of sexual behavior and violence. But, consider what you have to lose if you do not have this conversation. You could lose your son or daughter.
—From the Syracuse University Substance Abuse Prevention & Health Enhancement Office

Of all the prevention influences, appropriate parental communication and role modeling is probably one of the most powerful. Parental influence can even overcome the power of television. A recent study at Washington State University demonstrated that the potential risk of frequent exposure to persuasive alcohol messages on television was significantly moderated by parental counter-reinforcement messages.

"Parental notification" has been a controversial movement in an attempt to determine who is responsible for student welfare. Some say that the students themselves are responsible for what happens to them, and as adults, have a right to privacy. Others say that since many parents are footing the bill for college, parents have a right to know if their son or daughter is in trouble. Under a federal law passed in 1999, campus adminis-

---

The Higher Education Center recommends eight points for parents speaking with students about alcohol:

1. Establish clear and reasonable expectations for academic performance. Research indicates that alcohol abuse is largely responsible for academic decline, and if students realize that parents expect their best, they may be more likely to devote more time to studying.

2. Stress that alcohol consumed in high quantities can be fatal. Discourage high-risk drinking activities such as drinking games and chugging practices. Encourage students to intervene if they see others putting their lives at risk with these risky behaviors.

3. Tell students what to do if they see someone who is in trouble with alcohol. Share with them the warning signs of alcohol poisoning and to whom they can turn for help in this crisis.

4. Encourage students to stand up for their right to a safe, sanitary, and sane living and studying environment.

5. Know the alcohol culture of the campus and confront students' misperceptions. Students tend to grossly overestimate the percentage of students who get drunk on a regular basis. Let them know that many students are making good choices for themselves, but it is the most out-of-control students who usually are visible.

6. Avoid telling tales about "the good old days" when your drinking was out of control. This clearly sends a confusing message.

7. Encourage your son or daughter to get involved in service work in the community. Being a productive volunteer helps structure the student's free time, gives students a broader perspective, and creates natural connections with others.

8. Emphasize the point that underage alcohol consumption and impaired driving are against the law.

trators may disclose a student's disciplinary record without the student's consent. Supporters of this law favor the opportunity for early intervention with potentially high-risk behavior. An additional step that might improve the impact of this intervention would be to send parents information about helpful ways to talk to their son or daughter about alcohol.

Several experts have suggested open communication between parents and college students before the students even set foot on campus as a critical step in preventing alcohol abuse. The first six weeks of college often involve high consumption of alcohol as students are adjusting to having new freedoms while trying desperately to fit in. Kaiser Permanente advises parents to discuss issues of legality, high-risk behaviors such as impaired driving and sex under the influence, alcohol poisoning, and other consequences of alcohol misuse. Chris Wimmer, a substance abuse counselor at Kaiser stated, "Many parents treat this the same as they do discussions about sex—you have the talk with them, once, to explain the 'birds and the bees,' and that's it. Kids need an ongoing dialogue, especially once they are old enough to experiment on their own."

The Century Council, a national, not-for-profit organization dedicated to reducing drunk driving and underage drinking problems (www.centurycouncil.org), recommends that parents share their own drinking experiences, both positive and negative, without glorifying alcohol abuse. The first step in this process is becoming clear about one's own attitudes, values, and beliefs about alcohol and drinking. Parents should examine their own rituals and patterns around alcohol in order to recognize the influence their actions have on their children. Parents can talk about their own decision making related to how alcohol does or does not fit into their lives. Most importantly, parents must role model appropriate consumption of

alcohol and live by example. If the student is involved in an alcohol violation, parents should avoid the tendency to react, and rather respond to the opportunity for dialogue on the issue.

Coaches

Like parents, coaches play an unbelievably powerful role in shaping student behavior. At Regis University, coaches are notified when students receive their second minor alcohol infraction or any major substance abuse infraction. The intent of the notification is not to increase opportunities for punishment, but for communication. Coaches requested this notification because sometimes they were the last ones to know when one of their starter players was being asked to leave school for disciplinary problems. Coaches felt that they were in a good position to influence their players to make better choices for themselves off the field.

Students

Students are on the front line of this issue and see firsthand the patterns and areas of risk developing on campus. In order for prevention and intervention efforts to be effective, the students' voices—on all points along the drinking continuum—must be heard. Student focus groups are especially useful in assessing the campus alcohol culture.

Peer education, now a regular prevention strategy on most campuses, has proven to help the peer educators themselves in addition to the larger campus community. A 1998 BACCHUS & GAMMA Peer Education Network survey found that peer educators tend to make healthier choices about substances use. Seventy-eight percent believed they had positively influenced their peers, and most indicated that being a peer educator had positively impacted their relationships with others.

Community

It has been called "town and gown" collaboration. Leaders from city government, neighborhood associations, community resource officers, owners of drinking establishments, and others combine efforts with the campus task force to devise a comprehensive strategy of prevention.

A critical segment of this joint effort is getting the support of local bars and clubs. Campus and local law enforcement can encourage community drinking establishments to uphold drinking laws by not serving underage patrons or overserving those of age. In addition, campus prevention groups can ask the local bars to become more responsible in their drink promotions and advertising. The Center for Science in the Public Interest offers a free community action guide to help colleges stop irresponsible alcohol promotion targeting college students (download a free copy of *Last Call for High-Risk Bar Promotions That Target College Students* by logging on to www.health.org/pubs/lastcall/index.htm).

Offer Attractive Social Alternatives

"We drink because there is nothing else to do." For many college students, alcohol is the cheapest thrill in town. For the price of a movie ticket or a night of bowling, students can get very intoxicated. Substance abuse prevention personnel must figure out what students are getting out of their high-risk drinking episodes and find other ways to accomplish the same goals. When asked, many students say they like to go drinking at parties or bars because it gives them oppor-

tunities to meet new people, especially those with dating potential. Student activities departments can host other types of social events on Fridays and Saturdays where meeting new people is also possible. Some students like the excitement of high-risk behavior; they get a rush out of living on the edge. For these students, other forms of risk-taking such as skiing, rafting, and rock climbing may be attractive. If drinking is part of the social activity offered, it should not be the sole focus. Students should be involved in other activities as well such as a casino night or bowling.

Stop Enabling

Campus alcohol abuse prevention groups should encourage faculty to hold Friday morning classes. Tests too. Hangovers are natural consequences for overindulgence and performing poorly in a class might get students to re-evaluate their priorities. Front-line individuals such as security officers and residence life staff are often critical decision makers when it comes to getting problematic drinkers appropriate help and deserved consequences. These staff members should receive training on why enabling perpetuates the problem and how to effectively confront the problematic drinker. Finally, those in positions of imposing sanctions must be prepared to act consistently, regardless of the size of the sacred cow. The son of a board of trustee, the star basketball player, or the president of the student body all should be held to the same standards of behavior as the rest of the college community.

Restrict Access

Restricting access to alcohol has been shown to lower the prevalence of violence crimes and physical injuries linked to alcohol, according to a recent issue of *Contemporary Drug Problems*. Reduced availability of alcohol can take many forms–higher price, regulated serving, prohibited areas, and so on. The problem with restricted access of alcohol is that if the measures are unpopular with a large segment of the population, an illegal market will develop. This underground market adapts to the restrictions so that the type of alcohol favored will have a lower likelihood of being detected. Favored alcohol beverages will be higher in alcohol content so that they are easier to conceal and transport than large volumes of less potent alcohol. This means that students will be downing shot after shot of tequila rather than swigging from a keg. Students tend to have a more difficult time monitoring their intake of hard alcohol than they do from beer. They are more likely to succumb to alcohol poisoning when ingesting numerous shots in a short period of time than bottles of beer over the course of an evening. Thus, when restricting access, campuses must take into consideration this tendency for the underground market to develop, and take additional precautions.

The National Bureau of Economic Research came up with a novel way to raise money for the states and prevent alcohol abuse at the same time: increase beer tax. According to these economists, there is a clear cause-and-effect between the price of beer and student trouble. In their analysis, they determined that for every ten percent increase in the price of beer, the percentage of students who engage in problematic behavior such as fighting, sexual misconduct, and property damage decreases by four percent overall. In actuality, beer prices have fallen about 10 percent in the last ten years, and this trend may be contributing to college overindulgence.

Campus authorities have the power to regulate where, when, and how much alcohol is served. Banning alcohol from campus sporting events appears to be a current development on many campuses. According to the North American Interfraternity Conference, about 20 percent of fraternity chapters are going dry, and the number continues to increase. Sorority houses have always been dry and a new national rule will prohibit sorority members from attending fraternity functions where alcohol is served. Many residence halls are alcohol-free regardless of age of residents. Campus pub serving sizes and type of alcohol can also have an impact on how intoxicated students get.

Restriction policies must be well thought out in order for them to be effective. The University of Massachusetts, Amherst learned the hard way that sometimes the definition of a reasonable limit is complicated. Originally, the school had imposed a twenty-four-beer limit for any of-age student to keep in his or her room. Then they increased this limit to thirty at the request of student government who noted that liquor stores were selling thirty-beer cases. Upon reflection and substantial backlash from the alcohol abuse prevention community, the chancellor reversed his decision, which in turn caused student uproar.

Policies and Enforcement

Dr. Henry Wechsler of Harvard and the Department of Education suggest a "Zero Tolerance Policy" for alcohol-related violence including rape, assault, and impaired driving. Some schools go a step further and enforce a "Zero Tolerance Policy" for any underage drinking. Wellesley College has such a policy, and any underage student caught drinking by campus police is ordered to appear in court or is arrested.

Whatever policies campuses decide, the messages must be clear and consistent.

Separate policies for of-age students and staff or alumni can send conflicting messages of "do as I say and not as I do." A "dry" campus drenched in lucrative alcohol advertising or event sponsorship is equally confusing for the community.

The law enforcement departments patrolling the area's neighboring campuses have begun various crackdown efforts to curtail harmful drinking habits. San Diego State University students now know what it means to be "CAPPed." This term emerged after the local police department developed the "College Area Party Plan" and started issuing written notices to students hosting loud, unruly parties. If the CAPP is violated, the residents face possible arrests, property seizures, and fines.

Many schools also enforce "minor in possession" (MIP) violations. Any underage possession and public consumption violating community standards leads to mandatory sanctions. Examples of first-offense sanctions include a monetary fine, mandated counseling, a semester's disciplinary probation, community services, and an alcohol educational workshop.

In Colorado, several schools have jumped on the Department of Transportation's prevention bandwagon with the "College Crackdown" movement. In 1996, the Colorado Department of Transportation started "The Heat is On!" DUI enforcement campaign involving multiple enforcement agencies and high-profile media tactics. In the past year Regis University, the University of Colorado (Boulder), and the University of Northern Colorado have adopted similar strategies. During the week before traditionally heavy-drinking weekends, public announcements broadcast the upcoming presence of DUI enforcement circulate the campus. With the heightened awareness of enforcement presence, many impaired individuals chose not to get behind the wheel. Throughout Colorado, DUI arrests have increased 29 percent and alcohol-related fatalities have decreased 23 percent since the program's inception.

Positive Social Tactics

In contrast to the usual "health terrorism" approaches many campuses have used in the past, many schools are finding positive results by focusing on what students are doing right. Scare tactics in the past played upon people's fears—fears of death, fears of rejection, fears of embarrassment, fears of incarceration. For many college students, fear is a short-lived emotion, especially when the risks for such outcomes are relatively low in their perception. Besides, most of them have been hearing about the dangers of alcohol abuse since elementary school days and tune out to such messages by their college years. The shift in today's alcohol abuse prevention is toward supporting non- and low-risk drinkers, challenging misperceptions students have about high-risk drinking, and highlighting protective behaviors.

According to Dr. Wechsler, seven out of eight low-risk drinkers have been negatively affected by another's drinking, but a very small minority ever formally complain. Students at Cornell University, the University of North Carolina at Chapel Hill, and the University of Arkansas at Little Rock recently combined efforts with the Center for Science in the Public Interest to develop a media advocacy website called "HadEnough." The site (www.cspinet.org/booze/hadenough) supports student involvement in reducing high-risk drinking on college campuses.

Another student-based group called the "CIRCLe Network" (College Initiatives to Reinvent Campus Life) states that its mission is "to promote the development of healthy, responsible, socially-conscious individual . . . (by) advocat(ing) social programming and social structures that foster true community and de-emphasize the role of alcohol on college campuses." The group started at Duke University and sought to provide students with social options that did not focus around alcohol. The CIRCLe founders were not satisfied with impacting just one campus, and began reaching out to other schools to challenge widely held perceptions of what college life is supposed to be like. Again, through the means of the Internet, this group hopes to disseminate information of "best practices" and ongoing consultation.

"Social Norms Marketing" is another idea related to positive social pressure that seems to be catching on. The idea behind this approach is based in the theory developed originally through the work of Wes Perkins and Alan Berkowitz. Stated simply, students typically overestimate alcohol and other drug use on campus. As a result this illusion creates a partially self-fulfilling prophecy. Social norms marketing is used to correct these misperceptions and decrease high-risk drinking.

Underlying these social norms is a theory called "pluralistic ignorance" or the belief that one's private attitudes and judgments are different from others. In terms of substance abuse issues, this notion translates to this: individuals who choose not to engage in high-risk drinking, assume that everyone around them is. These low-risk or non-drinkers then adopt a "bystander" position and "stay in the closet" about how they really feel about others' high-risk drinking and their own choice not to do so. This behavior perpetuates the misperception that everybody is being irresponsible because these bystanders become, in a sense, invisible.

Another group that adds to the problem consists of "carriers of misinformation." These people are students, faculty, staff, and even parents who, regardless of their own personal use or attitudes about alcohol and other drugs pass on the misperceptions through conversation and comments. Through these carriers, the illusion gets reinforced.

When substance abuse educators continually focus on the problems of the minority of frequent high-risk drinkers, the misperception that all college students are problem drinkers gets perpetuated. Berkowitz and Perkins suggest that strategies for changing these misperceptions are threefold: (1) misperceptions must be corrected through repetitive and visible messages reflecting the truth about campus drinking patterns, (2) bystanders need to come "out of the closet" and be public in their responsible behavior, and (3) educators and leaders should balance their emphasis on the problems of high-risk drinking with the acknowledgment and reinforcement of those who do not drink.

"Social Norms Marketing" approach uses traditional marketing techniques to promote healthy messages about student behavior to challenge the misperceptions. Mass market media approaches often are used including posters, campus newspaper advertisements, bus banners, and so on. Messages are carefully developed to be positive, inclusive and empowering. Before mass circulation they are pretested in student focus groups. Evaluation of impact is a continuous factor.

This "social norms" model of substance abuse prevention has resulted in consistent and impressive patterns of results at Northern Illinois University, Hobart and William Smith Colleges, the University of Arizona, and Western Washington University. After years of substance abuse prevention efforts that resulted in no change in student behavior, the social norming approach impacted misperceptions of student drinking and a 10 to 25 percent drop in high-risk drinking followed.

Intervention with High-Risk Drinkers

The idea behind this last step is to identify those on campus who are most at risk for experiencing consequences related to their alcohol misuse and give them brief, focused interventions that will hopefully redirect their thinking. Like the earlier mentioned concept of placing trees in the way of those practicing violence, this method attempts to place trees in the way of those practicing high-risk drinking.

Research by one of the leading experts in the field of substance abuse, Alan Marlatt, has found impressive results with these brief high-risk interventions. Dr. Marlatt heads the Addiction Behaviors Research Center at the University of Washington in Seattle and has demonstrated that his approach of "harm reduction" can reduce drinking-related problems five years postintervention. At-risk students identified as those with a family history of alcohol problems and those interested in joining a fraternity or sorority underwent forty-five-minute individualized motivational sessions in their freshman year. Students who went through this process were less likely to engage in high-risk drinking than students in the control group were. Marlatt claims that his program significantly accelerates "maturing out" of drinking behavior.

According to Marlatt and colleagues, harm reduction is referred to as *indicated prevention* (or in more formal circumstances *secondary prevention*) because it focuses on students who are somehow identified as high-risk and are already showing evidence of a problem. The primary goal of harm reduction is to have the student reduce risky behaviors and harmful effects from drinking rather than focusing on abstinence. The objectives of this brief intervention are designed to be student-chosen, realistic, and achievable. This approach realizes that all risks will not be eliminated with this one intervention, but that lifestyle changes usually happen slowly over time through successive approximations.

Marlatt and colleagues designed the intervention model labeled BASICS (Brief Alcohol Screening and Intervention for College Students). This skills-based curriculum uses specific cognitive-behavioral strategies to guide students toward lower risk drinking. The courses are nonconfrontational, nonjudgmental, and nonlabeling. For more information about this approach, read *Brief Alcohol Screening and Intervention for College Students: A Harm Reduction Approach* (Dimeff, Baer, Kivlahan, & Marlatt, 1999).

Other campuses use the concept of "teachable moments" to intervene with high-risk drinkers. Students who are identified through the campus disciplinary system for alcohol abuse are sometimes mandated to the counseling center for a brief educational intervention. Effective intervention requires a combination of warmth, influence, resolution, and appropriate sanctions. Punishing, humiliating, or permissive interventions are not helpful and may make the situation worse. Those directing such interventions must carefully balance consistency with individualized approaches.

Brown University conducted a study of the effectiveness of this "teachable moments" approach conducted in emergency rooms. Again, medical providers conducted a forty-five-minute harm reduction session with teens being treated for extreme intoxication or injuries from an alcohol-related accident and compared the results to another group that received the standard ER intervention of assessment and referral. At a six-month follow-up, the group that received the "harm reduction" session had 32 percent fewer drinking and driving incidents, 50 percent fewer alcohol-related injuries, and far fewer alcohol-related consequences overall.

Other high-risk groups to consider are

first-semester freshmen, especially those pledging fraternities or trying out for athletics, and high school students on recruitment visits. At Stanford University, campus administrators have experimented with another controversial approach. Prospective freshmen must sign a pledge that they will abstain from alcohol and drugs during their visit to the campus. Opponents of this strategy claim that it sends a very hostile welcome to potential new members of the community. The contract developers state that this is the most effective way to get the message across that the expectation is that all members of the community will be responsible, even if they are only visiting for a couple of days.

Many athletic departments are beginning to consider the value of "student host contracts" when bringing in high school athlete recruits. These contracts clearly outline expectations for student conduct in regards to alcohol and other drug use. Both the recruit and the student host sign the contracts.

In summary, the issues of alcohol and the college campus are too complex and broad to cover in one chapter. Rather, we have highlighted the emerging trends, the relationships between alcohol and violence, and the most promising intervention strategies currently known. For more information consult these resources:

The Higher Education Center
Education Development Center, Inc.
55 Chapel Street
Newton, MA 02158-1060
www.edc.org/hec

Dr. Henry Wechsler
Harvard School of Public Health
677 Huntington Avenue
Boston, MA 02115-6096
(617) 432-1137
www.hsph.harvard.edu/cas

Brief Alcohol Screening and Intervention for College Students (BASICS): A Harm Reduction Approach by Linda Dimeff, John Baer, Daniel Kivlahan, & G. Alan Marlatt (1999). Guilford Press.

The Century Council
www.centurycouncil.org

A Social Norms Approach to Preventing Binge Drinking at Colleges and Universities by Michael P. Haines (1996). A publication of The Higher Education Center for Alcohol and Other Drug Prevention.

Part II

DEVELOPING ANTIBODIES:
GENERAL PREVENTION STRATEGIES
FOR THE COLLEGE COMMUNITY

Chapter 5

HEEDING THE SIGNS AND SYMPTOMS:
WHAT ARE THE RED FLAGS
FOR IMPENDING VIOLENCE?

IS VIOLENCE PREDICTABLE?

WHEN VIOLENCE OCCURS on a college campus, many respond by saying something to the effect of, "He (they) seemed so nice (quiet, normal, etc.). Who could have predicted this tragedy?" To be clear, violence is not predictable in the sense of being absolutely certain whether or not an individual will commit violence. There are too many intervening factors in our day-to-day lives that continuously influence decisions for behavioral science to ever be that accurate. But we can estimate violence potential based on a number of factors outlined in this chapter and throughout the book. Knowing these telltale signs can lead to effective prevention of violence; however, first we must overcome a basic myth many people hold about violent offenders.

MYTH: Violent perpetrators just snap.

FACT: Almost all violent perpetrators will give indications of violent intentions long before they act on them.

"He Just Snapped": Case Example at the University of Northern Colorado

On Tuesday, September 24, 1996, Joe Gallegos drove from Bayfield, Colorado to the University of Northern Colorado (UNC) in Greeley. Once there he held his ex-girlfriend and three other female students hostage for hours. He shot his girlfriend in the foot because he believed she had called the police. When negotiations with law enforcement began to deteriorate, Joe closed his eyes and stuck his head out the residence hall window. A SWAT marksman shot him. For twenty-eight minutes Joe remained alive and fired back at police. He was taken to the local emergency room and was pronounced dead.

His girlfriend was interviewed by the *Rocky Mountain News* the following day and next to a large color photograph of her on crutches the paper quoted her as saying, "Joe was a nice person. He just snapped. He was kind and caring and considerate." The statement fed into the widespread myth that violent individuals experience a sudden unexpected change of character before acting out.

It was also far from the truth.

Joe Gallegos began compiling a criminal record at the age of thirteen. His offenses included shoplifting, trespassing, criminal mischief, car theft, and assault. He was expelled from his high school because he participated in a food fight and set another student's pants on fire. Joe also had a problem with anger and alcohol. On one occasion, Joe and another youth visited the home of an acquaintance late at night. After breaking into the home through a glass window, Joe forced the victim to the floor and slashed him with a broken beer bottle. In 1995, he beat another man with a beer bottle. The assault resulted in a sentence of almost a year at a detention center, program for young offenders, halfway house, and supervised foster care.

Thirteen days before the UNC hostage situation in Greeley, Joe was paroled and claimed that he had found God. Joe went to visit his girlfriend on the day he was paroled, and she broke off the relationship. He told her, "I can't live without you. I love you too much."

Over the next few days, Joe began to show his true colors. He became violently jealous at a party and grabbed his ex-girl-friend, dragging her down some stairs. After returning to his home in southern Colorado, Joe obtained a 9mm semiautomatic gun previously stolen from the Cortez hardware store. On Monday, September 23, Joe called his girlfriend to attempt reconciliation, but she refused and he hung up on her. He then proceeded to dismantle and hide the kitchen phone of the home he shared with three young Christian men who took him in under the belief that Joe was turning his life around.

What happened over the next several hours is a matter of speculation and evidence interpretation as all of the witnesses are dead. Police officials surmise that Joe did not want any interference in his plan to kill his girlfriend. Furthermore, he needed a car. So he killed his three roommates execution style, and took the truck belonging to one of them. Joe drove straight to Greeley, consuming more than forty times the normal dose of ephedrine, a nasal congestion medicine with side effects of anxiety and impaired judgment. This pattern of behaviors was not indicative of a person who "just snapped," but rather one of an antisocial personality whose actions were premeditated and deadly.

ANALYZING THREATS

Threats, past interests and conduct, and current verbal and physical behavior can all serve as indications for violence potential. For many different strains of campus violence, perpetrators will make multiple threats before acting out. Therefore, it is imperative that protectors have some basic knowledge of analyzing threats. Understanding key aspects of three different types of threats—direct, conditional, and veiled—is a critical part of threat investigation.

When we look at certain forms of violence such as avenger and domestic violence, we find most perpetrators will make verbal or written threats before acting. For workplace violence and school avenger shootings, essentially all perpetrators made some sort of threat before they committed violence.

When analyzing threats, verbatim reporting is critical. The exact wording of the threat will give you a clearer picture of the perpetrator's motive. Both written and verbal threats should be preserved exactly as they are made. Background noises, accents, tone of voice, and rate of speech also contain important information about who the perpetrator is and should be documented. Any envelopes or packaging of written threats should be kept for fingerprint or DNA analysis if needed.

Protectors must take all threats seriously, even if they sound ridiculous or are presented in the form of a "joke." Why should we take threats so seriously? Because generally speaking, people tend to reward those who threaten. Receivers of threats tend to either back down or retaliate. That is, they give in to the threat demand or they fight back in anger. Giving in to the threat is clearly a reward for the perpetrator. However, even if the receivers of the threat retaliate with lots of public negative action, the perpetrator is still reinforced with attention. Threats that are ignored give the perpetrator the message that he or she is not being taken seriously. All of these approaches lead to the likelihood that perpetrators will continue to use threats to get what they want.

Most threats are harmless, just individuals blowing off steam and not thinking before they speak. However, what has one learned about a person who makes a threat on a campus where no threats are allowed? They may have impulse control problems. They may be trying to manipulate or intimidate others. They may be defiant of rules, or the threat may be a cry for help or attention. In any event, all of these motives are potential indicators of future violence. If the individual continues to make threats after being warned to stop, one has learned much more. Investigators have a stronger case for an individual who is intent on committing violence unless sufficient impediments are put in place.

Threats should always be analyzed for credibility, seriousness, and lethality. Threats can be nonverbal, verbal, or written, and fall into three categories: direct, condi-

tional, and veiled.

The following descriptions of threats and cues are adapted from *Violence Goes to Work* (1994) and *Violence Goes to School* (1999).

Direct Threats

A direct threat is a statement of clear intent to harm someone. There is no ambiguity or doubt in the statement. Examples are, "I'm going to kill you," or "I'm going to blow them away." A direct threat is punishable by law and the authorities should be contacted in this incidence. Individuals who make detailed threats regarding specific targets are more likely to become violent than those who make vague threats. Generally, the more specific the threat, the more concerned protectors should be. If the individual identifies types of weapons, names of targets, or an exact time or location of the violent act, immediate action should be taken. When individuals are that specific, we know that they have thought about their violent fantasy for a long time and have worked out all the details to their satisfaction. The potential for threat to become reality at this point is very real.

Conditional Threats

A conditional threat is made contingent on a certain set of circumstances. These threats contain the word "if," or the word "or." These types of threats are designed to manipulate or intimidate the target into compliance. Examples of these types of threats include, "You better do this *or* you're dead," and, "*If* you don't give me what I want, you will pay." If these threats are not met with resistance and clear signs of intolerance, they are likely to increase as they are often powerfully reinforced.

Veiled Threats

Veiled threats are the hardest type to address because they are often vague and subject to interpretation. These types of threats are very real for the recipients, but feel like they lose some of their impact when repeated to others. The perpetrator easily minimizes this type of threat, by refuting the receiver's interpretation. For example, the perpetrator may say the recipient just blew the situation out of proportion, or that they only intended the threat as a joke. An example of a veiled threat is the student who says, "I can see how something like the Texas sniper can happen. I'm surprised more people don't go off the edge."

Veiled threats are often used as a form of harassment in stalking situations. These threats were a consistent theme in Richard Farely's letters to Laura Black before he hunted her down and killed four people at his workplace. He wrote, "You cost me a job, forty thousand dollars in equity taxes I can't pay, and a foreclosure. Yet, I still like you. Why do you want to find out how far I'll go? . . . I absolutely will not be pushed around, and I'm beginning to get tired of being nice." Veiled threats are the most difficult to detect due to their vagueness and multiple interpretations. Again, the overall context and multiple signs are important when deciphering the significance.

In the aftermath of avenger-type violence, witnesses are often asked if they ever heard the perpetrator make any threats before the killings. These witnesses often say they "didn't know that they knew." In hindsight, these witnesses were able to say that the perpetrators often made comments or acted in ways that made them uncomfortable about possible violence, but they did not know they were dealing with veiled threats. Therefore, training for students and campus employees is critical to help them learn how to identify threats and how to report them.

NOTE: There is not a single variable capable of predicting violence. In the absence of disconfirming evidence one can tentatively assume that the profile characteristics are additive. That is, the more traits or behaviors people have, the greater the probability that they may act violently.

DISTAL CUES: GENERAL INDICATORS OF VIOLENCE POTENTIAL

The following list of warning signs associated with violence is neither comprehensive nor exhaustive. Rather, the list intends to offer general guidelines to determine whether a situation warrants the evaluation of a violence prevention specialist.

History of Violence

Past behavior is the best predictor of future behavior. This maxim applies to violent behavior as well. The probability of future violence increases with each prior violent act. Seriously violent individuals often have histories that include mutilation, torture, and killing of animals. Violent campus offenders might not have such a disturbing violence history, but they may have a series of disciplinary offenses or run-ins with the campus police. When a student transfers to a new campus, violent offenses and disciplinary records usually do not follow. Military disciplinary action, prior arrests or convictions, and prior violent disciplinary action at a previous college are all areas for concern.

Poor Impulse Control

Many violent actions are precipitated by a deterioration impulse control. From a developmental standpoint, by the time students are of college age they should have a reasonable ability to inhibit unacceptable social behaviors. By nature, younger children have less capacity for impulse control since their mental capacity is not yet well developed. Older adolescents and adults should have a better sense to think before they react. In daily conversation, most people are able to screen out inappropriate things to say and do, even when the thought crosses their mind. Violent individuals seem to have a poorer ability to do this. Perhaps this is partly because so many of the campus violence perpetrators are under the influence of alcohol and other drugs at the time of the crime. Some indications of poor impulse control include a high number of moving traffic violations, destruction of property, or making terminal statements such as "I'm quitting" without much forethought.

Unsuccessful Personal History

Individuals who have repeated failures throughout their life may be at risk for developing low self-esteem. A person continuously confronted with unattained goals, rejections, and unfulfilled dreams may choose antisocial avenues to reconcile the imbalance they feel in their life. Clearly, this factor is not the case for all perpetrators of violence when one considers the number of high-profile athletes and popular fraternity members who are accused of sexual crimes, brutal hazing, and other forms of campus violence. This is just one variable of many to consider when assessing an individual's potential for violence.

Perceived Injustice History

A perceived injustice history is frequently evident in workplace violence situations. Often the perpetrator has filed a series of grievances before killing. On campuses, perceived injustice may take the form of an irate student denied a passing grade or a group of students denied their "right" to drink on campus. These self-righteous individuals feel justified in their anger and blame others for their violent actions. They find validation in their role as a victim in an unfair world. Usually, these individuals will start by filing grievances, making protesting phone calls, or writing angry letters filled with statements of blame such as, "Look what you have made me do!"

Obsession

Obsessions are persistent thoughts, impulses or images that preoccupy the mind. Many types of campus violence perpetrators can have obsessions of one form of another. Avengers and predators can have obsessive thoughts as they became fixated on another person or activity. Stalking and persistent harassment are also forms of obsession.

Substance Abuse

As reviewed in Chapters 3 and 4, alcohol or drugs can interfere dramatically with reasoning ability, inhibition, anticipation of consequences, and the judgment to distinguish right from wrong. Alcohol has repeatedly been shown to have a strong link to violence on college campuses. Thus, someone with an alcohol or multidrug abuse history, may be at higher risk for committing violence.

Fascination and Proficiency with Weapons

Extreme fascination with weapons, extensive gun collections, and shooting skills are indicators to consider when assessing the potential for violence. The individual who continually discusses or carries weapons, names their weapons, or evidences an unusual enthusiasm for semiautomatic or automatic guns presents a greater risk. This type of obsession may also apply to other forms of destruction, such as explosives and bombs.

A clear red flag for violence potential is the proficiency with explosives. While generally speaking our culture is not concerned with ownership of guns for hunting and target practice, there are no prosocial uses for bombs. In civilian society, there would be no reason for someone to have knowledge about how to build and detonate bombs other than for destruction.

Personality Disorders

Personality disorders develop as maladaptive patterns of behavior become deeply entrenched over a long time. With violent individuals many precipitant and early warning signs of personality and emotional difficulties can be identified in childhood. Some of the early indications of antisocial tendencies include excessive lying, fire setting, bedwetting, and cruelty to animals. Narcissistic features also appear prevalent with this population, and their self-perception may vacillate between feelings of worthlessness and superiority. Personality problems can be identified by explosive tempers, irrational thought patterns, manipulative conduct, and rapid mood swings.

Some Elements of Major Mental Illness

Major mental disorders include a loss of contact with reality, and can be manifested in paranoia and severe depression. Behavioral indicators are delusions, hallucinations, bizarre thoughts, or talking to oneself about irrational subjects. Extreme paranoia can sometimes lead to violence when an individual believes that others are unnecessarily spying on him or her.

Preoccupation with Violence

Individuals who evidence a preoccupation with violence will constantly talk about the subject, and find ways to expose themselves to further violence. Examples of this could include violent musical lyrics, movies, the Internet and other media. Their ability to generate alternative solutions to their problems is diminished as they increasingly focus on details of violence and fantasies of violent rampages. Recently increasing numbers of violent and hate-filled websites are surfacing on the Internet. These websites fuel those who are obsessed with violence by giving them anonymity and a connection with other deviant individuals.

Other Situational Variables

An individual's overall "life context" is important in assessing their potential for violence. The individual who experiences multiple stressors appears to be at heightened risk to engage in violence. Specific factors to look for include:

• recent life and family stressors

- an inadequate or deviant social network
- medical or neurological disorders
- current psychological disorders
- a history of recent help-seeking behavior
- limited future opportunities

PROXIMAL CUES: VERBAL AND BEHAVIORAL INDICATORS

As humans, we are strongly verbal-oriented and tend to pay attention to what people say. Too often, however, we ignore the discrepancy between what is said and how it is said, and go only with the literal spoken word. When someone's verbal and nonverbal signals are incongruent, the nonverbal communication is almost always more reflective of the true emotional state. A person who says, "I'm not angry," but is red in the face and has clenched fists is showing nonverbal signs of anger. As people grow older they find ways to control verbal behavior, but most are unable to control the physiological changes that accompany anger. Many times people who are confronted about their anger are unaware of the messages their bodies are sending.

In addition to the discrepancy between the verbal and nonverbal, the *absence* of expected physical reactions to emotional situations can be an indication that the individual has serious emotional problems and may have little or no access to their feelings. We see these people in courtrooms yawning as they are given the death sentence. Or in the footage of the Columbine massacre when Eric Harris and Dylan Klebold seem to express intermittent icy and giddy demeanors as they perpetrate one of the most horrific crimes of our country. Individuals like this can commit heinous crimes because they lack empathy for others. In other words, they have no conscience. This type of discrepancy during violence is one of the most disturbing for most witnesses and others affected because it is so inconsistent with normal human responding.

Verbal Abuse Continuum

Language often reflects the emotional or mental state of an individual, and can warn of future behavior. Verbal statements can be placed on a continuum from compliant to assaulting. The following list explains the five categories on the verbal abuse continuum:

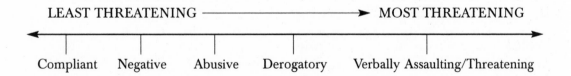

LEAST THREATENING ⟶ MOST THREATENING

Compliant   Negative   Abusive   Derogatory   Verbally Assaulting/Threatening

- *Compliant:* The least threatening verbal declarations indicate cooperation and compliance. The individual is not communicating any threat or resistance. This level reflects normal verbal interactions.
- *Negative:* This level of verbal communication is basically pessimistic. The individual frequently complains about a variety of things and responds negative-

ly to helpful advice. This level of negativity is not necessarily dangerous, and some might argue it characterizes much of adolescence.

- *Abusive:* As the individual becomes more upset and distraught, the verbal expressions escalate to abusiveness. This stage involves general nastiness and name calling. The individual appears intense, blames others excessively, and frequently uses the word "you" in an accusatory tone. For example, "You never understand," or "You don't know."
- *Derogatory:* The more the language deteriorates and becomes offensive, the greater the risk factor. At this level, the individual's conversation centers on making derogatory remarks, put downs, and harsh criticism of others' ideas. Language is marked by vulgar, racist, sexist, and slanderous words. For example, "You bitch," or "That dirty . . ." The purpose of this language is to dehumanize the target. By turning the person into an object, killers feel less connected to the consequences of their actions. This is a common defense mechanism during war when soldiers turn the individuals of the enemy forces into something subhuman, usually in the form of racial slurs.
- *Verbally Assaulting/Threatening:* This is the most serious verbal communication level. The individual is clearly threatening or attempting to intimidate others with language. Verbally assaulting behavior may include threats of physical assault and death. The more bizarre, destructive, and sadistic the language, the greater the risk of violence.

The lower levels of verbal abuse are designed to manipulate, intimidate, and otherwise control the behavior of others. These statements suggest the individual has minimal coping and/or interpersonal skills. While the lower levels of verbal abuse are not particularly dangerous, they do require attention and monitoring. The individual who makes verbally abusive, derogatory, or assaulting statements is a serious threat to the campus. This individual is likely experiencing an intense level of rage which could result in impulsive or destructive actions if timely intervention does not occur.

Physical Abuse Continuum

Physical behaviors are also rated on a continuum from least to most threatening. Physically destructive or abusive conduct could reflect a deteriorated internal state or poor impulse control. Either of these are potential warning signs of violence.

LEAST THREATENING ———————————➤ MOST THREATENING

Compliant   Passive Resistant   Active Resistant   Assault   Deadly Assault

- *Compliant:* A person who is fully cooperative demonstrates the least threatening form of physical behavior. This level reflects normal behavior.
- *Passive Resistant:* This type of behavior is also known as "passive aggressive" and is characterized by subtle defiance. Children and adolescents are masters at this type of behavior. They engage in resistive behaviors that are just under the threshold of noncompliance. They may follow directives but be extremely

slow, putting forth only minimally acceptable effort. In a physical manner, they may use their body mass to impede another's effort by blocking a doorway for example. On college campuses, this form of resistance may manifest as "sit ins" or student strikes.

- *Active Resistant:* This level of physical behavior involves a combination of actively resistant and passive-aggressive behavior. The individual actively resists any form of problem resolution or arbitration, and may engage in subtle or overt defiance or alternate between these styles. There is a noticeable shift in the scope and degree of resistance. The actively resistant individual is demonstrating signs of decreasing impulse control, and may show physical defiance toward authority figures. Examples of active resistance include slamming doors, turning over desks, or throwing objects. There is no actual bodily harm, but the threat of escalating violence exists.
- *Assault:* The physical threat at this level is high. The individual displays both verbally and physically aggressive behaviors, and is likely experiencing eroding impulse control resulting in a state of dangerousness. The individual's intention is to harm or destroy either property or people. Attempts to gain compliance at this point are met with hostile resistance or attack. For example, the individual may engage in an increased number of physical fights or attempt to hurt others with objects or vehicles.
- *Deadly Assault:* The final category is the most extreme of physical behaviors and represents the greatest level of danger to others. At this stage, the individual focuses on killing a specific target, harming a group of individuals, or committing suicide. The potential for critical harm or death to others is high and immediate remedial intervention is necessary in order to thwart violence.

NOTE: The above listed levels of verbal and physical compliance are provided for educational purposes only. A team of trained professionals should analyze the risk factors present in the individual's behavior.

PRACTICING

When violence is premeditated, the perpetrator will often engage in lower level forms of violence to "test out the system" and his or her own courage. These practicing efforts can happen either mentally through violent fantasies or physically against "lower level" targets. Without intervention, practicing efforts can escalate from fantasy to violence against property to harassment to deadly force. When practicing behaviors are noticed, protectors must work to create barriers to further escalation. As we discussed in Chapter 1, perpetrators often follow the analogy of skiing. At the top of the violence slope, the perpetrator begins slowly, but soon picks up speed. Increasing the intensity and frequency of violence, the perpetrator shoots down the mountain until he or she reaches a tree. When a tree is in the path, the perpetrator must make a decision. Do I slow down? Do I try a different trail? Do I turn a different way? The more trees or barriers in the perpetrator's path, the more difficult it is to continue on the violence mission. The rest of the chapters in this section are about "planting trees," or building barriers.

Chapter 6

BUILDING BARRIERS TO VIOLENCE, PART I: AMASSING THE ARMY

VIOLENCE IS AN ISSUE that almost everyone on campus is invested in preventing. Other hot topics on campus can come and go, or only light the passions of a few dedicated individuals, but violence touches the lives of many. There are many ways to channel this concern into effective action. A team approach is often the most effective tactic a campus can employ to prevent violence. Campus community members, whether they be students, faculty, or staff are likely to be more committed to prevention and intervention policies if they help design them and put them into practice. A team approach also helps in the planning by allowing for an overall view of problem areas and potential obstacles. The following chapter lists many ways for campuses to assemble their most valuable asset: the campus community.

CAMPUS-COMMUNITY COALITIONS

Campus-community coalitions consist of broad cross-sections of the university and surrounding neighborhoods. Campuses exist within larger communities, and as such, the larger community must be part of the solution when dealing with violence on college campuses. With campus-community coalitions, key stakeholders from the campus and community meet together to begin a discussion surrounding campus violence. This diverse group works toward the common mission of a safe campus and community.

The benefits of such a group are numerous. Members can get a very comprehensive picture of what is happening when so many interests are represented. Resources are shared and communication is enhanced to maximize the effectiveness of prevention efforts. Furthermore, cooperation is fostered when such diverse groups meet face-to-face. Credibility is enhanced when a wide range of individuals deems it an important issue.

Building and maintaining a coalition can be challenging. The reality of scheduling so many different individuals is daunting, and sustaining member motivation can be exhausting. Sometimes in such a large group, diffusion of responsibility settles in and getting things accomplished is difficult. Nevertheless, because of the benefits outlined above, a coalition is critical to the success of any prevention effort.

Effective coalitions share common characteristics, according to the Community

Anti-Drug Coalitions of America. This group studied the processes of eight successful coalitions and found them to be both highly flexible and structured. They concluded that the most successful coalitions operated with the following elements:

- a documented mission statement
- visionary and committed leadership
- willingness to share the spotlight
- a strategic plan
- a well-defined organizational structure
- an understanding of the local community leadership and volunteer networks
- representative membership and staff
- diverse partners
- recognizing accomplishments of member organizations
- clear expectations
- strong communication skills
- professional development opportunities
- diversified and relevant funding (often comes later in the process)

- up-to-date technology
- continuous evaluation

Potential coalition members may include:

- residence life
- health services
- personal counseling
- legal advisors
- upper-level administration
- campus security or police
- student leaders and other students
- athletics department
- faculty
- Greek life
- admissions
- public affairs
- alumni
- neighborhood and business associations
- local police
- alcohol retailers and bar owners
- city council
- feeder high school administrators

THREAT AND VIOLENCE ASSESSMENT TEAM (TVAT)

Another step in addressing violence prevention is the development of a Threat and Violence Assessment Team (TVAT). This team is smaller and more focused than the campus coalition. The team usually consists of those individuals dedicated to taking action roles rather than just providing input. The TVAT should consist of individuals trained in the evaluation of, and intervention with potentially violent situations. Other specialties that would benefit the team are policy development, media and public relations, human relations, and fundraising. While building this subcoalition, campuses should be selective in choosing the representatives. Solution seekers should be favored over status seekers.

The TVAT's objective is violence prevention and response. TVAT members are responsible for addressing threats and confronting violent behavior, and may assist in assessing potential for violence. They will serve as the primary decision makers in violent crises, and will be communication liaisons between internal and external responders. The TVAT is responsible for making critical decisions quickly. They will develop the protocol in case of a threat or violent incident and establish a plan for the protection of students, staff, and other potential targets.

In the aftermath of violence TVAT members help coordinate affected parties such as victims, families, employees, media, government, or law enforcement. For this reason they must have up-to-date knowledge about victim assistance and community service programs. They will be a primary referral source assisting victims with placement in immediate and ongoing counseling and support services.

Maximizing the Effectiveness of the TVAT

Due to the nature of the response duties of the TVAT, the group must be more efficient and purposeful than the broader campus coalition. For this reason, the TVAT must have a well-understood command structure and protocol. When campuses are developing the TVAT the groups should answer the following questions to clarify issues of command and response.

- Who assumes control when a dangerous situation develops? TVATs must establish an on-call leader who will activate the team when needed.
- At what point does the team begin activating the response plan? What happens to the chain of command at different points of responding to violence?
- How will information be communicated within and outside the organization?
- Who has final authority in decisions about the outcome for a violent or potentially violent student?
- Can the team negotiate with others?
- How will the team act as a liaison with all others involved?
- Who is responsible for the continuation of day-to-day business operations?
- Who will have the necessary information about students and staff (e.g., emergency contacts, phone numbers, addresses)?
- What alternative facilities are available if needed?

Adapted from *Violence Goes to Work* (1997).

The team must work in conjunction with local law enforcement to prevent guesswork in time of crisis. Authority and autonomy issues must be determined in advance. Specifically, when a campus is in a critical situation, law enforcement officials should be the incident commanders and assume authority. The scope of the other responsibilities of the group and particular individuals' tasks should be assigned. The TVAT may also serve as the Crisis Response Team as described in Chapter 9.

SPECIAL FORCES

Special forces are campus groups who have additional impact on preventing and responding to campus violence, and consist of groups already in existence. These groups usually have multiple objectives, of which violence prevention is one. Nevertheless, they can have critical influence by connecting with high-risk individuals or situations not accessible by the TVAT.

Upper Administration

Presidents and chancellors must be clear about their vision for their institution as a nonviolent entity. Ultimately many difficult decisions are placed in the hands of these leaders. Many decisions lead to no-win situations. Expelling a violent student could lead to campus and alumni uproar in the short run and retaining that student could lead to future episodes of violence in time. Stricter policies regarding alcohol may provoke riots while lax policies may invite opportunities for many forms of campus violence.

In addition to being clear and consistent in their messages about violence prevention, campus leaders must be visible as well. Top-down support for violence prevention efforts can often trickle into a downpour of support from other campus departments. At some of the most active campuses, presidents have been involved in a number of ways. They have written letters to parents and alumni on these issues. They have also addressed the current campus community through compassionate yet hard-line speeches.

Faculty and Staff

Faculty members are natural participants in violence prevention efforts. Often they are the most highly respected individuals on campus. They also have daily access to students and can be a fundamental means to address violence prevention issues. As such faculty may be first-line responders to violence. In their classrooms they may notice questionable student injuries or absenteeism. In writing assignments professors may read about self-disclosed victims of rape or other assault. In these cases, faculty must be knowledgeable and comfortable in handling these difficult situations and summoning the help of others if necessary.

Curriculum infusion has been a buzzword of the last decade. It refers to the process of bringing current social issues affecting students into the classroom. Originally, curriculum infusion efforts focused primarily on drugs and alcohol. Faculty members were encouraged to integrate these topics with the course material at hand. Chemistry professors focused on the chemical structures of substances, history professors discussed changes in attitudes and policies dealing with substances over time, psychology professors talked about the impact of alcohol and drugs on relationships and emotions, and so on. Other professors developed entire courses to address the issues of alcohol and drugs.

Similarly, curriculum infusion has been used to increase awareness about violence and violence prevention. Emory University offers an interdisciplinary minor in violence studies. This undergraduate course looks at the issues of violence from several different disciplines including history, sociology, biology, and literature. Beyond the classroom, students are required to complete an internship to gain hands-on experience with violence issues.

Many faculty members are also highly visible on campuses. They are well known by students and other staff, and their opinions are valued. When faculty share their own experiences with violence, the impact is powerful. At Regis University, faculty members joined students and other staff at an annual "Speak Out" on the library steps. During this forum, individuals voluntarily step up to a microphone and describe how alcohol and campus violence has affected their lives. Stories from faculty who talked about how they had been affected by these issues made a lasting impression on all those who witnessed the event.

Throughout this book, we speak to the numerous ways other campus staff can take a part in preventing violence. Most notably, counseling services, residence life, student activities, health services, athletics, campus ministry, and Greek life all play multiple roles in dealing with these issues.

Greek Life and Athletics

Greek life students and athletes are some of the most powerful students on campus. Many of them hold leadership positions and are respected role models. Others have charismatic personalities and are often in the spotlight. These groups also tend to have tremendous alumni support. For these and many other reasons, Greek life students and athletes can play a crucial role in violence prevention.

Because Greek life students, athletes, and respective advisors often feel scapegoated for all the problems of campus violence, they are often motivated to become part of a solution for change. Many Greek systems may be on the verge of being phased out, and thus, students who believe in the benefits of Greek life are actively trying to change the perception that all fraternity and sorority members are troublemakers. For example, some Greeks have formed chapters of GAMMA–a nationally organized peer-based health promotion organization designed to promote positive lifestyles.

Programs such as Mentors in Violence Prevention (MVP) target student-athletes to empower them to become active bystanders to gender violence. The presenters also meet with the entire coaching staff and athletic director to make sure these leaders are also supporting violence prevention attitudes through their comments and behavior. Throughout the program the facilitators focus on the social status of male student-athletes and the ways their leadership can create change in reducing all male violence against women.

Peer Educators

Peer education is an effective tool for creating awareness and supporting healthy lifestyles. The BACCHUS & GAMMA Peer Education Network has supported peer education efforts nationwide for decades and has demonstrated that peer education makes a difference. Campuses use peer educators to coordinate awareness weeks such as "Sexual Responsibility Week," "Alcohol Awareness Week," and "Safe Spring Break Week." Media campaigns, peer theater, interactive educational workshops, and informational displays organized by these students can have a positive effect on campus awareness and advocacy. Peer educators also work with students one-on-one by being active listeners and effective referral agents.

When asked how they made a difference:

- 82 percent said they taught new information.
- 64 percent said they changed an attitude.
- 60 percent said they caused a positive behavior change.
- 55 percent said they confronted a risky behavior.
- 25 percent said they caused a change in behavior that resulted in saving a life.

(From *The Peer Educator,* "Creating a home, making a difference: Studying our network" David Hellstrom, Director of Education, The BACCHUS & GAMMA Peer Education Network. September 1999.)

Peer educators not only have an impact on their campuses they are also positively affected by their experience. Many peer educators claim that being in the public light supporting healthy choices holds one accountable for making good decisions. Across the board, peer educators make healthier decisions regarding substance use than do their peers.

Parents

As a result of the 1998 Higher Education Amendment Act, colleges can notify parents about disciplinary actions involving alcohol and drug violations of students under the age of twenty-one. Many view this amendment as an opportunity to promote student health and individual responsibility by giving parents a chance to talk with their sons and daughters about the decisions they are making.

Parents can become active participants in preventing college violence. They are usually the most influential people in students' lives. Parents should ask for crime statistics of campus before sending students. By law, colleges and universities must release the information. With this information, parents can warn their sons and daughters about potential dangers on college campuses by being well versed about the risks students face. Parents can also talk about the fact that according to national surveys most students are not drinking to excess all the time and are not having multiple sex partners. Finally, parents can encourage effective coping and communication skills, and support their daughters and sons through this transition.

A resource for parents of college students is College Parents of America, a national organization providing a voice for parents of college students. This organization can be contacted by calling toll free 1-888-256-4627 or by visiting their website at www.college parents.org.

Campus Law Enforcement

Campus law enforcement has taken great strides in the recent past to become a more effective presence on college campuses. According to research cited in *Violence on Campus* (Schuh, 1998), three out of four campuses have enforcement personnel with arrest powers. Campus law enforcement personnel frequently come into contact with many different segments of the campus population in their work as protectors and emergency responders. They are often responsible for public safety programs, violence containment, investigations, escort services, and other protective measures.

When it comes to addressing campus violence problems, the breadth of responsibility for campus law enforcement personnel remains under debate. Should officers have a community resource mentality and lots of direct community-building contact with the campus members on a daily basis? Or should the officers take more of a militaristic stance, wearing more formal enforcement attire and carrying weapons? Many departments struggle with the boundaries between their roles and the roles of local law enforcement. When is it all right to keep security concerns and investigations within house and when should outside enforcers be called in?

In any event, campus security and police play a vital role in preventing campus violence on many levels. They are often first-line responders to campus violence incidents and have eyewitness accounts of the situation. Officers are often able to build rapport with students in a different way than faculty and other staff because security officers are present with students every day, all day long. Unlike most local law enforcement agencies, campus enforcers are frequently called upon to sit on committees and task forces where they have direct input to policy decisions and prevention initiatives. Additionally, security offices can serve as databases for campus crime information. Roles and responses of campus law enforcement are further discussed in Chapter 8.

TRAINING

A crucial component in violence prevention is the adequate training of students, faculty, and other employees concerning the dynamics of campus violence and effective preventive measures. Shared responsibility should be the emphasized message throughout the campus community. Three potential training seminars can help give the campus community an overview of the issues and potential solutions.

- **Campus Violence: What Is the Reality?** (2 hours)

Designed mainly for students, this workshop should help participants get a better understanding of the myths and realities of campus violence. Several different types of campus violence should be briefly discussed and broad potential solutions suggested.

- **Campus Violence: Become Part of the Solution** (4–6 hours)

This workshop should be designed for faculty, staff, student leaders, parents, and other concerned "protectors" who want to become more involved in preventing violence. Policies and prevention strategies should be covered in more depth and participants should leave with an understanding of what they can do to take the next step. This level of training is most appropriate for the campus-community coalition.

- **Campus Violence: Threat and Violence Assessment Team In-Service** (1- 2 day seminar)

The program should be designed to train the small group of individuals who will be responsible for making the critical decisions before, during, and after a violence incident. In addition to the previous topics, the training should go into great detail about threat analysis, perpetrator profiling, emergency preparedness, and crisis response.

Chapter 7

BUILDING BARRIERS TO VIOLENCE, PART II: DEVELOPING POLICY AND PROCEDURES FOR THREATS AND VIOLENCE

To PREVENT VIOLENCE effectively, colleges need to develop specific and well-known violence prevention procedures. There is no cookie-cutter approach to violence prevention. Each campus must adapt the following recommendations to their unique situations and concerns. In addition, interventions for different types of campus violence (e.g., sexual assault, hate crimes, hazing and so on) are more specific than strategies suggested here, and are dealt with in the chapters in the last section of this book. Campuses that have used the following general prevention and intervention strategies have been consistently more effective in dealing with campus violence than those that do not.

CONCEPTUALIZING PREVENTION AND INTERVENTION

Prevention and intervention occur at three levels:

1. *Detection and Awareness.* Protectors must have systematic ways of becoming aware of the signs and signals of potential violence. Anonymous tip lines and other streamlined reporting procedures can facilitate data gathering. Employee hiring practices, and to some extent admissions policies, must consider background patterns of violence when assessing the risk of bringing an individual to campus. Front-line responders must be aware of practice phenomena. They must be able to detect escalating threats and violent behavior to implement swift intervention before something more serious occurs.

2. *Delay and Insulation.* At this stage, "trees" and technology come into play. Protectors must be prepared with a range of trees or barriers as described in Chapter 2. Again, trees can question, confront, or implement consequences. The idea is to put a roadblock in the path of the violent individual. Technological approaches are designed to slow down the perpetrator and insulate potential victims. These include anything from ID cards to locked buildings to tear gas.

3. *Strategic Response.* Strategic responses must occur both on an individual level and on a campus-community level. Individuals must not only have the skills to escape or avoid violence they also must be able to give

themselves permission to act appropriately when the situation demands. On a community level, campuses must have well-coordinated response strategies both internally and with outside agencies.

GENERAL PREVENTION STRATEGIES

Multitiered Approach

All effective violence prevention strategies are comprehensive and broad-based. They go far beyond a single office or individual, and involve efforts on every level of the institution and many aspects of the community. Effective strategies target groups and individuals, employ large-scale and small-scale programming, and enact a host of different methods to create change. Each effort reinforces the next.

Clear Communication

Communication regarding violence, both written and verbal, must be clear and consistent. Messages must coincide with the mission of the institution and the image of the school. Catalogue descriptions, pre-frosh experiences, and orientation events set first impressions of the university. All of these must give new students the incoming impression: We do not tolerate violence here.

Evaluation

Both qualitative and quantitative evaluations are critical to the success of any violence prevention effort. Initially, a thorough needs assessment will give the prevention team a better picture of where the problems are and why. Focus groups and interviews with key stakeholders can flush out these descriptions and give important guidance on what might initiate change. Standardized questionnaires and university-developed supplemental surveys can be used to test pre- and post-changes in attitudes and self-reported behavior. Other indicators of campus violence such as disciplinary cases, personal counseling referrals, and campus security reports can be tracked to indicate trends in violence.

Not only are accurate campus incident records necessary to tally changes over time, this data can also relate important indicators of future violence or delayed violence impact. Violence does not happen in a vacuum. Ripple effects from one act of violence may lead to another related incident. Clustering of violent events during one period of time or around one general area may signify that new prevention techniques are needed.

Most importantly, in the evaluation process, the university must take a candid look at how certain systems or individuals may be contributing to problems of violence. This tactic is not done to lay blame, but rather as a place to start to take corrective action. If one area of the institution is working hard to make positive changes, it may be totally undermined if a more powerful segment of the university is sending a competing message.

Awareness and Skill-Building Efforts

Throughout this book, awareness raising and skill-building programs are suggested.

The professional staff members in the counseling center are natural resources for these purposes. Most counselors are experts in conflict resolution, understanding the impact of violence on victims, and a host of other relevant topics. They can work with victims and perpetrators, individuals and groups.

No violence prevention strategy will be effective without addressing the problems of alcohol abuse. Dealing with these issues must happen at many levels–individuals, high-risk groups, low-risk groups, and so on. A more comprehensive discussion of these issues is covered in Chapter 4.

As the Director of Prevention Institute in Berkeley, California, Larry Cohen advocates awareness programs because they effect the community on many levels, "Effective community education not only alerts individuals to new information, but it also builds a critical mass of support for healthier behavior, norms and policy change" (*Beyond Brochures: Preventing Alcohol-Related Violence and Injuries,* www.preventioninstitute.org).

Effective Response Mechanisms

Response mechanisms for violence or potential violence can run the gamut from mediation, to campus judicial codes, to civil and criminal action, to counseling and victim services. Mediation lets conflicting individuals or groups negotiate a resolution rather than resort to violence. This influential process allows participants to regain a sense of control in the situation.

Behavioral standards related to violence must be set and enforced. Once these codes are broken, the Threat and Violence Assessment Team may be called in to assess the situation and plan for further appropriate action. Emergency procedures must be spelled out and widely known. The first hour after a violent incident is most crucial for containing the situation, gathering information, and aiding the victim or victims. See Appendix for flow charts.

STANDARD OPERATING GUIDELINES

When it comes to rules and regulations, campuses seem to be coming full circle. The *New York Times* noted that before the 1970s many campuses had housemothers, curfews, and even dress codes. In the post-Vietnam era, many campus rules were discarded and the notion of campuses *in loco parentis* (or campuses as substitute parents) died out.

Today, the *zeitgeist* is shifting again. Possibly because of "boomer generation guilt," perhaps because of increased litigiousness, or maybe because of increased fears about dangers to students, policies and procedures are regaining popularity.

Rules and regulations regarding many specific factors leading to campus violence are suggested throughout this book. Alcohol

policies, hate crime policies, hazing policies, and so on are listed in their respective chapters. The following sections describe the necessary policies and procedures designed to monitor and detect potentially violent individuals. The prevention and intervention strategies listed below can assist colleges in developing a standard operating guide to avoid and respond to violence. Many campuses have implemented these and other techniques and have witnessed a positive response; however, there are no foolproof formulas for preventing violence. When people are 100 percent determined to carry out an act of violence, they will find a way. Fortunately, most violent individuals, like most suicidal individuals, experience some ambivalence. The more effective prevention and intervention techniques there are in place, the greater the likelihood that violence will be deterred because that ambivalence will be met with consequences and obstacles.

Much of the policy and investigation sections of this chapter were adapted from our book *Violence Goes to Work* (1997), while the emergency management section draws from our book *Violence Goes to School* (1999).

Bottom Line: Zero Tolerance

Campuses must be prepared to develop and enforce a zero tolerance stance against all threats and violence. What does zero tolerance mean? Does it mean that anyone who makes a joke about violence is automatically fired or expelled? No. What it means is that every questionable statement or gesture goes under the microscope. Every threat gets addressed, even if that only means investigation and documentation.

The airlines industry is currently the only trade that truly has zero tolerance for threats and violence. All threats or suspect behaviors are confronted. Even jokes. In the aftermath of the postal worker shootings of the early 1990s, many other workplaces have adopted zero tolerance programs involving tip lines and conflict resolution classes. The result? Homicides in the workplace have dropped significantly since 1993.

A zero tolerance message is clear and empowering. Creating the policy may seem relatively easy, but enforcing it becomes more complex.   Campuses must think through what zero tolerance means for them. What is fair? What is legal? What fits with the mission of the campus as a learning environment? Does it mean, "One strike and you are out?"   Many companies have learned the hard way that if you start shifting the line defining unacceptable behavior, the

zero tolerance policy becomes worthless. When you enter situations where it's one person's word against another, zero tolerance can become confusing. Effective zero tolerance policies take these issues into consideration, create effective means of enforcement, and train those affected by the policy to enhance civility.

Legal Considerations

According to the Higher Education Center, before 1980 colleges were generally not held liable for crimes occurring on their campuses. Today campuses are being held responsible for a number of violence incidents:

- The Nebraska Supreme Court ruled that the University of Nebraska had a duty to protect a fraternity pledge who was injured while trying to escape a hazing ritual.   The court determined that the university had been aware of previous hazing incidents involving this fraternity and was therefore obligated to take reasonable steps to protect against future acts of hazing.
- The mother of an Iona College freshman who died from alcohol poisoning sued the college and the owners of two bars. The suit stated that Iona administrators were negligent in their failure to control underage drinking and hazing activity.
- The Florida Supreme Court ruled that a university may be held liable for a student's injuries at an off-campus internship if the school knew in advance that the site was dangerous.
- The parents of John LaDuca have filed a wrongful-death suit against the fraternity and its alumni board. John hanged himself the day after the fraternity's initiation ended. Throughout the week leading up to initiation, John was subjected

to multiple dangerous and humiliating hazing practices.

Each of these cases calls into question a number of issues regarding campus liability. While this is not a legal manual per se, the following summary gives a brief overview of the concerns.

Definition of Campus

When people think about a college campus, they often think about the physical grounds of the school. But the boundaries of a campus are diffuse and permeable. Campus violence can involve visitors on campus grounds, students at an off-campus party or bar, individuals passing through campus property, Greek housing, interns at off-campus sites, and even study-abroad students. For example, in the aftermath of the campus riots, many schools found that their codes of conduct did not cover students' behavior in the local community. Many sought to rectify this problem by expanding the code to include behavior that was a reasonable distance from the institution. Then the question became what is a reasonable distance? Institutional responsibilities seem to be getting broader and broader.

And what about student behavior that is so discrepant from the established code of conduct, but occurs during spring break or summer vacation. According to the *Chronicle of Higher Education,* a 1997 survey of five hundred twenty members of the Association for Student Judicial Affairs determined that more than three out of four institutions have expanded codes of conduct to include off-campus behavior. What happens if a student or employee of the university is charged with a serious crime, but is awaiting trial? Should the school temporarily suspend the student or wait until the courts decide guilt or innocence? These are all difficult questions with which campuses have to struggle.

Negligent Hiring and Negligent Retention

Negligent hiring and negligent retention are legal terms that have received increasing attention in the wake of workplace violence incidents. The terms are usually used under certain circumstances when employees commit a violent act and employers are held liable. These situations occur when an employer has prior knowledge that people are at risk for committing violence but hires or retains them anyway. Thorough screening and background investigation, while not foolproof, can significantly reduce hiring risks. Swift and appropriate responses to threats and concerning behavior can minimize the potential of an escalating workplace violence problem. For more information regarding these issues, please consult *Violence Goes to Work: An Employer's Guide* (1997).

Violence Prior to Enrollment

At the time of this publication, no major case had demonstrated that a student's violent behavior prior to enrollment was cause for campus liability in a later act of violence while the student was at school. But plenty of schools are concerned about such exposure. The best known case concerns a woman named Gina Grant who was offered an early admission to Harvard University in 1995. Later the school discovered that in 1990 Gina had testified to the court that she had bludgeoned her mother to death with a candlestick and stabbed her mother in the neck with a kitchen knife. Gina was charged with voluntary manslaughter and served six months in juvenile detention before moving in with an aunt and uncle. This information was omitted from her application to Harvard. When Harvard discovered her history, they rescinded their offer of admission.

Arizona State University chose to admit a convicted murderer. James Hamm shot and killed a Tucson man in 1974. He also scored in the 96th percentile on his law school admissions test, and he is married to a former justice of the peace. Understandably, his enrollment sparked a heated controversy. Some see him as a criminal justice success story, others as an institutional liability and an unfair decision to the thousands of applicants who were rejected.

Failure to Protect/Failure to Warn

According to *Violence on Campus* (1998), when a university tries to control or prohibit dangerous behavior such as hazing or underage drinking, a court may find that the institution has a duty to protect those students. Several suits against colleges have resulted in monetary awards for damages such as failure to provide adequate security or prevent foreseeable harm.

Policy Development

Policies reduce the chance factors in campus operations by establishing a common body of knowledge. Colleges that develop a Standard Operating Guide before it is needed are more likely to avoid panic and disruption when an event arises.

As with most important human relation issues, an anti-violence policy requires careful analysis and review before implementation. Policy developers should include only criteria that can be administered consistently. Commitment from the upper-level administrators to develop and enforce the policy is essential. Policies cannot promise to protect students or employees from physical harm since this is not absolutely possible.

The choice of words in policy development is important. Many legal advisors suggest that it is preferable to use words such as "strive" rather than a promise to promote and maintain a school environment free from intimidation and threats of violence. Similarly, policy developers should consider using the term "may" over the term "will" in the text of the policy. The use of the word "will" can be a promise to act. If a complaint is received and not investigated, the campus could face a negligence claim.

Policy Development: General Questions to Ask

- Is the content of the policy within the scope of campus authority?
- Is it consistent with local, state, and federal laws?
- Have legal references been included?
- Does it reflect good educational practice?
- Is it reasonable? (Are any requirements or prohibitions arbitrary or discriminatory?)
- Does it adequately cover the issues?
- Is it limited to one policy topic?
- Is it cross-referenced to other relevant policy topics?
- Is it consistent with campus' existing policies?
- Can it be administered?
- Is it practical in terms of administrative enforcement and budget?

Source: Adapted from the National School Board Association (1993).

Who Develops Policies?

A violence prevention policy is most effective when it is created, implemented, managed, and evaluated by those who are directly involved with such assessments on a regular basis. A cross-section of the community should be involved to get varying viewpoints on the policy strategies. As always, legal council should be sought before any policies are put into practice.

What Policies Are Necessary?

Threat Policy. Campuses should create a written zero-tolerance policy that explains the position of the campus on intimidating, threatening, or violent behaviors. This policy should clearly define what constitutes threats (see Chapter 5 for a detailed description of various forms of threats), and establish appropriate procedures for investigating potential problems and determining appropriate consequences. One crucial component in the threat policy is the reporting procedure. Campuses must give students and staff clear instructions about what to do if they perceive a threat. An avenue for anonymous reporting should be implemented. Some prevention experts argue that language that guarantees strict confidentiality for reporting should be avoided for purposes of investigation.

Along these lines, campuses may consider developing the following additional policies:

- Search Policy
- Violence Communication Policy
- Hate Crime
- Hazing
- Sexual Harassment
- Sexual Assault
- Non-Sexual Assault
- Rioting

Sample Threats and Violence Policy

Our policy is to strive to maintain a campus environment free from intimidation, threats, or violent acts. This includes, but is not limited to: intimidating, threatening or hostile behaviors, physical abuse, vandalism, hazing, sexual assault, hate crimes, arson, sabotage, carrying or use of weapons, or any other act, which, in the administration's opinion, is inappropriate to the campus environment. In addition, bizarre or offensive comments regarding violent events or aggressive behaviors will not be tolerated.

Campus employees or students who feel subjected to any of the behaviors listed above should immediately report the incident to _____ [name of designated campus representative(s)]. All complaints will receive prompt attention and the situation will be investigated. Based on the results of the inquiry, disciplinary action which administration feels appropriate will be taken.

Campus employees or students who observe or have knowledge of violation of this policy should immediately report it to _____ [the appointed campus representative(s)]. All reported events will be taken seriously. If an investigation is warranted, we will request the cooperation of all incident-related individuals. An employee or student who believes there is a serious threat to the safety and health of others should report this concern directly to law enforcement authorities.

Source: Adapted from *Violence Goes to Work* (1997).

The "Vortex": Communication Policies

A *vortex* or *communication center* should be established to provide a knowledge base for all investigations. A standard reporting form and procedure will help ensure that reporting is complete and contains consistent information. This system organizes all incidents of violence by keeping record of the details of the incident, interventions, and outcomes. Any consultations, referrals, or other outside intervention should also be noted in these files. This documentation will help investigators determine patterns in perpetrators, targets, means, or other factors in their assessment of dangerousness.

In addition to documenting critical or threatening incidents, the communication center also can be a resource center for those concerned with violence prevention. The communication can serve as a clearinghouse to distribute current literature and data on campus safety issues. The center also can house a list of local and national experts or others known to assist in solutions to campus violence problems.

INVESTIGATION

A formalized plan for investigation of threats or violence complaints is necessary to prevent campus personnel from being caught off-guard and unprepared when a prompt response is most critical. A carefully thought-out investigation procedure helps ensure that facts about the incident are collected and examined in an expedient and thorough manner. Effective investigation can often defuse further violence potential.

Who Conducts the Investigation?

Those in charge of the investigation must have training in violence assessment and intervention. They must keep a neutral and objective attitude toward all parties, and have the ability to manage the investigation in a professional manner. At various points, the administration may wish to use outside experts who have knowledge and experience in evidence collection, and in conducting investigations, interviews, and interrogations. An alternative is to designate appropriately trained members of the Threat and Violence Assessment Team to conduct the investigation.

A series of steps that involve planning, conducting, documenting, and evaluating the investigation are necessary for an effective, thorough analysis of the evidence.

Planning the Investigation

Campuses should draft investigation procedures prior to conducting any actual investigation. Consistent and comprehensive inquiries result when a detailed methodology is followed in each case. Multiple sources of data are essential in determining risk. Thus, investigation of collateral witnesses (e.g., parents, roommates, friends, and so on), academic and disciplinary records, legal history, armament inventories all add critical information to complete the picture. The following step-by-step guide can assist investigators in their efforts to piece together the situation.

Step #1: Develop a preliminary list of witnesses or individuals involved in, or affected by, the incident.

Step #2: Specify the sequence of interviews

and appoint interviewers.

Step #3: Determine what evidence the investigator can obtain for the investigation.

Step #4: Decide what, if any, action is necessary before beginning the investigation. For example, consider implementation of security measures to protect targets and property, or the temporary suspension of an accused student or employee until the investigation is completed.

Investigators must take necessary steps to ensure privacy of each interviewee to the best of their ability. This is critical to ensure that students and employees feel free to discuss the problem.

NOTE: The investigator(s) should be careful not to guarantee absolute confidentiality about the information gathered. Witnesses must understand that if the allegations are serious, their statements could be reported to others. Assure them that the statements are treated as discreetly as is practical.

When planning the interviews, investigators should determine the type of information needed from each person. Possible reactions or responses from the alleged perpetrator or witnesses need to be anticipated as best as possible. Investigators should develop a list of questions in advance to ask each party, keeping in mind the objective of the interview. In particular, pertinent questions concern who, what, where, when, and how.

When beginning the investigation, it is important to establish rapport by remembering to be empathetic and calm. Victims and witnesses may be in shock, and may need ample time to answer questions. Investigator patience is paramount. Questions should be contained to the matters related to the complaint or event, unless past patterns of

this conduct have occurred in which case this history is open to questioning.

Investigators must be prepared to document what each party involved did, said, or knew. Follow appropriate questioning techniques such as:

- Ask open-ended questions, encouraging the individual to share more information.
- Listen to the response without interrupting the flow of details.
- Wait until the person has completed the narrative to ask for clarification.
- Keep each question brief and confined to one point or topic.
- Avoid leading questions that suggest or guide the answer.
- Keep questions simple, using words that are clear to the person being interviewed.
- Watch for nonverbal messages, and follow up with applicable questions to confirm or revise the received impression.

Conducting and Documenting the Interview

Begin the investigation with the individual who reported the occurrence. Ask for details regarding:

- What happened? What action did each party take? What did each person say? Where did it happen? Describe where the action took place.
- When did it happen? Get both the date and time of the incident.
- Who was present? List the names of any potential witnesses.
- What evidence exists to corroborate the story?
- Ask for a written statement summarizing the incident at the conclusion of the interview.

After this initial interview is completed, ask the same questions to the alleged perpetrator or perpetrators and any witnesses in an order appropriate to the situation. With witnesses or other involved parties, it is important to ask general questions first such as, "Are you aware of any problems that exist between students on our campus?"

Investigators should then prepare a confidential report of the findings in case of a filed charge or lawsuit. The investigative notes and statements of witnesses may be used as an official record. Therefore, investigators must ensure there are no extraneous comments, opinions, or statements cited as fact. The report should stick to the objective, verifiable data of the event and do not embellish.

To compile the documentation investigators should include all actual findings and their sources. Reports must be kept as confidential as practical. Only those with a legitimate need to know should have access to the report. No unnecessary copies should be made.

All those involved in the investigation must avoid defamation claims. Defamation is the unprivileged communication to a third person of a false statement intending to harm the reputation of another. To protect against the possibility of defamation, investigators should make the findings of an investigation and other pertinent documents available only to persons having a legitimate connection or interest in them. Precautions against needless publication of potentially defamatory statements minimize the exposure of the campus to liability.

Evaluating the Evidence and Taking Appropriate Action

The investigating team has an obligation to analyze the data collected and formulate a course of action. This is especially difficult when one person's word against another's is the only information available. Consultation with an outside violence assessment professional is often needed in evaluating the evidence.

To consider the credibility of the allegations, ask:
- When was the complaint made? If it was not immediately reported, find out why.
- Is the complaint specific and detailed? Are there any contradictions in the information collected?
- Are there things missing in the evidence that should be there? Is there any logical explanation for the missing data?

To consider the credibility of the accused, and any denials, ask:
- Has the student or employee accused simply made a blanket denial?
- Has the accused provided evidence that either supports or contradicts the allegations?
- Have other allegations been made about this person?

The type of corrective action needed depends on the nature of the incident and past practice. The more serious the allegation, the greater the need for law enforcement intervention. Failure to act can increase the liability of the campus. Overly severe discipline could lead to a legal suit from the accused or his or her family. When a campus needs to take immediate action to deal with a problem, suspending the student or employee provides time to investigate. As the team determines consequences, they should ask themselves, "Do the consequences fit the infraction?" Some examples of interventions include:
- Suspend student or employee pending investigation
- Individual is allowed on campus under close supervision
- Expulsion/Firing
- Probation
- Community service
- Psychological evaluation and/or man-

dated counseling
• Legal action
NOTE: If the campus plans to suspend or expel a potentially violent student or employee, escort the individual from the premises, deny the individual access to the campus, and take extra security precautions to impede attempted reentry. During this critical time, there should be a concerted effort to develop plans to keep the individual off grounds.

EMERGENCY MANAGEMENT

In addition to policy and procedures developed to prevent violence, emergency plans need to be designed as well. Each campus should develop systematic procedures for dealing with different types of crises. The purpose of these plans is to instruct key people on how to handle an actual crisis situation in an effective and efficient manner. In developing plans, take the following factors into consideration:

General Considerations

Emergency preparedness plans need to have both clarity and flexibility. Frequently, in the midst of a crisis, unforeseen obstacles will hinder the best thought-out plans. As much as possible, policy developers must attempt to identify any conditions or situations that can influence the emergency response and plan how these would be managed. These obstacles might include isolation or geographical location, critical functions the campus performs, or legal responsibilities.

We also have learned that the most effective plans are utterly useless unless people know them cold. The last thing campuses want at a time of crisis is key decision makers searching through file cabinets trying to find and then decipher the emergency manual. Campuses must evaluate the efficacy of the plan through regular "violence drills." While this concept may sound odd, it is no more outrageous than planned fire drills. As

with most planning processes, what looks good on paper may be lacking in a real situation.

In addition to the identified Threat and Violence Assessment Team and campus and local safety and rescue personnel, campuses should consider whether or not they may need these additional resources on-hand depending on the nature of the crisis:
• Building maintenance personnel
• Additional cellular phones and two-way radios
• Professional negotiators
• Locksmiths
• Specialized victim assistance professionals to counsel people in sexual assault situations and secondary victims of the violence.

Tools for Emergency Response

Emergency Management Kit for Responders

One of the important lessons learned from the Columbine High School tragedy was that emergency personnel responding to the scene were slowed due to a lack of information. They could not get a sense of the school's layout because blueprints were not readily available. Precious time was lost because of this confusion. Because of this lesson learned, we recommend that campuses compile blueprints of campus buildings and give them to proper law enforcement. These blueprints of campus buildings should have exit routes clearly marked as well as any potential concealment locations. While reviewing these blueprints, be sure to examine exit strategies. Most exits have been designed for fire escape and not violence escape. In addition to these blueprints, the emergency management kit should also contain important phone numbers, for example members of the Threat and Violence Assessment Team, and if practical, a current list of campus residents. Having several kits stored in more than one place will increase accessibility in the time of crisis.

Emergency Response Procedures

Other aspects of the emergency management plan to consider are procedures for intruders, hostage situations, and catastrophic occurrences. Planners should identify off-campus locations where students and employees might be moved and triaged and investigate crisis transportation issues—early closings, traffic flow, parking, emergency vehicle access. The Threat and Violence Assessment Team must identify a responsible party for each portion of the emergency plan.

Emergency Communication Plan

When developing a communication plan, clear command responsibilities including alternates are essential. An effective communication plan must be able to inform students, staff, and the community of the campus' plans in case of catastrophe. One tactic is a phone tree to enhance speed and thoroughness of communication. Another suggestion is some sort of signal to alert appropriate staff that a violent emergency has occurred or might occur. This signal should be unique for high-impact emergencies. A different signal can be used to alert staff that the emergency is over.

A command center serves as a communication vortex for an emergency. An easily accessible location and alternate must be determined in advance. One of the functions of the command center is to let people know who is where; thus, it is important to establish a procedure for creating a list of injured students and employees that includes their names and conditions. Procedures for alerting and providing supportive and counseling resources are also necessary. The command center also can serve as a location for reuniting students and employees with loved ones. The media liaison can gather and relay information obtained from the

---

Telephone Use During a Crisis

• Consider installing additional lines or temporary 1-800 numbers to handle incoming calls demanding information.
• Consider opening one line just for media contact.
• Staff "information hot lines" with informed professional staff with scripted informational releases.
• If professionals cannot staff phones, consider recording information and updating as needed.
• Give people who are answering phones frequent breaks as they may need relief from handling ongoing emotional intensity and the inability to sometimes give answers that satisfy the callers.

command center.

Particular importance must be given to communication between those within the campus and those outside the campus. Very often during a campus crisis, the telephone lines become jammed with incoming and outgoing calls of people trying to receive and relay information. For this reason, we have listed additional suggestions for telephone communication.

Disseminating the Emergency Plan

Again, all policies are in vain if no one knows them. Thus, it is essential that the plans be disseminated effectively. Informational brochures, special briefings, training videos, organizational newsletters, and staff meetings are some of the means of getting the plans out to the people who will be responding to the crises. But campuses should not rely on a one-shot approach to getting this information across. Regular reviews of the plan as conditions and staff change are necessary.

While these emergency preparedness plans are being disseminated, campuses must be sure to cultivate a supportive climate and not a panic climate. Violence prevention campaigns and recognition awards can help create a positive climate towards preventing violence on campus. Logos, slogans, and promotional items can help spread the message even further.

Chapter 8

BUILDING BARRIERS TO VIOLENCE, PART III: ENVIRONMENTAL PROTECTION AND SAFETY STRATEGIES

As we learned in Chapter 3 most institutions of higher learning in good faith inadvertently lull their community members into a false sense of security. We open ourselves to the greater community by having our libraries, athletic facilities, and other facilities open for public use. Campus events are open to the public. Students are encouraged to be open to diversity. These are all very positive actions that should continue. However, we sometimes fail to recognize that there are some legitimate dangers in our community. By doing so, we fail to teach our community members how to identify dangers and take appropriate steps to keep themselves safe.

While colleges and universities are making efforts with physical improvements and developing safety programs, they are also fighting a battle to correct bad safety advice that has run rampant. The following are examples of such bad advice:

"When being stalked, show the perpetrator that you are not afraid by remaining calm and collected."

Correction: You do not want to look like a target to a predator. Once the predator has identified you as a victim and is stalking you, you want to get away as fast as you can.

"If you are cornered in an elevator, hit the Emergency Stop button."

Correction: This button will stop the elevator and entrap you with the perpetrator for the attack. Instead, you want to hit the buttons for every floor and get out of the elevator as soon as possible.

"When you are being attacked, poke the attacker in the eye."

Correction: In a state of panic your fine motor skills become more difficult to use. Unless you are able to remain very calm in an attack, you need to depend on gross motor techniques. Another factor to consider is your psychological readiness to poke someone in the eye. The thought upsets most people, and yet in order to accomplish this effectively, there can be no hesitation.

"If you are wearing high heels, jam the heel into the foot of the attacker."

Correction: A great deal of pressure is required to jam a heel into someone's foot. If you are actually able to do this, you have succeeded in connecting yourself to the attacker.

"In the event that you are being chased, keep your keys in your hand so you can get into your car quickly and use the keys as weapons."

Correction: Again, when panicking, people often have difficulty with fine motor skills and sometimes experience blurred vision. When people attempt to put their keys in the keyhole, they find that the keyhole appears to shrink and move around. Unless you have a keyless entry system, these factors will make it difficult to get into the car. The better option is to run. Using a key as a weapon is also not a great idea, because in order to use the weapon you must get in close proximity to the attacker.

"If attacked, talk to the perpetrator and help them understand what they are doing is wrong."

Correction: During an attack perpetrators are past the point of being talked out their behavior. Again, the best option is to get away and get to help.

In addition to overcoming bad advice, colleges and universities often do not consider whom they are trying to protect and what violent behavior they are trying to prevent. For example, installing a blue light telephone for the purpose of helping someone who is being chased may not be effective. A blue light telephone is effective in those circumstances where people who are not in imminent danger can call in concerns. However, when people are being chased they will not take the time to stop, figure out whom to call, dial, and wait for an answer. They need to keep running.

If the same blue light telephone were equipped with a single button that could be activated by a gross motor hit as the person ran by, that might make the telephone more effective. The phone would then provide a safety responder with the location of the person being chased.

In this chapter we will examine guiding principles behind violent behavior and victim responses, how these principles influence prevention in environmental protection, safety services provided, and survival strategies.

GUIDING PRINCIPLES BEHIND VIOLENT BEHAVIOR AND VICTIM RESPONSES

Violence Is a Learned Behavior

As we mentioned in Chapter 5, people say things like, "He just snapped!" in the aftermath of violence. The reality is most violence perpetrators have a violence history and have worked up to the incident. Violence is a learned behavior. Perpetrators usually practice by engaging in behaviors that become increasingly violent. Practicing helps them feel more comfortable with the violent action. Most perpetrators provide veiled or direct threats before an incident occurs.

Responding Is Preferable to Reacting

Violent perpetrators have the upper hand because action is faster than reaction. Violent perpetrators are always one step ahead of potential victims because the victims cannot predict exactly what the perpetrator will do next. That leaves the potential victim in a position of guessing or waiting for the action. When people decide to become violent, they have crossed the line of social acceptability and the "rules" of human behavior are usually discarded. Because pro-social norms no longer apply, predicting the perpetrator's actions is challenging.

While violent individuals have an advantage, potential victims are not helpless. When potential victims are equipped with survival strategies, they become contenders. *Responding* is much more effective than *reacting*. When people react in a knee-jerk fashion when faced with violence, chances are they will make a decision that places them in greater danger. When people respond to a violent situation they are able to pull from a repertoire of appropriate skills and options. These survival skills are well understood and practiced beforehand. While reacting can bring on escalating panic, responding helps the victim remain focused and flexible in problem solving.

Performance Under Stress Is Compromised

As we noted in our previous books *Survival-Oriented Kids* (1998)and *Violence Goes to School* (1999), under extreme stress, the human body prepares itself for fight or flight. Blood rushes from the extremities to the heart and large muscle groups. Senses become very sharp, sometimes to the point of distortion. Because of these changes, human beings often experience a set of difficulties that make responding to the stress challenging.

Fine Motor Skills Are Impaired

Under extreme stress, the blood is drawn to large muscle mass, and fingers fumble. For this reason, tasks such as unlocking car doors, punching in phone numbers, and poking people in the eye become difficult. Typing in codes for alarm systems is also unpractical at this time. Even dialing 911 can be a challenge. When building a response plan for violence, it is important to rely on gross motor movements like the arms and legs rather than the fine motor movement of the fingers.

Perceptions Are Distorted

When individuals are under extreme stress, the brain switches to a different mode of information processing called *cerebral acceleration*. The brain begins to sort through tremendous amounts of information quickly

so that the best decisions can be made. The senses become very acute and amplified. The experience of this phenomenon is that it feels as if the world has turned into a very surreal, slow-motion movie.

Because the brain is working so quickly, reality is altered. The brain attempts to make sense out of extreme circumstances. As a result, objects in the environment seem to appear and disappear. Gunfire sounds like firecrackers. What looks like a soda can is actually a gun. Victims sometimes recall that during an attack they thought the perpetrator was coming to shake their hand. In reality, the perpetrator was coming at them with an outstretched hand holding a gun.

Tunnel Thinking Limits Adaptive Problem Solving

When people are in traumatic situations, their thinking often gets locked into one mode. For example, in a violent situation on campus, people will try to call for help by dialing 911. On most campus phone systems, a 9 must be dialed first to obtain an outside line. They instinctively dial 911 as opposed to 9-911. This error may be repeated several times in frustration before the individual either gives up or figures it out.

Survival Instincts

People cannot rely solely on instincts to survive a dangerous situation. As people become more civilized and technically advanced, they rely less on instinctual survival skills. We have become more dependent on external alarm systems and less sure of internal alarm systems.

Some human instinctive reactions are inappropriate. For example, notice how crowds tend to behave when there is a fire in a movie theater. Typically, a mass of people will run hysterically toward the nearest exit, causing a big jam. Another example of poor survival instincts in people is indicated by how they run. When a predator is chasing prey in the wild, the prey will attempt to escape by running in a serpentine pattern. That is, running in zigzags or erratic movements. However, when people are pursued, they tend to run in a straight line. This pattern of attempted escape gives the pursuer the advantage because predicting direction of travel is easy. In order to survive a violent incident, people need to learn how to overcome such inappropriate instincts.

"The Bump"

The bump is a term that describes when a perpetrator engages a person to assess whether or not the potential victim will be a good target. Perpetrators may ask for the time when they are wearing a watch. By enacting this form of contact, perpetrators are assessing how friendly or passive the potential victim is. In another example, perpetrators feign weaknesses to lure in victims. Ted Bundy wore a fake cast and found young women to help him to his car.

When we are in these situations we instinctively know something is not quite right. Most of us, especially women, have been socialized to be friendly and helpful. Given the choice of listening to our internal fear alarm and potentially offending someone, many choose to override the fear and be nice. Perpetrators know this. We must retrain ourselves to listen to our instincts.

PERPETRATOR CHARACTERISTICS AND RESPONSE STRATEGIES

Predatory

Most campus security measures are designed with the predator in mind. Predators are motivated by the hunt and attack and do not want to bring attention to them. Like wild animals, predators target what they perceive as easy prey. They will seek out the most vulnerable, the most impaired, and the least assertive.

Prevention strategies should create barriers to the hunt and train potential victims to present themselves confidently. Locked doors, card key locks, adequately lighted campus areas, and frequent rounds of safety personnel all make the hunt more difficult. Individuals who appear strong and sure encourage the predator to seek other prey. Once a predator has honed in on a target, that target must then focus on escape. Knowing that the predator does not want to be noticed, any escape strategy should involve creating as much of a disturbance as possible to elicit help.

Avenger

Avengers are motivated by righting what they perceive to have been a grave injustice. Avengers will often threaten prior to their action. They will often plan for and fantasize about their attack in detail before acting it out. Unlike predators, avengers usually want to be noticed. Also, unlike predators avengers may have greater access to and knowledge about the campus facilities because avengers have often been part of the system. Thus, barriers designed for predators often will backfire with the avenger.

Prevention strategies for the avenger are therefore somewhat different than for the predator. When an avenger type has been identified as a risk to the campus, his or her identity must be made known to those who will be in a place to intervene. If possible, the perceived injustice must continue to be addressed and resolution attempted. As long as avengers are engaged in a process of mediation, they are less likely to plot their revenge.

If the injustice is not able to be resolved to satisfaction, and the avenger continues to make threats, then the perpetrator must be removed from the community and blocked from return. This step is critical to preventing violence from an avenger. In many cases of workplace violence, disgruntled employees were allowed back on the work premises after termination or disciplinary hearings, and the results were deadly. Under these circumstances, campus-community members need to be made aware that the threatening individual is not permitted to return and that they should notify safety personnel if return is attempted. Any access codes or keys held by the potential avenger should be changed.

The escape strategies in an avenger situation are also different than the perpetrator. When an avenger attacks, victims should be advised to draw minimal attention to themselves. If they cannot escape, they should attempt to conceal themselves from the avenger.

Relationship-based

Perpetrators of relationship-based violence are motivated by the needs to control and dominate. In extreme cases, they become totally myopic. They believe no one can understand their need for the relationship. Their world revolves around this other person, and they do not care about anything else. This ability to block out other priorities and a rational world makes them unpredictable and dangerous. For this reason, police officers often consider domestic violence their most dangerous type of call.

Only one approach effectively deals with relationship-based violence that has reached these extremes. One must break off the relationship completely. Any contact with the perpetrator serves to reinforce an ownership mentality. The immediate aftermath of this break in the relationship is the most dangerous time for victims. The temptation will be great to reestablish contact directly or through other people. See Chapter 14 for more information on intervening in relationship violence.

Group-induced

Group-induced violence is based on diffusion of responsibility, herd mentality, and a need for belonging. Preventing group-induced violence can occur both from inside and outside of the group. For those in the group, members must feel comfortable setting boundaries. If the group pressures them to act beyond these boundaries, they must be willing either to confront the group or leave.

From outside of the group the following prevention strategies are recommended: (1) Decrease anonymity. When individuals in a group realize they will be held personally responsible for the actions of the group, they are less likely to behave out of character. (2) Identify the leaders of the group and negotiate alternatives to violence. (3) Attempt to find different means of reaching goals group members perceive they are gaining through violent means.

ENVIRONMENTAL PROTECTION TACTICS: PROS AND CONS

As discussed in Chapter 2, perpetrators need time to plan and the opportunity to gain access and carry out violence. Physical and human barriers between the perpetrator and the potential victim serve to slow down the perpetrator and reduce opportunity. The following environmental barriers are effective in slowing or stopping some but not all types of campus violence perpetrators.

Campus Lighting

Adequate lighting helps prevent predator attacks and should be properly maintained. Good lighting means fewer places to hide and to stalk prey. Bright, well-lit areas can also draw more attention to potential attacks. Proper maintenance requires nighttime assessments and timely repairs. Community members should be made aware of the areas that are and are not illuminated. Some campuses publish night maps that provide directions through well-lit areas.

There are some lighting systems that are motion sensitive. These systems save money in electric costs. However, if the system breaks down or is undependable, the prevention tactic has failed. Because these lights are not on all the time, individuals will be delayed in reporting the malfunction to appropriate authorities. There are definite pros and cons to this new format.

Emergency Communication Systems

Call boxes are good because they provide a convenient place to contact security services; however, as mentioned earlier they are not necessarily productive for someone who is being chased. Call boxes should transmit a location to safety responders. Call boxes should be able to be activated by running by and slapping a button. Personnel should be able to get to the location quickly. However, even with these provisions the chances are good that someone on the run will be long gone by the time help arrives.

Posting emergency information can improve speedy access to support and warn students of potential dangers. Numbers for primary support services should be posted in every building and near courtesy phones. Community alerts regarding potential dangers and reporting procedures should be disseminated when appropriate. This practice allows community members the opportunity to know when there is increased danger in their environment. This practice is extremely important in the case of a potential avenger who has been removed from the community. Finally, publicized information regarding what constitutes crime (such as hazing violations) can help community members by allowing them to make more informed decisions about when to intervene.

Routine Inspections

By conducting regular inspections of the grounds and buildings, potential danger points can be identified and resolved. Grounds inspections should be done in the evening as well as during the day. This enables staff to more accurately assess potential danger areas in the limited lighting. Rounds in residence halls should be done so that any lighting issues and locking difficulties can be identified and reported. Swift follow up on needed repairs is imperative. Sometimes the repairs may not be obvious because they are not reported. Inspecting staff should make it a point to periodically ask students and staff if all grounds and building maintenance is up to par.

Peepholes

Peepholes in residential hall rooms are helpful because they give the potential victim added time to decide how to respond. A door can be an effective barrier between a perpetrator and victim. Witnesses are more likely to be concerned when they see someone hanging out in a hallway. Witnesses are left to guess what is going on behind closed doors. Inside the room, the victim is barricaded and may have access to protectors via the phone. Peepholes are not particularly helpful if people neglect to use them or do not lock their doors.

Security Cameras

If surveillance cameras are continuously monitored, they can be effective in preventing violence. Monitored cameras can help locate propped doors. They can also speed up response time when a known perpetrator has entered a building. However, if they are not monitored, they are more effective in catching people stealing or other criminal activity but not very effective at preventing violence. Predators often carefully hide their faces when they know a security camera is watching them. The avenger, relationship-based, and group-induced violence perpetrators usually will not care that their picture is being taken. Indeed, their presence on the monitoring screen may not be cause for

alarm if the monitor is not aware of any potential danger. Cameras may be helpful in identifying perpetrators after the fact.

Building Lock-down

Card lock systems can be extremely helpful if the system is maintained properly. When cards malfunction, the locks slow down the potential victim in the same way they slow down the perpetrator. Desk systems with personnel in entryways can be helpful in this regard. However, propped doors continue to be a problem at many institutions.

Many campuses are moving to having their residence halls locked all the time. This practice does limit the ease at which guests can move through the building; however, it also limits the ability of a stranger to move through the building. Here again, this policy only helps if people do not prop open doors.

Appropriate key management is essential in promoting a safe environment. Key numbering systems should not be easily determined. As such, the numbers should not all fall sequentially and should not reflect room numbers. Lost keys should result in a lock change, not simply a key replacement. Master keys should be limited in number and issued only to essential personnel. Accountability for these keys should be strictly maintained.

SAFETY SERVICES AND PUBLIC SAFETY PROGRAMS

Campus Security and Law Enforcement

Different colleges and universities have used different security systems. Some have their own police departments, while others

have security departments. Many security departments have sworn law officers who have arrest powers. Some schools have chosen to arm their officers while others have not. Depending on the size and culture of the campus, each school develops a system that meets its needs; however, one element to success is an effective officer recruitment and training program. Most successful programs run thorough background checks on their candidates. Routine professional development keeps officers' skills sharp. Specific training to rape sensitivity is essential.

Safety Education Programs

Safety education is paramount in creating safer environments. Orientation programs for new students regarding safety should be implemented. When students first arrive on campus they are very vulnerable to violence. They are unaware of their surroundings, unfamiliar with their neighbors, and often overwhelmed and distracted by social and academic demands. Concise and memorable safety awareness briefings can alert students to appropriate reporting mechanisms and safety services.

Orientation programs for new and current staff members are equally important. These programs not only notify people of their resources and their options, they also slightly change people's operational mindset in a positive way. Programs should be offered to the community throughout the year, including self-defense programs. Given the challenges people face attempting to respond in situations of extreme stress, programs that offer opportunity to practice new skills are the most effective. These programs allow people to feel more confident and become less of a victim.

Environmental Safety Conduct Codes

There are a few policies that are critical in order to promote a safe environment. For example, door propping allows perpetrators

time and opportunity to commit violence. There have been multiple cases of violent crime happening after someone went through a propped door, the rape and murder of Jeanne Clery being a well-known example. A clear policy prohibiting door propping and consequences for violating this policy should be spelled out and enforced.

Another policy issue concerns guests. Campus guests are often the causes or the recipients of violence. Requiring guests to register increases their accountability and their host's accountability. A guest policy requiring registration and host responsibility for the actions of the guest should be created and enforced.

Everyone knows that a policy without enforcement is pointless, so adequate enforcement efforts are important. Many schools use central entrances with a staffed desk. Residence hall staffs make rounds checking for policy violations, propped doors, and other security breaches. Most hall staff members have radio access to security support services. Many campuses have security on foot or bike patrols. Thus, there are multiple options to provide adequate supervision and enforcement of policies.

Escort Services

Many campuses offer escort services, however, we caution people about providing this option. This service is very good in preventing a predator. However, in extreme relationship-based violence situations the perpetrator only cares about regaining the "property" and will eliminate any obstacles to the control of the target. Nationwide, there have been several tragic cases of good Samaritans attempting to intervene in a domestic violence situation, only to be killed. Nevertheless, this service can be effective if personnel are trained to ask why the escort is desired. The officers must carefully assess the situation to determine the safest course of action. If the escort is armed with a firearm and capable of providing the necessary force to overpower the perpetrator, they should be prepared to do so.

Other Services

In addition to programming and enforcement, many security and law enforcement offices provide other services. By publishing the crime statistics required by the Jeanne Clery Act, they bring awareness of violence trends to the community. Officers also advise individuals of the legal options in a case. As referral agents, officers help victims get to needed counseling and other services. Most security offices provide response to emergency situations.

GUNS ON CAMPUS

According to a recent Harvard study, 3.5 percent or about 490,000 of the nation's college students own guns. Put into perspective, this number is quite low considering approximately 25 percent of American households contain handguns. Nevertheless, most colleges and universities ban gun possession on their campuses. The fact that almost 90 percent of the schools involved in the Harvard study had at least one student who reported owning a gun on campus upsets many.

Harvard researchers estimated that two-thirds of student gun owners live off-campus. By law, students age twenty-one and older have the right to keep concealed guns in vehicles in campus parking lots and garages. Research cited in the Harvard study indicated that 6 to 7 percent of students admit to carrying some form of weapon while on campus. Guns accounted for 14 percent of the weapons carried.

Students who own guns are more likely to be male and white. They are more likely to live in southern and western regions of the United States. They tend to attend public institutions in rural areas. Slightly more fraternity and sorority members owned guns than non-Greeks.

More disturbing findings from the Harvard study also emerged. Students were more likely to own a gun if they had damaged property as a result of alcohol consumption, been arrested for DUI, or driving after drinking five or more drinks. Of the small number of students who said they needed an alcoholic drink first thing in the morning, 12 percent owned guns, a statistically significant finding. The Harvard study did not indicate that students were getting drunk and then firing their weapons. Nor is there any implication of a cause-and-effect relationship between alcohol and guns, but perhaps a third factor of sensation seeking or risk taking can account for the shared characteristics in this subgroup of gun owners.

While most guns are owned for hunting purposes or self-defense, some have resulted in campus homicide. Fatal campus shootings have been drug-related, while others were apparent revenge. Victims have been primarily students, but have also included professors, counselors, and other campus staff. Several of these cases are cited throughout the book.

Less known are the near misses involving guns on campus. For instance, in 1998 a student who said he needed an "A" in the class confronted a math professor at the University of Maryland at College Park. The student proceeded to lift his jacket, revealing a handgun in a shoulder holster.

The student threatened that if the professor did not cooperate the student would make him "disappear, leaving no evidence." The faculty member reported the incident to campus authorities who obtained search warrants and discovered the student possessed a loaded 9-millimeter semiautomatic handgun and three loaded ammunition clips on the seat of his car.

Most college officials stand firm in their prohibition of guns in residence halls and other campus property. The newsletter *Student Affairs Today* (August 1999) listed the following tips for confronting an individual suspected of carrying a weapon on campus:

1. Take every accusation seriously. Follow up on all tips.

2. Completely check the suspected area. When searching residence hall rooms or other areas, do not stop the search when you have found a weapon–there may be more.
3. Isolate the suspected individual during the search.
4. Treat the accused fairly.
5. Remain calm and flexible. De-escalation is a critical factor during these often-stressful situations. New safety precautions may need to be developed to handle these situations.
6. Training seminars can help faculty and staff members notice weapon concealment and what to do if they are suspicious.

SURVIVAL STRATEGIES

The first survival strategy is preventing violence before it occurs. The following is a list of tips, many of which have been adapted from the Campus Security website (www.campussafety.org):

- Project confidence and power in the way you hold yourself and the way you talk.
- Beware of and report "bumps" or inappropriate interactions with strangers.
- Decline freshman photos. Freshman photo collections can unfortunately become a catalogue for sexual perpetrators.
- Study the campus and the local area (day and night). Know how to access the protectors on campus.
- Share your class schedule and activities with family and close friends.
- Set up buddy system. During parties, buddies can commit to making sure the other does not become isolated or find themselves in situations they do not want to be in.
- Travel in groups or shuttles during

evening hours. Avoid shortcuts that lead you through poorly lit areas.
- Use alcohol moderately or not at all. Approximately 90 percent of campus crime involves alcohol and/or drug abuse.
- Do not leave valuables in open view.
- Know emergency telephone numbers and speed dial.
- Lock your doors while driving.
- Trust your feelings of fear and your instincts that things are not right.
- Avoid walking near bushes, trees, vines, shrubs, parked cars, or areas not visible.
- Be aware of your environment when you go to an ATM machine.
- Keep your keys with you and lock your door.
- Know your neighbors and report illegal activities or loitering.
- Let security know when you are in a location after hours.
- Attend safety programs and practice skills taught.

• Do not prop doors. Rather, remove props and report to the appropriate staff.
• Never admit strangers into a residence hall.

Unfortunately, prevention is not foolproof and learning escape methods is important. We learned earlier that under extreme stress, people encounter a number of difficulties. We also know that people cannot rely solely on their instincts to survive a dangerous situation. People need to learn to overcome inappropriate instincts, impaired senses and motor skills, and tunnel vision. People can learn a great deal about survival tactics from animals. Running, scanning, camouflaging, and distracting are all skills that animals use to escape their predators. Those specific tactics are included in four main strategies (also listed in *Violence Goes to School* (1999): Get out, barricade, hide, play dead, and fight.

Get Out

If there is enough distance between the potential victim and the perpetrator, this is the safest course of action. While attempting to escape a violent environment seems like common sense, many potential victims are not effective in their efforts. In one case cited in research by Kelly Asmussen and John Creswell, a heavily armed gunman entered a classroom at a large public university. He pointed his rifle at the students, swept the barrel across the room and pulled the trigger. The gun jammed. The gunman attempted to dislodge the gun, but was unsuccessful. After about twenty seconds, a student was able to push a desk into the gunman and students ran out of the classroom. The gunman followed the students out of the building to a nearby car he had left running. Police eventually caught the gunman.

In the weeks after the incident, investigators and researchers interviewed the witnesses and discovered themes in their responses. One of the main themes was denial. Students who were in the building and heard a gunman was present either ignored the warning or denied that the student could be a threat to them. For those students who exited the building, most just huddled together close to the exit doors rather than search for a safe place of protection. Curious on-lookers gathered too to see how the situation would play out.

Some of the following tactics are suggested to help potential victims overcome these unsafe tendencies.

Scanning

When most people scan, they check quickly from left to right. This method leaves many unchecked areas open for danger. All senses are important when trying to locate a threat, but humans primarily use vision. When scanning the environment, it is important to look for possible areas of concealment, shadows, or movement. Scanning a 360-degree circle is another valuable technique. By dividing the space into "pie slices," an individual can methodically check the entire space from floor to ceiling, one slice at a time. Sounds can also indicate areas of danger. Thus, potential victims can avert harm by cueing into any movement or breathing.

Distraction

The squid is known for its ability to distract its pursuer with an inky black substance. Distraction is a very effective tool because it creates an opportunity to escape. Doing something unpredictable throws the perpetrator off guard. Perpetrators must first process the distraction before they can continue being aggressive. The pause may give the individual the opportunity to escape. In the above-mentioned case, one student was able to push a desk at the perpetrator to distract him. Visual distractions are especially effective because people are largely visually oriented. Eyes tend to follow the fastest moving object. Therefore, if a perpetrator is pursuing a potential victim and the victim throws something to the side, the aggressor's eyes will instinctively follow the object. Even if this is only for a second, the opportunity to escape may be provided.

Running

As mentioned earlier, many animals use running as a means of escaping their predators. Darting back and forth makes it very difficult for pursuers to anticipate the next move, and thus slows the perpetrators down. Unfortunately, the natural tendency for people when they are fleeing is to glance over their shoulder. This can throw off the center of gravity and increase risk of falling or slowing speed.

Persist in the Pursuit of Protection

Once individuals are outside the immediate area of danger, they should continue running until they are in a protected area. Sometimes, people get curious and want to stay in the periphery of the violent environment to see what will happen next. This choice could prove deadly. In the case mentioned earlier, the students who hung around the exit doors were lucky that the gunman did not return with another loaded gun.

Barricading

If it is impossible to get out of the environment, the next best thing is to barricade. Barricading means putting as many obstacles as possible between the perpetrator and the

potential victims. Perpetrators who are on a spree killing will not stop their momentum to tear down a barricade. Therefore, potential victims must close and lock doors and close blinds. When perpetrators are aimed at taking out victims of opportunity rather than victims of choice, "out of sight, out of mind" can help protect potential victims in the perpetrator's path.

Hide

The chameleon is known as the master of camouflage in the wild. This animal blends in very well with the environment so that the predator will overlook it and not attack. The human predator is not an effective scanner and will most likely miss the person who is hiding above or below a straight line of sight. Within reasonable safety parameters, people should try to find hiding places that are not in direct view of the perpetrator. When hiding, it is important to remain still and silent. Individuals should check to make sure nothing is sticking out where it could be seen. Clothing, hair, limbs, shoelaces, strange lumps, or shadows may call attention to their presence.

Play Dead

If there is no other way to escape, playing dead is an option. The individual must remain totally motionless. Controlled slow breathing and minimal startle response are difficult to achieve under extreme stress.

Fight

If getting out, barricading, and hiding are not options and playing dead is not feasible, the final alternative is to fight. When fighting, an individual should fight to create an opportunity to escape. The end goal is not to beat up the perpetrator. If an option to escape becomes available, it should be taken. Given the difficulty with fine motor skills, gross motor skill movements should be used, such as kicking. Most important to fighting, people must give themselves permission to do what they need to do to escape.

PERSONAL SECURITY OPTIONS

Some individuals choose to protect themselves with nonlethal weapons of self-defense. People have purchased stun guns, pepper spray, body alarms, and other similar devices. But are these tools effective? Without proper training and practice, these devices can sometimes be more detrimental than helpful. Caution should be heeded using some of these devices. For example, perpetrators can take pepper spray from victims and use it against them. Furthermore, individuals who own these devices must be ready to use them at the appropriate time. Digging into a purse or backpack at the time of a crisis will only serve to slow down and fluster the victim. Pepper spray canisters clog and dry up without regular use, and so users must monitor these devices on a regular basis to maintain effectiveness.

Body alarms sound good in theory, but may not help the victim at all. We are so accustomed to hearing car alarms on a regular basis, most of us tune out such sounds and are not likely to respond.

SELF-PROTECTION FOR INDIVIDUALS WITH DISABILITIES

Individuals with disabilities are often even more vulnerable to campus violence than others. The term disabilities encompasses a multitude of impairments: physical disability resulting from injury, chronic disease or congenital conditions; sensory impairments (e.g., hearing or visual); cognitive impairments (e.g., mental retardation or brain injury); or mental illness. Individuals with disabilities may be targets of hate crimes, or they may experience miscommunication that escalates into conflict.

Only a few North American studies have investigated this issue, mostly in regards to violence against women with disabilities. In many ways the results are reflective of violence against women without disabilities. Most notably, perpetrators of violence against women with disabilities are largely spouses or other partners. There are significant differences, however, that are important to consider. Many women with disabilities reported being abused by service providers, and many did not report violent episodes because of fear and dependency. Treatment services for these women were often inadequate. Programs were architecturally inaccessible, interpreter services were lacking, and so on.

Often campus violence prevention strategies are devised with the able-bodied individual in mind. Consideration and accommodation must be made for those campus-community individuals who have disabilities as well. Escape routes must be planned to be accessible to wheelchairs. Panic buttons must be available and comprehensible to those with motor and sight impairments.

Campus call boxes must be equipped to handle calls from the hearing impaired.

Students with disabilities can be coached in adapting behavioral and sensory safety strategies to work from their functioning abilities. For example, when scanning a room the blind can scan with their ears rather than their eyes. Those in wheelchairs can learn to equip their chairs with safety devices such as pepper spray (as long as they follow the suggestions listed earlier).

Many of the general prevention strategies can easily be adapted to working with individuals with disabilities. Nevertheless, violence prevention with individuals with disabilities remains an underresearched area. Increasing numbers of students with disabilities will continue to enroll and colleges and universities must be prepared to ensure that their safety is met.

Chapter 9

PREPARING FOR THE VIOLENCE AFTERMATH:
A COMMUNITY AFFECTED

THE ROLE OF THE UNIVERSITY community after a violent incident is just as critical as in early interventions. Initially, most of the attention in the immediate aftermath is focused on the victims and perpetrators. Secondary and tertiary victims are often overlooked. Beyond that, most campus-community members are often affected by known campus violence, and need support systems in place. Grieving and healing as a community can have a synergistic effect.

Violence is like an earthquake. The epicenter of the damage pinpoints on the immediate victims. From there, rings of impact are radiated depending on the physical or emotional proximity to the event. People who did not know the victim may be affected because memories of their own traumatic experiences were triggered. Emergency responders may be affected because of the youthfulness of the victims. Depending on the media coverage of the event, the impact could be nationwide or even international. The depiction of the ripple effect illustrated on page 107 is inherent in a violent event. This diagram shows the overwhelming number of people that can be affected by just one incident.

CRITICAL POSTINCIDENT FACTORS

After experiencing a violent incident or trauma, many people are immobilized by the shock and are uncertain what to do next. The following guidelines are to help survivors know what to expect and what to do in the days and weeks following a critical incident. Analysis of colleges and universities that have successfully dealt with violence revealed the following factors and themes in their approaches.

Leadership

Presidents, faculty, key administrative personnel, and student leaders should be highly visible and demonstrate intense personal involvement. In the aftermath of highly publicized violence, people not directly involved begin to make assumptions about the community in which the perpetrator resided. For example, the murder of Matthew Shepard at the University of Wyoming led to misperceptions about the Laramie, Wyoming, community and ram-

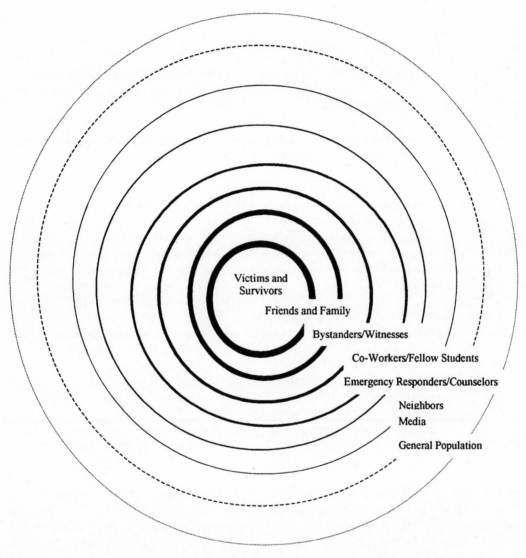

Source: Adapted from *Violence Goes to School* (1999).

pant homophobia. Perceptions such as these are frequently unfounded and become detrimental to the survivors. A truthful message from the leaders of the community must override such misperceptions. Leaders must repeat with clarity and conviction what the campus stands for and what it will not tolerate.

On November 1, 1991 two professors and

one graduate student were shot and killed at the University of Iowa. In a summary of the crisis in *Campus Violence: Kinds, Causes and Cures* (1993), Gerald Stone, the Director of the University Counseling Service, describes the importance of campus leadership uniting the community. The President and the Vice President for Academic Affairs defined the tragedy as a community experience. The campus leadership spoke of healing as a community and set the tone for the team-work that would be required to deal with the tragedy.

Crisis Response Team

In the aftermath of a tragedy, a predeter-mined team can be instrumental in address-ing the needs of affected individuals and the community. The crisis response team usual-ly consists of a cross-section of university representatives who are highly invested and trained in handling critical incidents. This team may have significant overlap or may even be identical to the Threat and Violence Assessment Team (TVAT) described in Chapter 6.

A common experience after a violent tragedy is a search for direction. In Stone's description of the tragedy at the University of Iowa, he remembered hearing "Who is in charge?" "What can I do?" and "Where is the plan?" Responses like these are com-mon. The crisis response team can serve as a locus of control for communicating with departments, community members, sur-vivors, and the media as well as for planning and organizing the many postincident events. The team should be representative of the community affected including faculty, staff, administration, students, and local community members when appropriate. The team should be flexible in membership to meet the needs of the violent crisis.

In his *About Campus* article on the Matthew Shepard tragedy, Dr. Jim Hurst, Vice President for Student Affairs at the University of Wyoming, cited this kind of flexibility as being a critical contribution to the healing of the community. For instance, professional staff members gave up offices and resources to student groups who were facilitating memorial planning for Matthew. The crisis response team may be responsible

for organizing the debriefing and victims assistance needs described below.

Debriefings and Victims' Assistance

The purpose of debriefings is to offer a group discussion that incorporates educa-tion, information, and crisis intervention techniques with the goal of minimizing the psychological disturbance resulting from the traumatic event. The debriefings are usually offered in a timely manner and may need to be repeated over time. The participants come together to discuss their roles, experi-ences, thoughts, reactions, and symptoms. Frequently, voicing the perceptions of the events, in a chronological order, helps par-ticipants piece together a coherent account of what feels like a fragmented, surrealistic event. Interventions should also focus on survivor strengths, coping skills, and social support. The scheduling of the debriefings should take into consideration services for the victims of the crime.

Professional mental health staff should be present to help facilitate the discussions and educate group members about normal stress reactions, symptom management, and when to seek additional help. In addition, on-cam-pus experts may be more likely than outside experts to understand the social circum-stances and organizational factors particular to the participants. Community referrals and readings for further assistance and infor-mation should be provided as well.

In addition to debriefings, other forms of victims' assistance are appropriate and should be offered as options. Mandatory counseling under these conditions is likely to be counterproductive. Colleges and univer-sities should identify specific mental health resources beforehand to respond in such cir-cumstances. A trend in post-violence situa-tions involves the flocking of "helpers" to the scene of the crime. Some are well meaning, others are sensation seeking. Few are invited.

In the Iowa tragedy, Dr. Stone shared that the number of phone calls he received from experts offering support was overwhelming. He went on to share that some of the agendas of the experts were questionable. This is not uncommon. Following the crash of TWA Flight 800 July 1996, the American Red Cross announced they had gathered almost five hundred volunteers, mostly mental health counselors to help families. At the same time, another welfare agency was sending their grief counselors to the airport. Counselors ended up outnumbering victims at the scene.

Crisis tends to attract people who are excited by the event and not always motivated by genuine concerns to help others. Many inexperienced counselors will abandon the situation when the novelty wears off or when they realize that they are in over their heads. The Emergency Support Network recommends the following steps to provide effective psychological assistance following traumatic events:

- *Plan who will provide psychological services.* These individuals may be internal or external to the college or university. Ad hoc responses can attract people who may be inappropriate to the task.
- *Use an appropriate response time-frame.* Sounding the alarm for professional mental health workers immediately after the violent incident, given the expectation that this will facilitate a rapid recovery for the victims, ignores the practical needs of both the victims and the counselors and may even inhibit the normal crisis recovery process.
- *Practical assistance and referrals are appropriate first responses.* In the immediate aftermath of violence, victims may need mundane assistance. Instead of counsel-

ing, transportation and financial assistance may be more beneficial. In his article on the Matthew Shepard tragedy, Dr. Jim Hurst described how even though the University of Wyoming Counseling Services were prepared for an outpouring of students in crisis, the number of students needing support relating to the tragedy was significantly low. Professional counseling is more likely to have a role after the immediate impact has passed, and the victims are looking for something more than their friends and family can provide.
- *Provide a "menu" of services from which victims and their families can choose.* Such services can include a twenty-four-hour crisis hot line/information line, psychological debriefings, educational seminars on "how to help someone who has been through a trauma," posttrauma counseling, follow-up debriefings or telephone contact, and trauma-anniversary assistance.

Working with Victims' Families

According to Gene Zdziarski of the NASPA Task Force (2000) both in the immediate aftermath and over the long term, families play an important role. Families can be an integral part of the campus healing and campus life can help families heal as well. The first question to answer is what if any connection between the campus and family is appropriate given such tragic circumstances. To determine this, family members must be found and contacted. In some cases, such as in extended blended families, this is not an easy task and everyone might not be agreeable to the involvement.

One or two campus contacts should provide a link between the family and the campus to facilitate communication and help coordinate memorial services if needed.

These contacts should stress that their role is one of a caregiver and not a legal advisor. Depending on the circumstance families may want to have varying degrees of connection with the campus after the tragedy. They may wish to have their own written statements distributed via letter or newspaper editorial. They may wish to speak at rallies or services held on campus. They may desire to set up scholarships in the name of their son or daughter. Families may also need help from the campus contacts. They may want to get information from sources on campus such as faculty members, roommates, and student life officials. They may need help gathering personal belongings from the residence halls. In essence, these contacts are there to ask the family members the question, "How can I help you right now."

Reestablishing a Sense of Security: The Role of Law Enforcement

Increasing security efforts in the weeks and months postincident will help reassure the community that serious efforts are being implemented to prevent tragedy from reoccurring. To deter copycat violence of high-profile cases such as the Florida A&M University bombing or the avenger massacre at Concordia University, security and law enforcement officers should be readily available to provide positive information quickly, and to weed out rumors regarding potential acts of further violence. In general, law enforcement officials should interact with the campus community informally on a regular basis in order to build trust. This community outreach contact by security must be magnified in the aftermath of a crisis.

To work effectively with law enforcement agencies outside of campus, campus officials must establish and nurture an ongoing con-

tact with their local department. Usually, a community resource officer can be a good liaison between the two institutions. This contact person must be familiar with the procedures and key personnel at the university and be able to communicate effectively the needs of each agency.

When a violent crisis occurs on campus, it is important to note that law enforcement officials may have different objectives than other campus administrators. Usually, law enforcement is focused on tracking down and stopping the perpetrators while other groups on campus are focused on responding to the needs of the victim. Sometimes these roles collide. For example, in the instance of sexual assault, campus security officers work to build a case against the perpetrator while residence life and counseling staff members strive to empower the victim and ensure privacy. Law enforcement professionals are trained to take control in crises, victims may not be willing to surrender that control. As long as the different agencies responding to the crisis are aware of the potential conflict of roles and are willing to work through them, the interference to an appropriate outcome should be minimal.

Constructive Outlets

Often, people can find a sense of purpose and meaning in terrible events if they can channel their sorrow or anger into action. Additionally, tangible symbols of the tragedy can provide a sense of solidarity for the community. In the weeks after the Matthew Shepard tragedy, students distributed yellow ribbons to symbolize the community's loss. These yellow ribbons were still noticeable months later on students' backpacks. Community retail stores became involved by donating ribbon materials to the students. The yellow ribbons became a healing project for everyone involved.

In the aftermath of the Florida A&M University bombings (see Chapter 15), students organized a march demonstrating their fears and concern over the safety of their campus. Similarly, in the aftermath of assaults at the University of Massachusetts (see Chapter 10), students gathered to protest what they perceived as an under-response by the university. These gatherings helped students to feel empowered and gave them a tangible way to become part of the solution so quickly after the event.

Media Management

The news media are perceived in many roles: adversaries demanding schools give them information; ghouls searching for victims to televise and situations to sensationalize; noble guardians of the community demanding details so a public can better protect itself. Universities court them, avoid them, befriend them, and need them.

– *Campuses Respond to Violent Tragedy*
(Siegel, 1994, p. 247)

The media can have a positive or negative impact on the community in the aftermath of a violent tragedy. On a positive note, the media provides the quickest, most efficient way to inform the surrounding community and concerned others far away about what is happening on campus. Parents who cannot reach their children have means by which they can find out information during the intense stages of a crisis. Likewise, the media can help inform the community on ways to keep safe during a time of crisis and alert them to resources for help.

Without doubt, many violent incidents on campuses attract the full force of the press. In the case of rioting, campuses' reputations have been damaged by the highly publicized footage of a few out-of-control individuals. Alcohol-poisoning deaths and hazing cases have also received close scrutiny by the

media. Therefore, it is important to have a preplanned strategy to handle this phenomenon, and to know the rights survivors and the campus community have with the media.

Much of the information included in this section is adapted from the suggestions of Dr. Jim Hurst of the National Association of Student Personnel Administrators (NASPA) Task Force of Violence and the book *Campuses Respond to Violent Tragedy* (Siegel, 1994). General guidelines for media management include the following goals:

1. Communicate the truth.
2. Control for and correct error in communication.
3. Prevent the media from becoming part of the crisis.

As we have mentioned earlier in Chapter 7, a *communication vortex* is a critical factor in controlling communication that goes out to the community as well as assessing and organizing information coming into the campus. This vortex or communication center should be known as the keeper and sharer of information. Highly visible representatives should be located in the main traffic pattern on campus so that media personnel can find them easily. These appointed communication representatives must diligently verify all incoming and outgoing information for accuracy. If the information cannot be verified, it should not be released. Speculation of any kind is discouraged.

Once accurate information is established it should be vigorously promoted both within and outside campus. Campus officials should not wait until inaccurate information has surfaced. Periodic information sheets, letters from the president, or mass email can help keep the campus up to date on developments. Key individuals who will be most likely sought after for quotes and perspectives on the situation should be coached and given written scripts to be communicated to ensure that a consistent message is being sent from university officials. To avoid a "No comment" response to a question that cannot be answered, provide the reason that answer cannot be given at this time. Appropriate campus officials should always return media calls, even when the tone may be hostile.

Well-trained spokespeople can be a tremendous asset to the campus in these circumstances. Each campus should identify one spokesperson and an alternate to handle the press in the aftermath of a crisis. All inquiries should be directed to this spokesperson to minimize confusion and contradictory statements. The crisis management team should establish guidelines for sharing appropriate information ahead of time.

This appointed spokesperson must be prepared to clarify questions before speaking into the microphone. To avoid potential distractions, the spokesperson should select a time and location based on comfort level, not the convenience of the reporter. Cold call interviews in the home, or during the normal business day are unacceptable. In order to prepare for the interview, the interviewee should ask beforehand what questions will be asked, and what direction the interviewer is planning to take.

Most reporters and other media personnel appreciate courtesy and professionalism, and will often reciprocate this treatment. That said, it is appropriate to put parameters on what is allowable for media coverage. For privacy reasons, campus administrators should prohibit the media from access to residence halls and classrooms. Campus-community members can be advised as to limits they can impose on the media. For example, community members can be given the permission by campus officials to tell the media, "I don't want to talk to you."

Rights with the Media

The campus community has the following rights with the media. While they may not all be granted, they should be requested to protect the campus and victims.

- The right to grieve and recover in private.
- The right to say "no" to an interview.
- The right to request a specific reporter.
- The right to refuse an interview with a specific reporter even if the interviewee has granted interviews to other reporters.
- The right to avoid a press conference atmosphere and speak to only one reporter at a time.
- The right to refrain from answering any questions with which the interviewee is uncomfortable or feels are inappropriate.
- The right to ask to review quotations in a story prior to publication.
- The right to demand a retraction when inaccurate information is reported.
- The right to ask that offensive photographs or visuals be omitted from airing or publication.

Source: Adapted from Slover, C. & Tasci, D. (1999). *Trauma Recovery Handbook,* published by Nicoletti-Flater Associates.

Follow-Up Services

For the most part, society responds well immediately after a crisis, but once the fanfare dies down, the victims are left wondering, "Where did everybody go?" Periodic check-in points for students, faculty, and staff will let survivors know they are supported in their continued struggle and healing. Be prepared for significant dates for the survivors: graduation, birthdays, special events, the beginning of the school year, and especially the anniversaries of the trauma (e.g., one week, one month, six months, annually, and so on).

Evaluate the Process

After the intensity of the crisis has passed, all parties involved in the violence prevention, intervention, and aftermath should conduct a tactical de-briefing as a group. Pertinent questions are, "What worked?" and "What didn't?" The analysis and discussions of these committees should yield a report of "Lessons Learned" from the incident. Recommendations from the report should be implemented as soon as possible, and shared with others. See the Appendix for a flowchart of violence aftermath responses.

KNOW WHAT TO EXPECT: UNDERSTANDING POSTTRAUMA RESPONSES

Each person who is victimized by a life-threatening situation is not necessarily traumatized. Responses to emotionally intense experiences are strongly influenced by past history and personality makeup. Therefore, it is unreasonable to expect that everyone who endures the same traumatic experience will exhibit symptoms and posttrauma reactions. In fact, suggesting there is something wrong with people who are not grossly affected may prove detrimental. People should be encouraged to "feel what they are feeling." The truth is, there is no standard way to respond to extraordinary events, and each person will evidence an individual reaction. The following sections of this chapter are based on our own experiences and observations and a combination of sources: *Trauma Recovery Handbook* (Slover & Tasci, 1999), *Violence Goes to School* (Nicoletti, Zinna, & Spencer-Thomas, 1999), the American Psychiatric Association's *Diagnostic and Statistical Manual of Mental Disorders* (1994), and *Trauma and Recovery* (Herman, 1992).

Trauma Symptoms

A violent incident is certainly a traumatic event and will likely cause strong physical and emotional reactions in those involved. These aftereffects are considered, "normal reactions to very abnormal events." During this time, the mind and body are trying to adapt and cope with a life-threatening situation. People can remain in red-alert survival mode for a prolonged period of time. The defensive guard remains up and ready for action at all times. Irrational fears, discomfort with previously enjoyed activities, and worries about family members and loved ones, are examples of the unwillingness of the body and psyche to be victimized again.

In addition to this activation of survival instinct, there is the impact of shattered assumptions. All people hold assumptions about the world and themselves. These fundamental beliefs are often not conscious, and they are quite resistant to challenge and change. According to trauma specialist Dr.

Janoff-Bulman (1992), these assumptions usually center around three themes: "The world is benevolent," "The world is meaningful," and "I am a good and worthy person." Most people believe the world is a safe and fair place, and people are moral. From these core beliefs, people derive the adaptable sense of trust, security, and invulnerability. These traits enable us to go through the day and interact with others without distress.

When a person experiences a traumatic event these assumptions are dramatically challenged and often shattered. This is especially true when traumatic events are perpetrated by another human being. Research has consistently shown that trauma inflicted by another person, as opposed to resulting from natural disasters such as hurricanes, tornadoes, and floods, are more damaging and tend to complicate and prolong recovery. The disillusionment and "depressive realism" that can stem from such events can be paralyzing. In other words, the individual's sense of trust, security, and invulnerability is gone. The survivor becomes aware of the reality of surrounding danger and loss potential. The implications can be overwhelming.

In the process of trauma recovery, survivors learn to rebuild their assumptions by integrating the new traumatic experience. Talking with others or writing about the event are effective ways to impose order on a chaotic event. By nature, humans are very verbal creatures, and need to put words to experiences. This is even truer for emotionally loaded incidents.

Another phenomenon associated with trauma is *survivor guilt*. When survivors blame themselves for what happened, it is often in an attempt to find some degree of control over an out-of-control situation. "If only I had done this . . ." or, "If only I had not done that . . ." or "Why did I survive when others didn't?" are statements often heard repeated by the victims of a traumatic incident. This attempt to regain control and predictability over one's life re-establishes a sense of fortitude and the belief that people can control their own destiny.

Finding some benefit or purpose in the experience can also assist with the "meaning-making" process for survivors. It is important to know that the event had a purpose. The benefits found in the aftermath of a crisis often involve a rediscovered appreciation for life, one's family and loved ones, and oneself. This drive for resolution can be aided by the community activities previously discussed.

According to the American Psychiatric Association's *Diagnostic and Statistical Manual* (DSM-IV), posttraumatic stress disorder (PTSD) is a psychological syndrome that affects individuals who have experienced a critical incident. The cluster of symptoms including nightmares, flashbacks, hyperarousal, dissociation, depression, and avoidance, was first noticed in World War I veterans returning from combat. It was initially labeled "shell shock," and then later "battle fatigue." Over the last several decades, research in the area of psychological trauma has discovered that other life-and-death situations, such as earthquakes, rape, domestic violence, airplane crashes, car accidents, and violent crime, can produce similar effects.

For many individuals, the symptoms gradually disappear with time, but for others, the symptoms can persist with varying intensity for decades. Many people experience a traumatic reaction that spans from two days to four weeks. This is known as an Acute Stress Disorder. People experiencing Acute Stress Disorder report "feeling in a daze" and the symptoms they experience cause significant impairment in their functioning. Usually, these symptoms resolve after one month.

In order to be diagnosed with PTSD post-trauma symptoms must have persisted for at least four weeks. The symptoms of PTSD fall into three categories:

1. *Intrusive symptoms:* These symptoms occur when the images, sounds, smells, tactile, or taste sensations related to the traumatic event unexpectedly "intrude" into the person's consciousness. These vivid memories may be manifested during sleep in the form of nightmares. Others are "triggered" by internal or external cues that resemble some part of the trauma. When this happens, the trauma is repeatedly re-experienced. These experiences can be quite distressful to the individual. In fact, many survivors report that these "flashbacks" make them feel like they are going crazy. The truth is, the intrusive memories are part of the normal healing process. The brain is desperately trying to make sense out of an unfathomable situation by searching memory banks for any related information. This is an unconscious process that often shocks and deeply upsets victims.

2. *Avoidance Symptoms:* Re-experiencing the traumatic event is usually painful, so many individuals develop avoidance patterns to dampen the intensity of the uncomfortable feelings. For example, an individual with PTSD may avoid situations that are reminiscent of the traumatic event. Others may become numb to emotions altogether. Depression and a loss of pleasure in life are common results of the withdrawal and "emotional shutting down" that occur.

3. *Hyperarousal Symptoms:* Individuals with PTSD often demonstrate hypervigilance as they feel constant pressure to be on guard for danger. *Hypervigilance* is the constant scanning of the environment for danger cues. Victims who have hyperarousal symptoms also experience exaggerated startle responses, irrational and new fears, increased irritability, and sometimes explosive anger. They may have difficulty concentrating or remembering new information.

Sleep disorders and disrupted appetites are common. It is commonly believed that the survivor of a trauma remains in hyper-alert mode to prevent future danger. All systems are revved at full throttle in case the individual should need to react again to a life-challenging event. After a while hyperarousal begins to wear on the individual's body and mental capacity.

There are several associated symptoms that may be present when one develops PTSD. These include:

- Alcohol or drug abuse (the individual's attempt to "self-medicate" painful feelings)
- Anxiety and panic attacks
- Suicidal thoughts, gestures or attempts
- Extreme guilt
- Feelings of alienation or intense loneliness

If these or other symptoms persist for longer than one month and interfere with the individual's life, professional counseling services with a therapist who is well versed in trauma should be sought.

Trauma Recovery Phases

Individuals who are traumatized proceed through different phases during the recovery process. While each person may vary widely in their clinical presentation and array of symptoms, the general process among individuals is similar. Sometimes traumatized individuals will recycle through earlier stages when their traumatic experience is triggered. Others will proceed through the stages sequentially. There is not necessarily a right or wrong way to go through this process, and all time parameters mentioned here are general guidelines. Some people may move quickly through the phases while others may take years to come to resolution.

1. Shock

The first phase begins at the onset of the traumatic event, and can continue for up to a week. The perceived threat of death or injury is very real. Sensory information floods the brain. Sights, smells, sounds, and feelings overwhelm the individual's entire being. The brain is unable to process it all, and emotional numbness sets in. At the time of the traumatic event, there are often distortions in time and space, as well as auditory and visual misperceptions. The experience of events is in "slow motion," there is an unreal or dreamlike quality to them. Sounds may be intensified, muted, or absent. Things may look different and unfamiliar, and there may be an intense focus on only one part of the visual field. There may be a strange sense of calm due to a survival mechanism of extreme denial in the presence of overwhelming danger. There may be some physical symptoms, including agitation, hyperalertness, overactivity, or biological disruption (e.g., sleeping and eating patterns).

2. Impact

This phase often begins when an individual leaves the location of the critical incident, and can persist from a few days to several weeks. This phase frequently triggers confusion and a sense of being overwhelmed as full realization of the extent of the danger, damage, death, or injury is made conscious. The individual may become highly emotional when leaving the scene of a disaster. They will likely feel a strong need to isolate, but should be with others for support and to ensure a reconnection with people.

3. Recoil

This phase begins with return to a near-normal routine pattern, accompanied by stable days. There will be a decrease in the symptoms of the impact phase, and attention, concentration, reasoning ability, recall, and emotional expression gradually return. This phase often resembles an emotional roller coaster with good days and bad days interspersed. At this stage, individuals often feel as though they will never regain a "normal" life. Each time they begin to get on their feet, another wave of memories sets in.

4. Posttrauma Resolution

This phase occurs after returning to one's routine pattern. Here the trauma's impact will show longer-term changes in behavior, thought patterns, beliefs, emotions, and perception. These changes may be irreversible. There are two possible outcomes of this phase: positive resolution, or negative reaction with no resolution. The positive course will lead to acceptance of the event and the individual's actions, along with a positive reevaluation of goals and values. Keep in mind, this may be a lengthy process and the continuum of resolution is broad. Without any trauma resolution, there is a strong likelihood of a chronic struggle throughout life with distress, family problems, job difficulties, chemical dependency, and potential suicide.

Counseling Approaches with Survivors

At the first stages of shock and impact, when the victims are feeling a lack of control in the situation, the most effective counseling approach is crisis management. At this time the goals of crisis management are to restore some sense of order to the person's life and to initiate referrals for help. This process might involve finding a safe place to stay, addressing physical and health issues, or initiating any investigation procedures. During this time, the victim may need support and someone with whom to discuss important decisions. The victims may remain highly symptomatic throughout these stages.

The second level of counseling occurs during the impact and recoil stages. The goal is to move the individual from victim to survivor. Here counseling addresses the unwanted symptoms and underlying causes. This may be achieved in a number of ways. Social support networks are often the most powerful healing mechanisms. Social support can be obtained through family and friends or through support groups. These caring helpers may have good intentions, but they also must have sensitivity and awareness about what victims are experiencing and how best to support them. Thus, counselors can have family sessions or consult with other significant others in the victim's life. Counseling also can help survivors unlearn maladaptive thinking processes and behaviors and work through upsetting emotions.

Trauma recovery work, while very rewarding, can be very complicated and draining for the counselor. Counselors with specialized trauma intervention training are best qualified to work with more difficult cases. As mentioned earlier in Chapter 2, counselors can sometimes become vicariously affected by the trauma themselves. It is essential that these therapists receive ongoing support and supervision for this demanding work.

The final level of counseling survivors is maintenance. Inevitably, new situations may trigger past traumatic memories, and survivors may need to check in with counselors periodically for booster sessions. The purpose of these sessions is to help remind the survivor of the strengths they have built from the experience and that setbacks do not mean they have to relive the whole process again.

Some Basic Coping Strategies

Recovering from a traumatic event can be a difficult process. Some survivors find they are able to use the following coping strategies to get through the tough times. Others find that professional counseling is most beneficial. Each survivor must determine what is the most helpful course of action. The following strategies are also recommended for the victims' significant others.

- *Education.* There are many excellent self-help books on the market today which describe the course and treatment of Posttraumatic Stress Disorder (see Bibliography section for resources).
- *Understand that healing occurs in stages over time.* After a traumatic event, life may not return to the way it was due to permanent losses and changes in views of the world and the self. Many assumptions about life have been destroyed, and developing a new set of beliefs will take time. Don't expect the traumatized individual to just "snap out of it."
- *Get support.* Victims, their families, and others affected by the violent event should talk about their experiences and feelings with others who are supportive. An organized psychological debriefing or support group could be arranged to help with this process. If there were others involved in the traumatic experience, it may help to establish regular contact when dealing with life after the event. Professional counseling should be considered if symptoms persist.
- *Empowerment.* After the turmoil and intense emotional processing has passed, many people find they can derive strength from the knowledge gained from the trauma. Some people volunteer to help other trauma survivors. Others write about and publish their experience. Some pursue legal avenues for compensation as an avenue for their empowerment.

Part III

STRAINS OF CAMPUS VIOLENCE

Chapter 10

SEXUAL ASSAULT

I thought college was about two things: studying and partying. When I left home to go to a small liberal arts school in the Northeast, I was very excited about the freedoms I would experience. I was an exceptional student, but did not want to appear a geek to others. So I partied hard. As long as my grades did not suffer, I felt that any amount of partying was just fine.

In the first few weeks of school, I became associated with a fraternity in hopes of meeting new people. I spent most of my nights in a drunken state, dancing, flirting, and hooking up with men. My sexuality felt like an unleashed power, and while some nights I regretted, others were very exciting encounters. I developed a reputation among the brothers of the fraternity, and soon found they would seek me out for easy sex. When I was in control of the situation, I had no problem turning down most of the propositions.

One night early in the fall of my freshman year, there was a party at the fraternity. It was a special occasion so we were serving hard alcohol in addition to the kegs in the basement. One of the senior fraternity brothers introduced me to another senior, Steve, who was visiting from a neighboring fraternity. I was very flattered with the attention. Here these senior guys were spending time with me. They started bringing me very strong drinks, one after another. As the night wore on, I became very intoxicated. Most of the party is erased from my memory. When people started to leave, Steve asked if I wanted to go back to his house. I said, "yes." He asked me if I knew what I was getting into. I said I didn't know what he meant. He laughed.

He drove me to his off-campus house, at which point my memory becomes very spotty. I remember getting sick in his bathroom. I remember being carried up to his bedroom. I remember not wanting to have sex but found someone on top of me. I passed out, and when I came to, someone else was on top of me. I am not sure who I had sex with or how many people that night. When I woke the next morning, there were two naked men on the bed. Shaken and shamed, I got dressed and left. When I got back to my room I realized that I had left a watch my grandmother had given me at the house. My grandmother had died during my first week of college, and this was a very precious memento. I called Steve's house to see if I could get the watch back and I was told, "no." A couple of years later Steve returned to school as an alumnus to attend a party and I confronted him. "What exactly happened that night?" I asked him. "Oh I guess you'll never know," he replied.

I never told anyone. How could I? I had no marks or bruises. Hell, I didn't even fight them. Anyone I told would have thought I had it coming to me. Besides I didn't even know who the perpetrators were. Nor could I accurately account for what happened. Telling anyone would have just gotten me more humiliation, that's all. In some ways I felt I had consented to the events by not challenging Steve's question about knowing what I was getting into. It took me years to actually call it rape. To this day images of the night haunt me—the slick smiles of the introductions, the vomiting, the lost watch. Despite numerous self-help books and self-talk, I cannot get rid of the self-blame and shame. How could I have been so stupid? It bothers me that he and whoever else was with him have gotten to go on with their lives without any consequences for what they did, while I am still troubled by what happened all these years later.

−Anonymous Female Student

THIS IS A TRUE STORY and a single example of a very common problem. According to the Crime Clock, an illustration in the 1998 FBI Uniform Crime Report, the relative frequency of occurrence of Forcible Rape is one every six minutes. This figure represents only reported rapes and does not include rape of men.

As we begin to delve into the problem of rape we must recognize some trends reflective of decades of research.

- The sheer number of rape occurrences has elicited descriptors such as epidemic and crisis.
- Rape is underreported by both men and women for varying reasons.
- Rape is committed by strangers, acquaintances, and groups.
- Drugs and alcohol are often factors involved in rape. Alcohol use is highly prevalent with both victims and perpetrators.
- Men rape women, men rape men, women rape men, and in rare instances women sexually assault other women.
- Many victims of rape are traumatized and impacted for life.
- There is significant debate about why people rape.

In this chapter we will examine each of these facts more closely, identify prevention strategies, and address appropriate methods of responding to rapes.

DEFINING RAPE

The definitions of rape vary among state laws and among different research studies. The FBI's current definition of Forcible Rape is "The carnal knowledge of a person, forcibly and/or against that person's will; or not forcibly or against that person's will where the victims is incapable of giving consent because of his/her temporary or permanent mental or physical incapacity," as stated in the 1999 Uniform Crime Report. As the FBI has done, many states have now included both genders as potential victims of rape; this was not always the case. Additionally, the idea of capacity for consent did not always exist in definitions. Many states now include the following acts in their definition of rape: oral, anal, or vaginal penetration by a person or object without the recipient's consent or if the recipient is unable to provide consent (intoxicated, unconscious, and so on).

Broader still, some rape researchers define rape as coercing someone to have sex using any of the types of sexual coercion defined in the Sexual Experience Survey developed by Koss and Oros in 1982. These types of sexual coercion include psychological pressure in addition to physical force or failure to consent due to intoxication from alcohol or drugs. A 1998 study on the prevalence and characteristics of male perpetrators of acquaintance rape conducted by Samuel Rubenzahl and Kevin Corcoran defines acquaintance rape using both broad and stringent definitions. The broad classification includes in its definition of rape forcing someone to have sexual intercourse with psychological pressure or threats of violence. This definition includes continual arguments or constant verbal harassment as part of psychological pressure. The stringent definition defines rape as forcing someone to have sexual intercourse using only threats of violence. This definition does not include those who only use psychological pressure. Research suggests that the variance among definitions is critical in the determination of what constitutes a crime, but not so much in what causes significant trauma for victims.

Since we know that sexual assault happens to both men and women and that unwanted sexual intercourse results in significant consequences, we will utilize the following working definition. Sexual assault is forcing someone to have sexual intercourse using any of the following types of coercion: psychological pressure, physical force, or taking advantage of a person's inability to give consent due to intoxication, loss of consciousness, or mental impairment.

The number of rapes occurring in our country is staggering. According to the FBI's Uniform Crime Report, 93,103 people were raped in 1998, of these 402 occurred on college campuses. A distressing notion discovered by The National Victim Center was that 35 percent of men indicated some likelihood that they would commit a violent rape if they were assured of getting away with it.

The FBI statistics include only those cases reported, so this figure is most likely a gross underestimate. Nathan Pino and Robert Meier conducted a study on gender differences in rape reporting in 1999 and determined that 54 percent of female rape victims and only 42 percent of male rape victims reported the crimes to the police. The National Victim Center presents an even more discouraging picture about campus rape reporting. In their survey of college women, 38 percent reported sexual victimization that met the legal definition of rape or attempted rape, yet only one out of twenty-five reported their assault to police. Thus, we know the FBI numbers are exceptionally smaller than the actual occurrences. The mass of these numbers and the issue of underreporting have justifiably earned rape descriptions ranging from crisis to epidemic.

Why Is Rape Underreported?

Using the National Sample Rape Subset for the years 1979–1987 and the National Crime Victimization Survey in their 1999 study on gender differences in rape reporting, Pino and Meier found some answers to the question, "Why is rape underreported?" Women stated they did not report because they did not want to face the prospect of being blamed for the incident–she didn't resist enough, she was promiscuous and asking for it, or she should have seen it coming. Women were reluctant to report because they feared the potential of being mistreated by authorities and being further victimized through interrogation and disbelief. Because women have difficulty identifying what has happened to them as rape unless it fits a stereotypical definition, they are less likely to report rape that does not incorporate physical force leaving marks and bruises.

Women also feared that the process of reporting rape will be traumatizing. These concerns included both the investigation of the crime and the medical examination. When victims were made aware of their reporting options–to campus authority or police–they often feared that their sexual history would be on trial rather than the perpetrator's. Sometimes investigation questions can seem harsh, invasive, or insensitive. Police may even ask sexual assault victims to take a polygraph test to help with the investigation even though results are not admissible in court.

Another reason women are hesitant to step forward is their concerns about the medical exam or "rape kit." The medical exam is done for both the purpose of assess-ing needs for immediate medical attention (e.g., physical trauma, sexually transmitted diseases, pregnancy, or HIV) and for gathering medical evidence. It can be very upsetting to the victim. Even with the gentlest caregivers, the "rape kit" can make the victim very uncomfortable. During this process a nurse conducts the following procedures as part of any standard rape kit:

- Conducts HIV testing and blood collection (to check for pregnancy).
- Gathers and documents evidence from clothing and injuries and takes pictures of the victim.
- Collects loose hairs or debris from pelvic area and then plucks fifteen to twenty hairs from the victim's pelvic area and head to compare.
- Collects fingernail scrapings for blood or tissue samples.
- Inspects the victim's thighs, abdomen, buttocks, and face for semen, and may take swabs from vaginal, oral, and anal areas.
- Performs a pelvic exam.

Anyone would probably loathe this exam, let alone someone who just had the worse sexual experience of her or his life.

Men's reasons for not reporting rape overlap with women, but men also have unique concerns. Men have trouble believing male rape happens outside of prison or violent homosexual relationships; as such, they have difficulty identifying their situation as rape. Men face the prospect of their masculinity being called into question. As with women, men are less likely to report a rape that does not incorporate physical force leaving marks and bruises. Despite efforts made to increase the support mechanisms for women who are raped, underreporting for both women and men continues to be a problem.

DYNAMICS OF RAPE

Who Rapes and Who Is Raped?

Before we address the types of rape and the characteristics of rapists, we need to acknowledge both who is raped and who is doing the raping. Men rape women. Men rape men. Women rape men. And in rare cases women sexually assault women.

The rape of women by men has received the most attention by far, and most models of conceptualization, prevention, and intervention are based on this form of rape. The remainder of this chapter will go into great length the different types of rape of women by men (e.g., stranger, acquaintance, and gang) and the effect rape has on victims.

One dynamic that has not received adequate attention is the rape of lesbian women by men. In the 1994 National Lesbian Health Care Survey (1994), 9 percent of college-aged lesbians stated they had been raped as adults, and the overwhelming majority reported their assailant was a man. Less that 1 percent of lesbians acknowledged other females had sexually assaulted them. The motivation of men who knowingly rape lesbians appears to be either an attempt to degrade lesbian sexuality or to "convert" lesbians to heterosexual women.

Contrary to traditional theories of the sexist nature of rape, some research has indicated a significant number of women sexually assault other women. A study published in 1989, found that 31 percent of lesbian students reported being victims of forced sex by their current or most recent partners. The main difference between this and the previously mentioned study conducted in 1994 (citing a 1 percent prevalence) was the terminology. In the 1989 study, subjects were asked about "forced sex" and in the 1994 study, subjects were asked about "rape."

In any event sexual assault is a greater problem for gay, lesbian, and bisexual students than many previously considered. In one study published in 1990, gay, lesbian, and bisexual college students reported significantly higher lifetime prevalence of sexual victimization than heterosexual students.

Men rape men, but the topic has received very little attention on college campuses. Like women, male victims of rape can be heterosexual, gay, or bisexual. From the scant research that exists on gay male rape by Ford Hickson and colleagues (1994), we know that about one-third of gay men admitted to being forced into sexual activity, usually by men with whom they had previously had or were currently having consensual sexual activity. They suggest that the idea that male rape (adult against adult) is committed by heterosexual men as an expression of power, is not supported by the data. To even complicate the matter more, according to research by Caroline Waterman and colleagues (1989), men who reported being victims of forced sex were also more likely to report that they were perpetrators as well, than men who did not identify themselves as victims of forced sex. The researchers interpreted this finding to mean that there was some degree of mutuality of abuse in these relationships.

Most sexual assault experts assume that while reported rapes for women are an underestimate of actual rapes, the reported rapes for men are an even greater underestimate. Gay men may be at greater risk for being raped than was previously thought because they are more reluctant to report the assault. Gay men have little faith that the criminal justice system will take their account of acquaintance rape seriously. While the impact of sexual assault on men has not been fully explored, some researchers speculate that the emergence of

HIV in the gay community may cause additional trauma for the victim, especially when the perpetrator does not use a condom.

Gay and lesbian victims of rape face the additional challenge of having limited specialized support services to help them cope with the aftermath of the rape. Furthermore, the goal of most anti-rape education efforts is to reduce a woman's risk of being assaulted by a man in the context of heterosexual relationships. Clearly, our research, prevention, and intervention strategies dealing with sexual assault and gay, lesbian, and bisexual populations are woefully inadequate.

What has received more attention recently is the idea of women raping men. This topic has been controversial as it challenges traditional concepts of interpersonal violence. Again, men are reluctant to come forward to report rape for fear of being disbelieved or trivialized, so actual prevalence rates for this crime are unknown. In fact, when the issue of women raping men is brought up in discussion with other men, it is often ridiculed with comments such as "I wish it would happen to me." Many have difficulty seeing it as a form of violence because there is usually no penetration into another's body.

The rape of men by women is a real issue though and research supports it as such. In *The Sexual Molestation of Men by Women* published in 1982, Sarrel and Masters concluded that men can be sexually aroused in a situation of unwanted sexual contact. The same study showed some women admitted to gaining control in sexual situations by physical force as well as psychological pressure.

A separate study by Sorenson and colleagues of the Los Angeles Epidemiologic Catchment Area Project, revealed that more men were assaulted by women than by men. More recent studies support the frequency of

occurrence of male rape by women. In 1994, as a result of their study on men pressured and forced into sexual experiences, Struckman-Johnson and Struckman-Johnson found that 10.8 percent of men reported experiencing some form of sexual coercion from a woman acquaintance. Larimer, Lydum, Anderson, and Turner (1999) conducted a study on male and female recipients of unwanted sexual contact in a college sample. The results indicated that the men in the sample were just as unlikely to report unwanted sexual coercion as the women.

The impact of rape by women on male victims is similar to women victims of male rape with some notable exceptions. According to research by Sorensen and Siegal and Struckman-Johnson, men are less likely to recall the event as threatening; however, they are more likely to develop alcohol dependence after the sexual assault and are more likely to experience depressive symptoms than men who did not experience these events. Men believe that they should be able to protect themselves and experience tremendous self-blame in the aftermath of an assault. Additional information about the impact of rape on both men and women is discussed in the Impact of Rape section of this chapter.

The National Center for Victims of Crime notes that men may be bothered by the fact that they became sexually aroused during an assault, either by another man or by a woman. In fact, rapists frequently succeed in getting male victims to ejaculate. These are normal, involuntary physiological responses to stimulation, yet both the victim and perpetrator may misinterpret this reaction to mean that he wanted to be raped. The perpetrator may use this reaction as evidence that the victim enjoyed the experience.

TYPES OF RAPE

There are three types of rape: stranger rape, acquaintance rape, and gang rape. Stranger rape is a predatory form of violence—perpetrators seek out a victim and attack. Acquaintance rape is a form of relationship-based violence—perpetrators seek to control and dominate victims to meet their needs. Gang rape is a form of group-induced violence—perpetrators have a reduced sense of responsibility and accountability and allow themselves to believe the action is acceptable because the group endorses it.

Stranger Rape

In stranger rape, the perpetrator wants to avoid attention. The perpetrator will look for dark areas outside or unlocked doors within a building as these options provide easy entry and easy exit. The hunt and the attack motivate the predator. As with predators in nature, the perpetrator of a stranger rape is generally looking for easy prey.

Stranger rapes do happen on college campuses, but they are rare. When they do happen, they are more likely to get reported than other forms of campus rape. If the information reaches public consciousness, it often results in a campus panic.

In 1997, a serial rapist at the University of Tennessee (UT), Knoxville, caused terror when UT students reported four off-campus rapes during a six-week period. In each case the perpetrator entered the victims' homes in the dawn hours on weekends while the women slept on the couch. The assailant choked or attempted to suffocate his victims and usually stole a purse or wallet. One of the victims was forced to take a bath after the assault. Before he left he told her he would see her at school. This predator took a "raptor" approach to the attack—swooping and scooping the victims without warning.

Just because a "raptor" attack seems to come out of nowhere, that does not mean the assault was not planned. According to a review of sexual assault research compiled by sexual assault experts at the University of California, Davis, 75 to 90 percent of rapes are planned and premeditated acts.

Other perpetrators of stranger rape might use the "ambush" attack of luring prey in with various verbal and nonverbal tactics. The perpetrator may try to size up potential victims through conversation or casual contact, seeking someone who is more passive, more uncomfortable, and less forceful. We call this a *bump*. As we discussed in Chapter 8, bumps give perpetrators an opportunity to learn about your limits and your ability to take care of yourself.

A bump feels out of place and leaves the victim with the strange sense that something is off. A bump can be a progression of inappropriate comments or out-of-context questions. A stranger may start a conversation and drive it in an overly personal direction to see the reaction. Predators also may test the waters by touching a person, when touching is inappropriate. A bump often puts the victim in an awkward bind between the need to pay heed to instincts saying "this situation is not right" and the strong socialization to be nice. Women especially fall into this trap of not wanting to offend or appear put-offish. But like violence expert Gavin DeBecker suggests in *The Gift of Fear*, those hairs raising on the back of the neck are doing so for a reason—attuning to survival signals can save lives.

Sexual homicide by strangers, like the cases of Jeanne Clery, the Gemini murders, and Ted Bundy described in Chapter 1, constitute a small percentage of all homicides and all sexual assault cases, but the horror they cause for family and friends is too great to be neglected. According to Harold Hall author of *Lethal Violence* (1998) predators of sexual homicide experience great hostility toward women, feel sexually inferior or inadequate, and have a powerful urge to completely possess the victim. There is a strong potential for repetition of this crime if the perpetrator is not caught. In some instances, the desire to carry out these sex-murder fantasies is so strong that the perpetrator's attempt to suppress it brings on anxiety and physical problems.

While the predatory form of campus rape is the most rare, it is also the crime most addressed in prevention workshops and security measures. Self-defense classes, personal alarm systems, keyed entrances to buildings usually are geared at deterring the stranger from access to campus and not the acquaintance. The idea of "stranger danger" seems to create more fear than the thought that the guy you are sharing a beer with might rape you.

Acquaintance Rape

The term *acquaintance rape* means that the victim knew the assailant even in a slight way. This term is preferred by many to the term *date rape*, as many victims of rape became confused when they were assaulted by someone they knew, but not on a date. In cases of campus acquaintance rape, the perpetrator can be a classmate, someone who lives down the hall, a roommate's boyfriend, someone to whom the victim was just introduced, and so on. According to research published in the *Journal of American College Health* (1999), acquaintance rapes account for 80 percent of all rapes on college campuses.

Acquaintance rape is unarguably the most common type of rape although it is less reported than stranger rape. In *Acquaintance Rape: The Hidden Crime* (1991), Christine

Gidycz and Mary Koss reviewed several studies dealing with rape–all of which indicated that high percentages of sexual assaults, 78 to 89 percent, were committed by acquaintances. Dr. Koss' research also revealed that one in every twelve men admitted to having forced or attempted to force a woman to have intercourse through physical force or coercion. Very few of these men, however, identified themselves as rapists. In cases of acquaintance rape, victims often do not report because believe they are at fault for trusting someone they thought they knew.

In acquaintance rape, the violence is relationship-based and the perpetrator is motivated to gain control over the victim in order to meet the perpetrator's desires. The perpetrator experiences a sense of ownership or entitlement to the victim as property. According to 1999 research by Mary Larimer and colleagues, the three main reasons both men and women give for why acquaintance rape occurred are: (1) feeling that it is useless to stop an aroused partner, (2) feeling pressure to have sex from continuous arguments with partner, and (3) being unable to consent due to intoxication from alcohol or other drugs. Each of these reasons gives evidence of an unequal power dynamic between the assailant and the victim.

Acquaintance rapes usually happen when a woman and a man are alone together, and alcohol or other drugs are present. Sometimes, as in the opening story of rape, the woman passes out and awakens to find a man having sex with her. Other times the victim is not impaired, but the perpetrator is intoxicated and sexually aggressive.

Communication problems are another critical aspect of acquaintance rape. Many women are socialized to be friendly, submissive, and complimentary. Men are often socialized to take charge of situations and be aggressive. In sexual situations, these lines often get crossed. A man misinterprets a woman's kindness as a flirtatious invitation for sex. The woman does not want to offend the man by telling him she is not interested in his advances. A mild protest may be interpreted as a signal that more persuading is needed.

Interpretation of sexual cues is also different for men and women. For women, going to a room with a man alone, and even kissing him does not mean that sex is inevitable. Women often feel justified in stopping behavior at any point along the sexual continuum. For many men, the accumulation of sexual signals tends to indicate one outcome. If the situation gets hot and heavy and the woman changes her mind, the man may become angry and feel that he has been misled.

Because of the degree of impairment of typically both victim and perpetrator and the "he said, she said" nature of these cases, adjudication is very difficult. Cases are hard to prove because there usually are not any direct witnesses to the crime, and alcohol or drugs alter many witnesses' memories. At three prestigious campuses–Harvard, Brown, and Bates–sexual assault adjudication has erupted in public controversy.

At Harvard, a student was found guilty in a criminal court of indecent assault and battery for raping a woman in an alcohol-induced sleep. Harvard expelled the student and received backlash from both students and faculty for overreacting. The protesters stated that different degrees of punishment should be instated for those who commit date rape as opposed to other forms of sexual assault.

In 1998, the Bates College president was confronted by three hundred angry students who wanted to know why alleged sexual assaults were not made public knowledge. They contended they had a right to know that one male student was responsible for one rape and three assaults. Furthermore,

they claimed had they known about the earlier assaults, the later assaults might have been prevented. Shortly after, the student accused of the crimes withdrew from Bates. At the same time two other men were held accountable by the college disciplinary system for separate sexual assault charges. None of the eight women who pursued complaints with the college filed police reports, and all cases involved alcohol intoxication and some degree of consensual sexual behavior before the rape. Defendants and their lawyers declared the school to be in mass hysteria over the rash of incidents. Bates' policy, however, states "If you take advantage of the fact that someone is drunk or drugged to have sex with her or him, you may be guilty of rape." The two remaining students faced expulsion from the college.

One of the most controversial cases occurred in 1996 at Brown University. A man claimed he had sex with a woman who appeared sober even though he found her in a puddle of vomit during a party. He claimed that he brought her to his bed where she initiated sexual contact and asked him to get a condom. After sex they talked for four hours and she gave him her phone number. He attempted to call her during the following week because he wanted to see her again. He was stunned to find out she had no recollection of the event. She stated she was drunk, did not remember anything about the night, and filed a complaint with the Office of Student Life.

The defendant was found guilty of sexual misconduct even though the complainant did not dispute the above version of the story during university proceedings. The disciplinary council on the case gave him a minor penalty of one semester probation and mandated counseling, but the dean of student life felt this was too lenient and increased the penalty to six months suspension. A music professor at Brown led a campaign to clear the defendant's name and stated, "When a woman cries rape, a rape has taken place. The charge automatically becomes a fact, and there is no defense against it."

The student then appealed the case to the provost who overturned the sexual misconduct finding and found him guilty of "flagrant disrespect"—a lesser charge. Suspension was once again reduced to probation. In 1997, the student sued both the complainant and the university for accusing him and punishing him of a crime he claims he did not commit. He withdrew from school on the basis of a medical leave and returned to his parents' home in Iowa. Two years after the incident the lawsuit was dropped and the student accused of rape was removed from probation at Brown.

Gang Rape

In *Fraternity Gang Rape: Sex, Brotherhood, and Privilege on Campus* (1990), Sanday highlights some of the cultural phenomena that occur in gang rape. For instance, gang rape euphemisms include "pulling train," "gang banging," "working out a yes," and "she asked for it." Within this terminology there exists group endorsement and justification of certain behaviors and practices. Unfortunately, this slang still exists, lending credence to the theory that group support of this form of violence is still prominent.

Gang rape is a form of group-induced violence and has as its primary causes diffusion of responsibility, group modeling, and a need for belonging. Gang rapists are less concerned with the welfare of the victim or with the potential consequences of their actions, because of the involvement of oth-

ers. Gang rape, like other forms of violence, is a learned behavior. As O'Sullivan indicates in the chapter on acquaintance gang rape in *Acquaintance Rape: The Hidden Crime* (1991), the participation of other group members is not only implied support for the action, but also modeled behavior of how to complete the crime. Furthermore, O'Sullivan suggests that engaging in gang rape provides perpetrators with a sense of camaraderie, via competition and challenge, and acceptance with other group members.

Men who would not rape alone, may rape in a group. Following is an example taken from O'Sullivan's chapter on acquaintance gang rape in *Acquaintance Rape: The Hidden Crime* edited by Parrot and Bechhofer and published in 1991.

> One of the Kentucky State defendants told the police that he left the woman alone when he found her partially clothed in his room because she was unwilling to have sex with him. When he returned and found his friends assaulting her, he joined in. (p. 145)

According to O'Sullivan, the perpetrators and victims of gang rapes have some common factors within their groups respectively. Most perpetrators are college-aged men. Perpetrators often identify themselves with a perceived elite group and have a greater sense of being privileged or have special rights or entitlements. Victims of gang rape are perceived as sexually promiscuous and naive. Often the perception of sexual promiscuity may be inaccurate; for some reason though, the perpetrators have convinced themselves that this is the case. For example, she was dressed a certain way and very flirtatious.

METHODS OF COERCION USED TO RAPE

There are several methods of coercion used by both male and female perpetrators: psychological pressure, threat of physical force, physical force, use of drugs, use of alcohol, and abuse of mental impairment. Psychological pressure is where the perpetrator actually wears down the resistance of the victim by continuing to push the issue until she or he gives in to the perpetrator's desires. In this situation, consent is not provided; rather, the victim finally stops resisting. The threat of physical force can be made with or without the use of a weapon. Actual physical force can be exercised with or without a weapon. Abuse of mental impairment is not as frequent on college campuses but can occur. In this case, the perpetrator takes advantage of a mentally challenged adult or a child–an individual lacking the mental understanding of the situation or the choices available.

physical force used against them and were more likely to report having been given drugs or alcohol by their partner with the intent of promoting sexual intercourse.

Muehlenhard and Linton conducted a study on date rape and sexual aggression in dating in 1987. They found that 55 percent of men who admitted to being sexual aggressors and 53 percent of women admitting to experiencing sexual aggression on a date had been drinking alcohol leading up to the attack. Larimer and colleagues also indicated that both men and women reported higher quantities of alcohol per occasion, greater numbers of alcohol-related negative consequences, and more alcohol dependence symptoms than those who did not experience or perpetrate sexual aggression. Women victims also reported higher weekly drinking frequency than women who were not sexual assault victims were.

Alcohol and Rape

Alcohol reduces inhibitions and the ability to resist or fight. Campus rape often happens when people are intoxicated and making poor decisions as well as when a person has passed out from alcohol use. Alcohol is a contributing factor in an overwhelming number of campus rapes. As in the opening rape example, the victims are often given large quantities of alcohol by the perpetrators.

In 1999 Larimer and colleagues conducted a study about male and female recipients of unwanted sexual contact. In this study a Greek pledge class of 165 men and 131 women were assessed as to degree of unwanted sexual contact, form of unwanted sexual contact, degree of alcohol use, and depression symptoms. The results indicated that women were more likely to have had

Date Rape Drugs

In the 1990s a new rape phenomenon began to make an impact on campuses: date rape drugs. These drugs are given to unknowing victims who then quickly find themselves in a very impaired state. Most cause profound "anterograde amnesia" or the inability to remember events that took place while under the effects of the drugs.

In "'Roofies,' The New 'Date Rape' Drug of Choice" posted in January 1996 on the Emergency Net News website, Clark Staten alerted the public about Rohypnol, a brand name for flunitrazepam (a benzodiazepine). Rohypnol produces a sedative effect, amnesia, muscle relaxation, and a slowing of psychomotor responses. Sedation occurs twenty to thirty minutes after ingestion and can last for hours. Roofies are placed in punch, beer, and other party drinks. Some people take it voluntarily to get a quick buzz. On the website Battalion, Megan Wright identified some other names used for Rohypnol: "the forget pill," "Mexican Valium," "R-2," "Rib," "Roaches," "Rope," Roofenot," and "Roofers." Most often Rohypnol is found in tablet form stored in "bubble packs." Sometimes the pills have been ground into powder. Rohypnol is sold as a prescription drug in other countries and smuggled into the United States.

In 1997, Staten posted information about another date rape drug of choice, GHB. GHB, or gamma hydroxybutyrate, is a central nervous system depressant. On the website Battalion (1999), Megan Wright reports that used in small amounts the drug can produce the effects of being drunk. The drug is colorless, odorless, and salty. GHB often leads to serious physical consequences. As Staten noted, acute GHB toxicity can manifest as coma, seizures, respiratory depression, and vomiting. There is no antidote for GHB. According to the February 1, 2000 issue of *USA Today,* the use of GHB has resulted in a minimum of 58 deaths and 5,700 overdoses from 1990 to 2000. Wright indicated the following other names for GHB: "GBH," "Grievous Bodily Harm," "Cherry Meth," "Liquid X," "Liquid

Ecstasy," "Easy Lay," "G-Juice," and "Energy Drink."

A third "date rape drug" is called Ketamine or "Special K." Veterinarians used this drug originally on farm animals. It usually comes in liquid form, but may also be found as a white powder or pill. According to the National Institute on Drug Abuse (NIDA), Ketamine is a central nervous system depressant and a rapid-acting general anesthetic. Ketamine is usually snorted, but may be sprinkled on tobacco or marijuana and smoked. Some users describe intense hallucinations while using this drug. Other effects can include convulsions, potentially fatal respiratory problems, and delirium.

In 1996, Congress passed the Drug-Induced Rape Prevention and Punishment Act of 1996. Under this federal law, the mere possession of Rohypnol can lead to three years in prison and fines. The February 1, 2000 issue of *USA Today* further reported that the House of Representatives passed a bill taking a strong stance on the use of GHB. The bill will authorize the DEA to seek federal criminal prosecutions against people possessing and distributing the drug. The bill will also increase prison time for the offenders.

CYBERSTALKING AND SEXUAL THREATS VIA THE INTERNET

Increasing numbers of individuals are finding romantic connections on the Internet. Most of these encounters are harmless, but some can prove to be dangerous. For sexual perpetrators, the Internet is a dream come true. They can spend as much time as needed to groom their victims to trust them and then to be vulnerable to them. Perpetrators can remain relatively anonymous and present whatever information is needed to convince the victim.

Vulnerable individuals are at risk of falling prey to the Internet connections, because in many ways they believe their desires will be met. They feel loved–some maybe for the first time, and they will risk anything to keep that feeling going. As with the couple in the cybersex case described later in this chapter demonstrates, the face-to-face meeting of these individuals often falls short of the fantasy created in cyberspace.

Sexual perpetrators are also well connected with each other via the Internet. Porn rings, many of them circulating illegal material, are a constant source of frustration for the authorities who attempt to control them. Some of the people who participate in these porn rings are individuals of our campuses. In 1995, a woman in Moscow was browsing the Internet and found a disturbing story. It was a description posted on an open bulletin board of a graphic rape and murder of a young woman. Through some investigation, authorities were able to determine that the author was a male student at the University of Michigan. He had posted three rape and murder stories, and in one the victim's name was the same name as a student in one of his classes. He was subsequently suspended. Further investigation uncovered the fact that he was in contact with a known porn enthusiast from Canada who was facing prosecution for transmitting threats via the computer. In one email between them, the student confessed to his mentor, "Just thinking about it doesn't do the trick anymore, I need to do it."

WHY RAPE?

The debate on why people rape is fierce and circles around two schools of thought. One school believes that the need to rape is based in the evolution of man. The other school believes the desire to rape is based in sociological development. To ignore either one of these schools completely would only serve to limit our ability to understand and address rape. However, we contend that once we address the fears elicited by the first argument, this argument actually plays a very limited role in addressing the problem of rape.

Thornhill and Palmer published their highly controversial book, *A Natural History of Rape* in 2000 and caused quite a storm in rape prevention circles. These authors contend that the basis of sexual coercion is biological and stems from evolution and natural selection. In an oversimplified form, the gist of their argument is that the reason men rape stems from their desire to procreate and perpetuate their lineage. From their perspective, rape is an instinctive desire and needs to be acknowledged as such, in order to be appropriately addressed.

According to many biologists, the argument is inherently flawed in many ways. One needs only to look at the fact that children are the number one victims of rape to dispute the "need to procreate" motive for rape. Nevertheless, those invested in the debate wonder how this theory will impact the rape prevention and intervention field.

The "biological predisposition to rape" argument calls for five immediate questions. One, does assuming an instinctual desire to perpetuate lineage presuppose a certain level of permission for men to rape women because it is natural? Two, does assuming this instinctual desire mean women of childbearing age are responsible for their being raped if they dress provocatively or choose to live their lives freely? Three, does assuming this instinctual desire mean all men are rapists? Four, does assuming this instinctual desire mean rape has nothing to do with power or control? Five, does assuming an instinctual desire presuppose that societal norms and culture have no bearing on the choices men make?

Men and women have the ability to think, reason, and make choices. Believing that men have permission to rape is correlative to believing that men have permission to randomly murder based on belief of survival of the fittest. An instinctual desire does not mean that men are no longer responsible for their actions regardless of the age or appearance of women they choose to be around. An instinctual desire does not imply follow through or a complete lack of control over your desires. An instinctual desire to procreate does not exclude the need for power and control in rape, and it does not exclude that the victim of rape is experiencing a loss of power and control. An instinctual desire does not exclude the possibility of the environment and culture playing a role in the choice a person makes to rape.

The majority of the literature on rape for the last several decades chooses an alternative explanation for rape in our culture. The sociological perspective contends that rape is a crime of power and is highly influenced by cultural, societal, and group norms. These norms support rape through poor role modeling, difficulty in holding perpetrators accountable, and a lack of support for victims of rape. Rape is a learned behavior, and people learn what is acceptable from watching others around them. Rape is often unreported, and proving rape is difficult. Consequently, most rapists are not held accountable. By reporting the crime, victims face the prospect of being victimized again, by being interrogated in the investigation or suffering social consequences for reporting.

This argument also calls for some questions. Does this argument ignore the biological standpoint that all men are capable of rape? Does this argument ignore the possibility that there could be an instinctual desire behind rape? Would we suggest that an instinctual desire behind rape is not as important as the choices based on alleged desires?

Clearly the debate about the motives for rape is not totally resolved. Nature-nurture perspectives run in conflict on a number of sociological and mental health issues, and usually the answer involves some of each argument.

THE IMPACT OF RAPE ON WOMEN AND MEN

Rape impacts women and men both physically and psychologically. The physical impacts of rape span the gamut. Rape victims can experience tissue damage from their arm being twisted or from being choked. They can also experience vaginal or rectal bleeding or sexual dysfunction. Those who attempt escape and fail can be injured from the attempt or the retaliation. Rape victims often experience a form of Posttraumatic Stress Disorder (PTSD) called Rape Trauma Syndrome. According to the National Victim Center 31 percent of all rape victims develop Rape Related Posttraumatic Stress Disorder sometime in their lives.

According to the UC Davis web site, http://pubweb.ucdavis.edu/Documents/RPEP/rts.htm, Rape Trauma Syndrome occurs in three phases: acute, outward adjustment, and resolution stage. The acute phase often begins immediately after the rape and can persist from a few days to several weeks. The victim may seem agitated, hysterical, or appear totally calm. Emotional ups and downs are common. Victims have difficulty concentrating, making decisions, or accomplishing everyday tasks.

The outward adjustment phase begins with return to a near-normal routine pattern. Inwardly, there is still turmoil which can manifest itself in many ways: anxiety, sense of helplessness, fear, depression, vivid dreams, insomnia, recurring nightmares, physical ailments, variations in appetite, vomiting, nausea, preoccupation with safety, denial, hesitation to forming new relationships, sexual problems, or disruptions to everyday behavior.

The resolution phase occurs after returning to one's routine pattern. The rape is no longer the central focus in the victim's life. Victims recognize that although they will never forget the rape or the pain and memories that go with it, it is a part of their life experience and they are choosing to move on. They have moved from victim to survivor.

Since the most common type of rape is that of women by men the Rape Trauma Syndrome model is most reflective of the response of a female victim to having been raped by a man. Struckman-Johnson indicated that male victims respond similarly to female victims with a few exceptions. She highlighted the findings of Kaufman and colleagues in 1980, by stating that male victims were more likely to exhibit a controlled rather than an expressive response. Men were more often quiet, embarrassed, withdrawn, or unconcerned. Speculation for the reasoning of this occurrence is that men are socialized to be inexpressive and stoic in the face of adversity. Men also feel guilt over a sense of losing their masculinity. In addition, Struckman-Johnson highlighted a finding by Myers in 1989 unique to men raped by men. Men raped by men experience a chronic "male gender identity" crisis related to the loss of masculinity or confusion about sexual orientation. Other than those exceptions, men typically respond similarly to the original Rape Trauma Syndrome model.

The most devastating consequence of rape is the victim's suicide. According to the National Victim Center, rape victims have been found to be almost nine times more likely to attempt suicide than nonvictims.

RAPE AND THE LAW

Holding perpetrators legally accountable for rape is difficult. For example, in rape cases the perpetrators have the right not to testify against themselves. This right allows defense attorneys the opportunity to grill victims about the details of their testimony regarding a traumatic event. As we discussed earlier, a victim's perceptions during a rape can be shaky. This combination of factors calls the jury to weigh questionable information from the victim versus a stable plea of not guilty from the perpetrator. In a gang rape scenario, the expectation is that the victim renews her objections with every perpetrator as they take their turn. Often the victim surrenders before all the perpetrators are done raping her.

The Rape Shield Law

In rape cases the victim is protected by the Rape Shield Law. This law, passed in 1975, precludes any testimony of the victim's sexual history that does not bear immediate relevance to the current case. The law was implemented to keep the jury focused on the case at hand and not information that has no bearing on the rape being tried.

Serious legal debate surrounds this law. Some suggest that the law interferes with an individual's right to a fair trial. Others state that sexual history is usually not relevant to the case at hand and the anticipation of disclosing such information will prevent women from pursuing legal recourse due to fears of humiliation. There have been cases where many legal experts have felt past history had a direct bearing on the credibility of the witness testimony. For instance, sexual history involving past consensual sexual activity between the victim and defendant may be deemed as relevant.

In a sensationalized case between a Columbia University graduate student and a Barnard College student, the Rape Shield Law played an important role. During the summer of 1996, doctoral candidate Oliver Jovanovic and Jamie Allyson met in an Internet chat room and exchanged email over the next several months. On November 2, 1996 they had their first date. Seventeen months later Oliver was convicted of kidnapping, assault, and sexual abuse and sentenced to fifteen years to life in prison. The Rape Shield Law was evoked in this controversial case and suppressed key evidence from the trial.

During the months before their first and only in-person encounter, Jamie emailed Oliver on several occasions openly acknowledging her interest in sadomasochism, snuff films (type of pornographic film in which the victim is murdered on screen), and dismemberment. Oliver's side of the email correspondence was allowed in the trial and served as the only other proof besides the word of the victim against him.

What actually transpired during their time together is subject to dispute. According to her testimony, Jamie said that Oliver tied her to his futon and for twenty hours gagged her, choked her, burned her with hot candle wax, bit her breasts until they bled, and sodomized her. After the ordeal she delayed seeking medical attention for several days and wrote Oliver several ambiguous emails such as:

Quite bruised mentally and physically, but never been so happy to be alive, not if I'm happy simply because I'm not dead, well some may question that. But nonetheless, all's well on 116th street . . . [William] Burroughs best sums my state,

saying something about rotting eggs or rotting cheese, the taste is so overpoweringly delicious, and at the same time, quite nauseating so that one will eat and puke and eat and puke until collapsing from exhaustion.

On the stand she admitted she willingly submitted to some of these tortures. During the trial Jamie denied sending Oliver emails expressing interest in participating in violent sex. Many experts believe that the Rape Shield Law was misapplied in this case as it wound up only shielding perjury.

The Violence Against Women Act

Another legal debate has surrounded the Violence Against Women Act (VAWA). VAWA passed in 1994 and among others things it allows rape victims to sue their attackers in federal court, because it is argued, rape impacts interstate commerce. The premise is that rape impacts the ability of women to work and do business across state lines, thus rape is a federal matter. Several women have pursued cases against the perpetrators and colleges under this act. There has been a great deal of debate about this act and its constitutionality. Some courts have upheld these cases and some have overturned these cases.

In June 2000 the United States Supreme Court overturned a provision of the act that allowed victims of gender-motivated violence to sue their attackers. Two days later members of Congress and federal leaders appealed the decision. They cited the significant drop in cases of intimate partner violence since VAWA passed as justification for its renewal.

The case that has brought this controversy to the spotlight is a case of alleged campus rape: *Brzonkala v. Virginia Tech*. According to her testimony, in 1994 two male athletes raped Christy Brzonkala before the end of her first month as a freshman at Virginia Polytechnic Institute and State University, also known as Virginia Tech. She had met the men fifteen minutes prior to the rape. Afterwards she withdrew socially for months. Several months later she went to the Women's Center and reported the rape. She filed charges under the school's Sexual Assault Policy. The hearing was held in May. One of the accused players denied having intercourse with Christy and was not penalized. The other admitted to having sex with her, was found guilty of sexual misconduct charges, and was suspended for a year.

According to Christy's testimony, in July 1994 the school notified her that the suspended football player was threatening to sue the school and that they had made a mistake during the previous school hearing. They told her a second hearing would be necessary. After the second hearing, the accused player was found guilty of a reduced charge of "using abusive language," and was allowed to return to Virginia Tech on a full athletic scholarship with the varsity football team.

Christy then filed suit against Virginia Tech in December 1995 under the civil rights provision of the federal Violence Against Women Act, which happened to pass legislation just months before the alleged rape occurred, and the Title IX gender discrimination law. Due to her emotional distress and fear for her safety, Christy withdrew from Virginia Tech. In July 1996, the federal district court ruled that the civil rights provision of VAWA was unconstitutional. That decision was appealed and reversed in December 1997. In March 1999, the decision was again reversed and claims against Virginia Tech and the accused students were dismissed based on the grounds that the relevant portion of VAWA was unconstitutional.

In June 1999, Christy filed a petition with the U.S. Supreme Court to review the constitutionality of the VAWA civil rights provision. In February 2000, Virginia Tech agreed to pay Christy $75,000 to settle the claims of the Title IX suit. On May 15, 2000 the U.S. Supreme Court released their 5–4 vote to invalidate this portion of the VAWA, meaning that Christy will not be able to further her case.

PREVENTION AND RESPONSE STRATEGIES

Even though sexual assault has been one of the longest recognized forms of campus violence, and schools have been working to successfully prevent such crimes for decades, the task still proves extremely difficult. A recent situation at the University of Massachusetts is a case in point.

Within a period of a few weeks during November 1999, the University of Massachusetts (Amherst) endured a series of reported assaults that sent shock waves through the community. On November 2, a female student reported that a man wearing a black ski mask near the Campus Center Pond had raped her. Exactly one week later on November 9, another woman reported that she had also been grabbed from behind and assaulted near the Student Union. On November 14, a third female student reported that she had been sprayed with a toxic substance like pepper spray by three assailants near Campus Pond. The assailants then wrestled her to the ground and beat her with their fists before she was able to flee the scene. On November 16, a female student reported to university police that she had been assaulted in a parking lot by a knife-wielding man. Later, the woman recanted this report and stated that the cuts on her face were self-inflicted.

The campus responded to these incidents in a number of ways including increased security all over campus; the installation of a HELP box near Campus Pond; frequent communications from the chancellor to the campus community and parents; the staging of a safety rally co-sponsored by numerous campus groups; the distribution of thousands of personal "shriek" alarms; and the formation of a group of student volunteers called "Pond Watch" who patrolled the campus and provided escort services. Despite all these interventions, the students were not satisfied with this response and members of the Student Government took a vote of no-confidence in the Dean of Students.

When developing prevention and response strategies, prevention specialists must consider what we know about rape. We know that the most common form of campus rape is acquaintance rape, a relationship-based form of violence with a primary motive being power and control. Less common forms of campus rape are stranger rape, a predatory form of violence, and gang rape, a group-induced form of violence. As mentioned earlier, the motives and perpetrator profiles for these crimes are diverse. We also know that rape impacts straight, gay, lesbian, and bisexual individuals as both victims and perpetrators. The Rape Trauma Syndrome defines the aftermath experience for many raped women, with a few additions for male victims. Given these facts, prevention and response efforts must have multiple target groups and a comprehensive campus strategy.

Community Education

Community members need to be aware of the many scenarios of rape in order to understand what can be done to prevent and respond to rape. In *Acquaintance Rape: The Hidden Crime* (1991), Parrot makes the following suggestions for community education: Information about sexual assault, prevention methods, and policies should be included in written material put out by admissions. A letter can be sent to parents explaining that all institutions wrestle with the problems of rape, how their child can help prevent rape, and the policies regarding rape. A comprehensive education can be created and coordinated being inclusive of community representation. Community members can be trained as resources.

Positive Modeling and Positive Peer Influence

Peer group dynamics are powerful. They can be used to create an atmosphere that supports rape, but they can also be used to help stop rape. Role modeling is a critical tool in developing leadership. When leaders from various different groups, clubs, fraternities, teams, students, staff, teachers, and coaches are involved in positive education, good communication, and positive practices, members will follow. When inappropriate actions take place and organization leaders step up, challenge the action, and hold perpetrators accountable, members will pay attention. The concept is to make inappropriate behavior the unpopular thing to do. When acting inappropriately becomes unpopular, the group can help some to do the right thing.

Social Norms Marketing, as described in Chapter 4, traditionally is used to target high-risk drinking, and now is being used to shape attitudes about sexual violence. When campuses survey men and women they find the overwhelming majority have respectful beliefs and actions in sexual situations. Campuses then filter this information back into campus consciousness through media campaigns proclaiming such findings as "most men on campus stop sexual activity the first time their date says, 'no.'" Research on this prevention technique is still in its infancy; however, early results are supportive of the fact that this strategy is effective in improving harmful attitudes and behavior.

Programming for Men and Women

Prevention programming can be a first step in increasing awareness about campus rape. Most experts suggest that educational efforts take place during the critical period between orientation and the school's fall break. This time is known for a high occurrence of sexual assaults. Programs should be targeted to particular audiences, including freshmen, athletes, Greeks, international students, and so on. Co-educational sexual assault programming can include the following information:
- Communication and assertiveness skills
- The connection between alcohol and other drugs and the incidence of acquaintance rape
- Correct social norms about the prevalence of those who do respect their dates and stop sexual activity when they hear "no" the first time
- Information about the different types of rape that happen and potential perpetrators and victims
- General safety prevention techniques (see Chapter 8 for additional techniques)
- Socialization patterns of men and women and how these norms can come into conflict with one another
- Dating rights (e.g., men's and women's right to say no)
- How to respond to a person who has been assaulted

Other types of programs for men and women together include a "safety walk" or a "take back the night" march. The purpose of the walk is to evaluate the general status of campus safety and to demonstrate active concern on the part of the campus community for safety. Along these lines, "Sexual Assault Awareness Week" or "Sexual Responsibility Week" can help raise campus awareness about the issues involved in campus rape. Activities might include educational programs, candlelight vigils, panel discussions, peer theater skits, informational tables, keynote speakers, and so on.

Programming for Women Only

Most college women have been receiving safety programming since they were children. By the time they reach college age women are overly aware about the dangers of potential rape. Usually, however, these fears are based on stranger danger. Many will tell you they protect themselves from rape by not walking alone at night, and by carrying keys ready to poke someone in the eye. What they know is not sufficient. Walking with the strange man you just met at a party and bonded with over shots is not necessarily better than walking alone, and as we stressed earlier unless a woman is fully willing to poke someone in the eye, she is not likely to do it.

Self-defense classes highlighting realistic prevention methods, effective responses to an attack, and actual practicing of the methods seem to have yielded positive results. This same information is helpful for men as well, however, we have seen them more successful as women-only programs.

Programming for Men Only

Historically, sexual assault has been thought of as a "woman's issue" and health educators have not usually included programming directed toward men. When men attended the programs aimed for a female audience, they often left feeling blamed and misunderstood. In the 1990s new programs began to emerge that looked to men to become part of the solution in preventing sexual assault on campus.

There are two programs for men that seem to have had some success and national recognition. The first, the Mentors in Violence Prevention (MVP) Project was established in 1993 at Northeastern University. The second, Stealing Home was created by John Foubert, the Assistant Dean of Students at the University of Virginia. These programs both begin by using a technique that gets men to think about how violence can impact a woman they care about. They are encouraged to imagine how they would feel if their mother, sister, or girlfriend just told them they had been raped. Some have criticized this strategy for placing men in this rescuer role because it reinforces the unbalanced gender power dynamic and ignores the occurrence of male rape. While these criticisms may be true, the technique has shown to open the door for the conversation when otherwise men are reluctant to speak about this divisive topic.

Men are socialized not to believe that they can or ever would be the victim of sexual assault. As such, it is hard for men to identify with any role but the perpetrator in many sexual assault programs, a role that does not fit with how most men see themselves. This situation leaves men feeling helpless and ostracized at traditional sexual assault prevention programs. The helper role approach allows men to see themselves as being a part of the solution and not just a part of the problem.

The MVP program focuses on highlighting the role of bystanders and changing masculine norms. The program presents a series of gender violence scenarios where participants are asked to choose a course of action.

The options available to participants range from doing nothing to full action. The choices are designed to help men identify what they think is right. From that point, the group talks about their choices. This structured opportunity to talk about what it really means to be a man is the most important part of the program. In this setting, positive peer pressure plays a significant role. Instead of diffusion of responsibility, an increased responsibility to the group occurs. Strong male role models are important for this process to work.

The MVP project has targeted primarily student-athletes across the country. Later they began working with fraternity groups and campus leadership groups. As the project grew, MVP developed another program for female athletes. This program approached women not as potential victims of rape but as empowered helpers who can confront and prevent violence too.

The Stealing Home program focuses on rape identification and what men can do to help prevent rape. The program uses a Seattle Police Department video in which a police sergeant describes a scene in which an officer is raped by two men on the street. The descriptions are portrayed in graphic detail with the goal of attempting to have men appreciate the physical and emotional impact of rape and its aftermath.

The program has received critical feedback that the video inaccurately depicts male rape. However, experience indicates that it is helpful in facilitating a frank discussion between men about a difficult topic. Following the video, the group talks about how the presented scenario is similar to female rape. The next part of the program discusses various different things men can do about the problem: improve communication, look out for people at parties, stop telling rape jokes, and so on. In particular, the roles bystanders play are important. The program allows men to see the opportunity and responsibility to prevent rape as a bystander.

Individual Prevention Tactics

Individual sexual assault prevention methods must be tailored to the different types of sexual assault. For stranger rapes predators are motivated by the excitement of hunt and attack and do not want attention drawn to themselves. Several self-protection techniques exist to make an individual less appealing to the predator. First, individuals should be coached to carry themselves with confidence and power in order to avoid presenting like a potential victim. Second, if the predator identifies someone as a target, that person should draw attention to the situation and get away if he or she can. Third, safety programs must stress that individuals should make decisions that maximize their ability to keep themselves safe. Some of these choices may limit freedom. For example, people should avoid dark or secluded areas, travel in groups, stay sober, and make sure doors are locked and not propped.

To prevent the occurrence of date rape drugs, the Rape Treatment Center of UCLA Medical Center suggests the following:

- Do not drink beverages that you did not open yourself, including drinks from punch bowls.
- Refrain from sharing drinks with others, and do not leave your drink unattended at any time.
- Do not drink anything that has an unusual taste or appearance.
- If you feel a lot more intoxicated that you usually do for the amount of alcohol you consumed, you may have been drugged.
- If you choose to go to the hospital request that a urine sample be taken for drug toxicology testing. A special test must be conducted to detect Rohypnol

in urine.

The motivation in acquaintance rape is control and domination, and clear communication may help an individual identify a potential problem at an earlier stage. To prevent acquaintance rape people must be able to set and communicate clear boundaries and to find language with which they are comfortable. Consistent boundary violations are a clear red flag of disrespect.

Over time, the submissive partner in these relationships can fall completely under the domination of the other. The only effective response to an escalated relationship-based violence situation is to completely detach from the relationship. Any form of contact, from gestures trying to make it better, to neutral conversation, to yelling and screaming will serve as reinforcement for the perpetrator.

Gang rape is a group-induced form of violence. Individuals are most vulnerable to this form of violence when they become isolated from potential helpers and are in a vulnerable state. Many rape prevention specialists encourage women to have buddies when they go out, and to make the pact beforehand that they will not leave the party without each other. At all times they will have an awareness of where their friend is and will intervene if they feel that the situation is becoming dangerous.

Most importantly, individuals must give themselves permission to do what they need to do to escape harm. Fighting, fleeing, and freezing are all potential responses during an attack. The bottom line is, if an individual has survived a sexual assault, they have done the right thing.

Policy Development

The following policy and practice recommendations are a compilation of suggestions from Rutgers University; Katie Koestner sexual assault prevention keynote speaker; and Andrea Parrot, editor of *Acquaintance Rape*.

Sexual Misconduct Policy Language

A clear policy regarding sexual misconduct should be created and should be separate from the sexual harassment policy. Policies should indicate minimum sanctions for violation, including such language as, "potential sanctions include but are not limited to." Penalties for sexual assault should be severe. Conduct codes should include a glossary of definitions including the following terms: "sexual abuse," "sexual assault," "acquaintance rape," and "consent."

Visitor Policies

Visitors should be included in the conduct code as a protected group. A policy should be created that holds students accountable for the behavior of their non-student guests.

Organizational Accountability

A policy should be developed that holds organizations accountable for their contributions to policy violations. The need for group accountability as well as individual accountability is paramount in combating the impact of diffusion of responsibility.

Anonymous Report Forms

Anonymous report forms should be accessible throughout campus. These forms allow victims to disclose information about sexual assault without either identifying themselves or their perpetrator. This information will give campus authorities a better picture of sexual violence that is not reported to them. Good locations for these forms include the library, the health center waiting room, the student union, and in residence halls. Extra safety measures can be taken when campuses have better information about the frequency of sexual assault in certain locations or during specific times of the year.

Once the anonymous form has been completed, the person reporting the sexual assault should have several options to deliver their report. A locked box with a drop slot should be secured next to the place where the report forms are offered. In addition, the report form should indicate other places on campus the individual can bring the report to. This may include campus security, a faculty advisor, the counseling center, and so on. The individual should be encouraged to bring the report to a person or department that she or he believes will act in accordance with the reporter's desires. That is, if reporters simply want to document the case and nothing more, they might bring it one place and if they want action but do not want to get involved they might bring it somewhere else. Staff members receiving these reports also must know what to do with them once they have them in their possession. Eventually, they should all be channeled to a central location so that accurate data may be compiled and any trends analyzed for prevention purposes.

The anonymous report form may include the following statements and questions as adapted from the Rutgers University "Creating a Safer Campus" brochure published by the Department of Sexual Assault Services and Crime Victim Assistance.

Adjudication

Parrot and Bechhofer (1991) also made recommendations for improving judicial

boards:
1. Cases should be heard and sanctions should be administered in appropriate time frames.
2. The judicial board should be well trained on a clearly defined sexual assault policy as well as the procedures for hearing such a case.
3. Appropriate elements of the rape shield law should be incorporated into the judicial code, and the board should be trained on these elements.
4. Since many boards have students on them, victims should have the option of having the case heard by a specially assigned hearing officer to protect confidentiality.
5. The board should be trained in showing the appropriate sensitivity toward the victim.

Responding to a Victim of Sexual Assault

First and foremost, the victim needs to be made to feel safe. Medical needs should be addressed as soon as possible. Legal and judicial options should be made available. Confidentiality must be maintained as much as possible.

When counseling sexual assault victims, constant reassurance that the rape was not their fault is appropriate. Victims may have been responsible for putting themselves in a vulnerable situation, but they did not asked to be raped. During rape, power has been taken away from the victim. During the healing process, the victim should be supported in making decisions and remain in control as much as possible. Finally, the victim needs to be made aware of all available choices and resources. In order to ensure that all the choices and resources are made available, a written response protocol should be developed to help responders cover all

bases of response. The following items should be included in such a protocol packet:
1. The sexual assault policy.
2. Names of people to notify and the specific notification procedures.
3. The legal reporting options and requirements.
4. Counseling services available.
5. Medical services and options available.
6. Information about Physical Evidence Recovery Kit (PERK) or "rape kit."
7. The confidentiality policy.

If appropriate, the counseling center might consider offering a support group for sexual assault survivors. Usually, facilitation by a professional counselor can help group members work through the difficult issues involved in recovery and help the group process stay focused in an effective direction. Professional counselors can also help support groups by intervening when a member becomes a threat to self or others. Support groups should be focused to the needs of the individuals. Thus, childhood sexual assault survivors should meet separately from adult survivors, male survivors will have different needs than female survivors, and so on.

Sample Protocol Checklist

The preceding checklist has been adapted from the Residence Life department of Allegheny College and materials from the State Council of Higher Education for Virginia.

In conclusion, rape is clearly a significant problem that impacts college campuses on many levels. Significant research on the problem has and continues to happen. Because of this research, we continue to make progress in becoming aware of the scope of rape and the causes. Programmatic efforts have opened new opportunities to impact students. Strong and clear policies and communication of these policies increase awareness of rape, prevention methods, response methods, and potential judicial consequences. Providing community members with these tools can serve them in being safe and protecting each other. We know that working toward preventing rape and better responding to rape will require a multitiered effort. Individual community members as well as groups have the power to prevent rape; each person's role is significant.

ANONYMOUS REPORT FORM FOR SEXUAL ASSAULT

The purpose of this form is to collect relevant information about sexual assault that affects members of our community. This report is anonymous and should be completed by anyone who receives information about a sexual assault. The location and date of the assault are the coordinating pieces of information on this form. In order to protect confidentiality, a generic description of the location is acceptable rather than a room number. Filling out this form will not result in an investigation.

1. Date of report: _____
2. Date of assault: _____
3. Location of assault: _____

Information about the Victim/Survivor:
Circle appropriate responses

4. Sex: Male   Female
5. Affiliation to University:

   Undergraduate Student
   Graduate student
   Relative or friend of student
   High School student visiting campus
   Faculty
   Staff
   Not affiliated with University
   Other

6. Current residence

   On-Campus Residence
   Off-Campus Residence
   Greek Housing
   Parent/Guardian
   Other

Information about the Assailant:

7. Was there more than one assailant: YES   NO

8. Was the assailant(s):   acquaintance   stranger

9. Sex of assailant: male   female

10. Assailant's affiliation to University:

    Undergraduate Student
    Graduate student
    Relative or friend of student
    High School student visiting campus
    Faculty
    Staff
    Not affiliated with University
    Other

Information about the Assault:

11. Type:
    Sexual Assault: oral vaginal anal other
    Sexual Contact: non-penetration penetration

12. Sought Medical Attention:
    YES   NO

13. Reported to other agencies:
    Campus Security/Police
    Local Police
    Counseling Center
    Health Services
    Don't Know

SEXUAL ASSAULT RESPONSE PROTOCOL

This protocol checklist serves to outline the critical steps for staff members responding to a victim of sexual assault. The checklist serves both as a reminder to which you can refer in order to ensure that victims have been made aware of all available resources as well as a document recording actions taken by staff members. Remember at all times the decisions remain in the victim's control.

Date each item when completed:

1. _____ *CONFIDENTIALITY.* Explain the limits of confidentiality with the victim and that you are required to:
   a. Report the incident to your supervisor in strict confidence.
   b. File an Anonymous Sexual Assault Report form with Campus Security.
   c. Inform student that no records of reports of sexual assault are kept in permanent academic records.

2. _____ *IMMEDIATE COUNSELING SUPPORT AND SAFETY.* Inform the victim of immediate available support from the on-call staff of the Counseling Center or other crisis services. This support person can give the victim additional information of services available. If appropriate walk victim over to the Counseling Center for an emergency evaluation. Ask victim if she or he has a safe place to go. If not look into temporary housing options.

3. _____ *MEDICAL SERVICES.* Discuss with victim medical resources available at the campus health center and local hospital. Inform the victim how current decisions about a medical evaluation and treatment may affect other options later (e.g., a "Rape Kit" is recommended if the student wants to pursue the case through the courts). Tell victim that the school will help provide transportation to any off-campus service if desired. Tell victim that physical evidence should be gathered within 72 hours of the assault, and recommend that they not change clothes, douche or shower during that time.

   Medical Options:
   Physical Exam: Helps determine the existence of sexually transmitted diseases, unknown injuries, and/or pregnancy. Some evidence of assault can be documented, but not to the extent of a "rape kit." Physicals can be conducted at the campus health center or local family planning agency or hospital emergency room.

   "Rape Kit": Otherwise known as a PERK (Physical Evidence Recovery Kit) involves a protocol to gather physical evidence (hair, blood, saliva, semen, etc.) that can be documented to be used later if the student chooses to press civil and/or criminal charges. It is only recommended if the student wants to preserve the option to prosecute through the court system; however, completing this evaluation does not mean that the victim MUST prosecute. Rape Kits are administered at the hospital.

4. _____ *HOSPITAL.* If the victim decides to go to the hospital, remind her or him to bring an insurance card. Call the emergency room before leaving. Tell victim to bring a fresh set of clothes to change into. If the victim has already changed, tell her or him to place soiled clothes in a paper bag (plastic damages evidence).

5. _____ *REPORTING OPTIONS.* Inform the victim about options for reporting the incident. The victim may file an anonymous report form for information gathering purposes only. No investigation will ensue. The victim may choose to report through the campus judicial system. Details of this process may be confidentially discussed with professionals in Student Life. The victim can choose to file a report with Campus Security. Usually the department can advise the victim about options to pursue the case through the legal system outside of the college. Remind student that any reporting options are entirely her or his choice.

6. _____ *ACADEMIC SUPPORT.* If the victim is a current student of the school, offer academic support as needed and make appropriate referrals for issues such as rescheduling tests and other academic expectations. Provide information on course withdrawal and medical withdrawals.

7. _____ *LIVING ARRANGEMENTS.* If the victim lives on campus explain that changes in living arrangements can be accommodated to reduce chances of continuing contact between the victim and alleged perpetrator.

8. _____ *LONGER-TERM COUNSELING RESOURCES.* Give victim a list of potential on- and off-campus resources for support groups and individual counseling. If known, explain any costs involved and other information known about the services. Offer to assist in making and accompanying the victim to the appointment.

9. _____ *DISCLOSING INFORMATION TO OTHERS.* Discuss with victim options for disclosing information about the sexual assault to family, friends, and significant others who may provide a source of support.

10. _____ *SECONDARY VICTIMS.* Assess if any secondary victims (e.g., roommates, witnesses, friends) were affected by the crisis and arrange for assistance and resources for them.

11. _____ *PHONE NUMBERS.* Give victim list of relevant phone numbers to call for further assistance. These resources could include:

> Counseling Center
> Emergency Room
> Health Services
> Campus Ministry
> Residence Life
> Security
> Local Police
> Rape Crisis Center
> Family Planning Center

12. _____ *FOLLOW UP.* If appropriate, arrange a follow-up meeting time with victim.

Chapter 11

RIOTING

PERSPECTIVES:
HERE'S WHAT PEOPLE ARE SAYING ABOUT CAMPUS RIOTS

For all activists who seek drastic social change, the university is an obvious target and a potential instrument of the greatest value. It is filled with young people whose natural idealism is as yet untempered by the patience and tolerance of maturity. These students are at a time of life when a normal feeling of revulsion against all authority easily can be diverted into violent antagonism toward existing political and economic institutions and policies. . . . The noisy clamoring of a handful of students may capture the headlines, but the vast majority of their fellows is either indifferent or even hostile toward them. . . .

–Columbia University President Grayson Kirk
June 1, 1965

Tired of a few skittish cops turning a mildly out-of-control party into a life threatening riot? Do your tear ducts still burn after last weekend's big soiree? Well, dammit the cops are going to bust up your party anyway so you might as well validate their aggression. Just follow the steps below to ensure a proper riot. By the time you're done the EPD won't be using tear gas, they'll resort to Napalm . . .

–The Official *Commentator* Riot Guide
Feature in University of Oregon's
Oregon Commentator
October 2, 1997

They treat us like animals, we'll act like animals.

–Freshman at University of New
Hampshire (UNH)
May 8, 1998

If everyone is so puzzled as to why UNH students are rioting, I think the answer is pretty simple–they're fighting back.

148

. . . We seem to have this understanding with the national press now: UNH = trouble. . . .

> −Cathleen Genova, student at UNH
> The New Hampshire Forum
> October 7, 1997

Over the years, colleges tended to wink at the alcohol policies, and then they started enforcing and changing policies without involving students in the decisions. It was the ideal set of circumstances to bring about these riots.

> −Arthur Levine& Jeanette Cureton, authors (1998)
> *When Hope and Fear Collide: A Portrait*
> *of Today's College Student* (Jossey-Bass)

I think the police made an utter mockery of the state, as well as the nation. We disagree with what's happening here. We think the students of UNH should stand up for their rights.

> −UNH Senior
> September 1997

The thing that is stupid is they did it for no reason other than to go into the street and set trashcans on fire. It's like their parents never taught them anything better to do.

> −Athens Police Chief about the
> Ohio University riots
> April 2000

When you have 23 officers injured, some of them with broken bones, and you see the size of the objects being thrown . . . We're not out there for fun and games.

> −Pullman Police Chief Ted Weatherly
> Commenting on the
> Washington State University riot
> May 4, 1998

It was a blast in all senses of the word. We came together as a school, burned some things, showed some skin and that's fine. It was Spartan pride.

> −Michigan State University junior
> March 29, 1999

What I have to say to East Lansing is that the riot is a symbol of freedom and we deserve it.

> −Michigan State University senior
> September 9, 1997

We're all moving out. I don't think you'll find any other permanent residents around here after this thing's over.

> −Beth Van Liere, East Lansing resident and former
> Chairperson of the Bailey Neighborhood
> Association about the MSU riots
> September 1, 1997

"Students Demonstrate for Their Right to Bear Beers"
  —*Times Union* (Albany, New York) headline
                         May 13, 1998

"College Protests are Sophomoric: All We Are Saying is
Give Beer a Chance"
                    —*Cincinnati Enquirer* headline
                         May 13, 1998

CAMPUS RIOTS OF TODAY

The above perspectives on rioting demonstrate the wide range of conflicts campuses and communities are currently facing. Finger pointing abounds and emotions run high. The students blame administration, the police and the media. Administration blames the student's upbringing and irresponsible attitudes. The media obtains dramatic photos and catchy headlines. The police find themselves in a no-win situation. The community residents and alumni of these schools are disgusted. What is going on here?

Many students involved in today's rioting liken the uproar of the 1990s to the campus unrest during the 1960s and 1970s. Some believe that their rights have been violated and they are protesting unfair university and law enforcement policies. One Michigan State University student wrote an editorial to *The State News* drawing similarities between the student rioting and the Boston Tea Party stating students may have a voice, but not a vote, "Clearly, we the students of Michigan State are being taxed without representation. Sound familiar? The founders of this great country also threw a party, and it was even more costly than a few windshields and a street light. . . ."

Here are some similarities and differences between the riots of the 1960s and 1990s:

Riots of Two Generations

1960s	1990s
Challenge values of authority	Challenge values of authority
Located on campus, heavy student involvement	Located on campus, heavy student involvement
Peaceful and violent demonstrations	Parties and violent demonstrations
Alcohol intoxication not a major contributing factor	Most participants drunk
Race and War central issues	"Right to Party" central issue
Targets of destruction—ROTC buildings, police	Targets of destruction—College towns, police
Media focal point—Four students killed at Kent State	Media focal point—"Real TV" footage of the MSU riot as part of segment on party schools

DOONESBURY® 1998 G. B. Trudeau. Reprinted with permission of Universal Press Syndicate. All rights reserved.

The chart below profiles some of the major riots affecting our campuses from 1996 to 2000. In this analysis we chose only the riots that either caused major damage or resulted in numerous arrests. Many other lower intensity incidents occurred on these and other campuses that still had a significant impact but were not included. Several campuses experienced "anniversary rioting" that occurred at lower intensity either before or after the more intense riot included in this chart. For instance, a couple of the campuses had annual riots around Halloween, some years worse than others. The riots analyzed here involved between 500 to 10,000 people and resulted in damage estimates ranging from $5,000 to $500,000.

Characteristics of Campus Riots 1996-2000

Number of Campuses Analyzed = 11
Number of Riots Analyzed = 20

Geographic Location			
	South	0	0%
	Northwest	2	18%
	Northeast	4	36%
	Midwest/West	5	45%
Possible Triggering Event	Alcohol Restriction Imposed	10	50%
	Athletic Victory/Loss	6	30%
	Tradition	4	20%
Time of Year	August-October	8	40%
	November-February	1	5%
	March-May	9	45%
	May-July	2	10%
Town-Gown Dynamics	Students Outnumber Permanent Residents	3	27%
	Students Roughly Equal to Permanent Residents	5	45%
	Permanent Residents Outnumber Students	3	27%

Characteristics	# YES	# No	# Unknown	% YES
Alcohol major contributing factor	20	0	0	100%
Campus enrollment 10,000+	10	1	0	91%
More then 15 people arrested	11	4	5	58%
Police injured/Police cars vandalized	9	4	7	45%
More than one riot at the school	6	5	0	54%

Intriguing observations emerge from this chart. Geographically, the rioting campuses seem to be clustered together indicating that copycat behavior may be occurring. Two schools were in New Hampshire, two in Colorado, and three in Ohio. Interestingly, so far no major riots have occurred in the South, a part of the country known for civil rights campus rioting in the 1960s and 1970s.

While it is difficult to pinpoint possible triggers for the riots, student interviews shed some light on the climate before behavior became out of control. "Alcohol restriction" rioting occurred after campus officials imposed a tighter reign on underage drinking, banned tailgating, or developed other drinking restrictions on the students. Police crackdowns on unruly parties also fell into this category. Limiting access to alcohol seems to be the biggest trigger for rioting at this time. There are many perspectives on this controversy, and we will address them later in this chapter.

Athletic victories or defeats also triggered rioting on several campuses. On large campuses where athletic teams are the source of school pride and identity, wins or losses of important games can result in an outpouring of out-of-control fans. Sometimes the athletic match does not even have to involve college sports. Many campuses in Colorado experienced student riots and disturbances after the Denver Broncos Superbowl victories.

Sometimes the rioting becomes a tradition. Schools tend to have annual big party weekends, and rioting can evolve out of these celebrations. As mentioned earlier, Halloween rioting seems to be a particularly favored pastime at some schools. Costumed rioters are especially difficult for investigators to identify and prosecute. With traditional rioting, students anticipate that rioting will occur at these times, and they prepare ahead of time, stockpiling bonfire kindling and spreading rumors of the riot repeat. Out of curiosity, groups of students will turn up just to see what will happen. Once the crowd has gathered a few instigators act outrageously and the riot is on.

The time of year also seems to have an important influence on rioting. Springtime seems to be the most popular time for campus riots. Many occur around the last days of school or spring party weekends. The beginning of the school year ranked second with Halloween weekend coming in a close third.

The campus and community relations or "town-gown dynamics" may be a critical factor. In many of the most destructive riots to date, the student population outnumbered or closely matched the population of the permanent surrounding community. Michigan State University, Penn State University, University of Connecticut, Washington State University, and Ohio University are large schools in small towns or cities. In some ways this setup may give students an inflated sense of "owning" the town and doing what they please. Often the students have an educational and economic advantage over many of the residents. Community members may be reluctant to confront students as the university may employ townsfolk, or local businesses may heavily depend on student patronization. Building resentment and tensions can easily escalate into fuel for the riots. One East Lansing resident commented on the MSU students' rioting by saying, "These kids do not seem to get the picture of what it means to be a resident in a community."

College students are not the only ones participating in these campus riots. High school students, alumni, community residents have all been involved. In the aftermath of a big sporting event, rival college students are also present. Nevertheless, we look at arrest rates as an indication of who is causing the trouble; college students of the campus where the riot took place usually account for about 75 percent of the arrestees.

The subsequent chronology details some of the more devastating riots on campuses in the last few years.

University of Colorado (CU) Boulder, Colorado May 2-4, 1997

Just before midnight on Friday May 2, police were called when two house parties at 14th Street and College Avenue overflowed into the street. A crowd of four hundred to five hundred people gathered around a bonfire in the middle of the street. They greeted police by throwing bricks, rocks, and bottles. The mob moved into the commercial area of

University Hill and began smashing store windows and vandalizing cars. By dawn the crowd had swelled to more than 2,000 people and one hundred officers were called to the scene. Police wore riot gear and used tear gas and rubber bullets to disperse the crowd.

The rioting continued into early Sunday morning when University Hill bar patrons left their establishments after "last call" and entered the streets to find police officers positioned and ready. Another clash ensued. Damage estimates from the two nights was $300,000. Twelve officers and many students were injured including some head injuries.

The history behind this incident involves a chain of events familiar to many campuses. First, in 1994 the university experienced an alcohol-related tragedy. A sophomore woman was killed in a drunk-driving accident. This unfortunate event combined with numerous community complaints regarding unruly student parties led to a law enforcement crackdown on underage drinking. The police targeted big parties, usually those within the Greek system. Resentment and tension began to build. At the same time the university beefed up its campaign to address alcohol problems on campus and increased educational and enforcement initiatives within the campus system.

In the fall of 1996, campus officials boldly decided to ban the sale of beer at football games and restrict alcohol use at tailgate parties. At the same time fraternities and sororities agreed to ban alcohol-related parties in their residences. Less than a year later they retracted that agreement, causing further conflict between students, the community and the police.

In the aftermath of the riot, town meetings were held and four task forces were formed to address issues of police-student relations, community building, violence, and alcohol. Despite campuswide involvement

in dealing with this event, smaller riots have plagued the CU campus for the last few years. Halloween disturbances have occurred annually for as long as people can remember. In 1999 CU experienced a post-Superbowl outbreak after the Broncos' victory, and in the fall CU and Colorado State University students were involved in a major disruption at Mile High Stadium after the football upset. During August 2000, a riot involving up to 1,000 people erupted after a block party got out of control. A large bonfire threatened trees and one hundred-year-old structures in the neighborhood. This latest riot led CU to form a "three strikes and you're out" alcohol discipline policy. Coincidentally, the same week of the riot the *Princeton Review* revealed that CU ranked number 5 on their list of top party schools in the country.

Because all of this rioting has cost the school and city of Boulder hundreds of thousands of dollars, local leaders and campus administrators are floating around the idea of developing a "rioting fee" likened to the annual student fee to help pay for the damages. The latest policy suggested by administrators has been called the "film and fine" policy. This tactic would involve hiring private contractors with video cameras and halogen lights to film student bystanders at riots. These bystanders would then be charged a stiff fine—up to $1,000 each in hopes spectators begin to view rioting more as a crime to stay away from rather than a sporting event to revel in.

Ohio University (OU)
Athens, Ohio
April 5, 1998

Ohio University has the dubious distinction of having the most bizarre rioting trigger of all—daylight savings time. When the clocks were set to "spring forward" on April

5, 1998, 2,000 OU students and others protested the fact that bars were forced to close an hour earlier. The 1998 riot marked the one-year anniversary of a spontaneous protest against the early closings the previous April. After the 1997 incident, which involved about 1,000 people and was much less violent than the 1998 riot, police invested in costly riot gear because they felt the safety of the officers was in jeopardy.

In preparation for the 1998 riot, camera crews were set to capture the action as students chanted "CNN! CNN!" Because of this, many blamed the media for creating a self-fulfilling prophecy. OU prides itself as an outstanding journalism school, and many have remarked how effectively OU students staged a sensationalized media event.

Police began by shooting foam bullets at the crowd, but the plan backfired as students goaded police to fire at them. The police then moved to wooden bullets. The students fought back with bottles, asphalt, and bricks.

One student commented, "It's a year after the big riot and people will probably celebrate this every year. We came down because we knew the cops would be here overreacting if something did happen. It's been great to watch."

University of Connecticut (UConn) Storrs, Connecticut April 25, 1998

During the annual "University Weekend" a crowd of 2,000 people taunted police and hurled bottles, cans, and rocks at them while eighty officers stood their ground on the perimeter of the dirt parking lot. A couch was set on fire. A Honda Accord was overturned. Still the police were motionless. According to the university police chief the police were told to take the approach of, "You can have a party, and you're clearly going to break the law–just don't break it on

a massive scale."

When the rioters attempted to put the couch on the Honda, police moved in with pepper spray to disperse the mob. By the end of the night, twenty-seven police cars had been vandalized.

The traditional party weekend occurs during the last couple of weeks before finals each year and had a reputation for getting out of control. Police were prepared to step in if they were needed, but their mere presence enflamed the situation for those who saw it as a violation of students' right to have a good time.

The university tried to provide alternative entertainment for students, but their plan failed miserably. Only one hundred students attended the university-sponsored party. Students claimed they were not interested because beer was not available to underage students.

By the end of the ordeal, UConn and state police arrested one hundred one individuals and the university disciplined ninety-two students. Six people received criminal convictions resulting in jail sentences and probation, thirteen people received criminal convictions that included suspended jail sentences and probation, seventeen people were placed in programs for first-time offenders, and forty-four people paid fines for noncriminal offenses. From the university disciplinary side of things two students were expelled, six were suspended, twelve were removed from the residence halls, and scores of others received warnings and probation.

Washington State University (WSU) Pullman, Washington May 3, 1998

May 1–3, 1998 was the worst weekend for campus rioting for several decades. Plymouth State College in New Hampshire,

156

Violence Goes to College

University of Kansas (Lawrence), and Michigan State University in East Lansing all experienced fire-setting, rock-throwing, glass-smashing, police-clashing disturbances involving large crowds of students. The weekend's most violent riot was at Washington State University.

The riot began with a party at the notorious "Golf Patrons Only" house, a rental residence on Greek Row nicknamed by a stolen sign. Police were originally called to the party in response to an unfounded report of a drunk driver-pedestrian accident at 12:30 A.M. When the two officers arrived on scene, they were greeted by two hundred rock-throwing partygoers. The officers quickly retreated while several bonfires were set in the street. The crowd grew as curious onlookers began to gather.

Other Pullman police were called in to close the three bars in the area. Subsequently, several hundred more students joined in the gathering in the street. At 1:30 A.M. the Pullman police chief divided his thirty-seven officers into two teams of twenty-two and fifteen officers. The plan was to have the teams confront the crowd from opposite directions and meet in the intersection. The plan failed. Communications efforts were hampered because the two teams were using different radio frequencies. Aggressive, intoxicated students drastically outnumbered the officers. Hostile bottle-throwing individuals halted the larger team. Students surrounded the smaller team.

Police supervisors did not anticipate that students would charge the officers. But they did. Carrying sections of chain-link fence as shields, kegs, bricks, frying pans, and even a manhole cover were projected at police. An officer was knocked nearly unconscious when a chunk of concrete struck his riot helmet. All fifteen officers in the smaller team were injured, many of them seriously. A state of emergency was declared and the crowd ordered to disperse.

By 5:00 A.M. an additional sixty officers were dispatched to WSU. Nine state patrol officers responded ill equipped for a riot because they did not possess riot shields. Eight of the nine were seriously injured by thrown objects. A small National Guard contingent was activated but not used. By 6:00 A.M. the riot was over and twenty-three officers were in the hospital. Five of the officers were awarded a Purple Heart distinction for their injuries.

Police confiscated cameras and videos of bystanders for their investigation over the next several days. With this evidence, police declared to the student body, "We know who you are!" Students quickly proceeded to dye their hair and alter their looks in other ways to avoid arrest. Flyers circulated the campus making jokes about the incident such as "Top Ten Reasons to Start a WSU Riot."

Two years later WSU is still feeling the hangover of the riot. On March 3, 2000 several hundred students gathered outside the Golf Patrons Only house. Six officers responded and some individuals began throwing bottles. The police acted swiftly by setting up a command center and calling for backup law enforcement agencies. Chanting emerged from the crowd and rumors flew—there's going to be a riot. Onlookers began to gather. Six individuals attempted to agitate the crowd. Approximately one hundred fifty officers in riot gear gathered behind the scenes. But it was probably student leadership that snuffed out the riot before it began. Greek leaders circulated the crowd telling people to go home. By 3:30 A.M. all was quiet again.

WSU has suffered a major public relations problem in the wake of the riot. Enrollment has dropped since 1998, and the footage of the riot continues to roll. WSU alumni Randy Stegmeier was quoted on spoakane.net, "Once it's (the bad public image) spread across TV screens especially, that damage is done and it takes a lot to undo because anytime you have an incident that even slightly mirrors that, it's like peeling the scab off. There it is again." Others speculate that WSU is under the microscope for being the center of attention in a small town.

Nevertheless, campus officials and Greek leaders have attempted to change the culture of WSU and prevent future riots from happening. Task force members developed a forty-page plan to systematically deal with the problems. Examining alcohol policies, expanding education, restructuring Greek residence, and enhancing student leadership training are some of the strategies. Student affairs faculty members participate in a walking patrol of College Hill every weekend. Alternative activities are being developed to offset the large street party attraction.

Pennsylvania State University (Penn State) State College, Pennsylvania July 12, 1998

The Penn State riot is unusual because it occurred during the time of year most students were not in class. During this weekend in July, the State College community hosted the annual Central Pennsylvania Festival of the Arts, but a combination of too much alcohol and a crowd of 1,500 turned this event into a disaster. By the time the riot was over sixteen police officers were injured, twenty people were arrested, and $150,000 worth of damage had taken place.

The riot took place in a section of town nicknamed "Beaver Canyon" because student high-rise apartment buildings line both sides of the street. Police state that within ten minutes a Frisbee game involving one hundred fifty people swelled to a rowdy crowd of 1,500 after the bars closed at 1:30 A.M. Three storefronts were damaged, thirty-three streetlights were broken, and at least one stu-

dent was burned when the crowd pushed him into the bonfire. By some reports, police stood back initially hoping the mob would wear itself out. Instead, it just gained momentum. Rioters got right in the officers' faces, challenging them to take action. Some students stripped naked and threw their underwear in the fire. The balconies of the high-rises became a public safety hazard as people threw objects from their apartments and cheered on the rioters. Some balconies held up to thirty people. One high-rise spectator commented he was so grateful to have "front-row seats for a major sporting event."

Police had difficulty identifying the rioters. Many of them left town after the event because school was not in session, and they were living elsewhere for the summer. Shortly after the riot, State College police began purchasing thousands of dollars worth of riot gear and received special training in crowd control. Penn State President Graham Spanier received criticism for not expelling the eleven Penn State students who were arrested. He was quoted in the Lancaster *New Era* as saying, "To kick somebody out of college is a life-changing event." During the same event in 1999 students were planning on heading over to Beaver Avenue just to see what would take place, but this time State College was ready for them and the weekend went smoothly.

The Festival of the Arts 2000 did not have such a good outcome. Once again, police used pepper spray and other riot tactics to disperse a crowd of 2,500 who inundated Beaver Avenue. The high-rises again were cause for concern as beer bottles were thrown into the crowd from seven stories above. Police moved quickly and contained the riot within an hour. Because of this swift response, extensive property damages were avoided. After the riot, police requested video footage taken by witnesses, and many voluntarily turned in their videos. Campus leaders voiced their disappointment publicly

given the effort and planning that had gone
into both the Festival of the Arts and the riot
prevention.

Michigan State University (MSU) East Lansing, Michigan March 27-28, 1999

The largest and most damaging campus
riot to date occurred at MSU in March 1999.
This riot was MSU's fourth in two years, but
rioting history at MSU dates back to the
1980s. On September 7, 1997, the "Gunson
Riot" erupted after MSU beat Western
Michigan University's football team on
opening day. About five hundred people
participated and $5,000 worth of damage
was inflicted. In late April 1998, email messages spread across campus urging people to
gather at Munn Field to protest the recent
school officials' decision to ban alcohol there
during football season. On May 1, 1998,
3,000 people showed and the peaceful
protest evolved into a riot (known as the
Munn Riot). Shortly after MSU was ranked
in a national survey as one of the leading
"party schools" in the country. On March
21, 1999, 1,000 people took to the streets
after MSU defeated Kentucky to enter the
Final Four competition (known as the
Kentucky riot). After Duke beat MSU in the
final four championship on March 27, 1999,
10,000 people swarmed the streets of East
Lansing causing up to $1,000,000 in damage
(known as the Duke riot).

The mayor of East Lansing said March 27
was the worst night of his life. Everyone
knew the probability for a riot that night was
high. MSU basketball coach Tim Izzo taped
a message to the students asking them to celebrate responsibly; however, when the segment was aired to the 3,000 students in
Munn Arena the sound was not turned on.
The university had arranged for a pep rally
and fireworks display after the game, but too
many students descended on the site.
Chanting began and someone threw a police
barricade in the fire. The riot was on.
Seventy fires were lit across town, one three
stories tall. A group of people stood on top
of the local Taco Bell and tore the tiles off the
roof.

MSU had perfected rioting by the time
the Duke riot erupted. In preparation for the
event, students froze beer cans to throw
through windows, stockpiled kindling, and
even had T-shirts printed with the logo
"Absolut Riot" (a spoof on the vodka's
advertising). They also learned that
anonymity is difficult to maintain in the age
of videotaping and the Internet, so a few
wore ski masks. Still a riot website containing more than one hundred photographs led
to the identification of thirty-three defendants before hackers entered the site to
uncover informants' names. Through metic-
ulous and undying determination, investigators arrested one hundred thirty-two individuals of which one hundred thirteen were
convicted of their crime. Seventy-one of
those arrested were MSU students. Of those
convicted ninety-four went to jail and many
were ordered to pay back the owners of
property that was destroyed.

Not only had rioters and investigators
perfected their skills by the Duke Riot, the
campus community developed innovative
approaches to prevention as well.
Community residents and students banded
together to attempt to stop the rioting. A
community group called the "Peace Team"
consisted of a handful of brave East Lansing
citizens wearing yellow jackets who roamed
the streets during the riot and confronted
rioters who were trying to flip cars and start
riots. A small group of students who call
themselves "SPARTY" (Students Pissed
About Riots This Year) in recognition of the
school mascot, attempted to sell T-shirts to
raise money to help pay back East Lansing
for riot damages.

In the year 2000, MSU beat Iowa State in the NCAA Basketball Tournament, and the celebration was peaceful. The East Lansing mayor credits strong education and the multiple convictions of the previous year's riot as determining factors in deterring a riot. A new ordinance passed by the city council gave police authority to establish police lines and safety zones, which prevented people from entering a designated area. Another ordinance passed making standing within three hundred feet of an illegal fire a disorderly conduct misdemeanor. Continued efforts are being made to mend the torn relations between East Lansing residents and MSU students. The local University Lutheran Church sponsored a community-wide conference called "No Future Without Forgiveness" to begin the reconciliation process.

WHAT IS A RIOT?

Definitions and Dynamics

Throughout the history of America, rioting has been a catalyst for social change. The perspective of the individual largely determines what constitutes a riot. What may be a peaceful demonstration or, more relevant to today's riots, a wild party to one person may be seen as a riot to another. We choose to abide by the definition suggested by historical rioting expert Paul Gilje in his book *Rioting in America,* "a riot is any group of twelve or more people attempting to assert their will immediately through the use of force outside the normal bounds of law" (1996, p. 4). "Force" refers to both violence and the threat of violence and the determination of what constitutes "force" is often circumstantial. The concept of spontaneity is absent from the definition as many riots are premeditated by a small group of people.

Retired U.S. Lieutenant Colonel Rex Applegate adds to this definition in his landmark book *Kill or Get Killed: Riot Control Techniques, Manhandling, and Close Combat, for Police and the Military* (1962). He makes the distinction that a crowd is not a riot because members of a crowd think and act as individuals. When agitators manipulate a crowd, members begin to lose their identity and merge into a primitive cohesive group.

The larger the group the more the anonymity is protected and the more normal moral restraints break down. For instance, many women participating in the college riots of the 1990s flashed bare breasts or took off their shirts entirely.

Simultaneously, members gain strength knowing that large numbers of people support their actions. When riot offenses begin to happen in rapid succession, the rioters can easily overwhelm police who are usually scrambling to react. As Northwestern University Professors David Haddock and Daniel Polsby comment in their article, "Understanding Riots," "There comes a point at which the police pass from inadequacy to impotence" (*Cato Journal,* 1994). During some campus riots, police have had to retreat because they were so outnumbered. As noted in the Washington State University riot, police ended up being surrounded by rioters. At the Penn State riot one man allegedly grabbed a police officer by the collar and shouted, "What are you going to do?!"

Rioters tend to act like a stampede. A triggering event sends a few noticeable leaders in a direction, and the rest of the group blindly follows. The triggering event can range from an athletic victory to bars closing one hour early for daylight savings time.

Once the starting signal is given—a rock through a car window or a couch in a bonfire—most of the crowd knows a riot is imminent. Haddock and Polsby emphasize that crowd psychology is crucial in the early stages of the riot because usually people who are looking to commit violent crimes do not want to be in the presence of hostile bystanders. Thus, a critical mass of the crowd must expect and desire the riot to begin.

According to Haddock and Polsby, the location of the riot is usually not determined by chance. Usually one or more logical focal points exist, and people instinctively know where to congregate. At CU Boulder, riots have started in front of the Golf Patrons Only house. At Penn State, they commenced at Beaver Canyon. Sometimes the location is symbolic of the cause for the riot itself. The Munn riot at MSU started there because of protests on alcohol restrictions during games at Munn Field.

First Amendment: Rights and Responsibilities

College protesters, like other American citizens have the rights of freedom of speech and assembly. College administrators and enforcers must take these rights seriously. Nevertheless, students and other protesters must be aware that they relinquish these rights when they break the law. According to Col. Rex Applegate, when the crowd begins to block entrances or exits, prevent free passage of individuals, use physical force on a person, throw matter, disturb the peace, use offensive instigating language, or commit any criminal act, the demonstration then becomes an "unlawful assembly." After announcing this state of unlawful assembly to revelers and demanding individuals disperse, law enforcement officers are then empowered to use reasonable force to restore order.

PLAYING A PART: ROLES IN A RIOT

There are many different ways people contribute to the outcome of a riot. Some get it going. Others sustain it. Often a large group watches and a small group tries to extinguish it.

Agitators

When we look across different riots in our nation's history, the agitators of riots tend to be young adults (average age twenty) with prior offenses and almost exclusively male. Agitators often plan for the riot and plant the seeds for the uprising long before the event takes place. They will spread rumors through email and by word of mouth to pique the interest of the masses. When the climate is right and the crowd has gathered, they will be the ones to take the risk of throwing the first bottle or flipping the first car in hopes that others will follow. During campus riots the agitators are usually outrageously intoxicated.

Haddock and Polsby suggest that agitators are often motivated by their need to uphold their reputation. Some students pride themselves on having reputations for hard partying or acting crazy. Witnesses may be surprised by who eventually gets sucked into the riot as these often unlikely participants have acted out of character, but they usually are not surprised by the ringleaders. Some agitators are chronic troublemakers who are

Agitator Excuses

Common Excuse	Agitator Quote	Additional Information
Authorities have blown this way out of proportion.	"I am not a bad person. The costs of my five seconds of stupidity are far overboard."	MSU rioter ordered to pay $5,000 for standing atop an overturned car.
Do I look like a rioter?	"Can we really look at [student] and say he is what a burglar looks like or what a rioter looks like? And I'd have to say he's not."	Attorney for Penn State rioter who defended his client on the basis that his actions resulted from recklessness not harmful intentions.
Wrong Place, Wrong Time	"I feel badly for [client]. It was just an unfortunate set of circumstances."	Attorney for another Penn State rioter who pleaded no contest to a misdemeanor charge of resisting arrest.
I don't remember what happened. I was too drunk.	"I was very intoxicated, more than I've ever been before in my life. I don't remember where we went or what happened to me."	WSU rioter's testimony during his trial for assaulting an officer. While he did not remember being actively involved in the riot, he did recall getting pepper-sprayed by police. Video cameras caught him pushing a dumpster toward police. He was eventually acquitted of the assault charges.
He said he's sorry, what more do you want!	"He apologized to his parents, for the grief he's brought them and the embarrassment they feel and the stress. Then he said he was very regretful and remorseful for participating in the so-called riot. . . . He wasn't out there yelling and screaming and leading a group of people with flags of anarchy, saying smash the machine. He just happened to be standing on the edge of a crowd when someone said help us tip this police car over."	Attorney for MSU student who pleaded guilty to flipping a police car. The student came forward after police posted a photograph of him on their Website. The crime is considered a 10-year felony, of which this student served 47 days.

looking to jump on the bandwagon of creating mischief or cashing in on crime opportunities (e.g., looting). Many of these individuals are not even college students, but local residents who want to get into the action.

In the aftermath of the riot, agitators and their lawyers will use a host of excuses to blend in with the "innocent bystanders."

As we will discuss in the solutions section of this chapter, campuses can not be seduced by this rhetoric if they are going to be effective in stopping agitators. A felony committed under the influence of alcohol is still a felony. If it only takes five seconds to commit the felony, it is still a felony. If you apologize for the felony, it helps, but it is still a felony.

Bystanders

Bystanders play a critical role in keeping the riot going. Curious on-lookers usually outnumber the agitators exponentially. Sometimes they will cheer on the destruction and treat the riot like a sporting event. Many are there because they just want to see what will happen next. In effect, they serve as an audience for the agitators. As the crowd grows and their chances of getting caught decreases, some will join in with the agitators.

Bystander apathy has long been an interest with social scientists, beginning with the Kitty Genovese case in 1964 when thirty-eight witnesses saw her being raped and murdered during an attack that lasted more than half an hour, and no one intervened. Initial research indicated that bystander apathy was an effect of the number of people present when an event was occurring. That is, a person would be more likely to give help if he or she were the only bystander present, than when there was a group. The larger the group the less likely any one person was to assume personal responsibility. This effect was labeled "diffusion of responsibility."

Later research by psychologist Mark Levine at Exeter University indicated that social presumptions of bystanders also play a role in the lack of intervention. In other words, people viewing violence will internally make a judgment as to whether or not the violence is legitimate. In the Kitty Genovese case, many witnesses assumed that the man beating and raping her was her husband or boyfriend and it was not their place to step

in. With campus rioting, we would argue, a similar social excuse crosses the minds of those who might otherwise step in. "Boys will be boys," or "college students are just having the time of their lives" are common comments that excuse normally inexcusable behavior.

In addition to cheering on agitators and failing to intervene, bystanders add to the riot by their sheer mass. Assistant City Attorney for East Lansing commented, "Once the fires started [during the riot] they became a point of congregation. The streets became so crowded and people became so unruly that the crowd impeded emergency vehicles. Not all the 10,000 people were acting unruly, but the problem is that there were 10,000 people."

For these reasons we make the bold statement that there are no innocent bystanders during a riot. The few brave counter rioters are not bystanders because they are actively involved in the resolution. Like the old saying goes, "If you are not part of the solution, you are part of the problem." We also support the notion that bystanders should be held accountable in part for the riot and should receive consequences.

Thin Blue Line

Many campus security officers and law enforcement officers of small towns are not prepared to handle a riot. Eugene Methvin, author of *The Riot Makers: The Technology of Social Demolition,* states, "Inexperienced and undermanned for riots [paralyzed law enforcers] fuel the fires, first by bumbling or inaction and then by overreaction" (1970, p. 84).

Even if the departments are adequately prepared for a riot, they remain paralyzed because they know their every move will be documented on someone's video camera. Witnesses at the Ohio University riot filmed officers spraying a student in the face with mace six seconds after he apparently complied with the arrest. The footage was aired repeatedly on news broadcasts.

Attempting to contain a riot is extremely stressful work for officers. Monitoring students' parties is not nearly as gratifying as other lines of police work. Students and other participants harass police officers and often attempt to embarrass them in order to get the attention of the media or to bait them into aggressive action. Officers are always outnumbered, and the power of the faceless mob can be overwhelming. In more than one campus riot, officers suffered serious injuries and were hospitalized.

Increasing numbers of campus security and police officers are receiving training and equipment to improve their crowd control tactics. Many of these strategies are listed in the recommendations section of this chapter.

Media

One need only look at recent history and the tremendous social changes that have occurred during the past thirty-five years to see how and why demonstrations are increasing. Extensive television coverage came into being at the same time these changes were occurring and service to communicate the turmoil of the times to the country.

–Capt. Charles Beene, Ret. 1992
Police Crowd Control, p. 14

The role of the media in campus rioting has hit the spotlight as both instigating the problem and providing evidence for intervention. Some campus administrators blame the media for creating a self-fulfilling situation by making such a big deal out of the anniversaries of riots. When the cameras show up, the students do too. In some ways, the media attention to campus rioting has helped make it a trendy thing to do.

Students compete for media attention by providing on-scene interviews and violent performances for the news crews. When the camera is on, the audience increases from a couple thousand to potentially millions. The power of this attention is too much to turn away. Often the footage of riot performances comes back to haunt the participants.

In East Lansing, the issue of using journalism footage as crime evidence caused a great controversy. A local newspaper objected to a judge's order requiring the paper to hand over three hundred unpublished photographs of the March 1999 riot. The newspaper claimed that this form of evidence gathering interfered with journalistic integrity. Student journalists were the most vocal in their objection. They claimed they would be violating trust they had with students who let them record the riot from their apartment windows and gave them interviews because they knew the reporters as fellow students. Prosecutors stood their ground and claimed that journalists have a legal obligation to testify to the court what they witnessed. Just because these reporters are students, they are not excused. They are journalists who witnessed crimes taking place and should not take sides in the issue. Some student reporters and photographers felt so strongly about the issue, they agreed to spend time in jail, if necessary.

The East Lansing Police posted fifty photographs confiscated by a freelance photographer on a special task force website. They hoped to ask the public for help in identifying the people in the pictures. More than 60,000 people accessed the site over the course of a month, and police received over five hundred tips. However, they closed down the site because hackers had found their way into a file that revealed confidential tip-offs from informants. The photographer, armed with three pro bono attorneys from Washington D.C., demanded the site cease existence due to copyright infringement. Despite the fact that the site helped lead to the successful convictions of dozens of riot participants, it was taken down.

There is another issue some people have with the media. Many see the coverage of the campus riots as a race issue. While the overwhelming majority of participants are white, no one has made note of this. Astute observers argue that if people of color were represented in larger numbers, the incidents would be called a "race riot." But because it is mostly young white men, the incidents are often described as "disturbances," "frat parties gone bad," and "youthful melees."

Counter Rioters

Fraternity brothers stand guard over a neighborhood business to protect it from rioters. Student leaders urge spectators to go back to their homes. Community residents attempt to distract rioters by engaging them in everyday conversation during the riot. Many stories emerge of brave individuals who attempt to take the speed out of the raging stampede.

Eugene Methvin calls this group "the decent majority." He claims in many riots counter rioters outnumber rioters, but that police fail to back up the counter rioters in the early stages of the riots.

RIOT STAGES

While riots appear spontaneous and unpredictable, most tend to develop in apparent stages over time. Much of our understanding of riot stages comes from Eugene Methvin, author of *The Riot Makers: The Technology of Social Demolition* (1970), and others who have analyzed decades of riots in our country. While they have not typically included campus riots in their investigation, many similar patterns can be identified. In describing these stages we have likened the riot process to a wildfire, because the analogy is compelling.

Stage I: "Drying the Tinder"– Preconditioning

Let's Get Gassed!
Spectator chants at the Colorado State University versus University of Colorado football game riot
September 1999

CNN! CNN!
Rioter chants during the Ohio University riot
April 1998

In the weeks, days, and hours before a riot, events take place that set the stage for violence to occur. Rumors pique curiosity. Agitators gather potential missiles (e.g., frozen beer cans) and bonfire kindling (e.g., old couches). A sense of in-group and out-group is fostered by editorials in the campus paper and social discussion. "Look at all the (administration, police, etc.) are doing to interfere with our rights," is the general theme. Gossip about impending restrictions and consequences can become highly exaggerated during this time.

Tension and excitement start to build as students anticipate what will happen next. Music and chanting can help fuel the emotion. During several of the campus riots, students blasted the Beastie Boys' lyrics "You've gotta fight for your right to party" out of apartment windows. Many participants baited law enforcement by shouting "F** the police." One Penn State student called the catchy chants "infectious." When Penn State president Graham Spanier arrived on scene, the chants became "Graham, Graham." Chants filled with loaded language and repetition have been known to have a hypnotic effect on some rioters. The emotional intensity of the chanting moves people to get caught up in the moment. Some have likened riot chants to war cries.

Stage II: "Striking the Match"– Precipitating Event

The precipitating event is the signal to all that now would be the appropriate time to get things going. In several cases, the precipitating event has been a campus athletic event or an annual party. In one case the riot was precipitated by a peaceful protest on alcohol restrictions. Students anticipate something big is going to happen with the buildup leading to this upcoming event. This anxious awaiting further sets the stage for the next phase of rioting.

Stage III: "Igniting the Fire"– Instigating the Riot

Someone has to make the first move. If the climate setting has been handled well by the instigators, it usually will not take much– an anonymous bottle thrown in the direction of the police officers, furniture dragged out of apartments onto bonfires, a rock thrown through a window. The behavior confirms what the spectators have been waiting for. The riot has begun.

The next few moments can be tenuous for the riot depending on how authorities handle the situation. If the police cannot or do not respond, the crowd reads anarchy and the situation becomes a "moral holiday." Most of the violence will take place within the first couple of hours of the riot.

Stage IV: "Feeding the Flames"–Magnet to Mayhem

At this point, the riot becomes a wildfire out of control. Law enforcement officers become quickly overwhelmed by the sheer mass and power of the mob, and usually must retreat or call for reinforcement. The riot takes on a life of its own as hoards of people are drawn into the chaos. As when handling a fire (real or symbolic) the enforcers can only hope for one of two things at this time–it rains (an outside force changes the momentum), or the fire loses its fuel (the students get too tired to participate anymore).

Stage V: "Wild Fire Containment"–Re-establishment of Order

At some point, the riot begins to lose its muscle and law enforcement moves into a better position to take over. When this shift of power occurs, rioters tend to jump ship quickly as the anonymity becomes diminished.

PREVENTION, INTERVENTION AND POST-RIOT STRATEGIES

The following suggestions are a compilation from several sources including Captain Charles Beene, Col. Rex Applegate, David Haddock and Daniel Polsby, and interviews describing "lessons learned" from campuses where riots have taken place.

Prevention

According to deterrence theory there are two tactics that effectively discourage potential criminals. First, there must be an increased probability that the perpetrator will be caught and the means for doing so must be visible and widely known. Second, the consequences must be harsh enough to make the costs of committing the crime outweigh the benefits.

Effective Code of Conduct and Appropriate Consequences

The student handbook must explicitly detail the type of rioting behavior that students will be held accountable for within campus policies. Many campuses have found themselves in a difficult position in their attempts to discipline students who were riot participants because the code of conduct did not take into consideration off-campus behavior. These schools then found themselves in the position of having to reinstate suspended and expelled rioters because their code of conduct did not encompass off-campus rioting. One MSU student was caught on videotape at an epicenter of the 1999 riot, was arrested for unlawful assembly, and did admit that what he did was wrong. Nevertheless he disagreed with the university's decision to suspend him because

he was not convicted in a court of law. He stated to the *State News*, "It was really against my constitutional rights. They basically kicked me out of school for nothing." MSU, like other schools, found rioters were indeed a "clear and present danger" to the campus and were able to hold them accountable to established conduct codes.

Students have admitted that being suspended or expelled from college is a far worse fate than any legal consequences they would most likely face. They know that when an individual is expelled from an institute of higher education it becomes virtually impossible to get readmitted somewhere else.

Finally, campuses must determine their stance on bystanders. As we have indicated, there are no innocent bystanders at a riot. If you are not actively trying to counteract the problem, you are part of the problem. However, handling bystanders is even a more difficult issue than disciplining rioters. At the very minimum, campus policies should indicate that those witnessing or encouraging riot activity will be held accountable for contributing to the riotous climate. Bystanders should then receive consequences appropriate to their behavior, from letters of warning to probation or more. Bystanders who refuse to disperse should have more severe consequences.

Training Student Leaders

Many campuses have found that student leadership is a very effective method for taking the steam out of an escalating situation. People tend to follow directions of others with whom they are familiar and who symbolize the interests of their group. The WSU riot fizzle of 2000 supports this claim. Here Greek leaders effectively convinced their fellow students to go home without incident.

Building Bridges

Conversations around the conflicts at hand can help minimize misunderstandings between parties. Schools should attempt to find mutually agreeable arrangements between students and campus officials that are legal, moral and effective. This last part must be stressed. "Agreeable arrangements" does not mean accommodation to student demands. Some schools retracted appropriate policies because of student pressure. Others altered enforceable policies so that they became loopholes. When negotiating with disconcerted parties, campus officials must be able to stand by their bottom line.

One school had a particularly difficult time with the rowdy section of their athletic stadium. The fans perceived the college crackdown on their section as unfair and the enforcement measures fuelled their anger. This school chose to have a conversation with some of the student participants and found that the students just wanted to have a good time. The officials replied along the lines of "we will not get in the way of your having a good time as long as you don't involve alcohol or destruction of property." This interaction became a first step in building bridges between these two usually adversarial groups.

If students are not open to a discussion with campus officials about potential solutions and no tangible roadblocks are identified, the prognosis for a positive outcome is poor. These students should seriously consider why they will not cooperate with efforts to prevent further destruction and bloodshed on their campuses.

Professional Development and Equipment for Law Enforcement and Campus Security

Depending on the size of the campus and each campus' potential for rioting, enforcement officials may need minimal protection and training or may need full riot preparation. As first-line responders with the need to take action quickly and decisively, campus enforcers cannot always depend on local authorities' ability to mobilize forces as quickly as needed. At a minimum, most at-risk campus enforcers should receive basic training in crowd management and control.

From there, tactics for intervention become increasingly invasive, and campuses will have to weigh the pros and cons of having such equipment at their disposal. Nonlethal riot control methods offer several options for officers. Tear gas canisters can be an effective means of dispersing the crowd, but often these canisters are thrown back at the officers. Plastic or rubber pellets fired at the rioter's torso can bring offenders into pain compliance, but drunken individuals can sometimes be immune to pain, so this technique might also backfire. Other strategies are outlined in the intervention and aftermath sections.

Protective gear for officers is essential if they are going to be handling riot situations. Multiple unprotected officers were seriously injured during campus riots because they lacked basic riot protection gear. Shields have proven to be one of the most effective protection devices in campus riots due to the brutal nature of the projectiles launched by students. As mentioned in the case studies earlier, officers have been hit not only by bottles and rocks but by manhole covers and concrete bricks as well. Other protective gear include riot helmets with visors, fire resistant jumpsuits, and body armor to protect knees, groins, thighs, forearms, and shoulders.

Intervention

At some point campus enforcers must make a decision to move from crowd management to crowd control when a riot situation is escalating. Two signals help officers make that decision. The first is the tone of the crowd. When celebratory exuberance turns into angry chanting, enforcers need to begin a different tactic. The second has been called the "upping the ante" phenomenon. This occurs when revelers begin to try to outdo each other through increasingly outrageous activity. When this behavior crosses the line of putting people in danger, especially the officers, crowd control is needed. Throwing of missiles is a good indicator that the crowd is getting unruly.

As mentioned earlier, as Americans, we have the right to demonstrate peacefully, but we lose that freedom when criminal activity takes place. At that time, enforcers must make it known that the gathering has become an "unlawful assembly" and that those who do not disperse immediately will face possible arrest. These announcements should be made slowly, deliberately, and repeatedly. The information should contain the reasons for the announcement and what students can expect if they do not disperse. Announcements should be repeated every three minutes and also be posted on highly visible banners. Photographs of the banners will serve as evidence that the police did declare the situation as a riot before acting.

The following list contains brief descriptions of interventions campus enforcers can use to bring an out-of-control crowd back into containment. For a more comprehensive review, the reader should consult Captain Charles Beene's *Police and Crowd Control: Risk-Reduction Strategies for Law Enforcement* (1992).

Show of Force

Once the riot has been declared, officers must be prepared to act swiftly. One of the first lines of offense is to present the crowd with an authoritative show of force. Large numbers of riot-prepared officers assembled in riot formation give many the intimidating presence needed to leave the area. Officers should remain as machine-like as possible, not showing any expression on their faces and definitely not retaliating with remarks or threats.

Divide and Conquer

As officers begin to take control of the crowd they should move to divide the group into smaller and smaller subgroups. Through the use of roadblocks and barricades, officers can direct rioters in a direction that makes it more difficult for them to assemble as a large group. Officers should also limit access by outsiders to the riot area. These tactics are along the lines of herding sheep. At all times, officers must be aware of an escape route for both themselves and the group they are trying to direct. A mob that is cornered will come out fighting. Pullman officers who responded to the Washington State riot learned that large mobs can easily surround small groups of officers, making for tragic consequences.

Decreasing Anonymity

Anonymity is a factor that fuels an out-of-control mob. Rioters do not believe that they will be held accountable for their actions, and thus, they are free to act without a social conscious. When we are able to put a face and a name to the rioters, the game changes. Photographs and videotapes have become instrumental weapons in the efforts to combat rioting. Plainclothes officers can mingle with the crowd or be posted on rooftops to detect the instigators behind the scenes. Anyone in the role of recording the events of the riot must be prepared to become targets of violence themselves as rioters attempt to destroy the evidence.

Take Out the Leaders

Just a few agitators are responsible for creating the energy that eventually involves thousands of people in destruction. Most rioters are ambivalent about their participation, and would not engage without the urging of the instigators. When these leaders are no longer in a position of influence, the followers drop out. As Eugene Methvin stated, enforcers must act by, "pinching off the criminal spearheads with precise and overwhelming force."

Effective Communication

During the escalation of a riot, clear lines of communication and command must be established. Most agencies will need to simplify their command structure to give appropriate individuals authority to make decisions quickly.

Riot Aftermath

During the riot aftermath several strategies can help expedite the investigation and assist in damage control.

Handling the Media

Campus authorities must be savvy in their reactions to the media. On one hand, several campus leaders have been criticized for their public minimization of the campus violence. Pictures of students flipping cars and hurling bottles does not fit in with the public's perception of a mild campus disturbance. On the other hand, visible outrage and mass condemnation of the student body will further alienate the fragile student–administration relationships. Negative buzzwords like "catastrophic" and "devastating" can create a very damaging image for the campus.

Campuses should appoint a well-trained spokesperson to get accurate facts about the riot to the media before others fill in the holes with misinformation. The spokesperson must refrain from saying "no comment," as this phrase has been associated with covering up a larger story. Bluffing and lying to the media never works as experienced journalists often can discover the truth very easily. Comments to the media should be contained to short sound bites of twenty to thirty seconds that fall into one of two categories. Either, "We are very concerned about what has happened, and we are doing the best that we can under the circumstances," or "We are trying to gain cooperation on this matter to get a better understanding of what has happened and what we can do to prevent it from happening again."

Investigation

In addition to the investigation tips suggested in Chapter 7, campus officials may consider additional tactics when facing rioting. Many campuses have had great success in identifying perpetrators by posting photographs on websites. Tipsters are even more forthcoming with information if reward money is tied to the eventual conviction of a rioter. However, anonymous means of reporting must be ensured so informants do not become targets of revenge. Conducting door-to-door interviews in the neighborhoods where the riots have taken place has also helped investigators. Very often these informants are motivated to seek justice on the individuals who destroyed their property and community.

Clean Up

Some believe that immediate clean up is necessary to remove the negative image of destruction from campus consciousness. Others suggest that those who have been identified as contributors to the riot work toward putting back together what they have torn apart. In any event, the clean up process while sad, can help bring communities back together by working hand in hand on a common goal.

Chapter 12

HATE CRIMES

"You shouldn't be most shocked that 9,235 hate crime offenses were reported to the FBI in 1998. You shouldn't be most disturbed that 212 of these crimes occurred in our colleges and universities. And you shouldn't be most concerned that a study on sexual orientation biased hate crimes showed that victims of these hate crimes suffered greater effects for a longer period than victims of non-biased crimes of a similar nature. What you should be most shocked, disturbed, and concerned about is the fact that research suggests that these discoveries reflect only a small fraction of the hate crimes that occur in our country and on our campuses because underreporting is so prevalent."

–Chris Bollinger
Director of Residence Life Heidelberg College
Presentation to the BACCHUS & GAMMA Peer
Education Network Regional Conference, April 14, 2000

WHAT IS A HATE CRIME?

CAMPUS VIOLENCE EXPERTS Hoffman, Schuh, and Fenske, editors of *Violence on Campus* (1998), define hate crimes as "words or actions that are intended to harm or intimidate a person or group due to race, gender, sexual orientation, religion, or other group identification." In the *Hate Crime Statistics* report the FBI identifies two categories of hate crimes: "crimes against person" and "crimes against property." Crimes against person include murder and non-negligent manslaughter, forcible rape, aggravated assault, simple assault, and intimidation. Crimes against property include robbery, burglary, larceny-theft, motor vehicle theft,

arson, and destruction or vandalism of property.

According to the U.S. Department of Justice, hate crimes can fall into one of three types. *Reactive hate episodes* occur in response to a triggering event the perpetrators feel justifies their anger. In these cases perpetrators of hate crimes believe they are standing up as pillars of justice for the whole community by acting in hate against a visible group. Perpetrators looking for excitement commit *impulsive hate episodes*. The payoff for these types of hate crimes is mainly social. The perpetrator receives ample approval from like-minded peers who believe such action is

171

fun. The third type of hate crime is the *premeditated hate episode*. In these cases, perpetrators actually declare "war" against another group of people. Usually, an organized group such as the Ku Klux Klan (KKK) or the White Aryan Resistance supports these perpetrators. Following are five recent examples of campus hate crimes, which show how hate crimes can vary in implementation methods and degrees of violence.

- "Die Faggot Die" is written on a residence hall room door.
- At Penn State several black, Asian, and Latino students received an email message directed at black students. The author described minorities as "savages." The message also stated, "Every time you scan your ID to the dorm, every time you eat on campus, and every time you log into your computer— we are watching." The message was signed, "Long Live Amerikka." – Reported by Scott Carlson in the 9/24/99 issue of the *Chronicle of Higher Education*.
- Two homemade bombs exploded at Florida A&M University, a historically black university. "The bombings occurred on campus in men's rooms and were followed by anonymous, racially charged phone calls to a local television station." –Reported by Bill Schackner in the 11/10/99 issue of the *Post-Gazette*.
- Matthew Shepard, a gay college student at the University of Wyoming, was brutally beaten into a coma and left to die tied to a fence. –Reported by multiple sources in October 1998.
- In 1999, Benjamin Smith, a former student at Indiana University, went on a hate-filled shooting spree that raged across Illinois and Indiana. During the rampage, he shot and killed a black man who was a former Northwestern University basketball coach. He also murdered a Korean graduate student and injured eight others including six orthodox Jews and two Asian Americans. Smith was a member of the World Church of the Creator, a white supremacist group. –Reported by the U.S. Department of Justice, Community Relations Service.

Unfortunately, these examples are not unique. They represent the spectrum of crimes that could occur on our campuses. In this chapter, we will conduct a close examination of hate crimes and what we, as campus-community members, can do to help prevent hate crimes from occurring. In the first part we examine an overview of campus hate crimes, the causes of hate crimes, and the impact of hate crimes on victims. In the second part of this chapter, we will provide suggestions for preventing and responding to hate crimes as a community. Our focus will be on the violence of hate crimes and *not* on the law versus freedom of expression debate. Regardless of the outcomes of such a debate, the violence inherent in hate crimes has a negative impact on college student communities and individuals.

CAMPUS HATE CRIMES

As noted in the 1998 FBI *Hate Crime Statistics* report, 7,755 hate crime incidents and 9,235 hate crime offenses were reported to the FBI by 10,730 law enforcement agencies. Of these offenses, 68 percent were crimes against persons. Intimidation was the most frequently reported. According to the same report, colleges and universities reported 212 hate crimes. Following is the breakdown by bias.

Bias Group	Number of Incidents by	
	Nation	Colleges and Universities
Racial Bias	4,321	97
Religious Bias	1,390	33
Sexual-Orientation Bias	1,260	67
Ethnicity/National Origin Bias	754	15
Disability Bias	25	0
Multiple Biases	5	0

Jessica Turco in a website article, "Campuses Challenged with Confronting Hate Crimes" indicates that colleges and universities are required to supply crime statistics of bias-motivated crimes by the Jeanne Clery Act of 1990 and the Higher Education Reauthorization Act of 1998. Even though this requirement exists, there is suspicion that hate crimes are underreported.

One reason for low numbers is the difficulty in proving that a crime is bias motivated. Even in the Matthew Shepard tragedy, the initial speculation of motive for his attack was aggravated robbery, not hate. A second speculated reason is that colleges are concerned about how a reported hate crime might affect the image of their institution. Hoffman and colleagues reference an article in the *Chronicle of Higher Education* in their book *Violence on Campus* that questioned reporting by colleges and universities:

Are colleges and universities oases of harmony, without any hate crimes? Or do colleges just hate to report them? The annual campus security reports submitted by colleges are supposed to tell whether any crimes were motivated by bias. But of the 487 colleges that sent reports for 1996 to the *Chronicle,* just over one-third listed the category of hate crimes. And only a handful of those colleges said they actually had a hate crime occur on campus. (1998, p. A57)

Sexual-orientation hate crimes may be a particularly damaging source of violence in our campus communities. Dr. Karen Franklin conducted a study of five hundred young adults in the San Francisco Bay Area on the motivations of hate crime perpetrators. In this study she found sexual-orientation-biased hate crimes seem to have a high degree of cultural acceptance. Dr. Franklin found that one in ten of the respondents admitted to physically harming or threatening people they believed were homosexuals. Another 24 percent stated they participated in anti-gay name calling. Of the men surveyed, 18 percent admitted physically harming or threatening, and 32 percent admitted name calling. While most of the population believes that violence and harassment is wrong, this study indicates that 10 percent of the population chooses to engage in the activity anyway. We can reasonably conclude that engaging in violence directed at perceived homosexuals receives more cultural support.

The Culture of Hate: Have We Made Any Progress?

1930s	1990s
A homosexual is interrogated about his male lovers. When he refuses to give details about them, he is beaten up.	Two suspected homosexuals—one black, one white—are attacked and beaten to racial and sexual epithets. One of the victims suffers from severe injuries to the face and head.
An influential academic study is published arguing that people of African descent show genetic defects in behavior and intelligence.	An influential academic study is published arguing that people of African descent show genetic defects in behavior and performance.
A newspaper article demands the death penalty for homosexual activities.	A high-ranking city government official tells a newspaper that a deadly plague killing hundreds of thousands of homosexuals is "divine retribution" for their ungodly lifestyle.
Swastikas and other racist graffiti are painted onto numerous shops, schools and residences.	Swastikas and racist graffiti are painted onto numerous shops.
Hundreds of synagogues are destroyed.	Hundreds of black churches are torched.
By law, Germans are forbidden to marry or have sexual relations with persons of "alien blood," later clarified as "Gypsies, Negroes, and their bastards."	By law, homosexuals are forbidden to marry or have sexual relations with each other.

Source: "Campus Current" of *Link* magazine.

CAUSES OF HATE CRIMES

The Sociological Perspective

Communities can support hate crimes through a cultural climate of intolerance. Knowing this, many educators and prevention-minded people encourage tolerance; however, the concept of tolerance challenges many. What it means to one person is not what it means to another. For some tolerance means, "I leave you alone, and you leave me alone." In order to prevent hate crimes communities must go well beyond this limited perspective. On the other hand a healthy co-existence among different cultures does not necessarily mean that everyone must agree to the same values and priorities. Rather the goal of diverse communities must be to strive toward an acceptance and even an embracing of differences among members of our community and members of the human race.

According to *Campus Violence: Kinds, Causes, and Cures* (1993) edited by Whitaker and Pollard, there are multiple factors that promote intolerance: lack of knowledge, peer group influences, increased competition for resources, inequity in opportunity, minority mistreatment, and an increase in voluntary separatism.

Lack of knowledge and experience can contribute to intolerance. College students come from a variety of different backgrounds and are thrust into a community of people with different values, experiences, ethnic backgrounds, races, and sexual orientations. In a study on Causes of Hate Crime: Economic Versus Demographic, Donald P. Green, found that large demographic shifts can be a predictor for hate crimes. The adage, "we fear what we do not understand," certainly applies to intolerance.

Peer affiliation is an important social need and a powerful force. No matter what the circumstances, people inherently seek out others like themselves. People associate with groups who share their perspectives. Sometimes this group association becomes negative when it causes hostility toward members outside of the group.

Carl Jung and Joseph Campbell stressed the need of the social group to foster the development of individual potential. When the individual is living primarily to glorify and protect the group (nation, class, community), the members become increasingly hostile, belligerent, narrow minded and mean spirited to all designated "outsiders." Whitaker and Pollard, *Campus Violence: Kinds, Causes, and Cures* (1993, p. 160).

Group influence is demonstrated by the fact that hate crimes are committed by multiple perpetrators. Group-perpetrated hate crimes are much less likely to be reported to the police and likely to be more violent, as noted in Dr. Dunbar's 1995 study on hate crimes. Although negative peer influence promotes intolerance, positive peer influence can be a productive force. Later in this chapter, we will address this prevention measure.

Increased competition for resources and the perception of unfair treatment have also been factors contributing to intolerance. Limited funding and space for diversity-oriented groups and programming when contrasted to highly-funded campus priorities (e.g., athletics) can create an "us against them" attitude.

Additionally, the perception of unequal aid packages also has created hostile feelings between groups. Many believe that students of color receive unfair advantages in scholarships and financial aid packages. According to at least one study, the perception does not reflect reality. In actuality, according to the Department of Education's study on the 1986–1987 school year, the difference in financial funding between minority and non-minority students was not considerable.

Inequity in opportunity creates division among students, and consequently, promotes intolerance. This concept goes beyond the idea that everyone should have a chance to apply for the same positions on campus or the same financial aid packages. Academic classes may not be inclusive of relevant material from minority scholars. Events on campus may not be inclusive or representative of the diverse backgrounds of community members. The school viewbook, the school newspaper, or the school radio station may not be representative of all students on campus. Each of these pieces play into a perceived, if not real, inequity in opportunity for diverse groups of the community.

Minority mistreatment creates a cycle of intolerance and violence. Writing on walls or doors, inappropriate joke telling, and name calling all serve to make the environment uncomfortable, if not hostile, for minority group members. More subtle forms of mistreatment lie in lowered expectations for minority group members, academically or otherwise. When minority students are mistreated, they can feel more hostile toward majority group members and mistreat them, thereby causing misperception about the minority group, causing minority mistreatment.

Voluntary separatism can contribute to intolerance as well. Voluntary separatism occurs when minority students choose to segregate themselves from the mainstream. This choice can reinforce the "we versus them" mentality among the different groups on campus. There are some significant positive aspects of voluntary separatism, though. Voluntary separatism allows minority students to gain personal support and validation as well as cultural experiences and knowledge that may not be accessible in the mainstream.

Lack of knowledge, peer group influences, increased competition for resources, inequity in opportunity, minority mistreatment, and an increase in voluntary separatism are factors that promote intolerance and contribute to hate crimes from a community perspective.

There are other factors that contribute to hate crimes, namely, the characteristics of the perpetrators. We must answer the questions "Who are perpetrating these crimes?" and "What is motivating them?"

The Perpetrator Perspective

Dr. Edward Dunbar conducted a study, Hate Crime Patterns in Los Angeles County: Demographic and Behavioral Factors of Victim Impact and Reporting of Crime involving 1,459 hate crime cases. In this study, he found that the perpetrators of the more violent hate crimes tended to be young white males with a history of violence and substance abuse issues. Less than 5 percent of these perpetrators were members of a hate gang (e.g., KKK, neo-nazi, and so on). In other words, contrary to popular belief this research shows that hate gang involvement is not a predictor for some of the more violent perpetrators. Nevertheless, Dr. Dunbar

also found multiple perpetrator hate crimes were significantly less likely to be reported to the authorities and multiple perpetrator hate crimes were significantly more violent than single perpetrator hate crimes.

Sexual-orientation-biased hate crime perpetrators may have their own set of motives. Dr. Franklin conducted a study entitled, Psychosocial Motivations of Hate Crime Perpetrators: Implications for Prevention and Policy. In this study, she found that perpetrators of sexual-orientation-biased hate crimes had four sources of motivation:

• Self-Defense—Perceived that a person of a different sexual orientation made a pass at them.
• Ideology—Believed it is their moral obligation to distribute justice for something wrong.
• Thrill Seeking—Thought it would provide some excitement.
• Peer Dynamics—Wanted to prove themselves to their peer group.

Further Dr. Franklin indicates perpetrators of hate crimes appear to have low self-esteem and an unfulfilled need for belonging. They tend to have a very narrow view of what is right and what is wrong, and limited ability to see things from another's perspective. Often their hateful belief system is fueled into action by diminished inhibitions either affected by substances or peer influence.

THE IMPACT OF HATE CRIMES ON VICTIMS

Hate crimes impact individuals and communities. Individual victims of hate crimes experience a heightened sense of vulnerability, a decreased sense of self-worth, and a loss of trust in people. Since victims of hate crimes are victimized due to their membership of a group and not because of personal actions or decisions, other members of the

same group who are not attacked also feel a heightened sense of fear and vulnerability.

The location where hate crimes occur is usually no accident. Perpetrators are intent on sending a message, and that message is, "Your kind is not welcome here." In his study on hate occurrence in Los Angeles, Dr. Edward Dunbar found that the majority of hate crimes were committed in public places. Those occurring in the victim's neighborhood were typically more violent.

Dr. Herek has authored multiple books in the area of hate crimes. In a study on the impact of hate crime victimization, he found that victims of sexual-orientation-biased hate crimes had higher levels of depression, stress, and anger for up to five years after the incident, where victims of nonbiased crimes experienced a drop in depression, stress, and anger after two years.

Additionally, he found that fewer hate crime victims reported the crimes than did the victims of nonbiased crimes. Given, Dr. Franklin's findings on the higher level of cultural acceptance of sexual-orientation-biased crimes, we can speculate that victims fear their cases will not be taken seriously and that they will not receive the same support as victims of nonbiased crimes.

PREVENTING HATE CRIMES AS A COMMUNITY

Although there is not a great deal of research on what prevention methods yield the best results, there are many different plans and approaches for hate crime prevention. All these plans agree that only a multi-tiered approach will be successful. The model we will examine requires a collaborative effort from the campus and surrounding community, utilizes multiple mediums, and targets both individuals and the campus culture.

Again, building partnerships both within campus agencies and among community agencies is critical in dealing with all forms of violence. Partnerships become even more imperative in the event of a hate crime, due to its further reaching impact. Campus and community alliances provide a greater network of resources for programming, training, prevention, and responding.

Our prevention model is a compilation of the following resources: *Stop the Hate* website: Hate Prevention Steps for Schools (http://www.stophate.org/preventionsteps.html); *Violence on Campus* (1998) edited by Hoffman, Schuh, and Fenske; *Campus Violence: Kinds, Causes, and Cures* (1993), edited by Whitaker and Pollard; *Responding to Hate Crimes and Bias-Motivated Incidents on College/University Campuses* published on the U.S. Department of Justice website (www.usdoj.gov/crs/); and *The Critical Years: Young Adults and the Search for Meaning, Faith and Commitment* (1991) written by Sharon Parks.

Sending Clear Messages

The first step in sending clear messages is to create a clearly stated hate prevention policy. The team creating the policy should have representatives from faculty, staff, administration, and students. If the policy is to be effective, it will need the support of the institutional leaders and community members. The policy should:

- Underscore the fact that each hate crime has many victims, not only the targeted victim, but also members of the same group.
- Provide clear directions for faculty, staff, administration, and students and outline the role each should play in preventing and reporting hate-motivated conduct.
- Reflect the value the institution places on respecting diversity.
- Define hate crimes and be inclusive of the categories covered by the law including race, sexual orientation, religion, and disability.

- Allow community members the freedom to express their thoughts, concepts, and ideas.
- Clearly define parameters and consequences for bias-motivated crime.

In order for the policy to be effective it must have the support of the community and be enforced by the community. Such a policy serves to connect community members on the most basic issue that bias-motivated harassment and violence is wrong and unacceptable.

Training the Campus Community

Once a policy is created, the campus community needs to be trained on what the policy states and how they will be involved in its implementation. Training can be facilitated by a number of resources: community members with an expertise in the area of hate crimes, campus security, or outside groups specializing in the area of hate crimes in cooperation with teams of representatives from faculty, staff, administration, and students. The specific knowledge being shared may require expert support, but the institutional, community leadership should be visible to the greater community.

The training should include the hate crimes policy, the causes of hate crimes, perpetrator motivations, how to identify potential issues, hate crime prevention, how to respond to harassment, how to report harassment and violence, and the different support resources available to a victim of hate crimes. For example, the institution community members, campus counselors, health center, campus safety, the local police, the Civil Rights Office, and so on.

Providing Diversity Programs

Diversity programming and a more balanced academic curriculum offers minority students the opportunity to identify with and feel valued for their cultural heritage and allows nonminority students a greater opportunity to expand their knowledge and experience of another culture. These educational attempts help to increase positive peer influence, can serve to decrease minority mistreatment, and increase the perception of equity in opportunities. Positive experiences of other cultures challenge community members to rethink assumptions used to justify mistreating people. When this experience occurs in greater numbers, it swings the peer influence in a more positive direction.

Diversity programming should not be left solely to a specific student club or a specific office. These programs are often more successful when there are collaborative efforts to bring them about. Diversity programs that are simply social interaction between members of different cultures have been proven to be less effective. Research indicates that a common goal or purpose shared by the two groups is important to make integration effective.

Diversity programs may take many forms: notable speakers and presenters, group discussions, role plays, cultural awareness games, musical performance, art exhibits, or roundtable discussions of issues of hate and prevention. The academic curriculum may include a diversity core, special presenters, various cultural studies, the use of "real world data" in economics or statistics classes (e.g., import/export ratios of a Third World country), the use of culturally different authors and writings, and so on.

One of the most powerful diversity programs to date has been the documentary *Journey to a Hate Free Millennium.* The program, promoted by Campuspeak (www.campuspeak.com) is the work of two Los Angeles filmmakers, Brent Scarpo and Martin Bedogne. Their documentary centers on many of the recent hate crimes that have captured national attention, and features interviews with family and friends of many of the victims. Scarpo is touring college campuses with a program centered around the documentary.

Reducing Existing Tensions

Sometimes the involvement of an objective third party can serve to reduce tensions between conflicting groups. The U.S. Department of Justice provides a Community Relations Service that offers both emergency services as well as ongoing technical assistance to campuses experiencing bias conflict.

Seeking Structured Integration Opportunities

Integration opportunities bring together diverse students, faculty, staff, and administration for a common purpose or goal. Successful integration experiences are active not passive. They work together sharing ideas and the chores of a common project. Integration helps increase the experiences individuals have with others from different backgrounds and cultures, create more positive peer influence, decrease minority mistreatment, and limit the division that can come from voluntary separatism. As stated earlier, integration will not be effective unless these various groups have a common goal or purpose. Some possible integration opportunities include community service programs, mentoring programs, neighbor-

hood clean-up programs, or art appreciation programs.

Finding Meaning

Sharon Parks, in her book *The Critical Years,* identifies a critical developmental process college students engage which she calls "meaning-making." She discusses how faith development is greatly impacted by making meaning out of life occurrences, especially challenges to our core belief systems.

Hate crimes can often pose such challenges to the campus community as individuals wrestle with their own beliefs, religious teachings, and morals. As such, university ministries and religious groups on campus can play an important role helping people put such events into a helpful spiritual perspective. As students make meaning out of life occurrences, they have an opportunity to learn how to treat people as human beings even if they are in disagreement about some of their choices or values.

In the aftermath of the Matthew Shepard tragedy, hate groups gathered under the guise of religion, and may have confused some who were trying to grapple with their own religious teachings about homosexuality and morality. Spiritual organizations on campus can play an active role in helping people make sense out of all the mixed messages they are receiving.

Allowing for Voluntary Separatism

As mentioned earlier, voluntary separatism can be part of the problem in fostering misperceptions and "in-group/out-group" mentality. However, voluntary separatism can also have positive effects on a diverse culture. Voluntary separatism allows students to find support and validation in their beliefs. It increases the opportunity for individual and group cultural development. The potential benefit of voluntary separatism is a feeling of belonging for some minority students and an increased sense of self-esteem. If structured well, one culture does not suffer at the expense of others. At a school with a small population of minority students, these students have even less opportunity to find validation in the mainstream. The potential positive benefits seem to outweigh the potential drawbacks.

RESPONDING TO HATE CRIMES

Perpetrators look for a reaction from the community after they have committed a hate crime. If the hate crime is ignored, they will interpret the inaction as implicit support for their beliefs. Thus, a swift acknowledgment and response by campus officials is crucial.

A first step in this process is to have an effective reporting procedure. As we mentioned at the beginning of the chapter, most campus hate crimes go unreported. This is largely due to the fact that most victims are not aware of or do not have access to proper resources that can offer assistance. Anonymous reporting is helpful in many cases, and some universities offer email reporting. Furthermore, reporting does not necessarily have to go directly to campus security. Sometimes students have built relationships with other departments on campus such as the Dean of Students or club officers and may feel more comfortable reporting the incident there first. These staff members then can serve as a liaison to direct the victim to appropriate resources.

For a comprehensive response to violent crimes, please refer to Chapter 9. Responding to hate crimes specifically, however, can differ from responding to other violent crimes. In this chapter, we have learned that hate crimes, by their nature, impact a wider population; therefore, we must consider a broader group when determining the support services to be provided. Also, the duration of stress, anger, and fear produced by a hate crime is significantly longer than the duration of stress, anger, and fear produced by a nonbias-motivated crime of a similar nature. Although, this is not an immediate response issue, it must be considered in the plans for long-term healing of the community and its members.

Finally, when hate crimes occur, the entire community should be part of the response. Perpetrators of hate crimes seek moral or peer group justification. Student, faculty, administrative, and staff leaders can oppose that justification with a united front of positive leadership opposing hate crimes. University ministries and religious groups can also be an integral part of the stand against violence and harassment. In the aftermath of a hate crime and necessary evidence collection, the community should work together to promptly clean up the damage and prevent further hate-filled activity or retaliation.

Case Example from *About Campus:* Matthew Shepard and the University of Wyoming

The Matthew Shepard murder of October 6, 1998, as described in Chapter 1, threw the small community of Laramie, Wyoming into upheaval. The months of media circus afterward compounded the damage. The University of Wyoming, through determined leadership and community compassion, brought from this tragedy tremendous healing and connection in a way that can serve as an excellent response model for schools facing similar devastation. Dr. James Hurst, Vice President for Student Affairs at the University of Wyoming, wrote a brilliant and deeply personal article in the July-August edition of *About Campus*. In the article he highlights several efforts by the University of Wyoming, which made the response to the tragedy a greater healing process for the community.

Campus Leadership Involvement

The university president was heavily involved and visible with the work of the Crisis Intervention Team and with the memorial services and vigils. His stance against hate and violence and his acceptance of differences among individuals were important to provide a sense of leadership in a time of crisis. Throughout the ordeal he was very visible to the campus and the media, and stood by his message that his university and community were about compassion, not hate.

Work of the Crisis Intervention Team

The team served as the focal point for coordinating media management, communications, memorial and vigil services, roles of varying community members, and the interactions with the Shepard family. When the tragedy occurred, the existing team was expanded to include members of the community and a mix of students, staff, and faculty from the campus. The flexibility for this expansion was important for effective response to a crisis that had such a wide impact.

Flexibility and Responsiveness of the Wyoming Union and Student Activities Staff

The staff members in this building turned over their offices and resources to the LGBTA (Lesbian, Gay, Bisexual, Transgender Alliance) membership. The media converged on these offices for the ten days after the attack on Matthew. Staff and students commonly worked eighteen-hour days to help with the crisis. Giving students such prominence and power during the time of a crisis was a critical step that propelled the community toward healing. The students felt empowered and validated by this recognition, and they exceeded all expectations in their ability to turn the situation around.

Involvement of Student Organizations

The LGBTA played a significant role in conveying to the nation that the University of Wyoming and the Laramie community members were not all filled with hate and hostility for gays. The LGBTA leadership served as voices of accuracy and reason. This student group was instrumental in their outreach and visible efforts in getting people to talk about the difficult issues this tragedy provoked. Their powerful and peaceful presence made a quite a contrast to the noisy hateful protesters during Matthew Shepard's funeral and memorial service and the perpetrators' trial.

Other student organizations, the United Multicultural Council, the Associated Students of the University of Wyoming, the Multicultural Resource Center, the Greek community, the residence hall association and other groups provided leadership to the community. One example of this leadership was the armbands created by these groups which became a significant symbol in the grieving as well as the healing process.

Symbols of Peace and Healing

One of the most powerful symbols and unifying forces of the tragedy was the yellow armband. The yellow armband was chosen because of its role in other national tragedies, namely the hostage crisis and the Oklahoma City bombing. The Matthew Shepard armbands were decorated with green circles reflecting the international symbol for peace. Student groups worked throughout the night creating these armbands and worked diligently to distribute them. When local storeowners realized what the materials were for, they refused payment for them and even helped produce the armbands.

Management of the Media Presence by University Relations

Most reporters represented their profession well and in good taste. Some of them, however, sought out sensational statements and constructed their stories around them. This experience makes it clear that centralized communication across campus with the media is imperative if an accurate picture is to be portrayed.

Provision of Discussion Forums by Faculty

Figure 4. October 16, 1998. Richard Osborn of Natrona, Wyoming held this sign up in protest at the funeral of Matthew Shepard, the twenty-one-year old gay student who was beaten to death in Laramie. Members of Osborn's VFW group (No. 9439), were angered by the fact that he wore his VFW uniform to protest. They stated that Mr. Osborn's views did not reflect that of the other members of VFW 9439 and indicated that Mr. Osborn's membership was in jeopardy of being revoked. Matthew's grandfather was also a member of that VFW Hall. Photograph by Nanette Martin.

A survey showed that half the student body had classes in which their instructor set aside at least one day to discuss the tragedy. In addition to classroom discussions, there were also universitywide faculty teach-ins. The faculty teach-ins took a more scholarly approach to the issues than the discussions. Interestingly but not surprisingly, the faculty who participated were in the social sciences. These teach-ins were provided over the noon hour during the weeks after the Matthew Shepard tragedy.

Work of the University Counseling Center

Although services were made available, fewer students than anticipated requested help regarding the tragedy. It was noted that this may have been because students are often more resilient dealing with crises than is assumed.

Planning for the Universitywide Memorial Service

On October 19, the university held the memorial service for Matthew Shepard. The planning for this highly emotional event was conducted by a Crisis Intervention Team committee selected to ensure appropriate representation of the constituencies interested in helping with the memorial service. The speakers included the president of the university, a friend of Matthew's from LGBTA, and a local poet. By the time this event was held, the intense critical media pressure seemed to have passed.

Involvement of Spiritual Organizations

Several campus-based religious and spiritual organizations were helpful throughout the process. In particular, the Canterbury House coordinated the communication between the university and the Shepard family. Great care was taken to ensure that university activities and plans were consistent with the desires of the Shepard family.

Efforts of the University of Wyoming Police Department (UWPD)

The service of the UWPD was pivotal in dealing with threats from organizations and people from all over the country. One anti-gay group made threats of attending the campus memorial service with signs saying "God Hates Fags," "Matthew is in Hell," and "Aids (sic) Cures Fags." Although the group did not attend the memorial service, the UWPD was thoroughly prepared. Finally, they were attentive to meeting the safety and protection of LGBTA members and others during Gay Awareness Week.

A Commitment to Continue Life at the University of Wyoming without Forgetting the Death of Matthew Shepard

Matthew's beating occurred just days before the annual homecoming events on campus. Campus officials decided to go forward with the planned events, but make special notice of the tragedy and its impact on the campus. At several points during the week, participants of homecoming activities were asked to pause for a moment of silence to reflect upon the tragedy. During the traditional homecoming parade, last-minute floats were added as tributes to Matthew. Faculty, staff, and community members gathered at the end of the parade behind a yellow banner with green circles. Many of the participants and spectators wept openly during this highly emotional demonstration.

In summary, hate crimes are prevalent in our national and campus communities. Of these crimes, those with a sexual-orientation bias seem to be more culturally accepted. The causes for hate crimes can be viewed from two perspectives: A community perspective and a perpetrator perspective. Victims of hate crimes are impacted with greater severity than victims of similar non-biased violence. Prevention plans need to be multitiered and need to be inclusive of the entire community.

Learning about the prevalence, dynamics, causes, and impact of hate crime can overwhelm us and promote a feeling of powerlessness. We now know, though, that we can have a positive impact on the issue. Working collaboratively, promoting tolerance, and valuing differences prevents hate crimes. By knowing some of the motivations of the perpetrators, we can anticipate their behavior and challenge their actions. Finally, we know the importance of working as a community in responding to hate crimes that occur. Together, we do have power to address the issue of hate crime.

Chapter 13

HAZING

- A young man or woman dies in a pledging-related activity every year since 1970, according to Hank Nuwer, a leading researcher on the subject of hazing.
- The University of Vermont (UVM) is publicly reprimanded by Vermont Attorney General William Sorrell for an inadequate investigation of a hazing incident involving the hockey team. Consequently, UVM cancels the remainder of their 1999–2000 hockey season.
- In 1999, the Nebraska Supreme Court rules that the University of Nebraska had a duty to protect a Phi Gamma Delta fraternity pledge who was abducted, handcuffed, and forced to drink alcohol. The university had been aware of past criminal conduct involving this same fraternity and of hazing activities of at least two other fraternities. The court determined the university could have foreseen the potential for hazing on its property. Thus, the university had the responsibility to take steps to protect its students.

As we moved into a new millennium, the topic of hazing made headlines. In August 1999, Alfred University released the results of a nationwide study in which 79 percent of NCAA athlete respondents indicated they were hazed as a part of a team initiation practice. This study exposed a significant hazing problem among NCAA athletes. At the same time a book, *Wrongs of Passage* by Hank Nuwer, topped the bestseller list directly confronting centuries of hazing traditions. Activists against hazing, such as Eileen Stevens, founder of C.H.U.C.K. (Committee to Halt Useless College Killings) continued to challenge institutions and organizations by speaking and lobbying. The number of states adopting hazing laws rose to forty-one. The body of hazing case law grew as college liability was scrutinized in civil court.

Despite these groundbreaking efforts in hazing prevention, old traditions are holding strong. Proponents of hazing do exist. These individuals believe that these practices have worked for generations and should not be infringed upon. Many claim that hazing rituals are a rite of passage that benefit individuals by helping them in their transition from nonmembers to group members. Some suggest that hazing weeds out people who lack commitment or loyalty to the group, creates a bond among group members that cannot be achieved in other ways, and helps keep members on a more equal level regardless of personal history. Others feel that hazing creates a sense of appropriate hierarchy and leadership and that humiliation breeds equality.

WHAT IS HAZING?

Definitions for hazing vary only slightly from one group to another. The Fraternity Executive Association defines hazing as "Any action taken or situation created intentionally, whether or not on fraternity premises, to produce mental or physical discomfort, embarrassment, harassment or ridicule." For the purposes of their study on athletic hazing in the NCAA, Alfred University defined hazing as "any activity expected of someone joining a group that humiliates, degrades, abuses or endangers, regardless of the person's willingness to participate. This does not include activities such as rookies carrying team balls, team parties with community games, or going out with your teammates, unless an atmosphere of humiliation, degradation, abuse or danger arises."

There are two areas of difference in how academic institutions view hazing and in how state legislators interpret hazing: definition and consequences. First, some schools and laws do not recognize hazing if the individual consents to being hazed while others differ and consider the actions to be hazing whether or not consent was provided. Second, the consequences for violating policies and laws related to hazing vary considerably from school to school and from state to state.

For the purpose of examining hazing in this chapter, we will define hazing as *any action related to an individual's admittance or membership in a group that produces mental or physical harm, embarrassment, harassment, or ridicule, regardless of the location of the activity or the individual's willingness to participate.* Furthermore, we will examine how hazing relates to the following categories: mental games, degrading activities, physically abusive activities, sexually violating activities, activities that require consumption of alco-

hol, and activities that place people in hazardous situations.

(NOTE: The following list of initiation activities was created from information taken from the following resources: Material from Eileen Stevens, books and articles written by Hank Nuwer, the Alfred University study on athletic hazing in the NCAA, an interview with Judge Mitch Crane, interviews with Greek members and advisors, and multiple reports on hazing activities at various institutions. Eileen Stevens is the mother of a young man killed in a hazing incident, a leading activist in the fight against hazing, and the founder of C.H.U.C.K. (the Committee to Halt Useless College Killings). Hank Nuwer has authored two books on hazing, the latter of which has topped the bestseller list. Judge Crane, in addition to his legal role on the bench, is a prominent speaker on risk management issues for Greek organizations. The Alfred University study on athletic hazing has been groundbreaking in demonstrating that athletics are far from immune to hazing.)*

Common Hazing Activities

Mental Games

- Initiates are required to jump on what appears to be a nail sticking out of a board; in reality it is aluminum foil and no physical harm results.
- Initiates are instructed to drop their pants expecting to be hit by a brother with a paddle and the brother hits something directly next to the initiate, not hitting the initiate.
- Initiates are required not to speak with anyone outside of the organization.

Degrading Activities

- Initiates are required to be a personal servant or provide favors to someone.
- Initiates are forced to wear funny clothing in public spaces.
- Initiates are yelled at, cursed at, intimidated, or insulted.
- Initiates are prohibited from bathing.
- Initiates are required to participate in racist or sexist activities: singing songs, keeping notebooks, etc.
- Initiates are required to conduct pranks or illegal activity, such as stealing signs.
- Initiates are required to ask members or alumni to sign books, clothing, or flesh.
- Initiates are required to carry objects with them at all times, such as paddles, balls, live animals, etc. . . .

Physically Abusive

- Initiates are branded or burned by cigarettes, cigars, chemicals, or other means.
- Initiates are paddled, beaten, or subjected to electric shock.
- Initiates are forced to eat or drink overly spicy or disgusting foods.
- Initiates are required to stay awake and fast.
- Initiates are doused in liquid or nonhygienic substances.
- Initiates are forced to do excessive physical activity–push-ups, sit-ups, boxing, swimming, etc.
- Initiates are required to play football without the protective gear that the current members wear.
- Initiates are required to sleep in a closet or other uncomfortable place.
- Initiates are subject to head shaving, tattooing, or piercing.
- Initiates are tied up, taped, or confined.

Sexually Violating Activity

- Initiates are required to strip and walk in a circle holding the genitalia of other initiates.
- Initiates are required to strip to their underwear, put on a blindfold, and lie on the ground while members of a related fraternity come in and mark on her where she needs to lose weight.
- Initiates are required to engage in or simulate sexual acts.
- Initiates are bound to a chair while strippers gyrate in their laps.

Required Consumption of Alcohol

- Initiates are required to drink a case of beer in a day.
- Initiates are required to drink until they fill a trashcan with vomit.

Placing People in Hazardous Situations

- Initiates are taken to a strange city and abandoned without money.
- Initiates are forced to hike in wilderness without proper protective gear.

PUTTING INITIATION PRACTICES INTO PERSPECTIVE: THREE DIMENSIONS

As we conceptualize hazing, it might be helpful to think of it as a phenomenon that resides somewhere in the cross-section of three dimensions or continuums. The first continuum, Rites of Passage, deals with self-growth on one end of the continuum and self-harm on the other. The second continuum, group development, deals with team building on one end of the continuum and brainwashing on the other. The third continuum of power or influence, deals with empowerment on one end of the continuum

and powerlessness or control on the other. Together, the cross-section of these continuums could represent initiation rites as a whole. Hazing is a subsection of this whole picture of initiation practices. Hazing constitutes the subsection that causes harm to individuals or groups.

Rites of Passage

Self-Growth   **Self-Harm**

●————————————————————————————————————●

Increased understanding of self and   Causing unnecessary
self-in-relation to community.   harm to oneself.
Coming into one's own.

Rites of passage take on many forms in cultures, religions, communities, and organizations signifying a transition to a new point in an individual's life. Most religions have some form of ceremony and celebration as young people take on their adult faith. Members of the military endure and complete boot camp and graduation. Greek organizations have the pledging process and induction ceremonies. High school, college, and professional athletes have held initiation events to induct new team members. Are these rights of passage so different from one another?

Not all rites of passage are pleasant or positive. Stephanie Welsh, author of "A Dangerous Rite of Passage" in the October 1995 issue of *World Press Review,* opened our eyes to a rite of passage passed on for centuries. Welsh reported on Female Genital Mutilation (FGM) taking place in Africa. In Kenya when a woman comes of age, she sits with her legs held open while a circumciser makes rapid cuts on her genitals. The woman receives no anesthesia and is forbid-

den to cry or show fear. She bites down on a cloth until the ten-minute operation is complete. The wound is then cleansed with cow urine and smothered in fat to stop the bleeding.

Although FGM is an extreme and horrifying example, it clearly demonstrates how a rite of passage can be seen as inhumane to a group outside of the culture and normal and appropriate to a group inside the culture. Welsh reported that multiple organizations, including human rights groups, were involved in working to eradicate FGM. But eradication will not be easy as Welsh noted two examples of the depth of cultural commitment to FGM. In one example, a mother responded to her daughter crying out from pain, "Keep quiet! You should be able to withstand this thing. You are not a coward." In another example, when a circumciser was asked why she laughed throughout the operation, she said, "The pain doesn't kill. We laugh because it is our culture, and we have all passed through this stage. . . . She is so beautiful because she is a clean woman now. She is a grown-up." These statements certainly do not represent all women in this culture; however, the fact that the practice continues demonstrates cultural support.

Group Development

Team Building

Choosing to depend on each other out of a sense of trust. Expanding the support network. Individuality is recognized as a strength in the context of the group.

Brainwashing

Forced dependency and reduction of individual choice. Limiting the support system.

One of the arguments for hazing is that it fosters team development and team loyalty, while one of the arguments against hazing is that it serves to brainwash its members into sacrificing their personal identity, dignity, and will. Some of the commonly cited techniques within this dimension are sleep deprivation, abusive treatment, and forced dependency. Sleep deprivation limits individuals' ability to concentrate and make decisions. Thus, their inhibitions are reduced, and they need to depend on other members to look out for them and provide them with direction. A potential consequence of this technique is that it limits people's ability to make sound and independent decisions and their ability to accept the consequences of their

decisions. The intent behind abusive treatment is to create a negative experience that a group has to live through together, thereby creating a tighter and stronger group of initiates. Some unspoken consequences of abusive treatment are the division created between the abusers and the abused and the reduced self-esteem of the abused.

Forced dependency is a technique where members are taken away or prohibited from associating with people outside the group. This technique allows members to commit to learning about each other and their purpose. A possible consequence of this technique is that members' abilities to function productively outside of the group become more limited.

Power

Empowerment

Providing direction in the forms of expanding options, empowering people, and challenging harmful actions.

Powerlessness

Providing direction by limiting options, limiting or squashing individual expression, often motivating by fear of harm or humiliation.

Power and influence may be exercised in many forms of which empowerment and control are on opposite ends of the spectrum. In the process of empowering, an individual's choices or options are expanded and discussions are held to assist the individual in decision making. The motivation in empowerment is principle oriented, choosing to act a certain way, because it appears to be the most "right" choice. In the process of control, an individual's choices are limited, so the decision is no longer entirely his or her own. When there is only one way to achieve a desired goal, an individual must choose to follow the direction of another if she or he wants to achieve the goal. The motivation in control is consequence oriented, choosing to act a certain way to achieve a specific outcome or to avoid punishment or humiliation.

In our review of the issues concerning initiation, we found that people responsible for developing groups (e.g., Greek members, athletes, coaches, retreat coordinators, administrators, and trainers) have traversed the aforementioned continuums with both positive and negative outcomes as new members have become group members. We have noted a common factor in these initiation activities: The perception of what constitutes hazing held by group members, those inside the culture, varies considerably with perceptions of those outside of the group.

Many groups still see hazing as an integral part of creating group trust and loyalty, while many nonmembers see hazing as humiliating, pointless, and risky. This variance occurs much in the same way that many cultures see female genital mutilation as inhumane, while some of the culture in which it exists find the practice as a critical rite of passage for girls becoming young women. These varying perceptions challenge us with questions of needs and power: What is it about these activities that is good? What is it about them that is bad? What do we want to embrace and support? What do we want to stop?

In this chapter we will focus on these questions with regard to hazing. First, we will examine how hazing plays out in different contexts. Second, we will examine the motivations behind hazing. Third, we will explore how hazing relates to individuals and institutions. Finally, we will offer recommendations to address hazing.

HAZING IN DIFFERENT CONTEXTS

Greek Life

Although these practices happen in many different groups, fraternities and sororities have received the most public attention over the years; consequently, some of the more positive aspects of Greek life are overlooked. For many, fraternities and sororities provide a sense of history and connection. By providing a training ground for leadership and service, fraternities and sororities have sought to uphold worthy principles. They have served students by helping them find their places in society and develop social skills and connections. The legacy of alumni continue this service by providing connections and role modeling in the postgraduate world.

Fraternity and sorority legacy also has a dark side; years of tradition and principle have been accompanied by years of hazing and deception. According to *Wrongs of Passage* (Nuwer, 1999), fatal fraternity hazing incidents date back as early as 1873 when a brother of the Kappa Alpha Society fell to his death in a gorge after being forced to find his way back home in the woods. As mentioned in Chapter 1, in 1978 Chuck Stenzel died from intensive alcohol consumption which was required as a part of the Klan Alpine fraternity pledging event, prompting Chuck's mother Eileen Stevens to become an activist against hazing. From this point onward, fraternity and sorority hazing has received increasing press coverage to the present day. We now know from Nuwer's research that at least one fraternity or sorority member has died every year in a pledging-related activity since 1970.

Two recent cases of Greek life hazing have captured media attention, both resulting in legal action. The first case is unusual because it features women. This is not to say that women do not haze, but it is usually the men who get the bad press. In 1997, Brandi Nave was attempting to become a member at the Alpha Kappa Alpha chapter at Illinois State University. She alleges among other mental and physical abuse she was hit in the head, forced to swallow unknown substances, and stripped. After the initiation she was treated for minor injuries at a local emergency room. In 1998, the sorority sisters who inflicted the hazing were convicted of misdemeanors and sentenced to court supervision. Nave received a little over $10,000 in damages from the women involved in the hazing. The national sorority and local chapter still remain defendants in a civil suit seeking $50,000 in damages.

The other case is significant, not only because a student committed suicide allegedly in relation to his hazing experiences, but because of a number of disturbing discoveries made during the investigation process as well. In 1998, John LaDuca, a freshman pledge at the University of Washington's (UW) Delta Kappa Epsilon (DKE) fraternity, hung himself just hours after the fraternity's initiation rites were over. According to the testimony of some of the participants, the hazing involved eating questionable substances until they vomited, incredible sleep deprivation, and multiple mind games designed, according to the pledgemaster, "to confuse them." Even more concerning is the fact that several alumni ranging in age from twenty-five to sixty-two participated in the hazing activities. One alumnus allegedly even coached the younger fraternity members on how to hide hazing from the police. Another alumni wrote an email to the international Delta Kappa Epsilon director, "If it gets too ugly we'll roll out the big money men. . . . Greeks account for 80 percent of alumni giving at the U, so we can get nasty too."

On the night of his death, John LaDuca talked to both his father and a friend. His father recalls hearing his son distressed and wondering whether or not he should be attending UW. His father urged him to come home, but John said he was not a quitter. Later a friend from home called and John revealed what he had experienced the previous week. He said he was naked, exhausted, and just wanted a gun. Later a friend found that John had hanged himself in his room.

The UW officials conducted an investigation into the tragedy, but did not involve the local police. The Interfraternity Council (IFC) also investigated the incident, but found DKE members to be uncooperative initially. The parents of John LaDuca filed a wrongful-death lawsuit in August 1998, and it has yet to go to trial.

Unfortunately, these very few facts and isolated cases of Greek life do not even begin to address hazing-related deaths, nor are they remotely inclusive of all the hazing activities causing physical and psychological harm.

Athletics

While the Greek systems have been in the public eye for hazing, the Alfred University study on athletic hazing in the NCAA has demonstrated that athletics clearly faces similar issues. With the support of the NCAA, Alfred University conducted a national study in which two hundred twenty-four institutions participated. Even though there are more than a thousand institutions in the NCAA, the study utilized responses from institutions across the country and broke new ground in athletic hazing research. The study, inclusive of male and female sports, identified various initiation rites in college athletics, perceptions of what is appropriate or inappropriate, and strategies for hazing prevention.

At first look, the results are deceiving. In response to the provided definition, 45 percent of the respondents indicated that they have been or have heard of or suspected hazing on their campuses. Only 12 percent of the respondents reported having been hazed for athletics. However, when specific hazing behaviors were listed separately without the heading of "hazing," 79 percent of the respondents indicated that they were subjected to activities that clearly fell under the hazing definition. The reluctance to identify activities as hazing may be attributed to a fear of consequences (forty-one states now have hazing laws and legal liability is a real threat) or to a lack of awareness of what constitutes hazing.

The results of the Alfred study were categorized as acceptable, questionable, alcohol-related, and unacceptable activities. Acceptable activities included activities that form team unity but do not degrade or humiliate new members such as preseason training, dressing nicely for team functions, completing a ropes course together, keeping a specific grade point average, doing community service work as a team, and signing team standards agreements. Questionable activities included activities that were humiliating or degrading, but not potentially dangerous or illegal. These activities include yelling, swearing, wearing embarrassing clothing, tattooing, piercing, head shaving, branding, sleep deprivation, food deprivation, and not allowing association with people outside the group.

Unacceptable activities included activities that had a high probability of danger or injury, or the potential to result in criminal charges. Such activities include making prank calls and harassing people, destroying or stealing property, being confined, beating, kidnapping or abandoning, and other illegal activity. Alcohol-related activities include drinking contests and alcohol consumption on recruitment visits.

Severity of Collegiate Athletic Initiation

The following table adapted from the Alfred hazing study depicts the percentage of athletes who stated that they had been involved in acceptable, questionable, alcohol-related, or unacceptable initiation activities.

Activities	Percent
Acceptable initiation activities only	19%
Questionable initiation rites, no unacceptable activities	19%
Alcohol-related initiation, no other unacceptable activities	39%
Unacceptable initiation activities, other than alcohol-related	21%
Hazed (total of questionable, alcohol, & other unacceptable)	79%

Source: Alfred University National Survey: Initiation Rites and Athletics for NCAA Sports Teams 8/30/99. Principal Investigator–Dr. Nadine C. Hoover.

Athletes Involved in Alcohol-Related Initiation

The following table, adapted from the Alfred hazing study, indicates the percentage of athletes who said that they were involved in alcohol-related activities as part of their athletic team.

The study cited several comments revealing denial or ignorance embraced by many athletic directors and coaches. "This is a non-issue! It doesn't happen here;" "... this is one of the more ridiculous questionnaires I've ever been asked to complete ...," "... (hazing) has never come up at any meeting in student life committee. If it happened, it would be an isolated case."

There are significant differences between the percentage of students hazed and the percentage of coaches and athletic directors aware of hazing. The most glaring misperception by coaches and athletic directors is in the area regarding alcohol-related activities.

Whether this discrepancy is a true misperception of the behavior of the athletes on the part of the professional staff or a "see no evil, hear no evil, speak no evil" attitude, remains to be seen. In our informal interviews with athletes, it is their perception that the coaches and athletic directors have some sense of the type of drinking that takes place but do not want to get involved. The students seemed to take this lack of response as a tacit endorsement of their behavior.

The study also generated a media frenzy, not all supportive of the findings. Richard Hoffer wrote an article published in the September 13, 1999 issue of *Sports Illustrated* titled, "Praising Hazing." Hoffer highlights a difference between "good clean fun and felonious assault." He contends that the idea behind hazing is the destruction of status to foster teamwork.

We don't need a 36 page report from Alfred University (it's in Alfred, N.Y.) to tell us that 'humiliating, dangerous and illegal activity' should be curbed. But what's wrong with making a freshman carry a senior's suitcase? Taping a rookie to the goalpost, as the Browns do, may be borderline, but is making him do a skit in a skirt so bad? Maybe cross-dressing isn't the worst thing in the world if it makes for camaraderie. Hazing doesn't make sense in high school, where freshmen have no egos and need no embarrassment beyond that of being freshmen. But we're all for college and pro hazing, or whatever you want to call it when athletes of extraordinary privilege are treated just like the rest of the team." (p. 31)

Military Campuses

Although athletics has been the recent focus of the press, military campuses have had their own long-standing tradition of hazing. The purpose in military hazing is commonly accepted as an effort to break some-

Alcohol-Related Initiation Activities	Athletes	Coach Awareness	Athletic Director Awareness
Consuming alcohol on recruitment	42%	7%	5%
Participating in a drinking contest	35%	4%	4%

Source: Alfred University National Survey: Initiation Rites and Athletics for NCAA Sports Teams 8/30/99. Principal Investigator–Dr. Nadine C. Hoover.

one down, so as to build him or her back up stronger, more confident, and more committed to the unit. Preparing military personnel for combat readiness is the primary objective; therefore, the ability to follow orders blindly and immediately is required. Surrendering a level of your personal judgment is necessary.

The purpose of this book is to help the reader understand violence, how to prevent it and how to respond to it; this contrasts with the purpose of the military. Becoming combat-ready requires soldiers to learn how to be violent. Our hope for educational institutions is that students are being taught how to prevent violence. The military teaches blind obedience, whereas, we advocate freedom of choice. These purposes are at odds.

Our intent in this book is not to debate the need for and the purpose of the military. Nor is the intent to disregard the choices we are privileged to make because of the military's existence. That being said, military academies have hazed in ways that General Douglas MacArthur, himself, has found to be inappropriate and not in accordance with the purpose of the military. In *Wrongs of Passage* (1999), Nuwer reviewed a military hazing tradition that dates back to the civil war and continues to the present day. From the nineteenth century to today, the media has highlighted hazing abuses of U.S. service academies. Unless otherwise indicated, the following military highlights are adapted from Nuwer's Work.

- *West Point.* Major incidents were reported occurring at West Point in 1881, 1900–1901, 1907, 1917, 1973, 1976, 1979, and 1990. In 1900–1901 President William McKinley initiated a congressional inquiry into hazing at West Point. This inquiry demonstrated the dilemma of cadets torn between being loyal to the academy and telling the truth to a con-

gressional committee. The cadets included Douglas MacArthur, the sons of Ulysses S. Grant, and Philip Sheridan. MacArthur, on the recommendation of his mother remained silent; however, he did share with the committee that he felt the hazing was wrong and unnecessary. The committee uncovered the following practices toward new recruits:

- –Squatting over a bayonet pointed at his groin, sometimes for hours.
- –Completing up to four hundred exercises similar to knee bends at one stretch.
- –Wearing heavy clothing and carry bedding in the heat of summer.
- –Sliding on a floor covered with soapy water that entered the nose and mouth.
- –Stripping naked and running through a gauntlet while being doused with icy water.

MacArthur later returned to West Point as superintendent and tried to outlaw what he felt were the worst hazing practices. However, he was unable to eliminate all abuses.

- *Texas A&M.* Texas A&M was criticized for brutal endurance tests and beatings in the Corps of Cadets. In 1913, the university expelled four hundred sixty-six students for hazing, but took most of them back after they swore to stop whipping new cadets. A month later hazing began again and two of the perpetrators were sent home. Public attention was heightened in 1984 when a cadet died after an exercise session and in 1991 when a female cadet reported being abused. In 1996 a cadet reported that he was taped up, punched, kicked, and required to cut his own body. The university now specifies what actions can be taken toward cadets, during what time periods cadets may be made to exercise, and a limit to the number of exercises (e.g., forty push-ups or sit-ups) a cadet may be ordered to do by a higher ranking cadet.

• *The Citadel.* Similar hazing activities at the Citadel inspired Pat Conroy, an alumnus, to write *The Lords of Discipline.* This portrayal of hazing at a military academy brought media attention to the Citadel. This attention remained until the following key changes occurred: The institution stopped harassing African Americans, opened its doors to women, and underwent policy reform to address hazing. In 1996, the remaining all-male military academies, the Citadel and Virginia Military Institute, opened their doors to women after the Supreme Court ruled that preventing women from entering military academies was unconstitutional. This was not the end of the schools' problems. In the January 24, 1997, edition of the *Chronicle of Higher Education,* Lisa Guernsey reported that two female cadets at the Citadel, Jeannie Mentavlos and Kim Messer, were doused in flammable liquid and lit on fire. They were also subject to nighttime raids where male cadets entered their rooms and sang sexually explicit songs. While other female cadets continued on, these two withdrew. Citadel officials stated renegade cadets committed these acts and would be punished. Jeannie Mentavlos did not believe that these were the actions of just a few, but that they were institutionally supported. She stated that renegade cadets are not permitted to lead cadet companies. Public attention and lawsuits have encouraged the military to take a more

serious look at hazing and how the institution addresses hazing. After the hazing incidents of Messer and Mentavlos, the Citadel's interim president had a meeting with the entire student body to make sure there was no misunderstanding about how cadets were to behave and be treated. Citadel officials issued a statement publicizing the terms of suspension for two of the men involved. Panic bars were also installed in the female cadets' rooms.

• *Virginia Military Institute.* After the Citadel, media attention shifted to the Virginia Military Institute (VMI) in 1997 as women were granted admission. VMI officials were originally opposed to the entrance of women and were fairly public with their opinions. Frequent news articles on the hazing activities at VMI kept the institution in the spotlight. As a result, VMI officials began to be less publicly opposed to the admission of women. In 1998, the media reported the dismissal of six cadets–not for their hazing behavior (i.e., whipping cadets with belts and hangers) but for lying about the incident and violating the honor code. Although VMI continues to have some serious hazing issues, it appears to have been more successful with the integration of women. In 1998, the March 27 edition of the *Chronicle of Higher Education* reported that twenty-three women and three hundred sixty-one men successfully completed the year at VMI. Seven women and sixty-nine men dropped out or were expelled.

HAZING AND THE INDIVIDUAL

The dynamics of hazing vary somewhat as it relates to individuals and institutions. As such, we will explore these dynamics in greater depth in the next two sections.

The Vulnerable Recruit

People who haze rarely consider the physical or psychological state of the people they are hazing. People who haze often assume all recruits are well-adjusted people, both physically and emotionally. Reality suggests that recruits are drawn from a wider population yielding a group of people with all kinds of issues and vulnerabilities. Some recruits have medical conditions while others may be highly stressed and possibly suicidal. Hazing is not an activity that yields positive outcomes with these issues. Even the healthiest people can suffer the negative consequences of hazing.

Physical and Emotional Consequences

Hazing can result in serious physical and emotional damage. Many recruits have been hospitalized due to physical abuse such as paddling or beating. Many have been hospitalized due to accidents, which occur from intoxication or other dangerous activities. Some victims of hazing suffer from Posttraumatic Stress Disorder (PTSD), a clinical mental disorder that is highly debilitating.

Those who choose to report hazing are subjected to negative attitudes and behavior from the peer group and are often ostracized and harassed both physically and emotionally, similar to the ordeal faced by a workplace whistleblower. For example, in the workplace, when a person reports illegal or unethical activity being conducted by the company, he or she is often fired and blackballed from any similar employment. In the college setting, the group member is usually expelled from the group and the word is put out that the individual lacks loyalty and should not be allowed in any similar social circles.

Most hazing falls into the categories of group-induced violence or relationship-based violence. In group-induced violence there is a diffusion of responsibility. People just follow the crowd. In relationship-based violence, an individual is seeking to have control over another person. Both of these types of violence have the potential to lead to great physical harm.

Example of Group-Induced Violence

In 1994 at Southeast Missouri State, Michael Davis was a Kappa Alpha Psi fraternity initiate. Michael was asked to do sprints on a field barefoot. At the end, he was tackled by his brothers and beaten on his feet with a cane. They beat him in other ways until he died. (*Source:* Nuwer, *Wrongs of Passage,* 1999.)

Example of Relationship-Based Violence

There are multiple examples of control via personal servitude and humiliation. This kind of abuse often leads to greater physical abuse. In October of 1996, John Warren, a Kappa Alpha pledge at Texas A&M, was subjected to both humiliation and physical abuse. A fraternity member poured a beer on him, held him down while he was made to do push-ups, and yanked up his underwear. After a few painful days, a surgeon removed one of Warren's testicles. (*Source:* Ben Gose, "Efforts to end fraternity hazing have largely failed," *Chronicle of Higher Education,* April 18, 1997.)

HAZING AND THE INSTITUTION

Duck and Cover

People create and operate institutions; thus, the instinct of self-protection is very strong. This instinct can lead to denial and avoidance, neither of which is necessarily intentional. Earlier we noted the tendency for athletic directors and coaches to believe hazing was not occurring on their teams. As demonstrated in the DKE case and Vermont hockey team mentioned earlier, some Greek and athletic leaders lie about upcoming hazing plans and after hazing incidents. Institutions, as a whole, are no different.

As a result of hazing laws, civil litigation, and public scrutiny this tendency to duck and cover is slowly shifting to one of accepting responsibility. After being reprimanded by the state Attorney General, the University of Vermont cancelled their hockey season because of a hazing incident. Alfred University, where Chuck Stenzel died in an alcohol-related pledging activity in 1978, has chosen to face its hazing issues head on and is now spearheading leading research in the area. Amherst, Colby, and Bowdoin Colleges have already chosen to phase out their Greek systems and start something new. There are still many schools that fall back to concealing information, citing the Student Right to Privacy Act; however, the pressure of the media challenges these institutions to develop strong policies with articulated responses.

Sacred Cows and Sacred Herds

Every institution has a "sacred cow" to protect. At some institutions, the sacred cow is the star athlete that takes the team to a higher level filling the stands, making money for the institution, and providing a great deal of alumni support. The sacred cow is often protected and rewarded by the institution. Rewards come in the forms of camouflaged gifts and privileges. Protection comes in the forms of institutional blind spots when these star students violate school policy or the law. Universities may conduct substandard investigations into the actions of these students and issue lesser consequences to these students.

In addition, institutions protect their "sacred herds." These may take the form of a sports team, a Greek organization, or another not as popular group that has the support of the board of trustees. Why would an institution protect individuals or entities like these? There are at least two reasons: money and politics. Sacred cows often bring in money or offer an alliance to an individual or organization that has considerable political strength. These two reasons often accompany each other but not always. The money may take the form of revenue generated from games, alumni support, affluent potential donors, and potential lawsuits. Political strength has the potential to make the jobs of institution officials more difficult or easier. For these reasons, officials are often reluctant to harm the sacred cow.

Civil and criminal case decisions have many officials rethinking their philosophies on their sacred cows and sacred herds. No longer are college officials faced with the straightforward choice between acting, leading to lawsuits and money loss and not acting in hopes the problem goes away. Civil and criminal case decisions suggest that you may be sued for not acting appropriately with regard to an incident. Thus, the choice is now between which lawsuit you would rather face.

Regulations and Laws

Hazing can result in both judicial and legal consequences. Forty-one states have adopted hazing laws. Media attention and broader legal influence has put colleges and universities under the looking glass by evaluating their policies and their judicial follow-through. Case law addressing an institution's responsibility for the prevention of dangerous hazing continues to be made.

Increased attention to hazing has certainly elevated accountability; however, many maintain that simply adopting laws is not enough. The issues of enforcement, consistency, and consent need to be addressed. In his time on the bench, Judge Mitch Crane has seen very little use of anti-hazing laws and believes there needs to be greater enforcement. The reason is the variance from state to state on what is criminal and what is not, and there is a need for greater consistency. Hazing activists fight for laws that acknowledge that hazing yields negative consequences with or without consent of the victim, and often state laws do not hold this to be true.

The Issue of Consent

The debate of what constitutes consent and whether or not it mitigates hazing is a powerful one and is similar to the argument fought by prosecutors in sexual assault cases. Investigation often shows that the person hazing and the person being hazed share different viewpoints on whether or not consent was given. In many sexual assault cases, the person who exercised power over another viewed the consent or lack of consent differently than the person who did not have the power.

Consent has been an issue of confusion for sexual assault situations, and recently this issue has been clarified: the absence of refusal does not imply consent. The victim may be too impaired to refuse, and this debilitated state must be taken into consideration when determining consent. Hazing laws still are clouded on this issue. Hazing laws often do not reflect the notion that consent provided when the victim was sleep-deprived, intoxicated, or subjected to massive peer pressure is different from consent provided under normal circumstances. Activists against sexual assault fought for laws that protect potential victims from perpetrators who would take advantage of an altered mental state.

To take the analogy one step further, we are faced with the issue of progressive consent. Some states consider individuals who consented to one part of hazing and not to another to be less victimized. The assumption is made that if the person was comfortable with one form of hazing, the person must have been comfortable with all forms of hazing. In sexual assault cases, assumptions are often made that women who consented to fondling also consented to intercourse.

WHY DO PEOPLE HAZE?

Diffusion of Responsibility

The group dynamic involved in hazing interferes with members' ability to reason. Group members fail to recognize inappropriate activity for what it is when they see a whole group of people they trust acting in the same way. Group members also experience a diminished sense of responsibility for the consequences of their actions since multiple people were involved. There is a sense of anonymity in a group; members just follow along doing what everyone else is doing.

Reciprocity

For all the loyalty development and personal growth rhetoric spouted by people who haze, some of the reason they haze is clearly, "This happened to me, now it's going to happen to you." While few group members enjoyed being hazed, most do not believe that the goals of hazing can be accomplished in a less abusive way. Such an acknowledgment would require them to believe that what they experienced did not really need to happen. This pattern is seen in the cyclical patterns of abusive families. Abused children can grow up to be abusive parents unless they are able to come to an understanding that something was wrong with the way they were raised. The process of diverging from those you have loved and trusted can be very challenging.

Badge of Loyalty

Another reason people haze is because they have convinced themselves that they are doing a service for the people they are hazing and for the group. The philosophy is, "I am willing to get my hands dirty to make the group stronger and more loyal." Other members of the group value this commitment to the group and revere the hazing leader as a sort of guardian of the group. In return, the group members themselves start to believe that hazing makes them stronger and more loyal. Their philosophy is "I must be committed and loyal if I am willing and strong enough to endure this from the group."

WHY DO PEOPLE ALLOW THEMSELVES TO BE HAZED?

People naturally want a sense of belonging and support and find that sense in the organizations to which they belong. Organizations offer a built-in social group. On some campuses, they are the primary social group. Most students suffer from a sense of insecurity when they come to school, and being a part of a group offers acceptance and support. The need for acceptance, particularly for first-year students, is enormous. In order to gain acceptance and feel more secure about themselves and their social status, students are willing to endure that which they would normally avoid.

Hazers are in effect extremists; they justify actions that are outside the range of normal human behavior. People join extremist groups because they crave relationships and acceptance, not primarily because they respond to a group's particular ideology. People who are friendless, who move to a new locale, who lack focus, or who need a romantic attachment are vulnerable to the recruiting efforts of extremists. Fraternities and sororities "rush" predominantly first-year male and female students who find themselves in unfamiliar settings, away from family and childhood friends, and who seek a feeling of belonging. Part of the exhilaration some students experience upon their arrival at College involves their ability to choose a Greek group that offers them friendship, some of which are likely to endure for life. To these young people, enduring hazing beats the pain of loneliness.

–Hank Nuwer, *Wrongs of Passage,* 1999, p. 38.

RECOMMENDATIONS

We developed the following intervention model, drawing from what we know of group-induced violence and relationship-based violence and from recommendations from the Alfred University study, Hank Nuwer, Judge Mitch Crane, Eileen Stevens, multiple focus articles on hazing, interviews with Greek members and advisors, and interviews with administrators and coaches.

Work Toward Enforceable and Consistent Hazing Laws

There are currently three major concerns with hazing laws. One, there is not a high degree of consistency in the laws from state to state; consequently, clear messages are more difficult to communicate. Two, the question as to whether consent mitigates hazing is still highly debated. Activists continue to fight for greater recognition of the roles that social pressure, sleep deprivation, and vast alcohol consumption play with consent to hazing. Three, there are limited consequences for hazing resulting in death or severe injury. The reason forty-one states now have hazing laws is because of continued efforts of activists, increased public attention, and more legal action. Continued efforts such as these will be important for the development of stronger laws.

Stop Sheltering

Despite the demise of the *in loco parentis* doctrine, institutions still retain some responsibility for protecting students from foreseeable harm. Police departments and local law enforcement are often willing to allow colleges and universities to deal with illegal behavior internally. This partnership can unintentionally permit the inappropriate sheltering of "sacred cows." In an effort to help our students grow in a more protected environment, sheltering can prevent our students from feeling the full weight of appropriate consequences, and as a result, inhibit their ability to learn. Judge Mitch Crane has suggested that in the future, hazing will be eliminated as serious offenders are jailed and offending organizations are closed. As long as offenders are sheltered, this level of accountability cannot be achieved.

Improve Communication

The first step in communicating a clear anti-hazing message is creating and communicating a hazing policy. The policy should include clear definitions and appropriate consequences and a clear reporting policy. The policy should articulate the roles community members (staff, faculty, coaches, and students) should play in hazing prevention and reporting.

The second step in communicating a clear anti-hazing message is making information available to students. Keep accurate records of hazing and make the hazing records of groups available to potential recruits. Make sure students know that they do not have to consent to being hazed. Make it clear that actions will be taken against groups who expel students for not consenting to being hazed.

The third step in communicating an anti-hazing message is establishing a clear method of reporting. The reporting method should be identified in the hazing policy. Establish a hazing compliance officer. It is important to give the reporting and advising process a home.

The fourth step in communicating an anti-hazing message is establishing a record for strong action against hazing. Establish a zero-tolerance policy that leads to a review of all suspect actions followed by appropriate action. Consistently remit consequences that reflect the seriousness of the situation. Today, non-action is as likely (if not more likely) to result in a damaging lawsuit than disciplinary action has been. The regulation of this enforcement must come from within the Greek system itself. Regulations are limited in their effectiveness because administrators rarely know when hazing is going on until it is too late. Student leaders must be convinced to make and uphold these changes.

Behavior accountability should be incorporated into advising and coaching. Accountability is key to growth. If inappropriate actions are not challenged, passive approval is assumed. If the end goal is to develop and educate students, accountability for actions is paramount.

Establishing a philosophy and policy for pre-frosh recruitment visits, and training staff and hosts on this philosophy and policy con-

tributes toward community education. The Alfred University study clearly showed a problem with recruit visitations. The study has recommended that clear guidelines are established and exercised. They suggest training and close supervision of recruit hosts by the coaches. They also suggest that coaches screen applicants thoroughly for behavioral concerns.

Educate

The first step in educating the community is to provide training on hazing. Creating a structured format to discuss the hazing policy and the institution's philosophy on hazing with students, staff, faculty and coaches will help to increase understanding of what hazing is and what can be done about it. The campus speakers network Campuspeak (303-745-5545) hosts several experts on the topic of hazing, including Judge Mitch Crane, to help campus groups become more aware of the dangers and liabilities hazing presents.

Alcohol education and support programs are important to educating the community. All the research indicates that alcohol is a significant factor in hazing and in hazing deaths. Focusing attention on the issue of alcohol education will also have a clear impact on hazing.

Enhanced community awareness also helps education. Major changes have occurred in hazing laws and institutional practices toward hazing in the past ten years. These changes are the result of increased awareness and attention. Greater numbers of civil and criminal cases are resulting in consequences for hazing. Activists against hazing continue to present and educate. Media attention keeps institutions on their toes regarding their practices. Critics suggest that greater law reform still needs to occur and many institutional practices are still suspect. Awareness and attention of the issue remains important.

Encourage Alternative Initiation Rites and Focal Points

Providing alternative initiation rites that have no hazing will require education and effort. Educating faculty, staff, coaches, and students on the importance of initiation rites helps people recognize realistic needs of groups. Integrating initiation philosophy and goals into group or team goals empowers groups to be a part of the solution as opposed to part of the problem. Identifying positive initiation rites provides groups with examples they can emulate. Role modeling team building by creating and implementing positive initiation rites shows groups that you take the issue seriously and are willing to do the work necessary to help them meet their needs in positive ways.

For Greek life, a shift in focus to academics, leadership development, career connections, and service may draw individuals away from hazing traditions. The emphasis on such activities may through natural selection create an atmosphere where hazing is less prevalent.

Provide Appropriate Leadership

Leadership provides united support for addressing the issue of hazing and requires four components: Top-down support, role modeling, utilization of campus leadership, and a strong connection with students.

Addressing issues of hazing without unified support from campus leadership is ineffective. To make real cultural change, campus leaders need to be active participants in discovering and providing new direction. Without support from higher level administration, students will not give it a second thought and without student involvement, student acceptance and support will be very difficult to achieve.

Role modeling requires that we practice what we preach. We need to examine the initiation ceremonies and rites of passages we choose to exercise and ask the question, "Are these healthy or manipulative?" As we discussed earlier in this chapter, we are faced with questions of needs and power. We have the responsibility to take the time to build teams in healthy ways. In a student culture, perception is often equal to reality. We need to take care that our actions are beyond reproach.

The utilization of campus leaders is very important. There are many leaders on campus who can deliver a message, sometimes more potently, than a written policy. Once these people are on board, cultural change will come more quickly. Without the involvement of student leaders, students will be more reluctant to follow. Providing better guidance and empowerment is important; there is no substitute however, for having faith in their ability to help solve the problem of hazing.

Connecting with students and gaining their trust and respect is perhaps the most crucial and most challenging component to providing leadership. Authority does not instantaneously equate to trust and respect in a relationship. Trust and respect are developed as people feel they are being heard, understood, cared about, and treated fairly. Support and accountability are two forms of interaction that occur with students that highly contribute to trust and respect. There is no substitute for spending time with people and listening to them. Accountability needs to be consistent, appropriate, and compassionate. Compassionate does not mean looking the other way or issuing a "slap on the wrist" for a serious behavior. Compassionate means that you show care for all the people involved when issuing just consequences. Compassionate sometimes means being willing to suspend a student or organization in a caring way.

In conclusion, we recognize some of the positive intentions behind hazing practices; but there are other, better ways of accomplishing the same goals without the negative consequences. Plenty of challenging experiences exist that do not include acting abusively toward new members. There is merit in having a group focus on its members for a period of time. Healthy initiation activities do not need to be extended for long periods of time and should not serve to discount non–group members. While hazing is one of the final violence frontiers to be confronted on college campuses, prevention efforts now seem to be moving the issue along with persistence.

Chapter 14

HOMICIDE AND NON-SEXUAL ASSAULT

IN PREVIOUS CHAPTERS we have construct- ed patchwork themes in campus vio- lence—sexual assault, hazing, hate crimes, and rioting. The last two chapters attempt to pull together the leftover pieces—physical assault, homicide, bombing, and arson.

Some of these violence types are common. Some are rare. In comparison to the previ- ous topics, few experts have written on these issues. Our attempt is to begin to sketch a picture of what we know on these topics to help guide future prevention strategizing.

HOMICIDE

While the straightforward definition of homicide is relatively simple—the killing of one person by another—the permutations of campus homicide are multiple. Campuses have faced student-on-student, student-on- staff, staff-on-staff, stranger-on-student, stu- dent-on-stranger, and other combinations of homicide. The victims are more equally dis- tributed than other forms of campus vio- lence. In other words, students, staff, and strangers all have about an equal chance of being either perpetrators or victims of this form of violence. While men still outnum- ber women in being perpetrators, women perpetrators are represented in greater num- bers here than in other forms of campus vio- lence. In fact, they are highly represented in one form of campus homicide: infanticide.

Strategies for dealing with one form of homicide do not necessarily protect against others. The following analysis of clustered case examples lists the possible typologies of

campus homicide and type-specific recom- mendations.

Predatory Homicide

Predatory homicide occurs when perpe- trators stalk down victims with whom they do not have a prior relationship and murder the victims for no other motive than the sat- isfaction they get from the killing. The Florida cases described in Chapter 1, Ted Bundy and the Gemini Killer, are two of the most notorious mass murder perpetrators in our country's history, and both preyed on college students. The 1986 murder of Jeanne Clery, also described in Chapter 1, was also a predatory murder. Predatory murders are usually what people think of when they think of a campus homicide. Scary drifters lurking in the bushes, com- monly known as "stranger danger." These types of homicide do occur on college campuses, and they are rare. However, most security tactics are designed to deter the predator and not other types of perpetrators. Predatory homicides are not the only form of homicide campuses face–avenger, relationship-based, and other forms are also possible.

Avenger Homicide

While avenger homicides are also rare on college campuses, they do occur. When they do occur, the sequence of events is virtually indistinguishable from other forms of workplace violence:

- An individual has experienced a series of perceived grievances.
- Previous attempts to resolve the problem through prosocial means are not adequate.
- The perpetrator begins to develop fantasies of violent revenge.
- Often perpetrators will make veiled or direct threats about the plan of violence.
- Finally, they execute their plan following a well-scripted plot and murder their intended victims without much concern for witnesses or their own outcome.

Again, the permutations of who seeks revenge on whom are multiple. Students have sought revenge on disciplinary officers and on faculty, and faculty have sought revenge on colleagues.

Two prominent cases of avenger homicide demonstrate this pattern of violence. Each case was a mass murder by a disgruntled individual whose premeditated actions targeted the source of his anger. Both perpetrators chose to execute their victims in a public area during a workday, without concern for observers. One perpetrator was suicidal, another hallmark of the avenger. In the aftermath, copycat behavior was apparent in one of the cases.

Concordia University

In August 1992, Dr. Valery Fabrikant, a Russian-born engineering researcher at Concordia, walked into the Henry F. Hall Building on campus concealing a 7.65-mm Argentinean Bersa pistol, a snub-nosed Smith & Wesson revolver, and a 6.35-mm semiautomatic pistol. He proceeded to fatally gun down four of his professor colleagues and injured a secretary before taking two people hostage. After an hour-long standoff with police he was overpowered and arrested.

During his thirteen years as a professor at this large Canadian university, Dr. Fabrikant had been involved in a series of disputes surrounding his contract and allegations he filed against his colleagues. He claimed that the top echelon of faculty was engaged in significant academic and financial fraud. In the aftermath of the murders, his allegations were proven true, but before the murders, he was simply known as a troublemaker. A head administrator at Concordia commented in an interview with *Maclean* magazine, "He was always complaining about something." The administrator also noted that Dr. Fabrikant had made a series of veiled threats such as, "Don't you want to search my bag to see if I have a gun in it? I might have a gun." Concordia officials claimed they warned police about these threats and Dr. Fabrikant's potential for violence. One repercussion of the murders was a redrafting of gun control laws in Ottawa.

San Diego State University

During the summer of 1996, master's candidate Frederick Davidson allegedly killed three professors at his second thesis defense. Mr. Davidson failed the first defense several months earlier, and police speculate that he expected to fail this defense as well, a decision that would have led to a dismissal from the university. On the morning of the killing spree, Mr. Davidson planted his 9-mm handgun in a first-aid kit in a laboratory. When his thesis review committee was assembled, Mr. Davidson reached into the first-aid kit and began firing, killing all three professors. Three other students were in the room at the time, and they claimed that Mr. Davidson did not attempt to kill them. When police officers arrived on scene, Mr. Davidson begged them to kill him. They apprehended him and took him into custody.

Three months later, a copycat threat occurred. An unnamed black faculty member at San Diego State University received a death threat. The anonymous flier allegedly stated that a bomb would be placed in the professor's car and included racial insults. The notice made veiled references to the earlier Davidson murders.

Recommendations

While comprehensive strategic suggestions are made throughout Part II of this book, the following list highlights particularly relevant issues for an avenger situation:

1. *Zero Tolerance for Threats.* Unlike other forms of violence, avengers usually make multiple veiled, conditional, and direct threats before carrying out their violence. All threats should be taken seriously, and at a minimum investigated and documented.

2. *Track Injustice History.* The perpetrator usually has a reputation as a complainer or troublemaker. He rarely takes responsibility for his own actions (the overwhelming majority of the perpetrators in these cases are male). They can often reach harassing levels of pursuing their complaints, such as constant letter writing and phone calls.

3. *Notice Interest in Weapons.* Avenger per-

petrators often collect guns and exhibit intense interest in violence. By taking note of the potential perpetrator's discussion of his weapon collection, assessors can determine the lethality of the perpetrator's threats.

4. *"Fitness for Duty" Evaluation.* If enough evidence exists to warrant concern, universities should consider what has been labeled in workplace situations as a "Fitness for Duty Evaluation." For students it might be labeled "Fitness for Enrollment Evaluation." This evaluation, conducted by an outside, independent violence expert, takes into consideration all the factors for violence potential and makes recommendations for the campus to minimize risk.

5. *Warn Potential Targets.* When an avenger names a targeted individual, this potential victim should be notified immediately. In addition, law enforcement should be alerted and reasonable measures should be undertaken to protect the victim.

Relationship-Based Homicide

Relationship-based homicide occurs when a one-on-one relationship, such as romantic partnership or friendship, becomes obsessive. When the submissive partner attempts to leave the relationship, the dominant partner begins to think: "If I can't have you, no one will." When the mindset of partner-as-property is so strong, the threat of relationship termination becomes unfathomable to the perpetrator. No one will get in his way when he attempts to repossess what is rightly his (again, the majority of perpetrators are male). For this reason, relationship-based homicide is one of the most dangerous, especially during the initial period of separation.

The acts of relationship-based homicide tend to be horrifying acts of rage. A relationship-based homicide is more likely to be a stabbing or strangling, much more intimate forms of violence, than other forms of homicide. In addition, the perpetrator is much more likely to involve more force than necessary to kill someone. For instance, a relationship-based perpetrator might stab the victim dozens of times and beat the victim severely around the face.

Unlike the avenger, the relationship-based perpetrators will not take out many victims of opportunity. But like avengers they are not usually deterred by barriers of any sort. Perpetrators often start their quest to regain the relationship through harassment and stalking, and later escalate their behavior to violence. Police presence, witnesses, and security devises are often ineffective in stopping a determined relationship-based perpetrator. In many cases, perpetrators feel that they have nothing to lose and are suicidal.

The next several cases presented represent both the wide variability and common themes in this type of violence. The first two cases are examples of intimate partner violence on college campuses. Both of them are male perpetrators murdering female partners, a pattern that matches national trends. According to 1998 FBI statistics, 32 percent of women killed in the United States died at the hands of a husband, a former husband, a boyfriend, or a former boyfriend. Other experts consider this fact to be a gross underestimate and suggest that the true figure is closer to 50 or 70 percent. Both cases presented here also resulted in the perpetrator's death–one a clear suicide, the other an apparent suicide-by-cop.

The second set of cases illustrates apparently non-sexual relationship-based violence, those homicides committed by obsessive friends and roommates. These cases also follow patterns of relationship-based violence.

University of Michigan

On September 23, 1997, Kevin Nelson brutally stabbed his girlfriend Tamara Williams, a University of Michigan senior multiple times with a kitchen knife while neighbors watched in horror. Unlike the infamous Kitty Genovese case (see Chapter 2) decades before, bystanders this time became actively involved. Many neighbors attempted to intervene and twenty-five 911 calls were made. One neighbor even threw a baseball bat at Kevin to get him to stop attacking Tamara. When an officer arrived on scene and ordered Kevin to back off, Kevin refused and the officer shot him twice. Both Kevin and Tamara died in surgery. The autopsy report indicated that Kevin had several horizontal "sharp cuts" on his inner wrists, suggesting that he might have been suicidal on the day of the murder.

The history of their relationship is also typical of relationship-based violence. Tamara and Kevin had had an on-again, off-again relationship for a few years. In 1995, Kevin was convicted of a domestic assault on Tamara. In her letter to the court, Tamara stated, ". . . June 20, 1995 was not the first time that Kevin Nelson had been abusive to me. He has hit me many times before and once he even hit my infant daughter in his attempt to strike me. My main concern is that every time Kevin Nelson has been in trouble he has only received a tap on the wrist. . . ." This time Kevin was sentenced to eighteen months probation. According to Tamara's friend, the two "got over their differences" and Kevin moved back in with Tamara. Witnesses, however, reported that during the attack, Kevin shouted, "She won't have me. And I love her."

Columbia University

On February 5, 2000, Timothy Nelford allegedly stabbed his girlfriend Kathleen Roskot in the neck. Her body was found hours later when her lacrosse teammates became concerned at her absence from practice. Kathleen was a well-liked sophomore at Columbia. Timothy dropped out of Columbia in 1998 due to academic difficulties possibly stemming from drug abuse. According to friends, the two dated since the prior semester, although some thought they might have split up in recent months.

On the night of the murder, security cameras recorded Kathleen and Timothy entering the residence hall together. Kathleen signed in her guest, and he left his photo ID, standard security procedures. An hour or so later, neighboring suites heard noise coming from Kathleen's room, but did not think anything of it, since loud parties were common. Kathleen was found naked on the floor of her bedroom. The apparent murder weapon, a kitchen knife, was found in the bathroom.

Shortly after Kathleen's body was found, Timothy threw himself in front of a subway train. Police found Kathleen's wallet on his body. Acquaintances claimed they had no warning signs of violence potential in Timothy.

Harvard University

In 1995, during the final days of their junior year Sinedu Tadesse, a biology major from Ethiopia, fatally stabbed roommate Trang Ho forty-five times. Sinedu then hung herself in the bathroom of their suite. Five days before the killing, the *Harvard Crimson* received an anonymous envelope containing a photograph of Sinedu and a computer-printed note reading "Keep this picture. There will soon be a very juicy story involv-

ing the person in this picture."

Trang Ho was a premed student born in Vietnam who had been profiled in *Boston* magazine as one of "25 Who Can Save Boston." In the aftermath of the deaths, the press painted the picture of two quiet international students whose problems were "no different than thousands of disagreements that happen between roommates at every college" (*People Weekly,* 1995). Many asked, who could have predicted such a tragedy?

One reporter, a Harvard graduate who had actually met Sinedu years before, dug deeper. In her book *Halfway Heaven: Diary of a Harvard Murder* (1997), Melanie Thernstrom uncovered what actually took place during the months that led up to the murder-suicide, and all the tell-tale signs were there.

The summer after her freshman year, Sinedu wrote a long letter about herself and sent copies to strangers whose addresses she had found in the telephone directory. Here are some excepts from that document:

> Well, why am I writing this letter? Because I am desperate. . . . My problem is that I am not bonding with people. I do not make friends even with my relatives. . . . I live in my own shell, afraid to reveal my personality and to express my opinions. . . . As far as I remember my life as been hellish. . . . Year after year, I became lonelier and lonelier. I see friends deserting me. They would take every chance to show me that they did not have any love or respect for me. . . . You are one of the very few people who see me struggle . . . All you have to do is give me a hand and put into words what you already know. . . . I am sure one of your concerns, if you have gotten this far in the letter is, what if I am one of those criminals lurking around. But believe me, right now I am not strong enough. . . . I anxiously wait to hear from you.
>
> –*Halfway Heaven,* pp. 101–104

One woman who received this letter knew an administrator at Harvard and passed it on. The letter eventually reached the Freshman Deans Office and was forwarded to the Dunster House, where Sinedu would be living in the fall. It was then placed in her file.

In her sophomore year Sinedu moved in with Trang and became obsessed with her one-sided friendship. She referred to Trang as "a girl I would make the queen of my life." Trang was "spunky" and had lots of friends, and this angered Sinedu as she felt her bond with Trang slipping away. When Trang would invite friends over, Sinedu would sit in her room festering with jealousy. At the end of their sophomore year, Trang reluctantly agreed to live with Sinedu the following year and immediately regretted her decision. Sinedu became increasingly disorderly and Trang began spending less and less time in the room. During the second semester, Trang decided she would move in with another woman for her senior year. At this point, Sinedu stopped speaking to Trang and became increasingly difficult. As indicated by her journals, Sinedu's violent fantasies began at this time: "The bad way out is suicide & the good way out killing, savoring their fear & then suicide."

Thernstrom concludes in her book, "Through her single act of violence, Sinedu's reality became the ultimate one, linking the two girls through death in a common fate, so that in memory they are bonded in a way in which Trang has no choice, and which in life never existed" (*Halfway Heaven,* 1997, p. 7). If I can't have you, no one will.

Johns Hopkins University

People Weekly called it a "fatal friendship." During their time at Johns Hopkins University, students Bob Harwood and Rex Chao had an intense friendship and some wonder if it bordered on a sexual relationship. Rex, a nineteen-year-old sophomore, called Bob, a twenty-two-year-old senior,

"the older brother I never had." But when Rex developed a relationship with a woman, Bob became increasingly obsessive, demanding to know where Rex was at all times. Rex became so distressed by the rambling emails and accusations made by Bob that he filed a grievance with the Dean of Students. Rex felt that he was being stalked and told the dean that Bob owned a gun.

Bob proceeded to pass out flyers defaming Rex when Rex ran for chairman of the College Republicans club. On the night of April 10, 1996, Rex won the election. After the meeting, Bob followed Rex and his girlfriend outside and shot Rex in the head with a .357 Magnum. Bob then stepped over Rex and fired a second shot into Rex's chest. Bob then ran for a security guard to call for an ambulance and immediately requested a lawyer.

Bob was sentenced to thirty-five years in prison. Bob later sued the university for withholding his degree. The Maryland Court of Special Appeals supported the rejection of the lawsuit stating that Bob had violated the university's code of conduct, thereby breaking the contractual obligation to award a degree for completed academic requirements.

Understanding Relationship-Based Homicide as End-Stage Stalking

Stalking is legally defined as "willful, malicious and repeated following and harassment combined with the credible threat intended to make the victim fear death or serious injury." Experts estimate that one in twenty women will become stalking targets at some point in their lives. According to the National Victims Center, both men and women can be either perpetrators or victims of stalking, but the overwhelming majority of cases involve men stalking women (75–80 percent).

Psychologists have identified two categories of stalking behavior: (1) "Love Obsession Stalkers" represent about 20 to 25 percent of all stalking cases. These stalkers develop a love fixation on another person with whom they have never had any personal relationship. Some choose to stalk celebrities, others develop obsessions with regular, ordinary people. (2) "Simple Obsession Stalkers" represent about 70 to 80 percent of all stalking cases. These stalkers are differentiated from Love Obsession Stalkers in that they have had a personal or romantic relationship with their victims before the stalking behavior began. In most instances, the victim has become the stalker's sole source of self-esteem. When the victim tries to break off the relationship, the perpetrator's thinking evolves from "If I can just prove how much I love you" to "I can make you love me," to "If I can't have you, nobody else will." Stalking cases which developed from domestic violence patterns are the most common and potentially lethal.

Stalking usually progresses through predictable stages:

• Mental Obsession

At this level, the stalker is preoccupied with intrusive thoughts regarding the victim. The stalker is unable to stop thinking about him or her. This type of obsession often occurs at the beginning of a relationship during the infatuation stage, or at the end of a relationship when the stalker feels rejected.

• Surveillance

At the next level the stalker follows the victim to collect information. Surveillance allows the stalker to watch the victim in his or her natural habitat. Information about the victim is collected from various sources–observation, coworkers, friends, family, and unsuspecting others. Direct approaches range from reading the victim's mail to going through the victim's trash.

• Harassment

During harassment, the stalker attempts to either seduce or intimidate the victim into compliance. The stalker crosses the line from observation of to interaction with the victim. In the beginning, the stalker may attempt to be attentive, charming, or even romantic. The stalker remains congenial as long as the victim responds favorably. However, if the victim rebuffs or ignores the stalker's attempts at courtship or control, a more negative campaign of harassment may result.

• Extermination

This is a lethal phase of stalking because the perpetrator has now realized no possibility exists for any relationship with the victim. The stalker may not see any alternative but to kill the victim and frequently him or herself. While the progression of these levels is common, no stalking case is completely predictable.

It wasn't until 1990 that California became the first state to pass a law that made stalking a crime. This gave law enforcement officers legal leverage to intervene in stalking cases *before* offenders took action. Since that time, all fifty states have made stalking a crime.

When people file a complaint under the stalking statute, they must have sufficient evidence to establish "probable cause." In other words, the stalking victims are put in the position of having to prove their case to law enforcement before they are allowed to take their case to court. It is essential, therefore, to document every stalking incident very thoroughly. For example, victims should be advised to collect phone answering messages, letters, photos of the stalker, videotapes, audiotapes, photos of property damage, affidavits from witnesses, and any objects the stalker may have left.

Victims may seek to obtain a restraining order from the local court. These orders require the offender to stay away from the victim, and if violated, the stalker may be punished by a fine or jail time. Nevertheless, restraining orders are not foolproof and may create a false sense of security.

Victims may also use the arm of the law when they have determined that the perpetrator has broken the law by entering the victim's residence without permission, by stealing property, by destroying property, or by physically assaulting the victim.

Recommendations

Homicide is the worst case scenario of obsessive relationships. Unfortunately, there is not much campus administrators can do to prevent it from happening. This is especially true if the perpetrator is a part of the campus community and continues to have a relationship with the victim. Victims, however, are in a position to prevent violence, although it is usually a complicated and difficult endeavor. The following recommendations for victims are adapted from the National Victims Center guidelines. They are presented in order of escalating danger from preventive measures to responding to imminent danger.

1. Notify the stalker to stop. You or your attorney can send a registered letter to the stalker requesting that the behavior cease. Treat all threats as serious and notify law enforcement immediately.
2. Tell everyone you know what is going on. Give residence hall directors, campus security, friends, coworkers, relatives, and neighbors a description or picture of the stalker and vehicles, and

have them document everything they see. Warn them not to give the stalker any information about you. Have coworkers or family members screen visitors and calls. Give your address and phone number to as few people as possible.
3. Document everything carefully. Take pictures of destroyed property, injuries inflicted on the victim, or other evidence. Save all letters or notes written by the stalker. Save answering machine messages. Log dates and times of all unwanted contact.
4. Secure the residence. Change locks and secure spare keys. Install solid doors with deadbolt locks. Post a "no trespassing" sign on the edge of your property. Improve lighting and visibility around your house. Change your phone number to unlisted. Obtain a post office box.
5. Vary your behavior. Don't follow the same routine every day. Change your driving routes and times when you usually do things. Limit or eliminate walking or jogging alone. Try to stay in public places.
6. If you move don't leave a "paper trail" by having mail forwarded to your new address. Take all records (medical, financial, school) with you.
7. Take care of yourself. Join a support group or consider therapy to help you deal with stress. Develop your support system.
8. Develop a safety plan.
• Memorize or have quick access to important phone numbers including:
   – law enforcement
   – safe places (friends, shelters, etc.)
   – attorneys
   – trusted people to help you when safety is secured (childcare, pet care, etc.)

- Be ready for a quick departure:
  - pack a small suitcase for yourself (and children)
  - have reserve money stashed
  - gather critical documents (birth certificates, prescriptions, social security information, passports, creditors' numbers)
- Alert critical people of your situation:
  - family and friends
  - law enforcement/security
  - employers/coworkers
9. Victims in Imminent Danger: Attempt to locate a safe place:
  - police stations
  - residences of family or friends
  - shelters or local churches
  - public areas (stalker may be less likely to create a public disturbance)
10. Call 911 or other emergency number.

NOTE: The above information is not intended to be a strict set of guidelines, but rather to give victims options. Unfortunately, there is no guarantee that if you follow any or all of these suggestions that you will be safe.

Infanticide

Infanticide is a form of homicide that is often overlooked as a potential type of campus violence. There are numerous cases across the country where female students, sometimes with the assistance of their partners, kill their unwanted newborn babies. Amazingly, most of these women were able to hide their pregnancies from others, and thus, college officials are unable to reach out to these women to offer assistance. The women frequently claim that they are afraid to announce their pregnancy for fear that they will be asked to leave school. This fear seems to be pronounced at religious institutions.

These women often deliver their babies alone in their residence halls or nearby hotel rooms and can experience significant problems without medical assistance. According to an article in the *Chronicle for Higher Education* a woman who was a junior at Claflin College delivered a baby in her residence hall room and was later found unconscious. When doctors examined her and discovered she had just given birth, college administrators rushed back to her room to look for the baby. They found the baby dead in a gym bag under her bed. The housing policy at this particular school read, "Pregnant students . . . will be required to move out of the residence hall. The college is in no way responsible for any problem/complication that may arise out of this condition."

The highest profile case of college infanticide was "Baby Boy Grossberg." On November 12, 1996, Amy Grossberg, an eighteen-year-old freshman at the University of Delaware, gave birth in a motel with the assistance of her boyfriend Brian Peterson, Jr., a freshman at Gettysburg College. Autopsy findings revealed that the baby had been severely beaten before being wrapped in a garbage bag and thrown in the motel's dumpster. When Amy returned to school, she fainted and was taken to the hospital where they determined she had just given birth. Brian told campus officials where the baby was. While initially there was much talk about the death penalty for the two students, in July 1998 they were sentenced to brief prison terms (less than three years each).

Recommendations

Like many forms of violence prevention, colleges are again at the crossroads of protecting students' privacy and taking steps to intervene. Many schools see pregnancy as a moral issue as well as a medical issue, and these perspectives can complicate the picture further. Administrators are often at a loss as to how to intervene.

1. Colleges need to make sure that students know that medical treatment on campus is confidential.
2. Student conduct and residence policies should be reviewed to note any per-

ceived punishments for pregnancy.

3. Campus communities must offer safe places where students feel that they can explore their medical options without consequences.
4. Residence Hall staff must be trained on telltale signs of pregnancy and how to intervene effectively.

NON-SEXUAL ASSAULT

Non-sexual assault is another heterogeneous category of campus violence. We have chosen to divide this section into two categories—physical assault between people not in an intimate relationship and dating violence.

Physical Assault

For the most part physical assault that is not dating related usually occurs between male athletes or fraternity brothers who are under the influence of alcohol. In a recent study published in the *American Journal of Health Studies,* researchers found that 47 percent of college men surveyed reported non-sexual violent acts with those of the same sex. Alcohol was involved in 60 percent of the incidents. Furthermore, over half of these men indicated that they were involved in more than one violent act, with alcohol present in almost 70 percent of these instances.

At the University of Rhode Island, football players smashed windows and doors at a fraternity house. Campus administrators responded swiftly with significant consequences for the offenders. Ten days later thirty students, many of them football players, fought with fists and beer bottles. The university president punished the team by forfeiting the upcoming game against the

University of Connecticut.

Virginia Wesleyan College suspended twenty-three male basketball players from participating in competition after a brawl that was allegedly ignited by a fight over a woman at an off-campus bar. Shortly after, college officials reviewed the case and conceded to let some players seek reinstatement for some of the games for which they had been suspended. Instead, they were mandated to complete "meaningful community service." It was argued by proponents of this decision reversal that the suspensions could substantially hurt the basketball team's chances of a repeat NCAA Division III championship win.

Washington State University suspended two fraternities after a brawl involving golf clubs, flashlights, sticks, and other objects. The brawl apparently erupted after weeks of brewing conflict between the houses. Each house claimed that the other had damaged house property. During the fight, a half-dozen men from each house were injured and many required medical treatment.

Recently, the University of New Hampshire (UNH) experienced a bizarre case of drunken fighting. In March 2000, Walter Wilson, a twenty-one-year-old civil engineering senior got into a fight with another student. Hours later and intoxicated, Walter rounded up five fraternity brothers to seek revenge. Walter led his brothers to an apartment complex, barged through the door of Unit C1, and attacked the man sleeping there. Soon they realized they had the wrong apartment and left. Then they went to the next door and broke in, attacking the two men sleeping there. One victim received a blow from a barstool. Again, they had the wrong apartment. It turns out the student Walter was looking for did not even live in that particular complex. The six men were arrested and face disciplinary action by the school as well.

This UNH fraternity had quite a track record of violent offenses ranging from burglary to assault. The university also has a history of trying to tame the fraternity system. In the 1990s a campus administrator banned another fraternity for a number of violent allegations including hazing. Afterwards, this administrator received death threats, experienced car vandalism, and found drivers were attempting to run him off the road.

The most tragic case involved a man named David Shick from Georgetown University. In a campus parking lot on February 18, 2000, David was involved in a drunken brawl involving five members of the school's soccer team. According to witness testimony, David was punched in the face and fell backward, hitting his head on the pavement. Georgetown's campus police sent the other students home without taking names or statements, and David went to the hospital. He died four days later. His death was ruled a homicide; however, no criminal charges were made.

In the aftermath of David's death, faculty urged the provost and other upper administrators to convene a panel of deans to examine the party culture at Georgetown. Only half of the deans showed up for the first meeting; only one attended the second meeting.

While the majority of physical assault seems to come from athletes and fraternities,

one unlikely group has also made the headlines: marching bands. On September 19, 1998 two of the nation's most revered bands–Prairie View A&M and Southern University–battled it out, literally, during the halftime show. When Southern attempted to exit to the sideline the bands collided and three hundred seventy marchers got in a "full-on, 100-percent street brawl" for twenty minutes. Each band blamed the other, and three students were taken to the hospital. Both teams were suspended from the following two football games.

Given that non-sexual male-on-male violence was such a common occurrence, one would expect to find a plethora of research and articles on the topic. There were scarcely any–another indication that our culture adheres to the "boys will be boys" mentality.

Recommendations

1. Swift and decisive action against all parties involved in physical assault. It seems that many colleges have a much lower expectation for acceptable behavior of their students on campus than we have for other individuals in other contexts. For instance, we would not excuse this behavior as "boys will be boys" if it happened in a church or a movie theater.
2. Address alcohol abuse (see Chapter 4).
3. Be prepared to slay the sacred cows and stand by a zero tolerance position on violence.

Dating Violence

Experts in women studies claim that the distinction between sexual violence and battering in relationships is rather artificial. They contend that relationship violence is often sexualized in nature because it usually takes place in the bedroom, is triggered by sexual issues, and is considered erotic subject matter to some. For this reason we conceptualize relationship violence and sexual violence as overlapping; however, we limit this section to non-sexual forms of violence.

Dating violence can span a continuum from verbal abuse and threats to minimal injury contact to lethal force. Dating violence can take the form of physical abuse, emotional abuse, economic abuse, social isolation, and sexual abuse.

As identified by domestic violence expert Lenore Walker (1980), dating violence tends to pass through predictable distinct phases: tension building, explosion, and honeymoon. These phases vary in time and intensity for each couple and between different couples. Tension building refers to the time when minor incidents occur causing friction in the relationship. Explosion refers to the point where the tension building has reached uncontrollable levels, and the batterer explodes with an acute battering incident. The honeymoon stage, otherwise known as "hearts and flowers," is characterized by remorseful, loving, and contrite behavior by the batterer.

Verbal abuse is a category that often gets bypassed in discussions about dating violence. Verbal abuse occurs when one uses words to attack or emotionally injure another person. Often disguised in the form of "harmless jokes," verbal abuse is often the first step in the progression of dating violence and can take many forms.

Verbal Abuse	
Forms	*Examples*
Withholding Intimacy	"There is nothing to talk about."
Denying Victim's Reality	"No, that's not the way it is." (constantly saying the opposite)
Discounting Feelings	"You're too sensitive." "You can't take a joke."
Shutting Down Conversation	"I don't see where this is going. Discussion over!"
Blaming	"I've had it with your complaining. You're just out to get me."
Judging	"Your problem is you never stop nagging."
Eroding Confidence	"You wouldn't understand. It's over your head."
Threatening	"Do what I want or I'm out of here."
Name Calling	Even "sweetheart" or "dear" when used with a sarcastic tone
Convenient Forgetting	Promises, important occasions, agreements
Ordering	"Get over here and do this now." "You're not wearing that!"

Source: Adapted from Patricia Evans, *The Verbally Abusive Relationship*, 1992.

Heterosexual Couples

According to the National University Center for Law, Education and Public Policy, battering is the single greatest cause of injury to women in the United States. This cause of injury supercedes car accidents, muggings, and rapes combined. After reviewing several gender violence studies, Kay Hartwell Hunnicutt (1998) concluded that one quarter to one third of high school and college students have been involved in relationship violence–as victims, perpetrators or both. Even more disturbing is the fact that approximately 70 percent of female college students found some form of dating violence acceptable. This probably helps to explain findings cited in *Responding to Violence on Campus*–27 percent of college dating violence victims chose to continue the relationship with their abuser.

Like many forms of campus violence, the number of dating violence incidents reported to campus officials is significantly lower than the number reported by students. This pattern is largely due to either the reluctance of victims to come forward for fear of retaliation or the desire of the victim to continue the relationship.

According to a 1991 study published in the *Journal of Consulting and Clinical Psychology,* when we look at male violence against women, peer support of masculine hostility and abuse are stronger predictors of aggression than a remote history of a violent past. In addition, evidence exists to suggest other proximal influences like training in the military or violence on the streets "slip over" to affect personal lives.

Most of this section focuses on male violence against women, but we acknowledge that women inflict violence against men. Research seems to indicate that this is an increasing trend. In 2000, a study published by Purdue University researchers found that females were significantly more likely to report using physical force than were male students. "Physical aggressions" was defined as: throwing objects at partner; pushing, hitting, or grabbing partner; slapping partner; kicking, biting, or hitting partner with a fist; trying to hit partner with something other than a fist; beating up partner; choking partner; threatening partner with a knife or gun; or using a gun or knife on partner. Any endorsement of these items led to a categorization of "physically aggressive." It is not clear from this study what degree of violence was inflicted by the women.

It is generally understood by experts of gender violence that because of their greater height, weight, and muscular build most males have a greater propensity to inflict harm on women than vise versa. Thus, most research to date has been focused on males perpetrating violence against women.

The media has placed a great deal of attention on male athlete violence against women. This trend has led to heated debates: Are athletes being unfairly scapegoated because they live in the spotlight or are athletes more prone to commit acts of violence against women because of strong aggression socialization and a hypermasculine culture? Recent evaluations by social scientists of athletic involvement and violence against women suggest that both sides of the debate have validity.

It is true that on occasion the media has oversensationalized the problem. Athletes are highly visible and their criminal activity makes for interesting news. That said, research indicates that male athlete involvement in violence against women is significant. Todd Crosset and colleagues found that while male student-athletes made up 3.0 percent of the total male population at Division I institutions, they represented 35 percent of the perpetrators reported. *Sports Illustrated* noted that in the aftermath of the Nicole Brown Simpson murder, college athlete domestic violence mushroomed. At the University of Florida alone three football players were arrested for assaulting their wives or girlfriends, one of whom was pregnant. One of the players was expelled from school. For the other two, most charges were eventually dismissed and the Florida football program only suspended them for one game.

Researchers from Carleton University suggest the "DAD" model gives us insight as to why men perpetrate violence against their female partners. *DAD* stands for *d*ependency, *a*vailability, and *d*eterrence. Dependency refers to the "addictive" quality of the relationship. Dependent partners will experience physical and emotional withdrawal pains when their significant other is absent. Likewise, many men who abuse their girlfriends or wives also abuse alcohol and drugs, and this substance abuse is often related to the trigger of the violent events.

Availability refers to the amount of access that a man has to his partner. Those men who live with their partners are more likely to be abusive than those who do not because there are more opportunities for abuse. Deterrence refers to how much the man conforms to social and legal conventions prohibiting violence. Social isolation plays into the level of deterrence–men who are isolated are less concerned with negative consequences of abusive behavior. Furthermore, the more violence a man has engaged in during the course of his life, the more his deterrence has worn down.

Recommendations

1. Develop disciplinary policies that specifically deal with the unique dynamics of partner violence to make sure cases are not dismissed as "lovers' quarrels." The consistent message must be repeated: violence is unacceptable and those who commit it will be punished. According to Rosemarie Bogal-Allbritten, Professor of Sociology, Murray State University, and William Allbritten, Director of Counseling and Testing Center, Murray State University (1991), there exists a power differential in male-female violence, and thus, traditional disciplinary methods used in male versus male violence may not be appropriate in these cases.
2. If danger is imminent make sure that the victim has an effective safety plan (see stalking section earlier in this chapter).
3. Depending on the circumstances, counseling and mediation between victim and offender might prove beneficial in stopping the abuse. This would not be advisable in extreme obsessive relationships, but may be helpful in

first-time low-level violence incidents to increase awareness before patterns develop.
4. Establish connections with services provided in the larger community, for example, support groups for victims or battering prevention groups for perpetrators. Assign someone on campus to serve as the liaison between the school and community agencies, so that rapport is developed and referrals can be made more confidentially.
5. Provide educational programs for students on understanding patterns and consequences of dating violence. Include in these presentations a discussion on verbal abuse, a form of dating violence that often gets overlooked.

Gay and Lesbian Couples

According to *Violence in Gay and Lesbian Domestic Partnerships,* a book by Claire Renzetti and Charles Miley (1996), domestic violence occurs at approximately the same rate in gay and lesbian relationships as it does in heterosexual relationships. These findings clearly shatter many myths people have about same-sex partnerships. This research seems to indicate that partnership violence is less about gender and more about power and control. While very little is known about same-sex violence in the general population, even less is known about same-sex couples at our colleges and universities. Thus, the relationship between the findings reported and college life are speculative until future research is conducted.

Much of the dynamics of same-sex dating violence is similar to heterosexual violence. The types of abuse, the patterns, the consequences, and the reasons for staying in the relationship are all similar. Still, important differences exist. One form of psychological abuse for same-sex couples is the threat of "outing" the abused partner to family, employers, or others with "blackmail" potential. Another difference same-sex couples face is that the direction of violence can and often does go both ways between partners. Most state laws do not include language inclusive of gay and lesbian relationships, but rather use the terms "spouse" or "battered wife." Therefore, gay and lesbian victims do not have the same civil rights protection as heterosexual couples and their isolation from advocacy and other helpful resources is often magnified because of this.

Recommendations

The following recommendations are adapted from L. Kevin Hamberger's chapter in *Violence in Gay and Lesbian Domestic Partnerships* (1996).

1. Name the problem. Confront denial and challenge myths around same-sex dating violence. Community education regarding the incidence, prevalence, and dynamics of same-sex violence is essential.
2. Establish community networks. Task forces made up of local community and campus leaders, medical professionals, victim advocates, batterer therapists, law enforcement, and others can work together to advocate change, research the problems, and educate the community.
3. Safe-house resources must address the unique needs of same-sex couples.
4. Research campus same-sex dating violence.

Chapter 15

ARSON AND BOMBING

WHILE THEY DO NOT ALWAYS make national headlines, arson and bombing happen on college campuses. Perpetrators who gravitate toward these crimes are becoming increasingly sophisticated in their ability to inflict tremendous damage without getting caught. Universities often have ample firepower materials available in science labs, and experimentation is the natural consequence of curious minds. Students of the computer era are very savvy in finding information about building bombs and setting fires with delay devices.

SIMILARITIES BETWEEN ARSONISTS AND BOMBERS

In their book *Bombers and Firesetters* MacDonald, Shaughnessy, and Galvin (1977) noted some striking similarities between arsonists and bombers. The motives and agents of destruction are alike. The destruction of evidence and cover up of additional criminal activity causes similar frustration for investigators. Both compulsive bombers and compulsive firesetters can experience sexual excitement during their crimes, and many of these perpetrators return to the scene of their destruction. Few other crimes have the capacity to cause such widespread property damage and loss of life in one act. Like arsonists, bombers often seal their own fate. A large percentage of those who die from bombs are bombers themselves. In addition to intended victims and the perpetrators, arson and bombs often take the lives of innocent bystanders and rescue personnel.

ARSON

What We Know About Arson

• Each year, fire kills more Americans than all natural disasters combined (U.S. Fire Administration, "Facts on Fire").
• Arson is the second leading cause of death by fire in the U.S.–surpassed only by smoking–and the leading cause of property damage due to fires (www.fire-investigators.org)
• Arsonists usually escape punishment. In 1997, only 19 percent of arson offenses

219

led to arrest, and only 2 percent of those arrested were convicted (www.fire-investigators.org)

- Those twenty years of age and under account for about 50 percent of all arson fires in the United States (www.fire-investigators.org).

The FBI Uniform Crime Reporting System definition of arson is, "Any willful or malicious burning or attempt to burn, with or without intent to defraud, a dwelling house, public building, motor vehicle or aircraft, personal property of another, etc." A recent campus crime report published by the *Chronicle* indicates that arson happens more than most expect. In 1998, there were five hundred thirty-nine cases of reported arson, a 16.9 percent increase over the previous year. This makes arson a more frequent crime than reported murders, manslaughter, nonforcible sex offenses and hate crimes combined.

Arsonists are driven by a variety of motives. Curiosity, racial hatred, drunken vandalism, sexual excitement, copycat crimes, and revenge are some. The overwhelming majority of arsonists are male, and of the eight FBI Crime Index offenses listed in the Uniform Crime Report, arson has the highest percentage of adolescent involvement.

As forensic expert John MacDonald notes, firesetting is a hazardous undertaking and can often take the life of the arsonist. Arsonists often dump fire accelerant such as gasoline to help ignite their fire. Naive firesetters do not realize that gasoline evaporates quickly and increases the risk for explosion. Young arsonists tend to light paper and trash as incendiary materials. Other flammable liquids used by arsonists include paint thinner, kerosene, turpentine, alcohol, and ether.

Effects of Alcohol

The crime of arson is often committed by persons under the influence of alcohol. As with other crimes, alcohol affects judgment and inhibition and increases the potential for violence. In a monograph published by the Institute of Psychiatry, forensic psychiatrist Ann Barker (1994) cited research stating 54 percent of solo arsonists and 40 percent of those with partners were intoxicated with drugs or alcohol at the time of the crime.

Intoxication also significantly increases risks for victims of arson. Toxicological analysis of victims who have died in fires reveal that many of them had high blood alcohol levels, seriously affecting their ability to escape. Party pranks involving firecrackers and smoke bombs have sometimes turned deadly because of intoxicated victims. In 1996, at the University of Virginia in Charlottesville fire officials speculate that senior Elizabeth McGowen died when a fire swept through her off-campus apartment because she was too impaired to respond. The fire started when two of her friends threw smoke bombs into her apartment during a party. An autopsy indicated that Elizabeth's blood alcohol content was three times the legal limit for intoxication in Virginia.

Murray State and Other Campus Arson Cases

On September 18, 1998, Michael Minger, a sophomore music major at Murray State died in a residence hall fire that officials have ruled as arson. Fifteen other students were injured including Michael Priddy who suffered major burns and brain injury from oxygen depletion. The fire was the second one set in Hester Hall that week, the former was quickly contained and caused only minor damage. Fire authorities surmise the fatal fire began from gasoline poured on a carpet in the hallway. Hester Hall did not have a sprinkler system despite repeated warnings from Deputy State Fire Marshals.

As the case has unfolded, it has taken many unexpected turns, complicating the investigation. A couple of hours before the fire started, a group of rugby players and their friends decided to make prank calls to a freshman in Hester Hall. One of the calls recorded on an answering machine tape warned him that his door was on fire. A university police officer was summoned to talk to residents about the calls and reports of smoke. Sixty-eight minutes later flames were visible and students began fleeing in their nightclothes. Some students were rescued from their windows, while others found themselves trapped in stairwells.

The university offered a $30,000 reward for information leading to a conviction of the firesetters. In the weeks that followed one hundred students moved off campus. Toward the end of October, police indicted the seven prank callers, five of whom were Murray State students. The charges ranged from capital murder and arson to complicity and conspiracy. All admitted to participating in the phone calls, but vehemently denied the firesetting charges. Predictably, these students were seen as guilty by many and ostracized from the campus community. When officials realized they did not have enough evidence to tie the students to the fire, they dropped the charges.

Nine months after the fire, another student was arrested. Jerry Walker, a senior at the university and former member of a campus security unit, was charged with capital murder and first-degree arson. Ironically, Walker was one of the students injured and rescued in the fire. Police claim that after the fire, a letter written by someone stating to

know the fire's source was found on the windshield of Walker's girlfriend. Furthermore, a convenience store surveillance camera taped Walker buying a dollar's worth of gas on the night of the fire. Walker's trial is scheduled for October 2000.

Five of the seven previously accused students are filing suit alleging wrongful arrest on felony charges. Four of the seven were nevertheless convicted of making prank phone calls, a misdemeanor. Murray State has since installed sprinkler heads in each room of Hester Hall along with a new evaluation system. In the aftermath of this tragedy, Michael Minger's mother Gail Minger championed legislation requiring public and private institutions of higher education in Kentucky to publicly disclose information about serious campus crimes and restates the fire marshal's jurisdiction over these campuses. In July 2000, the Michael Minger Act took effect.

Other lesser-known campus arson occurrences include the following cases:

- In 1995, three arson fires caused more than $1 million in damage to Clark Atlanta University buildings. The fires were set over a five-day period during the university's spring break.
- In 1997, five fires ignited during one week at the University of Miami, Florida, one of them ruled as arson. The arson fire was set before dawn in the offices used by the men's basketball coaches and caused more than $100,000 in damage.
- In 1998, seven minor fires were set at Benedict College, five of them occurring within a ten-hour span. The arsonist lighted the fires in bathrooms and trash buckets.
- In 2000, a radical environmental group claimed responsibility for setting a fire that burned offices at Michigan State University. The targeted offices were in charge of a controversial project bring-

ing biotechnology research to agricultural scientists in the Third World. The fire cause $500,000 in damage.

Arson Investigation

Arson is a difficult crime to solve because the crime itself erases most evidence. In fact, most campus arson cases remain unsolved due to this aspect of the crime. Thus, motives for campus arson are unclear. As Bernard Levin (1976) notes in his article "Psychological Characteristics of Firesetters," "Unfortunately, our knowledge about the psychopathology of firesetters is limited to those arsonists who are caught or give themselves up. In short, we know the most about the least successful arsonists" (p. 43).

Generally speaking arsonists light fires to create a financial gain, cover up a crime, inflict revenge, or bring themselves attention. However, according to a recent review of the psychiatric literature on arson, the largest category of motives is "pleasure or excitement, vandalism, boredom, or relief from tension." These latter experiences are common for college students.

During the investigation phase of arson, firefighters look for certain clues to help them determine the cause. John MacDonald, coauthor of *Bombers and Firesetters* (1977) notes that fires that spread rapidly or irregularly are often suspicious. The color of the smoke can indicate what set the fire. Distinctive odors of gasoline, diesel fuel, kerosene, or turpentine are other clues. Sabotaged fire safety equipment such as fire alarms and sprinkler systems and obstructed entrances are further evidence of arson. Many times the person who first reports seeing the fire is actually the firesetter.

Recommendations

The following recommendations were compiled from the www.fire-investigators, and www.fire.org.uk and *Bombers and Firesetters* (1977). In general, arson prevention follows general burglar and fire prevention guidelines. One particular concern for college campuses dealing with arson is the high number of fire alarm pranks. The tremendous number of false alarms gives students, administrators, and even firefighters a sense of apathy. Some schools have a delay system when fire alarms are pulled to make sure the fires are real before fire crews are summoned. This delay can prove deadly. In the training video *How Fast it Burned* (University of Georgia, 1989) filmmakers demonstrate that fire from a lit candle can progress to engulf a residence hall room in three minutes.

1. Illuminate campus property and exteriors. Arsonists, like burglars and predators, fear light and do not want to get caught.
2. Do not publicly announce when campus buildings will be vacant.
3. Most arsonists work at night, so surveillance cameras may be the best method of capturing evidence. Note that arsonists sometimes carry liquid accelerant, like gasoline, in an inconspicuous container. Acts of vandalism may precede arson.
4. Ensure that firefighting equipment is in good working order and is protected against sabotage.
5. University policies should require total evacuation of residence halls and notification of the fire department for every fire alarm.
6. Fire safety education provided by local

fire officials can help students feel confident in using fire extinguishers and other fire safety techniques.

7. Take pictures of spectators who watch the fire burn. Arsonists often like to witness their act of destruction. If the fire takes place during normal sleeping hours, the arsonist may be the only spectator wearing normal street clothes instead of nightclothes.

BOMBS AND BOMB THREATS

Why should colleges be concerned about bombs and bomb threats?

• Because technology in the area of explosives has advanced tremendously and materials necessary to construct powerful devices are readily accessible via underground publications and the Internet.

• Bombing and bomb threats draw high media attention making these forms of violence susceptible to the "copycat" phenomenon.

• High school bombings such as at Columbine and bomb threats in high schools and workplaces are becoming increasingly common and may spill over to the college setting.

• Today, bombers are very creative and bombs can be constructed to look like almost anything. Most bombs are homemade and are limited only by the imagination and resources of the bomber.

Bombs have appeal for sensation seekers. The power of the explosion, the magnitude of destruction and the deafening noise can be thoroughly exciting for some. Investigators can infer the motive of the bomber from the choice of target. A small toilet bowl explosion is probably a prank. A middle of the woods explosion is most likely out of curiosity. A targeted car or office would indicate revenge of some sort. In the few cases of college bombings that have been made public, the motives have ranged from revenge to curiosity to racial hatred to a burglary cover up.

Campus Bombing

In 1996, a former student at the University of South Florida, Tampa, pleaded guilty to a bomb threat that essentially shut down the campus for three days. The perpetrator mailed the threat to the student newspaper stating that he intended to bomb a building and kill a professor if the former professor Ramadan Abdullah Shallah did not receive an apology from campus officials. What specific type of apology was unclear to investigators.

In 1998, David Rose, a student at the California Institute of Technology, was killed when a homemade bomb he had built with friend Matthew Roesle, a sophomore at Rose-Hulman Institute of Technology, exploded. David was visiting Matthew and the bomb detonated in a wooded area on the campus of Rose-Hulman Institute. Police evacuated Matthew's residence hall to find a second explosive device in his room.

In April of 1999, campus police at Georgia Southern University arrested five students who allegedly attempted to set off a bomb to divert attention while they robbed a campus office. The officers learned of the plan and defused the bomb minutes before it was going to explode. In the same month, three students at Bringham Young University were arrested for detonating a homemade pipe bomb outside their residence hall. The bomb's explosion shattered windows and injured the ear of a nearby student.

In a widely publicized case, Lawrence Lombardi, a forty-one-year-old white man, was convicted on six federal charges of setting off two bombs at the predominately black institution, Florida A&M University (FAMU). Two small explosives detonated within a month during late summer of 1999. There were no injuries in either blast, but racist phone calls accompanied each and forecasted future attacks.

The evidence against Lombardi was staggering. In the immediate aftermath of the bombings, Lawrence Lombardi called News Channel 27 and the *Tallahassee Democrat* to state that these bombs were "just the beginning." Later government agents secretly taped him discussing his alibi with his wife on the phone. Lombardi was videotaped buying PVC pipe at a home improvement store. He later claimed this pipe was intended to build a lawn sprinkler, but the pipe was identical to fragments found at the crime scene. Lombardi had been a snack vendor and this position allowed him access to the campus and a FAMU photo identification card. When he stopped working for the food vendor, he did not turn in his photo ID. The men's bathrooms where the bombs exploded were twenty to twenty-five feet from the vending machines Lombardi serviced. Lombardi was known to make racial comments and visit racist websites. He also owned a manual on how to make bombs and had expressed interest in explosives to friends.

Understandably, the bombings set the FAMU campus in a panic. After the first bombing, most students shrugged it off as a prank. But after the second bombing and subsequent racist phone calls, the campus community was terrified. In the days after the second bombing, students, faculty, and staff were required to wear the campus identification around their necks to get access to the campus. The governor increased funding to take extra security measures on campus including increased law enforcement presence and security cameras. Campus officials immediately began detailing written evacuation plans to be distributed to classes. During the year of the investigation and trial, hundreds of students withdrew from FAMU out of fear.

Bomb Threats

Bomb threats, especially those in the immediate aftermath of a bomb incident, can cause intense fear and serious inconvenience for those who receive them and respond to them. So many threats are made and never carried out that it becomes easy to dismiss them. Nevertheless, because of the significant damage bombs can inflict, all bomb threats must be taken seriously. Most threats are made via phone calls while a few are written or made in the presence of an intended victim. Schools are the number one target for bomb threats. Forensic expert John MacDonald estimates that two out of five callers of bomb threats give the time the bomb will explode. The time ranges from "right now" to a month away. Sometimes, the caller will give a location of the bomb or make taunting comments such as "Are you nervous?" MacDonald also notes that more than two thirds of those who answered bomb threats were women.

The Bureau of Alcohol, Tobacco and Firearms suggests that there are only two logical explanations for a bomb threat. Either the caller has definite knowledge or the caller wants to create mayhem. If the caller has a strong suspicion that an explosive has been planted, he or she may want to minimize personal injury or property damage. In this case the caller may be either the person who placed the bomb or someone who has become aware of the situation. An individual might become suspicious of a roommate's reading material or bomb-making equipment left in the room. In this "real" scenario (the threat of the bomb is real), the caller will present supporting information that can only indicate that the caller is legitimate. He or she may have detailed specifics about how the bomb was made or where the bomb was located. In the "fake" scenario the person making the threat wants to create panic and disrupt normal activities. In this situation, the caller will not usually have verifiable information.

Recommendations

1. Do not touch suspected explosive devices under any circumstances. A burned fuse may be a trick designed to deceive the discoverer into believing the bomb was harmless.

2. According to the Bureau of Alcohol, Tobacco and Firearms (ATF), agencies benefit greatly from a bomb incident plan. Proper planning will instill confidence in those who must take charge of the situation and reduce the sense of panic. The bomb incident plan calls for a definite chain of command with provisions for alternates. Updated blueprints must be made immediately available to responding emergency personnel. Evacuation and communication procedures should be developed. Contact the police department or fire department for assistance in developing the specifics of the bomb incident plan.

3. Training is critical in helping those who answer phones deal with a bomb threat. It is desirable for more than one person to listen to a threatening call; thus, a covert signaling system can

be advantageous. Callers should be kept on the phone line as long as possible. Call recipients should have those making threats repeat their message several times. All words spoken by the perpetrator should be recorded verbatim. The following Bomb Threat Telephone Report Form was adapted from Stanford University.

4. With written threats, all materials including the envelope or container, should be saved for the investigation. Great care should be taken in handling the evidence so as not to hamper fingerprint analysis.

5. Residence halls and college administrators will have diverging views when it comes to the decision to evacuate a building after a bomb threat. The ATF states that agencies have three alternatives: ignore, evacuate immediately every time, or search and evacuate if warranted. Ignoring the threat is not prudent as a few threats do turn out to be real. Evacuating with every bomb threat can seriously disrupt the campus environment and certainly reinforces the person making the threat. Students can quickly learn a foolproof method for getting out of exams. The third approach, initiating a search after a threat is received and evacuating the premises after suspicious evidence is found is the most desirable approach according to the ATF.

6. Using area occupants to search their own areas is another recommendation by the ATF. Occupants' concern for their own safety motivates them to conduct a thorough search, and they are the most familiar with what belongs and what is out of place in their space. Occupants should not move anything or attempt to investigate suspicious evidence; their only task is to search the area. If they have

BOMB THREAT
TELEPHONE REPORT FORM

Instructions: Be calm and courteous. Listen, and do not interrupt the caller. Notify your supervisor of your activity by a prearranged signal while the caller is on the line.

Date: _____ Time: _____ Person receiving the call: _____

Phone number receiving the call: _____

Exact words of person placing the call: _____
_____
_____
_____

QUESTIONS TO ASK:

1. When is the bomb going to explode? _____
2. Where is the bomb right now? _____
3. What kind of bomb is it? _____
4. What does it look like? _____
5. Why did you place the bomb? _____

Try to determine the following (circle as appropriate):

Caller's Identity:	Male	Female	Adult	Juvenile
	Age: _____			

Voice:	Loud	Soft	High-pitched	Deep	Intoxicated
Accent:	Local	Foreign	Region: _____		Description: _____
Speech:	Fast	Slow	Distinct	Distorted
	Stutter	Slurred	Nasal	
Language:	Articulate		Normal	Uneducated	Foul
	Other: _____			
Manner:	Calm	Angry	Rational	Irrational	Coherent
	Incoherent		Deliberate	Emotional	Righteous
	Laughing		Intoxicated	

Background noises:	Office machines	Factory machines	Trains	Animals
	Music	Voices	Airplanes	Street traffic	Party
	Other: _____			

Additional information: _____
_____
_____

Immediately after the call, notify police and tell your supervisor.

Source: Adapted from Stanford University.

any doubt about this or are frightened, they should be instructed to leave the situation alone and let professionals handle it.

7. As suggested by the National Bomb Data Center and John MacDonald, investigation of witnesses of bomb explosions should include the following questions:

Questions to Ask Bomb Witnesses

Before the blast:
- Where was the bomb?
- Were there any obstructions on the way to the bomb (stairs, doors, other hazards)?
- Are there alternative approaches to the bomb?
- What did the bomb look like? Smell like? Sound like?
- When was the bomb placed? Was there a telephone warning?
- Who might be the target?
- How long did it take the bomber to leave the bomb?

After the blast:
- How long were you in the area before the blast?
- Where were you when the explosion occurred?
- What did you see happening?
- What color was the flash and smoke?
- Was there more than one explosion?
- Did you notice any particular smell?
- What did the explosion sound like?
- Did you notice anything unusual in the area prior to the explosion?

EPILOGUE: THE FUTURE OF CAMPUS VIOLENCE

Overall, our campuses are one of the safest places to be. Nevertheless, as violent crime continues to wreak havoc on our society, its effects will continue to wash up on the shores of our campuses. Many of these forms of violence are difficult to comprehend. They are even more difficult to control. Because the majority of campus violence cases occur among people who know each other and who are often under the influence of alcohol, there tend to be many mitigating circumstances that make reporting violence complex and adjudication complicated. From the aftermath of high-profile campus cases of the recent past and the new legislation dealing with campus violence, many colleges and universities have made violence prevention a priority. Campuses are more aware and prepared than ever before.

As campus officials begin to address the issues of violence they are met with both support and backlash. Tighter controls and increased regulations are often met with resentment and in some cases outright rioting. Campuses should expect this and prepare for it. Rather than undoing effective long-term strategies in the face of immediate campus unrest, officials should seek to work collaboratively with all sectors of the campus community to find solutions that work for all. No violence prevention strategies will be successful without addressing the issues of alcohol abuse. This is an area that a small group of highly vocal students feels passionate about. They should be part of the solution-generating process.

The viruses of campus violence will continue to mutate. As campuses crack down on alcohol, students may move increasingly toward alternative drugs of choice–ones that are cheap, potent, and more easily concealed. We are already seeing the emergence of this trend through the growing attraction to the so-called club drugs. The proliferation of handguns in our society may work their way onto our campuses and into the hands of those seeking self-defense as well as perpetrators. As increasing numbers of students spend more time connecting with others via the Internet, we may see growing numbers of "cyberstalkers" affecting campus life. We bring up these possibilities, not to be doomsayers for campus violence, but to draw attention to the fact that violence changes. Campuses must be anticipating these changes so that they can stay one step ahead of the perpetrators. Or at least not too far behind.

College and university campuses are inspirational places. They offer developmental experiences and challenges, community spirit and support, and under the right circumstances can offer a chemistry that can energize the nation toward better alternatives. A main motive in writing this book is our hope that they stay that way.

APPENDIX

VIOLENCE RESPONSE FLOW CHARTS

Plan A: Violence Potential Exists But No
       Immediate Danger
Plan B: Immediate Threat Exists
Plan C: Aftermath Situation

Plan D: Large Scale Violence Situation
Adapted from *Violence Goes to School*
(1999), Nicoletti, J. and Spencer-
Thomas, S.

Plan A: Violence Potential Exists But No Immediate Danger

These situations develop when an individual uses abusive language and/or gestures and makes veiled or conditional threats without a death threat. In these instances, it is important to investigate, document, and confront the alleged perpetrator.

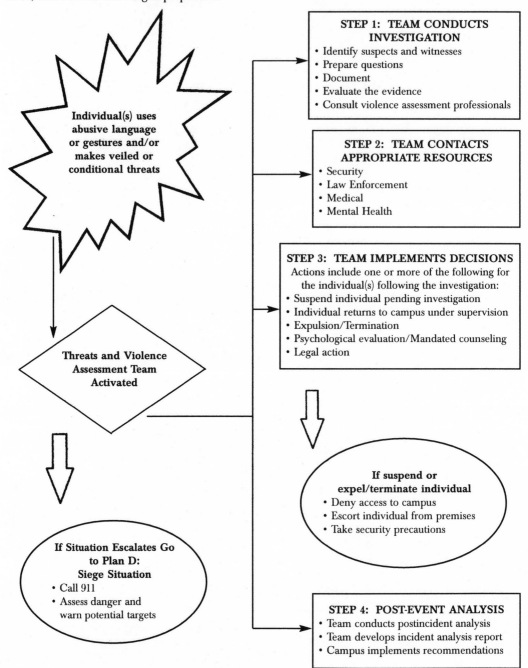

Plan B: Immediate Threat Exists

Immediate threat exists when the situation involves direct or conditional threats ending with a death threat, evidence of aggressive behavior, including brandishing a weapon on campus. The goal at this time is to limit the access of the perpetrator to the campus. Notification to targets is crucial, as is a thorough assessment of the alleged perpetrator's dangerousness.

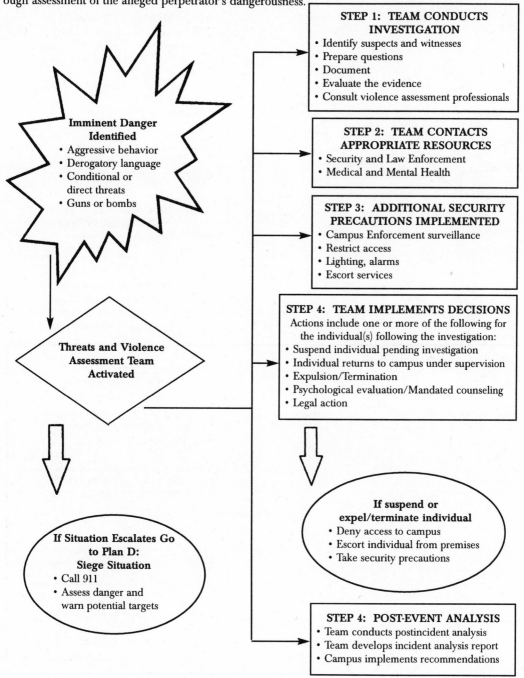

Imminent Danger Identified
- Aggressive behavior
- Derogatory language
- Conditional or direct threats
- Guns or bombs

STEP 1: TEAM CONDUCTS INVESTIGATION
- Identify suspects and witnesses
- Prepare questions
- Document
- Evaluate the evidence
- Consult violence assessment professionals

STEP 2: TEAM CONTACTS APPROPRIATE RESOURCES
- Security and Law Enforcement
- Medical and Mental Health

STEP 3: ADDITIONAL SECURITY PRECAUTIONS IMPLEMENTED
- Campus Enforcement surveillance
- Restrict access
- Lighting, alarms
- Escort services

STEP 4: TEAM IMPLEMENTS DECISIONS
Actions include one or more of the following for the individual(s) following the investigation:
- Suspend individual pending investigation
- Individual returns to campus under supervision
- Expulsion/Termination
- Psychological evaluation/Mandated counseling
- Legal action

Threats and Violence Assessment Team Activated

If suspend or expel/terminate individual
- Deny access to campus
- Escort individual from premises
- Take security precautions

If Situation Escalates Go to Plan D: Siege Situation
- Call 911
- Assess danger and warn potential targets

STEP 4: POST-EVENT ANALYSIS
- Team conducts postincident analysis
- Team develops incident analysis report
- Campus implements recommendations

Plan C: Aftermath Situation

Violence has just occurred. The primary goal at this stage is to prevent further violence and get assistance to the victims.

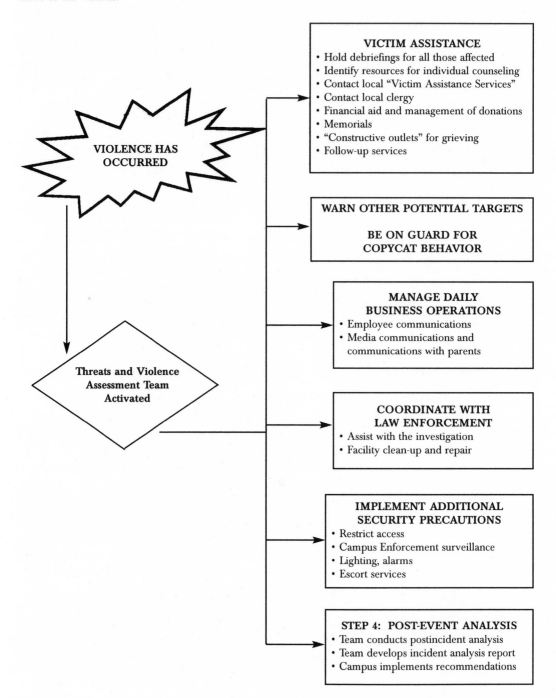

VIOLENCE HAS OCCURRED

Threats and Violence Assessment Team Activated

VICTIM ASSISTANCE
• Hold debriefings for all those affected
• Identify resources for individual counseling
• Contact local "Victim Assistance Services"
• Contact local clergy
• Financial aid and management of donations
• Memorials
• "Constructive outlets" for grieving
• Follow-up services

WARN OTHER POTENTIAL TARGETS

BE ON GUARD FOR COPYCAT BEHAVIOR

MANAGE DAILY BUSINESS OPERATIONS
• Employee communications
• Media communications and communications with parents

COORDINATE WITH LAW ENFORCEMENT
• Assist with the investigation
• Facility clean-up and repair

IMPLEMENT ADDITIONAL SECURITY PRECAUTIONS
• Restrict access
• Campus Enforcement surveillance
• Lighting, alarms
• Escort services

STEP 4: POST-EVENT ANALYSIS
• Team conducts postincident analysis
• Team develops incident analysis report
• Campus implements recommendations

Plan D: Large-Scale Violence Situation

Violence is occurring. The primary goal is to implement the previously developed safety and evacuation plans in order to contain the violence and reduce casualties. Law enforcement should be immediately notified and may direct many of these steps.

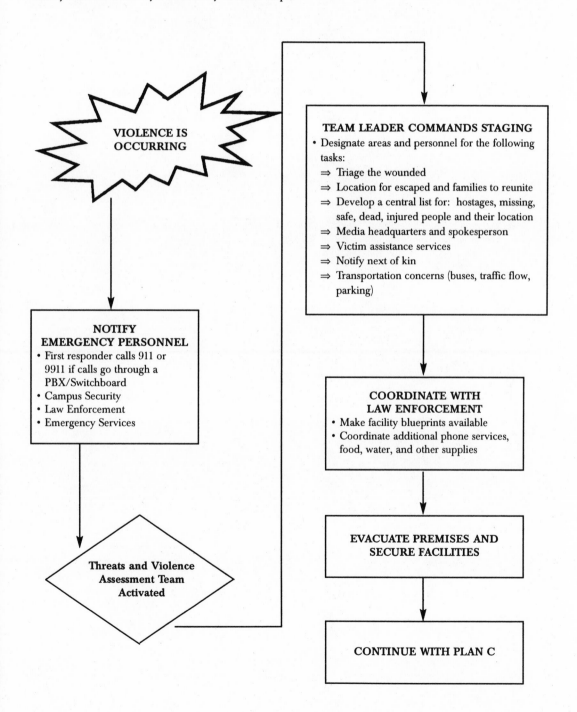

VIOLENCE IS OCCURRING

NOTIFY EMERGENCY PERSONNEL
- First responder calls 911 or 9911 if calls go through a PBX/Switchboard
- Campus Security
- Law Enforcement
- Emergency Services

Threats and Violence Assessment Team Activated

TEAM LEADER COMMANDS STAGING
- Designate areas and personnel for the following tasks:
  ⇒ Triage the wounded
  ⇒ Location for escaped and families to reunite
  ⇒ Develop a central list for: hostages, missing, safe, dead, injured people and their location
  ⇒ Media headquarters and spokesperson
  ⇒ Victim assistance services
  ⇒ Notify next of kin
  ⇒ Transportation concerns (buses, traffic flow, parking)

COORDINATE WITH LAW ENFORCEMENT
- Make facility blueprints available
- Coordinate additional phone services, food, water, and other supplies

EVACUATE PREMISES AND SECURE FACILITIES

CONTINUE WITH PLAN C

GLOSSARY

0-1-3 guidelines (Chapter 4) 0-1-3 guidelines are suggestions for low-risk drinking. These guidelines recommend that in some situations zero alcohol is appropriate. *Zero* alcohol consumption is important for those individuals dependent on alcohol, pregnant women, and most high-risk tasks such as driving. Otherwise, for most people *one* drink per hour with meals, and no more than *three* in any sitting will usually minimize consequences.

acquaintance rape (Chapter 10) A rape committed by someone the victim knows. The broad classification includes in its definition of rape forcing someone to have sexual intercourse with psychological pressure or threats of violence. This definition includes continual arguments or constant verbal harassment as part of psychological pressure. The stringent definition defines rape as forcing someone to have sexual intercourse using only threats of violence. This definition does not include those who use only psychological pressure.

active resistant (Chapter 5) A level of physical behavior that involves a combination of active and passive-aggressive behavior. Examples of active resistance include slamming doors, turning over desks, or throwing objects. There is no actual bodily harm, but the threat of escalating violence exists.

acute stress disorder (Chapter 9) A traumatic reaction classified as an anxiety disorder that spans from two to four days. Symptoms include "feeling in a daze," reexperiencing the trauma, avoidance of things that remind the individual of the trauma, and marked symptoms or increased anxiety. These symptoms cause significant impairment in day-to-day functioning.

agitators (Chapter 11) Agitators plan for and instigate riots. They are often motivated by their need to uphold their reputation. Some agitators are chronic troublemakers who are looking to jump on the bandwagon of creating mischief or cashing in on crime opportunities (e.g., looting).

ambusher (Chapter 1) A type of predator who takes the Bundy approach—feigning vulnerability and weakness or manipulating victims with charm and seduction in order to lure them into the trap.

anger-defensiveness (Chapter 1) A stage in an institution's readiness for change. It occurs when people begin to come forward with information about violence, and the initial reaction is often to find fault with the reporter or to otherwise discredit the information.

anniversary rioting (Chapter 11) Rioting that happens at predictable times each year. For example, Halloween rioting is a tradition on some campuses.

arson (Chapter 15) The FBI Uniform Crime Reporting System crime definition of arson is, "Any willful or malicious burning or attempt to burn, with or without intent to defraud, a dwelling house, public building, motor vehicle or aircraft, personal property of another, etc."

avenger (Chapters 1, 8, and 14) A type of violence perpetrator who perceives violence as the only possible recourse for perceived grievances. Avengers usually have particular targets in mind, although they may take down many others in their violent rampage.

avoidance symptoms (Chapter 9) A set of symptoms common in survivors of trauma that involve avoiding things that remind the victim of the trauma in order to dampen the intensity of the uncomfortable feelings. For example, an individual with PTSD may avoid situations that are reminiscent of the traumatic event. Others may become numb to emotions altogether.

barricading (Chapter 8) A survival strategy that involves putting as many obstacles as possible between the perpetrator and the potential victims.

binge drinking (Chapter 4) This catchphrase, used to describe high-risk drinking, is defined by researchers as five drinks or more in a row for men and four or more for women.

bump (Chapter 8) A low-level behavior that perpetrators engage in to assess whether or not the potential victim will be a good target. By enacting this form of contact, perpetrators are assessing how friendly or passive the potential victim is.

bystanders (Chapters 2 and 11) People who observe violent or pre-violent behavior. Regardless of their true feelings about the violent behavior, the silent presence of

bystanders has a strong influence in continuing a violent incident.

campus-community coalitions (Chapter 6) Campus-community coalitions consist of broad cross-sections of the university and surrounding neighborhoods. With campus-community coalitions, key stakeholders from the campus and community meet together to begin a discussion surrounding campus violence and to work toward the common mission of a safe campus and community.

carriers of misinformation (Chapter 4) Students, faculty, staff, and even parents who, regardless of their own personal use or attitudes about alcohol and other drugs, pass on misperceptions about campus substance abuse through conversation and comments.

catalyst for change (Chapter 1) Something that affects an institution's readiness for change. Often an event, person, or group of people that show the true colors of the violence in a way that it cannot be ignored.

cerebral acceleration (Chapter 8) A response experienced under extreme stress when the brain switches to a rapid mode of information processing. This occurs because the brain is attempting to sort through tremendous amounts of information quickly in order to make the best decision. Consequently, the senses become very acute and amplified. The experience of this phenomenon is that it feels as if the world has turned into a very surreal, slow-motion movie.

club drugs (Chapter 3) Drugs used recreationally at clubs or "raves" popular with teens and young adults. Ecstasy and GHB (gamma hydroxy butyric acid) are two of the most common. Rave participants usually take these drugs to induce a warm sense of well being accompanied by heightened senses.

communication center (Chapter 7) Otherwise known as the communication "vortex," serves as a knowledge base for all investigations. This system organizes all incidents of violence by keeping record of the details of the incident, interventions, and outcomes. In addition to documentation of critical or threatening incidents, the communication center can also be a resource center for those concerned with violence prevention. The communication center can serve as a clearinghouse to distribute current literature and data on campus safety issues.

conditional threats (Chapter 5) A threat is made contingent on a certain set of circumstances. These threats contain the word "if," or the word "or." These types of threats are designed to manipulate or intimidate the target into compliance. Examples of these types of threats include, "You better do this *or* you're dead," and, "*If* you don't give me what I want, you will pay." If these threats are not met with resistance and clear signs of intolerance, they are likely to increase as they are often powerfully reinforced.

counter-rioters (Chapter 11) The "decent majority" of a riot who is actively engaged in stopping or preventing further violence.

crisis response team (Chapter 6) In the aftermath of a tragedy, a predetermined team can be instrumental in addressing the needs of affected individuals and the community. The crisis response team usually consists of a cross-section of university representatives who are highly invested and trained in handling critical incidents. This team may have significant overlap or may even be identical to the Threat and Violence

Assessment Team (TVAT) described in Chapter 6.

culturally influenced violence (Chapter 3) Otherwise known as the "setting" influence of drugs and violence. Violence shaped by expectations or traditions of the social group using the drug separate from the actual effect of the drug. Of the three factors *drug* (biological effects of the drug), *set* (emotions or mental state of the user), and *setting,* the setting is often the most powerful predictor of violence.

curriculum infusion (Chapter 4) A substance abuse prevention practice attempting to get alcohol and other drug issues integrated into almost every syllabus. Faculty tie issues of substance abuse to their course topic. For example, "The Costs to Society" (Economics class) or "The History of Alcohol Advertising" (Mass Media class or History class).

cyberstalker (Chapter 10) A predator who finds and grooms prey via the Internet.

date rape drugs (Chapter 3) Drugs given to unknowing victims in order to induce a very impaired state. Rohypnol, GHB, and Ketamine are common examples. These drugs tend to cause profound "anterograde amnesia" or the inability to remember events that took place while under the effects of the drugs, making them very effective in preventing victims from coming forward after the fact. In 1996, Congress passed the Drug-Induced Rape Prevention and Punishment Act of 1996.

diffusion of responsibility (Chapters 1 and 11) The social psychology phenomenon of bystander apathy that occurs when a large number of people witness a distressing event. An individual would be more likely to give help if she or he is the only bystander present, than when there is a group. The larger the group the less likely any one person is to assume personal responsibility. Also contributing to this effect is whether the violent act is tacitly approved of by a majority of people. If there is some kind of consensus (usually unspoken and often misperceived) that a form of violence is legitimate, than few people in a group will step forward to stop it.

direct threats (Chapter 5) A statement of clear intent to harm someone. Examples are, "I'm going to kill you," or "I'm going to blow them away." Generally, the more specific the threat, the more concerned protectors should be.

dissociative anesthetics (Chapter 3) Drugs that diminish the sensation of pain while distorting reality. Ketamine and PCP are examples.

drunkenness defense (Chapter 4) A relaxed standard of accountability because "The beer made me do it." Those who buy into this line of thinking often excuse otherwise inexcusable behavior with the "drunkenness defense," and thereby promote the continuance of violence.

enabling (Chapter 4) An addictions term, referring to the situation when one person or group of people minimizes the short-term consequences for an addicted person without addressing the long-term problems. For example, between individuals enabling occurs when a friend or spouse calls into work for someone who is incapacitated by a hangover.

entrepreneurial violence (Chapter 1) Committing violence to gain a profit (e.g., robbery).

fads (Chapter 1) Patterns or perceived patterns in violence that gain much attention in a short period and fade out just as quickly. They are often created by urban myths. For example, during the mid-nineties many people thought they would be shot if they flashed their car's headlights at a car that was driving at them with no headlights in the dark.

forced dependency (Chapter 13) A technique often used in team building, brainwashing, or cults where members are taken away or prohibited from associating with people outside the group. The positive outcome of this technique is that it allows members to commit to learning about each other and their purpose. A possible consequence of this technique is that members' abilities to function productively outside of the group become more limited.

gang rape (Chapter 10) Sexual assault perpetrated by more than one person. Gang rape is a form of group-induced violence and has as its primary causes diffusion of responsibility, group modeling, and a need for belonging. Gang rapists are less concerned with the welfare of the victim or with the potential consequences of their actions, because of the involvement of others.

GHB (Chapters 3 and 10) A popular "club drug," also considered a date rape drug, gamma hydroxy butyrate, is a central nervous system depressant. When used in small amounts the drug can produce the effects of being drunk. The drug is colorless, odorless, and salty. Other names for GHB include "GBH," "Grievous Bodily Harm," "Cherry Meth," "Liquid X," "Liquid Ecstasy," "Easy Lay," "G-Juice," and "Energy Drink."

Greekthink (Chapter 4) A term coined by Hank Nuwer who found the following behavior common among fraternities. During a crisis when an individual has become hurt or is critically impaired by alcohol, there is a devastating pause. At the time when first responders should be racing to get appropriate medical attention, these individuals, who are often fairly impaired themselves, think, "oh shit." They pause because they are concerned about getting in trouble, about covering up evidence, and about taking care of the problem themselves. This pause often leads to lifesaving minutes lost.

group-induced violence (Chapters 1, 8, and 14) Violence that occurs when a group of individuals are swept into a mob mentality. Group-induced violence creates the perception of decreased accountability through anonymity. Group violence can be contagious, in that the excitement of the moment may overpower the better judgment of the on-lookers that chose to participate when they would have normally not behaved in such a fashion. Bystanders play a critical role in group-induced violence. Group-induced violence is often trigger-driven, that is, ignited by an external event or stimulus.

harm reduction (Chapter 4) A treatment and prevention strategy developed by Dr. Alan Marlatt and colleagues designed to reduce dangerous drinking behavior through brief intervention.

hate crime (Chapter 12) Words or actions that are intended to harm or intimidate a person or group due to race, gender, sexual orientation, religion, or other group identification (according to *Violence on Campus*) (Hoffman, 1998).

hazing (Chapter 13) Any action related to an individual's admittance or membership in a group that produces mental or physical harm, embarrassment, harassment, or ridicule, regardless of the location of the activity or the individual's willingness to participate.

health terrorism (Chapter 4) Scare tactics that play upon fears of death, rejection, embarrassment, or incarceration. For many college students, fear is a short-lived emotion, especially when the risks for such tragic outcomes are relatively low in their perception.

high-risk drinking (Chapter 4) An alternative and preferred term to "binge drinking." High-risk drinking is a term that many people are still trying to operationalize. For some, it means a large amount (e.g., 5+ drinks) of alcohol consumed in a short period of time (e.g., 0 to 2 hours). For others, it is the quantity of alcohol required to get an individual legally impaired. Less specifically, drinking that exceeds the "injury dose" for a person. Injury dose means the amount of alcohol that typically results in negative consequences for the consumer (e.g., vomiting, severe hangover, fights, falls, blackouts, etc.)

hunters (Chapter 1) A type of predator who stays within his or her own area or neighborhood to locate prey.

hyperarousal symptoms (Chapter 9) A collection of symptoms common in sufferers of PTSD (Posttraumatic stress disorder) including startle responses, irrational and new fears, increased irritability, explosive anger, problems concentrating or remembering new information, sleep disorders, and disrupted appetites.

hypervigilance (Chapter 9) Constant scanning of the environment for danger cues. Being constantly aware of potential danger.

impact (Chapter 9) A stage in posttrauma experiences when an individual leaves the location of the critical incident and feels confused and overwhelmed as full realization of the extent of the danger, damage, death, or injury is made conscious. This phase can last from days to weeks.

impulsive hate episodes (Chapter 12) A form of hate crimes defined by the search for excitement and spontaneity on the part of the perpetrators. The payoff for these types of hate crimes is mainly social. The perpetrator receives ample approval from like-minded peers who believe such action is fun.

injury dose (Chapter 4) The amount of alcohol that typically results in negative consequences for the consumer (e.g., vomiting, severe hangover, fights, falls, blackouts, etc.)

in loco parentis (Chapter 7) A notion of the 1960s that campuses were to act as substitute parents. A perspective that lost favor during the 1970s, 1980s and early 1990s and is regaining support today.

intrusive symptoms (Chapter 9) A cluster of symptoms common in people who experience PTSD (Posttraumatic stress disorder). Intrusive symptoms occur when the images, sounds, smells, tactile or taste sensations related to the traumatic event unexpectedly violate the person's consciousness. These vivid memories may include nightmares, triggered memories, flashbacks, and obsessive thoughts.

Ketamine (Chapter 3) A "date rape drug" nicknamed "Special K." Veterinarians used this drug originally on farm animals. It usually comes in liquid form, but may also be found as a white powder or pill. According to National Institute on Drug Abuse (NIDA), Ketamine is a central nervous system depressant and a rapid-acting general anesthetic. Ketamine is usually snorted, but may be sprinkled on tobacco or marijuana and smoked. Some users describe intense hallucinations while using this drug. Other effects can include convulsions, potentially fatal respiratory problems, and delirium.

limbo (Chapter 1) A stage in institutional change when, due to outside pressure institutions can no longer deny or excuse away violence, but they do not know how to proceed. The problem with the "limbo" stage is that resistance to acknowledging the violence remains, so any attempt to address the problem is usually half-hearted. Quick-fix band-aids are applied in haste usually more to show the public that "something is being done" rather than effective, comprehensive prevention. Very often, these attempts are phased out as soon as the public eye blinks.

liquid courage (Chapter 4) A person who intends to engage in a premeditated violent act may get intoxicated to create the "liquid courage" to act out.

love obsession stalkers (Chapter 14) Represent about 20 to 25 percent of all stalking cases. These stalkers develop a love fixation on another person with whom they have never had any personal relationship. Some choose to stalk celebrities, others develop obsessions with regular, ordinary people.

low-risk drinking (Chapter 4) A preferable term to "responsible drinking," low-risk drinking describes standard guidelines for decreasing consequences related to alcohol use (e.g., 0-1-3 guidelines).

maturing out (Chapter 4) A substance abuse term referring to the developmental trend many individuals experience as they get older and do not find the need to get intoxicated as frequently or as intensely as they did when they were younger.

meaning-making (Chapter 9) A term coined by Sharon Parks (1991), in her book *The Critical Years,* identifying this critical developmental process college students experience when faith development is greatly impacted by creating order out of life occurrences, especially challenges to our core belief systems.

MIP (Chapter 4) Abbreviation for "minor in possession," a legal infraction for those under the legal drinking age who are consuming or possessing alcohol.

negligent hiring (Chapter 7) A legal term referring to the situation when employees commit a violent act and employers are held liable because they did not conduct an adequate background investigation to discover patterns of violent behavior in the individual's past.

negligent retention (Chapter 7) A legal term similar to negligent hiring where an employer retains a known violent or threatening employee despite ample evidence that the individual is a risk to the company.

off-schedule (Chapter 3) Students switch majors, take time off to work or travel, and experience medical and emotional setbacks that often delay graduation anywhere from one semester to several years. This sense of being "off-schedule" is difficult for many. They become out of sync with their friends, school debts accumulate, and the destination of reaching a degree and prosperous career feels out of reach.

opportunists (Chapter 1) A type of predator who lures in prey by placing himself or herself in positions of trust or authority.

parental notification (Chapter 4) A substance abuse prevention strategy gaining popularity among many schools (albeit controversial) to notify parents when their sons or daughters (under the age of twenty-one) break alcohol policies on campus.

passive-resistant (Chapter 5) This type of behavior is also known as "passive aggressive" and is characterized by subtle defiance. These antagonistic behaviors are just under the threshold of noncompliance. Individuals using passive resistance may be extremely slow, putting forth only minimally acceptable effort. In a physical manner, they may use their body mass to impede another's effort by blocking a doorway for example.

pathways to violence (Chapter 1) Predictable patterns perpetrators engage in before becoming violent. Usually these patterns include testing limits and practicing out violence at lower intensity.

perpetrators (Chapter 2) Individuals who commit acts of violence.

pluralistic ignorance (Chapter 4) The belief that one's private attitudes and judgments are different from others. In terms of substance abuse issues, this notion translates to individuals who choose not to engage in high-risk drinking, assume that everyone around them is.

poachers (Chapter 1) A type of predator who surveys an area away from the home territory in order to find prey for violence.

posttrauma resolution (Chapter 9) A phase many people experience after a critical incident that is defined once victims return to routine patterns. Here the trauma's impact will show longer-term changes in behavior, thought patterns, beliefs, emotions, and perception. These changes may be irreversible. There are two possible outcomes of this phase: positive resolution, or negative reaction with no resolution. The positive course will lead to acceptance of the event and the individual's actions, along with a positive reevaluation of goals and values. Keep in mind, this may be a lengthy process and the continuum of resolution is broad. Without any trauma resolution, there is a strong likelihood of a chronic struggle throughout life with distress, family problems, job difficulties, chemical dependency, and potential suicide.

posttraumatic stress disorder (Chapters 9 and 13) A psychological syndrome that affects individuals who have experienced a critical incident such as combat, earthquakes, rape, domestic violence, airplane crashes, car accidents, and violent crime. The cluster of symptoms includes nightmares, flashbacks, hyperarousal, dissociation, depression, and avoidance.

practicing (Chapter 5) Behavioral and psychological precursors to violence imagined or acted out by perpetrators in an effort to prepare themselves for their violent act. These patterns may include elaborate fantasies, threats, vandalism, harassment, harm to animals, and so on.

precontemplation (Chapter 1) At this stage in readiness for change where an individual or institution is truly unaware of the problems. Some have called this stage "denial." When this concept is applied to campus violence, people in this stage do not believe violence is a concern because the violence is hidden or not believed. No one is assessing or addressing the problem, because it is thought not to exist.

predatory violence (Chapters 1, 8, and 14) A form of violence highly feared but relatively rare on college campuses in which a

perpetrator commits an act of violence for the sole reason that it gives him or her a thrill. There is no other desired outcome than to experience the violence and another's suffering. Otherwise known as "stranger danger."

premeditated hate episodes (Chapter 12) In these cases, perpetrators actually declare "war" against another group of people. Usually, an organized group such as the KKK or the White Aryan Resistance supports these perpetrators.

primary victims (Chapter 2) Individuals who have experienced the violence directly.

protectors (Chapter 2) Individuals who do what is in their power to prevent violence incidents from occurring or intervene when violent events are unfolding. Protectors include security officers, law enforcement officers, residence life staff, coaches, faculty, and others.

psychopharmacological violence (Chapter 3) Drug-related violence caused by the actual chemically induced properties of the drug itself. For instance, drugs can cause agitation and paranoia in perpetrators, and can cause sedation and memory loss in victims.

PTSD (Chapters 9 and 13)—See Posttraumatic Stress Disorder

rape (Chapter 10) Sexual violence defined by forced sexual intercourse using any of the following types of coercion: psychological pressure, physical force, or taking advantage of a person's inability to give consent due to intoxication, loss of consciousness, or mental impairment.

rape kit (Chapter 10) A medical exam given to victims after a sexual assault for the purpose of assessing needs for immediate medical attention (e.g., physical trauma, sexually transmitted diseases, pregnancy, or HIV) and for gathering medical evidence.

Rape Shield Law (Chapter 10) A law that precludes any testimony of the victim's sexual history that does not bear immediate relevance to the current sexual assault case. The law was implemented to keep the jury focused on the case at hand and not information that has no bearing on the rape being tried.

rape trauma syndrome (Chapter 10) A response some victims have to rape that occurs in three phases: acute, outward adjustment, and resolution stage. The acute phase often begins immediately after the rape and can persist from a few days to several weeks. Victims usually have difficulty concentrating, making decisions, or accomplishing everyday tasks. The outward adjustment phase begins with return to a near-normal routine pattern. Inwardly, there is still turmoil which can manifest itself in many ways: anxiety, sense of helplessness, fear, depression, vivid dreams, insomnia, recurring nightmares, physical ailments, variations in appetite, vomiting, nausea, preoccupation with safety, denial, hesitation to form new relationships, sexual problems, disruptions to everyday behavior. The resolution phase occurs when victims recognize that although they will never forget the rape or the pain and memories that go with it, it is a part of their life experience and they are choosing to move on.

raptor (Chapter 1) A form of predator who "swoops and scoops" victims without any warning or attempt to engage them socially.

reactive hate episodes (Chapter 11) A type of hate crime that occurs in response to a triggering event the perpetrators feel justifies their anger. In these cases perpetrators

of hate crimes believe they are standing up as pillars of justice for the whole community by acting in hate against a visible group.

recoil (Chapter 9) A phase many people experience in the aftermath of a critical incident that begins with return to a near-normal routine pattern, accompanied by stable days. During this time symptoms of the impact phase begin to decrease and attention, concentration, reasoning ability, recall, and emotional expression gradually return. However, this phase often resembles an emotional roller coaster with good days and bad days interspersed. At this stage, individuals often feel as though they will never regain a "normal" life. Each time they begin to get on their feet, another wave of memories sets in.

relationship-based violence (Chapters 1, 8, and 14) A type of violence that involves an exploited one-on-one attachment. Relationships that have both power differential and privacy are most vulnerable–parent-child, husband-wife, pledgemaster-pledge. In relationship-based violence, the dominant partner has an "ownership" mentality over the submissive partner. Because the submissive partner is perceived as property rather than a person of equal standing, the dominant partner employs certain strategies to ensure that "the property" is maintained under current control.

responsible use (Chapter 4) A controversial term in alcohol abuse literature loosely defined as use that does not result in consequences to the user or others.

right to party (Chapters 4 and 11) A trend on many campuses based on the belief (held mainly by students) that college students have a right to drink alcohol when and where they choose. This perspective comes as a backlash against institutes of higher education that are attempting to crack down on underage drinkers and out-of-control drinkers. On some campuses, those who assert their right to party are sometimes the agitators of riots.

riot (Chapter 11) A large group of people attempting to assert their will with violence and the threat of violence outside the normal bounds of law. When agitators manipulate a crowd, members begin to lose their identity and merge into a primitive cohesive group. The larger the group the more the anonymity is protected and the more normal moral restraints break down.

Rohypnol (Chapters 3 and 10) Called a "date rape drug," Rohypnol is a benzodiazepine that produces a sedative effect, amnesia, muscle relaxation, and a slowing of psychomotor responses. Sedation occurs twenty to thirty minutes after ingestion and can last for hours. Other names used for Rohypnol include "the forget pill," "Mexican Valium," "R-2," "Rib," "Roaches," "Rope," "Roofenot," and "Roofers." Most often Rohypnol is found in tablet form stored in bubble packs. Sometimes the pills have been ground into powder and either taken recreationally to enhance an alcohol buzz or they are slipped in drinks of unknowing victims. Rohypnol is sold as a prescription drug in other countries and smuggled into the United States.

sacred cows (Chapters 4 and 13) Individuals who are treated by a different standard than the rest of the campus community. The violent behavior of these people may be excused from consequences due to their perceived importance or influence of powerful stakeholders.

sacred herds (Chapter 13) Groups that are treated by a different standard like sacred

cows (e.g., athletic teams and Greek systems).

secondary victims (Chapter 2) People involved but not directly impacted by the violence (e.g., roommate, friends, rescue workers, resident assistants, etc.). These secondary victims are often overlooked in trauma recovery efforts, but many of them may experience a posttraumatic response that is very upsetting.

shock (Chapter 9) The first phase many people experience in the aftermath of a critical incident. Shock usually begins at the onset of the traumatic event, and can continue for up to a week. During this time, sensory information floods the brain. The experience of events is in "slow motion," there is an unreal or dream-like quality to them. There may be some physical symptoms, including agitation, hyperalertness, overactivity, or biological disruption (e.g., sleeping and eating patterns).

simple obsession stalkers (Chapter 14) A form of stalking that represents about 70 to 80 percent of all stalking cases. These stalkers have had a personal or romantic relationship with their victims before the stalking behavior began. In most instances, the victim has become the stalker's sole source of self-esteem. When the victim tries to break off the relationship, the perpetrator's thinking evolves from "If I can just prove how much I love you" to "I can make you love me," to "If I can't have you, nobody else will." Stalking cases that develop from domestic violence patterns are the most common and potentially lethal.

social norms marketing (Chapter 4) A substance abuse prevention strategy (currently being adapted to address other campus issues) based on the idea that students typically overestimate alcohol and other drug use on campus. Consequently, this illusion creates a partially self-fulfilling prophecy. Social norms marketing is used to correct these misperceptions and decrease high-risk drinking. Social norms marketing approach uses traditional marketing techniques to promote healthy messages about student behavior to challenge the misperceptions.

stalking (Chapters 1 and 14) Willful, malicious, and repeated following and harassment combined with the credible threat intended to make the victim fear death or serious injury.

standard operating guide (Chapter 7) A set of procedures used in the prevention and intervention of violence on campuses.

stranger rape (Chapter 10) Sexual assault perpetrated by someone the victim does not know.

student host contracts (Chapter 4) Agreements between campus visitors and residents or campus hosts that, depending on the circumstances, all parties will either commit to a drug- and alcohol-free visit (as would be the case with high school recruitment visitors) or the hosts agree to take responsibility for the behavior of their visitors.

suicidal avenger (Chapter 1) A type of avenger (see above) who believes that he or she has nothing to lose and is willing to die during the violence rampage. Many of the school shooters and workplace violence perpetrators fall in this category.

suicide-by-cop (Chapter 1) A form of violence where individuals use law enforcement officers as weapons of suicide by provoking the officers to use deadly force against them.

For example, a suicidal individual may threaten an officer with a plastic knife and the officer shoots the individual because the officer believes that he or she is in imminent danger.

survivor guilt (Chapter 9) In the aftermath of a violent tragedy, many people experience these feelings because they second-guess their actions or they wonder why they were not chosen as the victims.

synergy (Chapter 3) A term used in this book to describe drug interactions whereby two drugs that are used together have an additive effect and a more intense impact on the user than each drug's effect taken by itself.

targets (Chapter 2) The victims (or sometimes the property) harmed by the perpetrators.

tertiary victims (Chapter 2) Helpers who also become affected by the violent event. In the aftermath of a violent incident, student life staff may be flooded with individuals in crisis, needs for debriefing sessions, and requests for consultation. At the same time, these professionals may be dealing with their own reactions to the trauma. They may also be vicariously affected by listening to story after story from the survivors. In some cases these helpers may internalize others' pain and become overwhelmed. As a result, they may experience similar nightmares and distressing thoughts as the victims.

Threat and Violence Assessment Team (TVAT) (Chapter 6) A team of campus professionals dedicated to taking action roles rather than just providing input. The TVAT should consist of individuals trained in the evaluation of and intervention with potentially violent situations. The TVAT's objective is violence prevention and response. TVAT members are responsible for addressing threats and confronting violent behavior, and may assist in assessing potential for violence. They will serve as the primary decision makers in violent crises, and will be communication liaisons between internal and external responders. The TVAT is responsible for making critical decisions quickly. They will develop the protocol in case of a threat or violent incident, and establish a plan for the protection of other students, staff, and other potential targets.

T.O.A.D.S. (Chapter 2) A "formula for violence"–Time, Opportunity, Ability, Desire, Stimulus.

trends (Chapter 1) Culture patterns that build slowly and forever change the fabric of a community, nation, or world.

trees (Chapter 2) A symbolic concept used to represent barriers placed in the way of practicing perpetrators to stop or slow them.

trollers (Chapter 1) A form of predators that wander around to areas of vulnerability searching for viable prey (e.g., campus bars).

TVAT (Chapter 6)–See Threat and Violence Assessment Team

user-based violence (Chapter 3) A drug-induced violence concept that encompasses internal expectations or needs or the user. One example of this form of violence is economically motivated crimes. Illicit drugs often are expensive, and because of this, users may often engage in other illegal behaviors to obtain the drugs. Others may use drugs to drum up a false sense of courage before committing a violent act.

veiled threats (Chapter 5) A type of threat that is hard to address because it is often vague and subject to interpretation. Veiled threats are statements made to communicate the desire or intent to commit violence, but when taken out of context are often minimized or misunderstood. For example, "I could see why someone would want to shoot a professor" is an example of a veiled threat.

victims of choice (Chapter 2) Victims who are chosen by the perpetrator for a reason. The reason may be revenge, easy access, or the victim's likeness to a violent fantasy.

victims of opportunity (Chapter 2) Victims who are not intentionally targeted by perpetrators but are in the wrong place at the wrong time.

violence (Chapter 2) Behavior that by intent, action, and/or outcome harms another person.

Violence Against Women Act (VAWA) (Chapter 10) An act passed in 1994 that among other things allows rape victims to sue their attackers in federal court because, it is argued, rape impacts interstate commerce. There has been a great deal of debate about this act and its constitutionality.

vortex (Chapter 7)–See Communication Center.

zero tolerance (Chapters 4 and 7) An intervention stance used to address violent behaviors meaning that every questionable statement or gesture goes under the microscope. Every threat or practice behavior is addressed, even if that only means investigation and documentation. Alcohol-induced violence is no exception.

BIBLIOGRAPHY

CHAPTER ONE
SEEING VIOLENCE AS A VIRUS

Anonymous. *American Justice: Murder in a College Town.* (A&E) 55 minutes. Aired 22 March 2000.

Anonymous. Attorney general says Vermont failed in hazing investigation. 3 February 2000. http://www.acmi.canoe.ca/Hockey NCAA/feb3_att.html (27 February 2000).

Anonymous. *Investigative Reports: Campus Insecurity.* (A&E). Aired 22 March 2000. Documentary.

Anonymous. Charles Joseph Whitman. *Find a Grave.* http://www.findagrave.com/pictures/5921.html (27 February 2000).

Anonymous. Katie Koestner. *Campus Speak.* http://www.angelo.edu/~ucpc/kaite.htm (28 February 2000).

Anonymous. *Mayday: Kent State.* http://www.emerson.edu/acadepts.cs.comm/chrono.html (27 February 2000).

Anonymous. MIT accepts responsibility in Scott Krueger's 1997 death. *Security on Campus Update #224.* 13 September 2000. http://www.globe.com/news/daily/reporters/13/mit_settlement.htm (13 September 2000).

Anonymous. MIT Statement on the ABC 20/20 program on Scott Krueger. *MIT News.* 1999. http://web.mit.edu/newsoffice/nr/ 1999/alcohol2020.html (13 April 2000).

Anonymous. Remembering Matthew Shepard. *MSNBC.com.* http://www.msnbc.com/news/237387.asp (27 February 2000).

Anonymous. Richard Speck: Born to raise hell. *Court TV Online.* http://www.courttv.com/onair/shows/crimestories/q_z_.../richard_speck_born_to_raise_hell.htm (14 March 2000).

Anonymous. Ted Bundy: Murder on the run. *The Crime Library.* http://www.crimelibrary.com/bundy/murder.htm (27 February 2000).

Anonymous. U. of Texas tries to move beyond campus landmark's legacy of violence. *CNN.com* 15 September 1999. http://cgi.cnn.com/US/9909/15/texas.tower.ap/ (27 February 2000).

Anonymous. 2000. UVM captain sentenced in hazing scandal. *USA Today.* 30 August.

Anonymous. Violent crimes reported on campus increase slightly in 1998. *CampusSafety.org.* http://campussafetyorg/STATS/98ucr.html (25 October 1999).

Barr, A. *The Handbook of Texas Online: Charles Whitman.* 15 February 1999. http://www.tsha.utexas.edu/handbook/online/articles/view/W W/fwh42.html (27 February 2000).

Cullen, D. A dramatic moment of mercy. *Salon.com.* http://www.salon.com/news/feature/1999/11/05/shepard/index.html (27 February 2000).

Cullen, D. Killer: Shepard didn't make advances. *Salon.com.* http://www.salon.com/news/feature/1999/11/06/witness/index.html (27 February 2000).

Denlinger, K. Vermont hockey team's hazing earns major penalty. *The Washington Post.* 2 February 2000. http://www-wp9.washingtonpost.com/wp-srv/sports/daily/feb00/02/vermont2.htm (27 February 2000).

Dorin, R. Victim of anti-gay attack in Wyoming clings to life. *CNN.com.* 11 October 1998. http://europe.cnn.com/US/9810/11/wyoming.attack/ (27 February 2000).

English, B. From a daughter's death, a life's work: After Jeanne Clery's murder at Lehigh University, her parents have worked to change laws and change minds about campus safety. *The Boston Globe.* 20 October 1999.

Hammer, J. The "gay panic" defense. *Newsweek.com.* 8 November 1999. http://www.newsweek.com/nw-srv/printed/us/na/a59700-1999oct31.htm (27 February 2000).

Henry, B. "Revisions of the Manuscript." 28 September 2000. Personal email. (28 September 2000).

Hoffman, A., Schuh, J., and Fenske, R. 1998. *Violence on Campus: Defining the Problems, Strategies for Action.* Gaithersburg, Maryland: Aspen Publications, Inc.

Hussain, Z. 1998. Krueger's parents leave open option for civil suit against MIT, fraternity. *MIT News.* 118(42):1, 27.

Glover, P. 2000. Media circus back in Laramie. *Wyoming Tribune-Eagle.* 27 February.

Gregg, J. Why one murder makes page one and another is lost in the news briefs. *Time.com.* http://www.time.com/time/daily/special/look/0,2633,33788,00.html (27 February 2000).

Kaganoff, P. 1993. The crime of the century. *Publishers Weekly.* 22 March.

Lewis, J., and Hensley, T. 1998. The May 4 shootings at Kent State University: The search for historical accuracy. *The Ohio Council for the Social Studies Review.* 34(1):9–21.

Nichols, D. 1995. Violence on campus. *FBI Law Enforcement Bulletin.* 64(6):1–5.

Nuwer, H. Thank you survey! May I have another. And another? http://stophazing.org/nuwer/sept99column.htm (29 February 2000).

Nuwer, H. 1990. *Broken Pledges: The Deadly Rite of Hazing.* Atlanta: Longstreet Press.

Nuwer, H. 1999. *Wrongs of Passage: Fraternities, Sororities, Hazing, and Binge Drinking.* Bloomington: Indiana University Press.

Nuwer, H. The "Wrongs of Passage" Page. http://stophazing.org/nuwer/aug99column.htm (29 February 2000).

Phillips, J. 2000. Campuses fighting to change their party school reputation. *Alcohol: Issues and Solutions.* 2(7):1–8.

Port, B., and Lesser, B. The 25 highest-risk college campus neighborhoods. *APB News Online.* 10 November 1999. http://www.apbnews.com/safetycenter/childrens_safety/campus/01main.html (13 January 2000).

Pratt, M. 2000. Mother of student who died drinking at MIT sues fraternity. *Boston Globe.* 27 September.

Roark, M. 1993. Conceptualizing campus violence: Definitions, underlying factors, and effects. In Whitaker, L. & Pollard, J. (Eds.), *Campus Violence: Kinds, Causes, and Cures.* New York: The Haworth Press, Inc.

Rogers, T., and Stevens, E. Anti-hazing activist. *New York Daily News.* 15 September 1996. http://www.alphaphi.org/Featured/Daily_News.html (29 February 2000).

Rosellini, L. Unsporting athletics. *U.S. News Online.* http://www.usnews.com/usnews/edu/college/articles/sthazing.htm (3 September 2000).

Stevens, E. Hazing–A Greek tragedy. *Alpha Phi: Eileen Stevens' Message on Hazing.* 15 September 1996. http://www.alphaphi.org/Featured/tragedy.html (29 February 2000).

Suggs, W. Hazed hockey player will receive $80,000 from the U. of Vermont. *Chronicle of Higher Education.* 31 August 2000. http://chronicle.com/daily/2000/08/200083105n.htm (3 September 2000).

Watkins, T. Terror in Chicago, 1996: Richard Speck's twisted world and the murder of 8 nurses. http://home1.gte.net/deltakit/speck.htm (14 March 2000).

Whitaker, T. UW expects no ill effects from Shepard murder. *Laramie News.* http://www.uwyo.edu/a&s/comm/newsarc/shepenro.htm (27 February 2000).

Word, R. 1999. Decade after execution, survivors still mourn. *The Capital Journal.* 24 January.

CHAPTER TWO
VIOLENCE 101: UNDERSTANDING THE BASICS

Hoffman, A., Schuh, J., and Fenske, R. 1998. *Violence on Campus: Defining the Problems, Strategies for Action.* Gaithersburg, Maryland: Aspen Publications, Inc.

Mountain States Employers Council, Inc. and Nicoletti-Flater Associates. 1997. *Violence Goes to Work: An Employer's Guide.* Denver, Colorado: Mountain States Employers Council, Inc. and Nicoletti-Flater Associates.

Nicoletti, J., and Spencer-Thomas, S. 1999. *Violence Goes to School: Lessons Learned from Columbine.* Denver, Colorado: Nicoletti-Flater Associates.

Palmer, C. 1998. Violence at home on campus. In Hoffman, A., Schuh, J., & Fenske, R. H. (Eds.), *Violence on Campus: Defining the Problems, Strategies for Action.* Gaithersburg, Maryland: An Aspen Publication.

Roark, M. 1993. Conceptualizing campus violence: Definitions, underlying factors and effects. In Whitaker, L. & Pollard, J. (Eds.), *Campus Violence: Kinds, Causes, and Cures.* New York: The Haworth Press, Inc.

CHAPTER THREE
VULNERABLE TO INFECTION:
RISKS TO COLLEGE COMMUNITIES

Anonymous. Anabolic steroids. *National Institute on Drug Abuse.* 17 April 2000. http://165.112.78.61/SteroidAlert/SteroidAlert.html (4 August 2000).

Anonymous. Anabolic steroid abuse. *National Institution on Drug Abuse Research Report Series.* 13 April 2000. http://165.112.78.61/Research Reports/Steroids/anabolicsteroids4.html (4 August 2000).

Anonymous. Marijuana use among students at institutions of higher education. *Higher Education Center.* 11 July 2000. http://www.edc.org/hec/pubs/prev-updates/marijuana.txt (10 August 2000).

Anonymous. 1996. When violence follows employees to work. *Business Insurance.* 30(29):3.

Anonymous. Leveling the playing field. *MSNBC.com.* http://www.msnbc.com/news/230198.asp (17 January 2000).

Anonymous. Survey shows steroid use on decline. *News and Features.* 15 September 1997. http://www.ncaa.org/news/19970915/active/3432n01.html (4 August 2000).

Anonymous. NIJ Study questions link between methamphetamine use, violence. *Alcoholism &*

Drug Abuse Weekly. 17 May 1999, v. 11, i 20, p. 7.

Arbor, A. Drug trends in 1999 among American teens are mixed. *Join Together Online.* 17 December 1999. http://www.jointogether.org/sa/default.jtml?O=261301 (21 December 1999).

Benedict, J. 1997. Colleges must act decisively when scholarship athletes run afoul of the law. *Chronicle of Higher Education.* 43(35):B6–B7.

Feigelman, W., Gorman, B., and Lee, J. 1998. Binge drinkers, illicit drug users and polydrug users: An epidemiological study of American collegians. *Journal of Alcohol and Drug Education.* 44:47–69.

Fenske, R., and Hood, S. 1998. Profile of students coming to campus. In *Violence on Campus: Defining the Problems, Strategies for Action.* Gaithersburg, Maryland: Aspen Publications.

Haughney, C. 1999. LSD showing up on campus, court docket shows. *Mobile Register.* 22 December.

Hoffman, A. M. (Ed.). 1996. *Schools, Violence, and Society.* New York, NY: Praeger Publishers.

Leinwand, D., and Fielda, G. 2000. Feds crack down on ecstasy. *USA Today.* 19 April.

Leshner, A. Club drugs. *National Institute on Drug*

Abuse. 5 December 1999. http://165.112.78.61/ClubAlert/Clubdrugalert.html (5 December 1999).

McKenzie, S. Report shows officials' roles in investigations. *The Minnesota Daily Online.* 12 July 1999. http://www.daily.umn.edu/daily/1999/07/12/news/sex/> (25 October 1999).

McKinely, J. 2000. Decision on Knight shows the fine line that colleges walk. *New York Times.* 21 May.

Nicklin, J. 1999. Colleges report increases in arrests for drug and alcohol violations. *The Chronicle of Higher Education.*

Palmer, C. 1998. Violence at home on campus. In *Violence on Campus.* Gaithersburg, Maryland: Aspen Publications.

Parker, R., and Auerhahn, K. 1998. Alcohol, drugs, and violence. *Annual Review of Sociology.* 24:291–311.

Reeves, W. 2000. Police say use of club drugs at raves 'a growing problem'. *The Huntsville Times.* 9 February.

Reisberg, L. 2000. Rites of passage or unwanted traditions? *Chronicle of Higher Education.* 46(23):A49–A50.

Reisberg, L. Student stress is rising, especially among women. *The Chronicle of Higher Education.* 28 January 2000. http://chroni-cle.com/weekly/v46/i21/21a04901.htm (26 January 2000).

Reynolds, L. 1997. Fighting domestic violence in the workplace. *HR Focus.* 74(11):8.

Ritter, K. 1999. City strips MIT frat of dorm license. *Boston Globe.* 29 October.

Rivinus, T., and Larimer, M. 1993. Violence, alcohol, other drugs, and the college student. In Whitaker, L. & Pollard, J. (Eds.), *Campus Violence: Kinds, Causes, and Cures.* New York: The Haworth Press, Inc.

Roark, M. 1993. Conceptualizing campus violence: Definitions, underlying factors, and effects. In Whitaker, L. & Pollard, J. (Eds.), *Campus Violence: Kinds, Causes, and Cures.* New York: The Haworth Press, Inc.

Schuh, J. 1998. Campus vulnerability. In *Violence on Campus.* Gaithersburg, Maryland: Aspen Publications.

Spicuzza, M. Nightly grind. http://www.metroactive.com:80/metro/ecstasy1-0012.html (27 March 2000).

Tennant,C. Wonder drug, rape aid. *Student.Com.* http://www.student.com/article/ghb (28 February 2000).

Weiss, K. 2000. College freshmen more stressed than ever, poll finds. *Los Angeles Times.* 24 January.

CHAPTER FOUR
ALCOHOL: A VIOLENCE CATALYST

Anderson, D., and Milgram, G. 1996. *Promising Practices, Campus Alcohol Strategies.* Fairfax, Virginia: George Mason University.

Anonymous. Alcohol Alert. 1997. *National Institute on Alcohol Abuse and Alcoholism. no.38.*

Anonymous. Report finds binge drinking major college problem. *Join Together Online.* September 1998. http://www.jointogether.org/sa/wire/news/reader.jtml?Object_ID=255336 (22 October 2000).

Anonymous. Study shows ER counseling reduces teen drinking. *Join Together Online.* 6 December 1999. http://www.jointogether.org/sa/default.jtml?0=261159 (7 December 1999).

Anonymous. Survey eyes youth substance abuse. *New York Times.* 30 August 1999. http://www.nytimes.com/aponline/a/AP-Teens-Drugs.html (30 August 1999).

Anonymous. Northwestern U. sororities sever ties with frat drinking parties. *The Salt Lake Tribune.* 21 January 2000. http://www.sltrib.com:80/2000/jan/01212000/nation_w/19461.htm (24 January 2000).

Anonymous. Alcohol consumption in California declining. *Join Together Online.* 29 December 1999. http://www.jointogether.org/sa.default.jtml?0=261398 (2 March 2000).

Anonymous. Alcohol and violence. June 1998. http://www.ias.org.uk/theglobe/jun98/violence.htm (2 April 2000).

Anonymous. 2000. A round-up of current facts and findings. *Research Briefs.* 13 (54):2–8.

Anonymous. Addressing binge drinking in emergency rooms. *Join Together Online.* 18 April 2000. http://www.jointogether.org/sa/default.jtml?O=262751 (19 April 2000).

Anonymous. National college alcohol study finds college binge drinking largely unabated, four years later: 10 September 1998. http;//www.hsph.harvard.edu/press/releases/press91098.html (22 October 2000).

Anonymous. Beer seen as more dangerous than liquor, wine. *Join Together Online.* 11 August 2000. http://www.jointogether.org/jtodirect.jtml?U=52192&O=264055 (16 August 2000).

Anonymous. Alcohol-related death leads to debate over disclosure policy at Duke. *Chronicle of Higher Education.* 3 March 2000. http://chronicle.com/weekly/v46/i26/26a04702.htm (3 March 2000).

Anonymous. Circle network. *Circle Network Online.* http://www.circlenetwork.org/about.html (24 November 1999).

Anonymous. College parents of America. *Higher Education Center: THIS WEEK!* 13 September 1999. http://www.edc.org/hec/thisweek/tw990913.html (24 November 1999).

Anonymous. Have open communication with your college-age kids about alcohol. *New.Excite.com.* 9 September 1999. http://www.news.excite.com:80/news/bw/990909/oh-kaiser-permanente (11 September 1999).

Anonymous. A parents' guide to college and drinking. *Higher Education Center: LaSalle University.* 28 September 1999. http://www.edc.org/hec/parents/lasalle.html (24 November 1999).

Anonymous. What MIT has done to curb alcohol abuse. *MIT News.* 1998. http://web.mit.edu/newsoffice/nr/1998/factsalc2.html (13 April 2000).

Anonymous. Parents, you're not done yet. *The Century Council.* http://www.centurycouncil.org/parents/index.cfm (30 August 1999).

Anonymous. 2000. UMass reverses its ruling on beer in dorms. *Boston Globe.* 7 March.

Appel, A. Wellesley's crackdown will apply to colleges. *Boston Globe's West Weekly.* 28 November 1999. http://www.boston.com/dailyglobe2/332/west/Wellesley_s_crackdown_will_apply_to_colleges+.shtml (30 November 1999).

Austin, E., Pinkleton, B., and Fujioka, Y. 2000. The role of interpretation processes and parental discussion in the media's effect on adolescents' use of alcohol. *Pediatrics. 105*: 343–349.

Autman, S. Police put CAPP on parties that rile college neighbors. *San Diego Union-Tribute.* 10 October 1999. http://www.union-tribune.com/news.uniontrib/sun/metro/news_1m10capped.html (11 October 1999).

Azar, B. Avoiding alcohol in real-world settings. *American Psychological Association.* May 1995. http://www.apa.org/monitor/may95/prevent.html (7 November 1999).

Baker, J., and Ward, E. Ah, the rituals and rites of spring. . . *San Diego Union-Tribune.* 14 April 2000.

Borger, J. Regents focus on underage drinking. *St. Paul Pioneer Press.* 11 February 2000. http://www.pioneerplanet.com/seven-days/2/news/docs/028801.htm (14 February 2000).

Borges, G., Cherpitel, C., and Rosovsky, H. 1998. Male drinking and violence-related injury in the emergency room. *Addiction. 93*:103–112.

Branch, D. 1998. Brief counseling of freshmen may curb student drinking. *Clinical Psychiatry News. 26*(3):1.

Chen, H., and Hordern, B. Does school security scare students? *MSNBC Online.* http://www.msnbc.com/news/325616.asp (17 January 2000).

Childs, N. 1999. Brief counseling cuts college binge drinking. *Pediatric News. 33*(2):32.

Curtin, D. 1999. Beer-money Brouhaha at area schools. *The Denver Post Online.* http://www.denverpost.com:80/news/news1003b.htm (5 October 1999).

Davenport, A., Dowdall, G., Grossman, S., Wechsler, H., and Zanakos, S. 1996. Binge drinking, tobacco, and illicit drug use and involvement in college athletics: A survey of students at 140 American colleges. *JACH* 44.

Defenbacher, J. Anger, substance use, and the potential of anger management as a secondary prevention program. Department of Psychology, Unpublished manuscript, Fort Collins, Colorado: Colorado State University.

DeJong, W. Language matters. *Higher Education Center.* 28 January 2000. http://www.edc.org/

hec/thisweek/ (3 February 2000).

Deutsch, C., Dowdall, G., and Wechsler, H.1995. Too many colleges are still in denial about alcohol abuse. *The Chronicle of Higher Education.* (April).

Dimeff, L. A., Baer, J. S., Kivlahan, D. R., & Marlatt, G. A. 1999. *Brief Alcohol Screening and Intervention for College Students: A Harm Reduction Approach.* New York: The Guilford Press.

Edelson, E. Cheap beer linked to campus violence. *APBnews.com.* 26 January 2000. http://www.apbnews.com:80/safety/center/campus/2000/01/26/collegebeer0126_01.html (27 January 2000).

Elias, M. 2000. Does TV cause teens to drink? *USA Today.* 8 February.

Erb, R. 1999. Alcohol sweep nets 54 despite advance notice. *The Blade.* 26 October.

Feigelman, W., Gorman, B., and Lee, J. 1998. Binge drinkers, illicit drug users and polydrug users. *Journal of Alcohol and Drug Education.* 44(1): 47–69.

Gebhardt, T. Town gown cooperation. *Higher Education Center: Prevention File Spring 1998.* 13 no.2. (1998). http://www.edc.org/hec/pubs/articles/prevfile98.html (25 January 2000).

Glionna, J. College students' rites of passage can be fatal. *Los Angeles Times.* 10 April 2000. http://www.latimes.com:80/news/state.2000410/t000033802.html (11 April 2000).

Goff, K. 2000. Binge drinking. *Washington Times.* 6 February.

Gose, B. Harvard researchers note an increase in college students who drink heavily and often. *The Chronicle of Higher Education.* 15 March 2000. http://chronicle.com/daily/2000/03/200031501n.htm (16 March 2000).

Haines, M. 1996. A social norms approach to preventing binge drinking at colleges and universities. The Higher Education Center for Alcohol and Other Drug Prevention, U.S. Department of Education (Publication No. ED/OTE/96-18).

Henry, B. "Revisions of the Manuscript" 12 October 2000. Personal email (12 October 2000)

Herper, M. Binge and purge: Scolding students won't make them safer. *Reason Magazine.*

November 1999. http://www.reasonmag.com:80/9911/fe.mh.binge.html (11 October 1999).

Hernandez, R. Frat houses decide to go clean, sober. *The Oregonian.* 13 March 2000. http://www.oregonlive.com:80/news/00/03/st031302.html (15 March 2000).

Hilde, P., Rossow, I., and Wichstrom, L. 1999. Young , wet, and wild? *Addiction.* 94: 1017–1031.

Karasik, S. Notification law pits safety vs. privacy. *APBnews.com.* 28 January 2000. www.apbnews.com/safetycenter/campus/2000/01/28/notification0128_01.html (3 February 2000).

Kilbourne, J. *Calling the Shots: Advertising and Alcohol.* (Second Edition) Produced by Cambridge Documentary Films. 28 minutes. 1991. Videocassette.

Kirchoger, T. 2000. College drinking: Both extremes grow. *The Inquirer.* 15 March.

Mason, J. 1993. The dimensions of an epidemic of violence. *Public Health Reports.* (January/February):1–3.

Migneault, J., Velicer, W., Prochaska, J., and Stevenson, J. 1999. Decisional balance for immoderate drinking in college students. *Substance Use and Misuse.* 34: 1325–1346.

Milloy, R. Residents reassessing spring rite of students. *Port Arkansas Journal.* 9 April 2000. http://www10.nytimes.com:80/library/national/040900beach-edu.html (11 April 2000)/

Moss, H., and Tarter, R. 1993. Substance abuse, aggression, and violence: What are the connections? *American Journal on Additions.* 2: 149–160.

Mountain States Employers Council, Inc. and Nicoletti-Flater Associates. 1997. *Violence Goes to Work: An Employer's Guide.* Denver, Colorado: Mountain States Employers Council, Inc. and Nicoletti-Flater Associates.

Nicholson, M., Wang, M., Maney, D., and Jianping, Y. 1998. Alcohol related violence and unwanted sexual activity on the college campus. *American Journal of Health Studies.* 14(1): 1–10.

Nicoletti, J., and Spencer-Thomas, S. 1999. *Violence Goes to School: Lessons Learned from Columbine.* Lakewood, Colorado: Nicoletti-Flater Associates.

Nuwer, H. 1999. *Wrongs of Passage: Fraternities,*

Sororities, Hazing, and Binge Drinking. Bloomington: Indiana University Press.

O'Hare, T., and Sherrer, M. 1999. Validating the alcohol use disorder identification test with college first-offenders. *Journal of Substance Abuse Treatment.* 17:113–119.

Parker, R., and Auerhahn, K. 1998. Alcohol, drugs, and violence. *Annual Review of Sociology.* 24:291–311.

Parker, R., and Cartmill, R. 1998. Alcohol and homicide in the United States 1934-1995–Or one reason why U.S. rates of violence may be going down. *Journal of Criminal Law and Criminology.* 88:1369–1398.

Pearson, M. SIU restores drinking privileges to fraternity members. *Evansville Courier and Press Online.* http://www.courierpress.com:80.cgi-bin/view.cgi?200001/28+siu012800_news.htm l+20000128 (2 February 2000).

Perkins, H. W. Scope of the problem: Misperceptions of alcohol and drugs. *The Higher Education Center for Alcohol and Other Drug Prevention.* Fall 1995. http://www.edc.org/hec/pubs/catalst3.htm (10 August 2000).

Pernanen, K. 1998. Prevention of alcohol-related violence. *Contemporary Drug Problems.* 25 (fall): 477–509.

Reisberg, L. 1999. When do scare tactics become "health terrorism?" *The Chronicle of Higher Education.* 46(2):A79.

Rickgarn, R. 1989. Violence in residence halls: Campus domestic violence. In *Responding to Violence on Campus,* Jan Sherrill & Dorothy Siegel (eds.), San Francisco: Jossey-Bass Inc.

Ritter, K. MIT frat disbanded for alcohol violation. *Boston Globe Online.* 16 November 1999. http://www.globe.com/dailyglobe2/320/metro/MIT_frat_disbanded_for_alcohol_violation+.shtml (16 November 1999).

Rivinus, T., and Larimer, M. 1993. Violence, alcohol, other drugs, and the college student. In Whitaker, L. & Pollard, J. (Eds.), *Campus Violence: Kinds, Causes, and Cures.* New York: The Haworth Press, Inc.

Rossow, I., Pape, H., and Wichstrom, L. 1999. Young, wet and wild? *Addiction.* 94(7): 1017–1031.

Roth, J. Psychoactive substances and violence. *Schaffer Library of Drug Policy.* February 1994. http://www.druglibrary.org/schaffer/GOV-PUBS/psycviol.htm (4 August 2000).

Schevitz, T. 2000. Freshmen booze less, worry more. *San Francisco Chronicle.* 24 January.

Sondheimer, E. 1999. Time to remove alcohol from recruiting process. *Los Angeles Times.* 27 October.

Silverman, J. UCA suspends fraternity after alcohol-related deaths. *Arkansas Democrat-Gazette.* 2 December 1999. http://www.ardemgaz.com/weekly/Fri/Ark/B12xfrat3.html (6 December 1999).

Svaldi, A. Fake ID? You could face felony. *Denver Business Journal.* 3 January 2000. http://www.amcity.com/denver/stories/2000/01/03/story2.html (5 January 2000).

Urwitz, J. What every freshman should know. *Boston Globe.* 9 September 1999. http://www.boston.com:80/dailyglobe2/252.living/What_every_freshman_should_knowp.sht (10 September 1999).

Van Munching, P. 1998. *Beer Blast.* New York, NY: Times Books.

Veenhuis, P. 1997. Recent developments in alcoholism, vol. 13: Alcohol and violence–epidemiology, neurobiology, psychology, family issues. *American Journal of Psychiatry.* 155: 1453–1454.

Vivinetto, G. They'll drink to that. *St. Petersburg Times.* 5 December 1999. http://www.sptimes.com:80/News/120599/Floridian/They_II_drink_to_that.shtml (6 December 1999).

Walsh-Sarnecki, P. Drinking binge was deadly for student. *Detroit Free Press.* 17 March 2000. http://detroitnews.com:80/2000/metro/0003/18/03180043.htm (20 March 2000).

Warner, J. 1997. Shifting categories of the social harms associated with alcohol: Examples from late medieval and early modern England. *American Journal of Public Health.* 87(11):1788–1797.

Wechsler, H., Deutsch, C., and Dowdall, G. Too many colleges are still in denial about alcohol abuse. *The Chronicle of Higher Education.* 14 April 1995. http://www.hsph.harvard.edu/cas/test/articles/chronicle2.shtml (25 January 2000).

Wechsler, H., Nelson, T., and Weitzman, E. 2000. From knowledge to action: How Harvard's College Alcohol Study can help your campus

254

Violence Goes to College

design a campaign against student alcohol abuse. *Change: The Magazine of Higher Learning.* January/February 2000.

Wechsler, H., Davenport, A., Dowdall, G., Grossman, S., and Zanakos, S. 1996. Binge drinking, tobacco, and illicit drug use and involvement in college athletics. *JACH.* 44: 1–6.

Wechsler, H. Getting serious about eradicating binge drinking. *The Chronicle of Higher Education Online.* 20 November 1998. http://www.hsph.harvard.edu/cas/test/articles/chronicle.shtml (25 January 2000).

Wechsler, H., Dowdall, G., Maenner, G., Gledhill-Hoyt, J., and Lee, H. 1998. Changes in binge drinking and related problems among American college students between 1993 and 1997. *Journal of American College Health.* 47: 57–68.

Weiss, J. Alcohol agency probers laid off: State cites a shortfall in commission budget. *Boston Globe Online.* 1 February 2000. http://www.globe.com/dailyglobe2/032/metro/Alcohol_agency_probers_laid_off+.shtml (2 February 2000).

Workman, B. Stanford in turmoil over sobriety letter. *San Francisco Chronicle.* 11 February 2000. http://www.sfgate.com:80/cgi-bin/article.cgi?file=/chronicle/archive/2000/02/11/MN68546.DTL (15 February 2000).

CHAPTER FIVE
HEEDING THE SIGNS AND SYMPTOMS:
WHAT ARE THE RED FLAGS FOR IMPENDING VIOLENCE?

Anonymous. Massive pep-pill dosage found in Gallegos' system. *Denver Rocky Mountain News.* 8 November 1996.

Frazier, D., Levitt, L., and O'Keeffe, M. 1996. Greeley cops storm dorm, kill slayer of 3 hostage-taker at UNC had 'executed' roommates in Bayfield, authorities say. *Denver Rocky Mountain News.* 25 September.

Germer, F. 1996. He was going crazy. Ex-girlfriend says student describes horror in UNC dorm, says Gallegos blamed his mental anguish. *Rocky Mountain News.* 26 September.

Levitt, L. Suspect not on drugs when shot tests show Gallegos also not drunk during UNC hostage incident despite previous abuse. *Denver Rocky Mountain News.* 12 October 1996.

Mountain States Employers Council, Inc. and Nicoletti-Flater Associates. 1997. *Violence Goes to Work: An Employer's Guide.* Denver, Colorado: Mountain States Employers Council, Inc. and Nicoletti-Flater Associates.

Nicoletti, J., and Spencer-Thomas, S. 1999. *Violence Goes to School: Lessons Learned from Columbine.* Lakewood, Colorado: Nicoletti-Flater Associates.

Ryckman Levitt, L. 1996. Killer hid rage from kin, friends jilted lover was turning around his life of crime before Bayfield rampage, death at Greeley dorm. *Rocky Mountain News.* 29 September.

Ryckman Levitt, L., Frazier D., and Brennan, C. Friends knew a mellow Gallegos he killed the missionaries who took him in, and motive will be a mystery forever. *Rocky Mountain News.* 26 September.

Scanlon, B. Campus hangover. *Denver Rocky Mountain News.* 12 September 1999. http://insidedenver.com:80/news/0912booz7.shtml (14 September 1999).

Scanlon, B. 1997. UNC hostage crisis echoes in Greeley lives finally mending one year after gunman killed 3, took captives. *Rocky Mountain News.* 24 September.

CHAPTER SIX
BUILDING BARRIERS TO VIOLENCE, PART I: AMASSING THE ARMY

Anderson, D., and Napeirkowski, C. 1998. Substance abuse and violence. In *Violence on Campus*. Gaithersburg, Maryland: Aspen Publications.

Anonymous. Campus-community coalitions in AOD prevention. *Prevention Updates*. February 1998. http://www.edc.org/hec/pubs/prev-updates/campus-comm-coal.txt (20 August 2000).

Anonymous. Effective coalitions are flexible, deferential, structured. *Join Together Online*. 10 January 2000. http://www.jointogether.org/sa/default.jtml?O=261553 11 January 2000.

Cohen, L., and Swift, S. Beyond brochures: Preventing alcohol-related and injuries. *Prevention Institute*. http://www.preventioninstitute.org/alcohol.html (13 January 2000).

Deisinger, E., Cychosz, C., and Jaeger, L. 1998. Strategies for dealing with violence. In *Violence on Campus*. Gaithersburg, Maryland: Aspen Publications.

DeJong, W. Presidential leadership needed to advance prevention on campuses. *Higher Education Center: Prevention File Spring 1998. 13*(2). (1998). http://www.edc.org/hec/pubs/articles/prevfile98.html (25 January 2000).

Floyd, E. Get tough on student drinking: How to sober up the campus and reduce Alcohol abuse. *Detroit Free Press*. 10 September 1999. http://freep.com:80/voices/columnist/qefloyd

10.htm (11 September 1999).

Goff, K. 2000. Tough policy urged to curb bingeing. *Washington Times*. 6 February.

Hellstrom, D. 1999. Creating a home, making a difference. *The Peer Educator*. September.

Kassab, B. 1999. Police begin to stern flow of alcohol at UF. *St. Petersburg Times*. 3 October.

Katz, J. 1995. Reconstructing masculinity in the locker room. *Harvard Educational Review. 65*(2):163–174.

Mountain States Employers Council, Inc. and Nicoletti-Flater Associates. 1996. *Violence Goes to Work: An Employer's Guide*. Denver, Colorado: Mountain States Employers Council, Inc. and Nicoletti-Flater Associates.

Reisberg, L. 1999. Violence-studies program takes aim at social evils and student attitudes. *Chronicle of Higher Education. 46*(13):A60–A61.

Schuh, J. 1998. Campus vulnerability. In *Violence on Campus*. Gaithersburg, Maryland: Aspen Publications.

Sherill, J. 1989. Models of response to campus violence. In *Responding to Violence on Campus*. San Francisco: Jossey-Bass, Inc.

Wechsler, H., Nelson, T., and Weitzman, E. 2000. From knowledge to action: How Harvard's College alcohol study can help your campus design a campaign against student alcohol abuse. *Change*. January/February.

CHAPTER SEVEN
BUILDING BARRIERS TO VIOLENCE, PART II: DEVELOPING POLICIES AND PROCEDURES FOR THREATS AND VIOLENCE

Anonymous. Campus crime legislation in the 106th congress (1999-2000). *Campus Crime Legislation*. http://www.campussafety.org/publicpolicy/congress/106/index.html (17 April 2000).

Anonymous. Interpersonal violence and alcohol and other drug use. *The Higher Education Center for Alcohol and Drug Prevention*. June

1999. http://www.edc.org/hec/pubs/factsheets/fact_sheet4.html (2 April 2000).

Brennan, R. 2000. First college fined for campus security reporting violations. *Clinton Herald*. 22 June.

Brenner, E. 2000. Mother sues Iona College. *The New York Times*. 16 July.

Bronner, E. In a revolution of rules, campuses go

full circle. *The New York Times on the Web.* 3 March 1999. http://www.nytimes.com/library/national/030399college-supervision.html (25 October 1999).

Cohen, L., and Swift, S. Beyond brochures: Preventing alcohol-related and injuries. *Prevention Institute.* http://www.preventioninstitute.org/alcohol.html (13 January 2000).

Gose, B. 1995. Harvard's decision to withdraw offer to woman who killed her mother raises tricky questions. *Chronicle of Higher Education.* 41(32):A48.

Gose, B. 1998. Some colleges extend their codes of conduct to off-campus behavior. *Chronicle of Higher Education.* 45(7):A51–A52.

Gose, B. 2000. Court upholds right of a university to deny degree to student who killed another. *Chronicle of Higher Education.* 46(28):A52.

Greengard, S. 1999. Zero tolerance: Making it work. *Workforce.* 78(5):28–34.

Hansen, M. 1993. An ex-con goes to law school. *ABA Journal.* 79:19.

Hewitt, B., Wescott, G., and Duffy, T. 1995. Poisoned ivy. *People Weekly.* 43(16):42–44.

Hoffman, A., Schuh, J., and Fenske, R. 1998. Violent crime in the college and university workplace. In *Violence on Campus.* Gaithersburg, Maryland: Aspen Publications.

Hunnicutt, K., and Kushibab, P. 1998. The legal response to violence on campus. In *Violence on Campus.* Gaithersburg, Maryland: Aspen Publications.

Mountain States Employers Council, Inc. and Nicoletti-Flater Associates. 1996. *Violence Goes to Work: An Employer's Guide.* Denver, Colorado: Mountain States Employers Council, Inc. and Nicoletti-Flater Associates.

Nicklin, J. 1999. Colleges differ widely on how they tally incidents under crime-reporting law. *The Chronicle of Higher Education.* 45(38):A38.

Nicoletti, J., Spencer-Thomas, S., and Porter, K. 1998. *Survival-Oriented Kids in a Violent World.* Lakewood, Colorado: Nicoletti-Flater Associates.

Nicoletti, J., and Spencer-Thomas, S. 1999. *Violence Goes to School: Lessons Learned from Columbine.* Lakewood, Colorado: Nicoletti-Flater Associates.

Roark, M. 1993. Conceptualizing campus violence: Definitions, underlying factors and effects. In Whitaker, L. & Pollard, J. (Eds) *Campus Violence: Kinds, Causes, and Cures.* New York: The Haworth Press, Inc.

Siegel, D. 1994. Summary. In *Campuses Respond to Violent Tragedy.* American Council on Education. Phoenix, Arizona: Oryx Press.

Selingo, J. 2000. Florida supreme court says university is liable for intern's injury. *The Chronicle of Higher Education.* 4 April.

CHAPTER EIGHT
BUILDING BARRIERS TO VIOLENCE, PART III:
ENVIRONMENTAL PROTECTION AND SAFETY STRATEGIES

Anonymous. 1999. Gun studies serve as wake-up call for student affairs administrators. *Student Affairs Today.* 2(5):1, 8.

Anonymous. *Campus Safety: Tips and Evaluation Brochure.* Security on Campus, Inc.

Asmussen, K., and Creswell, J. 1995. Campus response to a student gunman. *Journal of Higher Education.* 66(5):575–591.

Estrin, R. 1999. The wild, wild campus? *ABC News.com.* 2 July.

Leo, R. 1999. 400,000 undergraduates in the U.S. own a handgun, study finds. *Chronicle of Higher Education.* 45(45):A40.

Lewis, C. 1999. Tracking students' guns is challenging for colleges. *The Fort Worth Star-Telegram.* 14 August.

Miller, M., Hemenway, D., and Wechsler, H. 1999. Guns at college. *Journal of American College Health.* 48:7–12.

Nicoletti, J., Spencer-Thomas, S., and Porter, K. 1998. *Survival-Oriented Kids in a Violent World.* Lakewood, Colorado: Nicoletti-Flater Associates.

Nicoletti, J., and Spencer-Thomas, S. 1999.

Violence Goes to School: Lessons Learned from Columbine. Lakewood, Colorado: Nicoletti-Flater Associates.

Nosek, M., and Howland, C. Abuse and women with disabilities. *Violence Against Women Online Resources.* 8 November 1999. http://www.vaw.umn.edu/Vawnet/disab.htm (20 August 2000).

Schneider, A. 1998. Student charged in armed threat. *Chronicle of Higher Education.* 45(10): A14.

Young, M., Nosek, M., Howland, C., Chanpong, G., and Rintala, D. 1997. Prevalence of abuse of women with physical disabilities. *Archives of Physical Medicine and Rehabilitation.* 78: S34–S38.

CHAPTER NINE
PREPARING FOR THE VIOLENCE AFTERMATH:
A COMMUNITY AFFECTED

Alexander, P. 1998. The real story of the cyber-sex trial. *Rolling Stone.* 7(97):94–104.

Anonymous. 1994. *Diagnostic Criteria from DSM-IV.* Washington D.C.: American Psychiatric Association.

Baily, A. 1998. A question of violence. *Arena Magazine.* 35:25.

Cerio, N. 1989. *Counseling Victims and Perpetrators of Campus Violence.* San Francisco: Jossey-Bass Inc.

De Becker, G. 1997. *The Gift of Fear: Survival Signals That Protect Us From Violence.* New York: Little, Brown and Company.

Herman, J. 1992. *Trauma and Recovery.* Boulder, Colorado: BasicBooks.

Hurst, J. 1999. The Matthew Shepard tragedy–crisis and beyond. *About Campus.* 4:3.

Janoff-Bulman, R. 1992. *Shattered Assumptions: Towards a New Psychology of Trauma.* New York: The Free Press.

Nicoletti, J., and Spencer-Thomas, S. 1999. *Violence Goes to School: Lessons Learned from Columbine.* Lakewood, Colorado: Nicoletti-Flater Associates.

Pennington, K., Duncan, M., Hurst, J., and Zdziarski, G. 2000. Violence on campus: Prevention and recovery. NASPA Task Force presentation at NASPA Annual Conference March 21, 2000 Indianapolis, IN.

Siegel, D. 1994. Summary. In *Campuses Respond to Violent Tragedy.* Phoenix, AZ: American Council on Education and The Oryx Press.

Slover, C., and Tasci, D. 1999. *Trauma Recovery Handbook.* Lakewood, Colorado: Nicoletti-Flater Associates.

Stone, G. 1993. Psychological challenges and responses to a campus tragedy: The Iowa Experience. In Whitaker, L. & Pollard, J. (Eds.), *Campus Violence: Kinds, Causes, and Cures.* New York: The Howarth Press, Inc.

CHAPTER TEN
SEXUAL ASSAULT

Alvi, S., and Selbee, K. 1997. Dating status variations and woman abuse. *Violence Against Women.* 3(6):610–628.

Anonymous. 1998. Canada: Rape shield law survives challenge. *Off Our Backs.* 28(6):7.

Anonymous. 2000. Date-rape bill sent to Clinton. *USA Today.* 1 February.

Anonymous. Rape Trauma Syndrome: An overview. *UC Davis Rape Prevention Education Program.* 15 February 1998. http://pubweb.ucdavis.edu/Documents/RPER/rts.htm (15 January 2000).

Anonymous. Gamma Hydroxy Butyrate use in New York and Texas, 1995-1996. *Morbidity and Mortality Weekly Report.* 4 April 1997. http://www.emergency.com/ghb-2.htm (15 July 2000).

Anonymous. Security on campus update–date

rape drug bill passes U.S. House. *Security on Campus, Inc.* 2 February 2000. http://campussagety.org (2 February 2000).

Anonymous. Virginia Tech settles lawsuit with Brzonkala. *Campus Safety.org #160.* http://campussafety.org/courts/BRZONKALA/index.html (25 February 2000).

Anonymous. Christy Brzonkala's Violence Against Women Act & Title 9 cases. *Campus Safety.* http://campussafety.org/publicpolicy/courts/brzonkala/index.html (1 August 2000).

Anonymous. 2000. Lawmakers urge renewal of Violence Against Women Act. *Nation's Health.* 30(6):5.

Anonymous. UMass Campus Safety. *Campus Safety.* http://www.umass.edu/umhome/safety/index.html (27 February 2000).

Anonymous. University of Massachusetts rallies against campus attack. *CNN.com* 24 November 1999. http://www.cnn.com/US/9911/24/amherst.rapes.index.html (27 February 2000).

Anonymous. Male rape. *Infolink.* http://www.ncvc.org/infolink/info38.htm (15 August 2000).

Anonymous. Rape statistics. http://www.cs.utk.edu/~bartley/sa/stats.html (15 August 2000).

Bradford, J., Ryan, C., and Rothblum, E. 1994. National lesbian health care survey. *Journal of Consulting and Clinical Psychology.* 62(2): 228–242.

Brzonkala, C. Prepared testimony of Christy Brzonkala. *Campus Safety.* http://campussafety.org/publicpolicy/congress/104/cbrzonkala.html (1 August 2000).

Carlson, S. 1999. Umass student concocts sexual assault during anti-rape rally. *The Daily Free Press.* 10 December.

Clinton, W. 2000. Statement on the Supreme Court decision striking down a provision of the Violence Against Women Act. *Weekly Compilation of Presidential Documents* v. 36 n 20. 22 May.

Crosset,T., Ptacek, J., McDonald, M., and Benedict, J. 1996. Male student-athletes and violence against women. *Violence Against Women.* 2(2):163–179.

Davis, T. 1999. Book review of the Men's Program: How to successfully lower men's

likelihood of raping. *Journal of College Student Development.* 40(6).

De Becker, G. 1997. *The Gift of Fear: Survival Signals That Protect Us From Violence.* New York: Little, Brown and Company.

Duncan, D. 1990. Prevalence of sexual assault victimization among heterosexual and gay/lesbian university students. *Psychological Reports.* 66:65–66.

Dunn, P., Vail, K., Knight, M. 1999. What date/acquaintance rape victims tell others. *Journal of American College Health.* 47(5):213.

Fischman, J. 2000. A fight over the evolution of rape, sex or power. *U.S. News and World Report.* 7 February.

Garnets, L., Herek, G., and Levy, B. 1992. Violence and victimization of lesbians and gay men. In *Hate Crimes.* Newbury Park: Sage Publications.

Gidycz, C. A., and Koss, M. P. 1991. The effects of acquaintance rape on the female victim. In Parrot & Bechhofer (Eds.), *Acquaintance Rape: The Hidden Crime.* New York: John Wiley & Sons, Inc.

Goetz, T. 1996. Cyberstalker, qu'est-ce-que c'est? *Village Voice.* 441(53):23.

Gose, B. 1996. Brown University's handling of date-rape case leaves many questioning campus policies. *Chronicle of Higher Education.* 43(7):A53–A55.

Gose, B. 1998. Men accused of sex crimes at Bates say they are victims of "hysteria". *Chronicle of Higher Education.* 44(38): A37–A38.

Gose, B. 1999. Harvard expels student for role in controversial date-rape case. *Chronicle of Higher Education.* 45(28):A45.

Grogan, D., Ramirez, S., and Garelik, G. 1995. Terror by e-mail. *People Weekly.* 43(9):59–60.

Hall, H. 1998. *Lethal Violence: A Sourcebook on Fatal Domestic, Acquaintance, and Stranger Aggression.* Boca Raton, Florida: CRC Press, LLC.

Hickson, F., Davies, P., Hunt, A., Weatherburn, P., McManus. T., and Coxon, A. 1994. Gay men as victims of nonconsensual sex. *Archives of Sexual Behavior.* 23(3):281.

Koss, M.P. and Oros, C. J. 1982. The sexual experiences survey: A research instrument investigating sexual aggression and victimization. *Journal of Consulting and Clinical Psychology, 50:*455-457.

Landolt, M., and Dutton, D. 1997. Power and personality: An analysis of gay male intimate abuse. *Sex Roles: A Journal of Research.* 37(5–6):335–359.

Larimer, M., Lydum, A., Anderson, B., and Turner, A. 1999. Male and females recipients of unwanted sexual contact in a college student sample: Prevalence rates, alcohol use, and depression symptoms. *Sex Roles: A Journal of Research.* 40(3):295.

McNair, J. Violence against women act thrown out. *The Associated Press.* 5 March 1999. http://www.abcnews.com (25 October 1999).

Monasteksy, R. 2000. Debunking the idea that evolution makes rapists. *Chronicle of Higher Education.* 46(28):A24.

Muehlenhard, C.L. and Linton, M. A. 1987. Date rape and sexual aggression in dating situations: Incidence and risk factors. *Journal of Counseling Psychology,* 34(2):186-196.

Myers, M. 1989. Men sexually assaulted as adults and sexually abused as boys. *Archives of Sexual Behavior,* 18(3):203-215.

Parrot, A., and Bechhofer, L. (Eds.) 1991. *Acquaintance Rape: The Hidden Crime.* New York: John Wiley & Sons, Inc.

Pino, N. W., and Meier, R. F. 1999. Gender differences in rape reporting. *Sex Roles: A Journal of Research,* 40(11-12):979-990, January.

O'Sullivan, C. S. 1991. Acquaintance gang rape on campus. In Parrot & Bechhofer (Eds.), *Acquaintance Rape: The Hidden Crime.* New York: John Wiley & Sons, Inc.

Rohde, D. 1999. Call for new sex-abuse trial is said to harm rape shield. *New York Times.* 23 December.

Rubenzahl, S., and Corcoran, K. 1998. The prevalence and characteristics of male perpetrators of acquaintance rape: New research methodology reveals new findings. *Violence Against Women.* 6(6):713-725.

Sanday, P. 1990. *Fraternity Gang Rape–Sex, Brotherhood, and Privilege on Campus.* New York: New York University Press.

Schmidt, P. 2000. Ruling in Virginia Tech case, Supreme Court rejects federal rape law.

Chronicle of Higher Education. 46(38):A42.

Staten, C. GBH, GHB- Unofficial report from the United Kingdom. *Emergency News Service.* 1 February 1997. http://www.emergency.com/ghb1.htm (15 July 2000).

Staten, C. Roofies, the new 'date rape' drug of choice. *Emergency Net News.* 6 January 1996. http://www.emergency.com/roofies.htm (15 July 2000).

Struckman-Johnson, C. 1988. Forced sex on dates: It happens to men too. *Journal of Sex Research,* 24 234-241.

Struckman-Johnson, C. 1991. Male victims of acquaintance rape. In Parrot & Bechhofer (Eds.), *Acquaintance Rape: The Hidden Crime.* New York: John Wiley & Sons, Inc.

Struckman-Johnson, C., and Struckman-Johnson, D. 1994. Men pressured and forced into sexual experience. *Archives of Sexual Behavior,* 23(1):93-114.

Thornhill, R., and Palmer, C. 2000. *A Natural History of Rape: Biological Bases of Sexual Coercion.* Cambridge, MA: MIT Press.

Ullman, J. 1998. Cyber sex. *Psychology Today.* 31(5):28–30+.

U.S. Department of Justice, Federal Bureau of Investigation. *Uniform Crime Reporting: National Incident-Based Reporting System.* (Vol. 1, *Data Collection Guidelines*). Updated February 1998.

Waterman, C., Dawson, L., and Bologna, M. 1989. Sexual coercion in gay male and lesbian relationships. *The Journal of Sex Research.* 26(1):118–124.

Willing, R. 2000. Court rejects rape law. *USA Today.* 16 May.

Woodruff, K. 1996. Alcohol advertising and violence against women: A media advocacy case study. *Health Education Quarterly.* 23:330–345.

Worden, A. Rapes, assaults stun Mass. campus. *APBnews.com.* 17 November 1999. http://www.apbnews.com/newscenter/breakingnews/1999/11/17/umass1117_01.html (27 February 2000).

Wright, M. Gamma hydroxy butyric acid. *The Battalion Web Site.* 27 January 1999. http://battalion.tamu.edu/archives/99a/1-27/fp6.html (15 July 2000).

CHAPTER ELEVEN
RIOTING

Acker, G. 1997. Students prove they won't be controlled. *The Opinion.* 10 September.

Anonymous. About Plymouth State College. *Plymouth State College Homepage.* 19 January 1999. http://www.plymouth.edu/psc/adm-serv/factbook/general_info.htm (23 May 2000).

Anonymous. 1999. After Web posts, police feared copyright infringement. *News Photographer.* 54(5):30.

Anonymous. Annual OU riot a hit. *The Miami Student Online.* 10 April 1998. http://mustu-dent.muohio.edu/1997/041098/ou.html (24 May 2000).

Anonymous. A brief history of Eugene. *Eugene Information.* 28 October 1998. http://www.ci.eugene.or.us/local/euggov.htm (23 May 2000).

Anonymous. Campus incident reports. *Campus Watch Newsletter Online.* 5 April 1999. http://campussafety.org/WATCH/watch0499.05.html (25 October 1999).

Anonymous. College rioters jailed at higher rate than rapists. *APB News.* 5 March 2000. http://www.apbnews.com:80/newscenter/breakingnews/2000/03/05/msuriot0305_01.html (14 March 2000).

Anonymous. Colorado State, city officials to coordinate following incident. *Colorado State University News and Information.* 30 August 1997. http://www.colostate.edu/Depts/PR/releases/news/incident.htm (23 May 2000).

Anonymous. Colorado State University establishes hotline to identify students involved in incidents near campus. *Colorado State University News and Information.* 8 September 1997. http://www.colostate.edu/Depts/PR/releases/nes/hotline.htm (23 May 2000).

Anonymous. Court tells Michigan newspaper to hand over photos of campus riot. *The Freedom Forum Online.* 6 April 1999. http://www.free-domforum.org/press/1999/4/6msuriot.asp (13 April 2000).

Anonymous. Enrollment history. *Oregon University System.* February 1999. http://www.ous.edu/irs/factbook/WEBstudent/hchist.htm (23 May 2000).

Anonymous. Facts about WSU. *WSU Facts.* http://www.wsu.edu/NIS/FactsAboutWSU.html (23 May 2000).

Anonymous. 1998. Halloween's a riot again at U. of O., despite extra police patrols. *The Columbian.* 2 November.

Anonymous. Just the facts. *University of Colorado at Boulder.* http://www.colorado.edu/Public Relations/JustTheFacts/jtf.html (23 May 2000).

Anonymous. 1993. Lesson in riot control. *National Review.* 45(1):14.

Anonymous. The 1997 University Hill riots. http://www.colorado.edu/geography/COGA/geogweb/universityhill/forum/riotpic2.html (23 May 2000).

Anonymous. The official Commentator riot guide. *Oregon Commentator.* http://dark-wing.uoregon.edu/~ocomment/ocarchive/oc97_98/oc2_97_4.html (23 May 2000).

Anonymous. Penn State quick facts. *Penn State Online.* http://www.psu.edu/ur/about/quick.html (23 May 2000).

Anonymous. 1998. Penn State riot damage estimated at $100K. *York Daily Record.* 14 July.

Anonymous. 1998. Penn State riot reported about 1,500 people flooded streets through the early morning Sunday after the Central Pennsylvania Festival of Arts. *York Daily Record.* 13 July.

Anonymous. 1998. Penn State should expel rioters. *Daily Collegian.* 14 July.

Anonymous. 1998. Police arrest eight more in July 12 Penn State riot about 1,500 people took part in the melee. *York Daily Record.* 28 August.

Anonymous. Prospective students. *Miami University Homepage.* http://www.mohio.edu/prospectivestudents/ (23 May 2000).

Anonymous. 1997. Riot act. *The Opinion.* 9 September.

Anonymous. 1998. Seventeen arrested in weekend riot. *The State News.* 4 May.

Anonymous. 1998. Sober thoughts as Penn State riots show, binge drinking has become the most serious drug problem on campus. It's time to address it. *Sunday News.* 19 July.

Anonymous. State College police make eight more riot-related arrests. *Intercom Online.* 3 September 1999. http://www.psu.edu/ur/archives/intercom_1998/Sept3/roit.html (23 May 2000).

Anonymous. 1998. Student rioters demand the "right to party." *Chronicle of Higher Education.* 44(36):A46.

Anonymous. 1998. Students demonstrate for right to bear beers. *Times Union.* 13 May.

Anonymous. Students involved in summer riot no longer in school. *Penn State Online.* 30 November 1998. http://www.psu.edu/ur/NEWS/news/riotsanctions.html (23 May 2000).

Anonymous. Three more sentenced for participation in riot. *Intercom Online.* 28 January 1999. http://www.psu.edu/archives/intercom_1999/Jan28/riot.html (23 May 2000).

Anonymous. Thumbnail facts. *University of Connecticut.* January 2000. http://www.uconn.edu/about.html (23 May 2000).

Anonymous. UNH profile 1999. *University of New Hampshire Homepage.* http://www.unh.edu/aboutunh.html (23 May 2000).

Anonymous. University weekend rioters disciplined. *University of Connecticut Advance.* 21 September 1998. http://www.advance.uconn.edu/09219802.htm (23 May 2000).

Anonymous. Oxford, OH. *U.S. Gazetteer.* http://www.census.gov/cgi-bin/gazetteer?city=Oxford&state=OH&zip= (11 July 2000).

Anonymous. U.S. Gazetteer. *U.S. Census Bureau.* http://www.census.gov/cgi-bin/gazetteer?city=Boulder&state=CO&zip= (23 May 2000).

Anonymous. What Jeanne didn't know. *Security on Campus, Inc.* http://campussafety.org/soc/jac,html (27 February 2000).

Anonymous. 1998. The yell. *The Post: Athens, Ohio.* 9 April.

Applegate, R. 1981. *Riot Control.* Boulder: Paladin Press.

Applegate, R. 1962. *Kill or Get Killed.* Harrisburg: The Stackpole Company.

Arden-Smith, T. Daylight saving is a riot. *Student.com.* 7 April 1998. http://www.student.com/article/ohioriot (23 May 2000).

Austin, D., and Hardy, K. 1999. Last riot case brings closure. *The State News.* 3 November.

Beene, C. 1992. *Police Crowd Control.* Boulder: Paladin Press.

Beutler, W. Oregon commentator riot guide. *Oregon Commentator.* http://darkwing.uoregon.edu/~ocomment/ocarchive/oc98_99/oc3_98_5.html (23 May 2000).

Blair, B., and Cole, P. 1998. 1,500 riot at Penn State; 20 arrested. *Daily Collegian.* 13 July.

Bloch, G. Prohibition, part II: At the University, and across the country, students are fighting for their right to party. *Oregon Commentator.* http://darkwing.uoregon.edu/~ocomment/ocarchive/oc97_98/oc13_97_4.html (23 May 2000).

Bradley, F., and Cichon, F. 2000. Police end riot near Penn State University. *Daily Collegian.* 17 July.

Brown, D. UNH takes action against possible riots. *The New Hampshire.* 24 March 2000. http://www.tnh.unh.edu/Issues/032400/News/riots.html (23 May 2000).

Brown, J., and Politsky, A. 1997. *The Post.* 24 April.

Brunt, J. 1997. Weekend fracas "total anarchy." *The State News.* 8 September.

Burden, M. 1999. Alumni hesitant with gifts after riot. *The State News.* 5 April.

Burden, M. 1999. Suspended rioter reinstated. *The State News.* 19 April.

Byyny, R., and Stump, R. Past points to possible solutions. *Carillon.* 13 November 1998. http://www.colorado.edu/Carillon/volume17/stories/2_alcohol_solutions.html (23 May 2000).

Caufield, K. 1999. Peace groups tried to stop riot, damage. *The State News.* 30 March.

Chen, H. Student jailed for role in campus riot. *APB News.* 10 June 1999. http://www.apbnews.com/newscenter/breakingnews/1999/06/10/riot0610_01.html (25 October 1999).

Cheng, V. 1998. Community wants to curtail drinking; Students binge drinking was blamed for fueling the July 12 riot at Penn State. *York Daily Record.* 3 September.

Clapp, A., and Hardy, K. 2000. Enforcement helps deter further riots. *The State News.* 27 March.

Cohen, J., and Pardo S. 1999. Riot wasn't spontaneous; students had stockpiled. *The Detroit News.* 29 March.

Cook, K. 1999. Field of screams. *Sports Illustrated.* *91*(10):32.

Corlene, D. Students riot. *The Post.* 1 April 1998. http://thepost.baker.ohiou.edu/archives/0401 98/aftop.html (23 May 2000).

Couch, G. 2000. The real March madness. *Chicago Sun-Times.* 28 March.

Curtin, D. 1999. Mile High will be dry for CU, CSU. *The Denver Post.* 21 September.

Curtin, D. 1999. CU regent proposes "riot fee." *The Denver Post.* 12 November.

Curtin, D. 1999. Anti-riot policy has initial OK. *The Denver Post.* 23 November.

Danchuk, E. Riots not a well chosen battle. *The Miami Student Online.* 14 April 1998. http://mustudent.muohio.edu/1997/041498/ri ots.html (24 May 2000).

Delgado, V. Two rioters suspended. *Lansing State Journal.* 14 July 2000. http://www.lansingstatejournal.com/features/riot/suspended.h tml (14 July 2000).

Donvan, J., Sawyer, F., Tate, R., Zeoli, R., and Coleman, M. 1998. The right to party. *ABC Nightline.* 11 May.

Drummond, D. School tightens rules to curb alcohol abuse, prevent repeat of riots. *The Toledo Blade.* 29 August 1999. http://www.toledoblade.com:80/editorial/ne ws/9h29msu.htm (30 August 1999).

Durbin, D. 1999. MSU suspends 2 rioting students. *South Bend Tribune.* 31 March.

Freile, V., and Mateen, M. Conference focuses on PSU riot. *The Digital Collegian.* 27 July 1998. http://www.collegian.psu.edu/archive/1998/0 7/07-27-98tdc/07-27-98d01-003.asp (23 May 2000).

French, B. 1999. Booze, rebellion fed rampage. *The Detroit News.* 29 March.

Gilje, P. 1996. *Rioting in America.* Bloomington: Indiana University Press.

Gonzales, P. Riots at Michigan State University. *Campus Safety Journal.* http://www.campusjournal.com/michigan-state-riot.htm (13 April 2000).

Gose, B. 1998. At Connecticut's party weekend, days of music replaced by nights of vandalism. *Chronicle of Higher Education.* *44*(36):A47–A48.

Haddock, D., and Polsby, D. Understanding riots. *The Cato Journal.* 14, no. 1 (Spring/Summer 1994). http://www.cato.org/

pubs/journal/cj14n1-13.html (23 May 2000).

Hamilton, L. 1997. Riot proves city is full of oppression. *The Opinion.* 9 September.

Hampshire, K. 1998. Campus clashes not uncommon occurrences. *The Post–Ohio University.* 29 April.

Howe, J. Reading the riots. *Link Magazine.* August/September 1998. http://www.link mag.com/Link/aug_sept_98/980820Riots.ht ml (24 May 2000).

Hudson, M. 1998. Students pleased by riot workshop. *The State News.* 12 August.

Hughes, K. 2000. Churches seek to help heal riot wounds. *The State News.* 24 March.

Imhof, H. WSU students spearhead efforts to curb alcohol abuse. *News from Washington State University.* 16 April 1999. http://www.wsu. edu/NIS/release2/hi125.htm (23 May 2000).

Imhof, H. WSU Greeks plan community party. *News from Washington State University.* 23 April 2000. http://www.wsu.edu/NIS/releases2/ hi131.htm (23 May 2000).

Jackson, C. Campus Riots Continue. *Student.com.* http://www.student.com/article/riotupdate (23 May 2000).

Kinney, D. 1998. Police gear up to prevent repeat performance of riot. Some men convicted for their part in the riot last year are being visibly punished. *York Daily Record.* 8 July.

Kron, M. Fight for your right. *Oregon Commentator.* http://darkwing.uoregon.edu/ ~ocomment/ocarchive/oc97_98/oc3_97_8.ht ml (23 May 2000).

Kuntz, J. Riots stupider than daylight saving time. *Student Advantage.* 4 May 2000. http://www.studentadvantage.com/article_sto ry/1,1075,c2-i39-t0-a25790,00.html (24 May 2000).

Levine, A., and Cureton, J. 1998. *When Hope and Fear Collide: A Portrait of Today's College Student.* Somerset, NJ: Jossey-Bass Publishers.

Levine, M. 1999. Rethinking bystander nonintervention. *Human Relations.* *52*(9):1133–1155.

Lively, K. 1998. At Michigan State, a protest escalated into a night of fires, tear gas, and arrests. *Chronicle of Higher Education.* *44*(36):A46–A47.

McCollum, K. 1999. Hackers attack Web site set up to nab student rioters at Michigan State U. *Chronicle of Higher Education.* *45*(33):A38.

Meese, J. How to stop a riot: Forum yields ideas. *The State News.* 1 April 1999. http://www.statenews.com/editionsspring99/040199/p1_forum.html (23 May 2000).

Methvin, E. 1970. *The Riot Makers.* New Rochelle: Arlington House.

Michelson, M. 2000. Potential Washington State U. riot repeat rebuffed. *Daily Evergreen.* 6 March.

Mills, D. 1998. Munn field riot latest in long string of uprisings. *The State News.* 2 May.

Mitchell, K. 1999. U. Colorado students riot after Super Bowl. *Campus Press–University of Colorado.* 5 February.

Mitchell, M. Official suggestions for safe student celebrations. *Carillon.* 5 May 2000. http://www.colorado.edu/Carillon/volume43/stories/5official.html (23 May 2000).

Morse, J. More violence near Miami. *Enquirer Local News Coverage.* 9 May 1998. http://enquirer.com/editions/1998/05/09/miami.html (23 May 2000).

Muir, P. Riot ordinance empower police. *The State News.* 22 April 1999. http://www.statenews.com/editionsspring99/042299/ci_ordinance.html (23 May 2000).

Murphy, P. 1997. City, 'U' disrespect students' rights. *The Opinion.* 10 September.

Nault, D. Overnight disturbance. *Miami News and Public Information Office.* 8 May 1998. http://newsinfo.muohio.edu/news_display.cfm?mu_un_id=298 (23 May 2000).

Olsen, N. 1998. Colorado State needs to cut party attendance to avoid police tear gas. *Rocky Mountain Collegian–Colorado State.* 19 October.

Owen, M. 1999. Riot footage shows up on 'Real TV' party school piece. *The State News.* 9 November.

Pardo, J., and Cohen, J. 1999. MSU vows to expel rioters: Police seek melee videos; students may face charges. *Detroit News.* 29 March.

Parfitt, M. Penn State riot aftermath: Officials clean up, assign blame. *Daily Collegian.* 14 July 1998.

Petura, B. Expulsions, suspensions, fines, probation included. *New from Washington State University.* 14 August 1998. http://www.wsu.edu/NIS/releases/bp129.htm (23 May 2000).

Phillips, M. 2000. Washington State U. aims for more students, money. *Daily Evergreen.* 20 June.

Piscitelli, A. 1998. Look around you: There's more to see. *The Post–Ohio University.* 18 May.

Platt, A. (Ed.) 1971. *The Politics of Riot Commissions 1917-1970.* New York: The Macmillan Company.

Quinn, S. Riots spark publicity, animosity. *The New Hampshire.* 8 May 1998. http://www.tnh.unh.edu/Issues/050898/News/riots.html (23 May 2000).

Reilly, R. 1998. And the band fought on. *Sports Illustrated.* 89(14):112.

Reisberg, L. 1998. Some experts say colleges share the responsibility for the recent riots. *Chronicle of Higher Education.* 44(36):A48.

Ripley, T. 1999. Riot control equipment. *Armada International.* 23(2):40–44.

Ritzo, N. UNH is a mess, but not because of riots. *The New Hampshire.* 14 October 1997. http://www.tnh.unh.edu/Issues/101497/Forum/badrep.html (23 May 2000).

Sanchezand, R., and Ebnet, M. "Fluke" weekend riot at WSU may be part of trend. *The Seattle Times.* 5 May 1998. http://seattletimes.com/news/local/html98/pull_050598.html (24 May 2000).

Schlosser, R. Riot act: Part II. *The New Hampshire.* 23 September 1997. http://www.tnh.unh.edu/Issues/092397/News/riot.html (23 May 2000).

Schneider, K. 2000. Video depicts questionable police actions during riot at Ohio U. *The Post.* 13 April.

Shepardson, D. Media fight to demand MSU riot photos. *The Detroit News.* 11 April 1999. http://www.detnews.com/1999/metro/9904/11/04110046.htm (13 April 2000).

Simpson, H. 1998. What a riot this weekend was! *The Post: Athens, Ohio.* 7 April.

Skertic, M. Arrested seniors' status in limbo. *Enquirer Local News Coverage.* 12 May 1998. http://enquirer.com/editions/1998/05/12/diplomas12.html (23 May 2000).

Smylie, M. 1999. One year later, Washington State U. remember May riot. *Daily Evergreen.* 6 May.

Sowa, J. 1997. Halloween party turns into riot. *Oregon Daily Emerald.* 3 November.

Sowa, T. 1998. Law enforcement cites mistakes in handling riot authorities lacked shields and failed to wait for backup, say officers involved in WSU melee. *The Spokane Review.* 20 May.

Stebbins, R. Who hath woe? *Plymouth State College English Department.* http://www.ply-mouth.edu/psc/english/special_projects/spir-its/stebbins1.html (24 May 2000).

Steele, J. 1999. Student look to extinguish negative image. *The State News.* 31 March.

Stockwell, J. Rioting: The new rage? *Student.com.* http://www.student.com/article/riots (13 April 2000).

Swavy, J. 1997. Gunson residents to challenge tickets. *The State News.* 11 September.

Swavy, J. 1997. Police brace for crowds. *The State News.* 9 September.

Tato, S. MSU officials defend riot suspensions. *Lansing State Journal.* 14 July 2000. http://www.lansingstatejournal.com/features/riot/msuofficials.html (14 July 2000).

Tato, S. New policy lets MSU suspend future rioters. *Lansing State Journal.* 14 July 2000. http://www.lansingstatejournal.com/features/riot/suspend.html (14 July 2000).

Terlep, S. City designs plans to deter future melees. *The State News.* 10 September 1997. http://www.statenews.com/editions-fall97/091097/p1_balance.html (13 April 2000).

Terlep, S. 1997. E.L. at odds with students. *The State News.* 11 September.

Terlep, S. 1997. E.L. turmoil angers city. *The State News.* 9 September.

Tio, A. Police hoping to avoid riot repeat. *The Miami Student Online.* 27 April 1999. http://www.mustudent.muohio.edu/1999/042799/festival.html (24 May 2000).

Viator, J. Riot aftermath hits professors. *The New Hampshire.* 7 October 1997. http://www.tnh.unh.edu/Issues/100797/News/profriot.html (23 May 2000).

Vogt, A. 1998. Ex-WSU student has dim recall of riot Jackson tells court of drinking binge. *Spokesman Review.* 11 September.

Vogt, A. 1998. Overnight riot injures 23 police at WSU students spill out of party house for fiery showdown with officers. *The Spokane Review.* 4 May.

Vogt, A. 1998. We know who you are, police tell WSU rioters investigators review videotapes. *The Spokane Review.* 5 May.

Vogt, A. 1999. WSU riot trial ends in acquittal Jamie Jackson not guilty of assaulting deputy. *Spokesman Review.* 22 October.

Vogt, A. WSU tries to polish its image. *Spokane.net.* 16 April 2000. http://www.spokane.net:80/news-story-body.asp?Date=041600&ID=s792186&cat= (17 April 2000).

Whaley, M. 2000. Three strikes, you're out, CU says. *Denver Post.* 29 August.

Wise, T. The kids are all-white: Riots, pathology, and the real meaning of color-blindness. *Something to Think About.* http://www.samrc.com/news/othernews.htm (24 May 2000).

Witkin, G. 1993. Ready for the worst. *US News and World Report.* 114(15):24–27.

Wolper, A. 1999. Newsies aren't police. *Editor & Publisher.* 132(27): 15.

Wyer, W. Riot retrospective. *Oregon Voice.* http://darkwing.uoregon.edu/~ovoice/riots.html (23 May 2000).

Xu, S. 1999. Sentences given in final Penn State U. riot trials. *Daily Collegian–Penn State University.* 17 March.

Zeigler, P. 1998. Entertainment value found in riot at Penn State. *Daily Collegian.* 13 July.

CHAPTER TWELVE
HATE CRIMES

Anonymous. Hate prevention steps for schools. *Stop the Hate.* http://www.stophate.org/preventionsteps.html (5 January 2000).

Anonymous. Responding to hate crimes and bias-motivated incidents on college/university campuses. *CampusSafety.org.* http://campus-safety.org/resources/police/hatecrimes.html (31 July 2000).

Carlson, S. F.B.I. investigates second bombing at historically black Florida ACMU. *The*

Chronicle of Higher Education. 24 September 1999. http://www.ede.org/hec/ (28 September 1999).

Della, C. College by numbers: Hate crimes. *Link Magazine.* April/May 1998. http://www.link mag.com/Link/apr_may_98/rap_sheet.html (26 September 2000).

Dunbar, E. Hate crime patterns in Los Angeles County. *APA Public Policy Office.* http://www. apa.org/ppo/pi/dunbar.html (24 January 2000).

Franklin, K. Psychosocial motivations of hate crime perpetrators. *APA Public Policy Office.* http://www.apa.org/ppo/pi/franklin.html (24 January 2000).

Herek, G. The impact of hate crime victimization. *APA Public Policy.* http://www.apa.org/ ppo/pi/herek.html (5 January 2000).

Hoffman, A., Schuh, J., and Fenske, R. (Eds.) 1998. *Violence on Campus: Defining the Problems, Strategies for Action.* Gaithersburg, Maryland: Aspen Publications.

Hurst, J. 1999. The Matthew Shepard tragedy–crisis and beyond. *About Campus.* 4:3.

Miller, M., Hemenway, D., and Wechsler, H. 1999. Guns at college. *Journal of American College Health.* 48(1):7–12.

Parks, S. 1991. *The Critical Years: Young Adults and the Search for Meaning, Faith, and Commitment.* New York: Harper Collins.

Schackner, B. Wave of Internet hate mail hits Penn State Minorities. *Post-Gazette.* 10 November 1999. http://www.post-gazette. com/regionstate/199911ohhatemail.asp (10 November 2000).

Sherrill, J., and Siegal, D. 1989. *Responding to Violence on Campus.* San Francisco-Oxford: Jossey-Bass.

Siegal, D. 1994. *Campuses Respond to Violent Tragedy.* Phoenix: American Council on Education and The Oryx Press.

Whitaker, L., and Pollard, J. 1993. *Campus Violence: Kinds, Causes, and Cures.* New York: The Haworth Press.

CHAPTER 13
HAZING

Anonymous. Attorney General finds University of Vermont hazing occurred. *CampusSafety.org.* 4 February 2000. http://CampusSafety.org (16 December 1999).

Anonymous. 1997. Citadel punishes cadets for hazing 2 women. *Chronicle of Higher Education.* 43(28):A12.

Anonymous. 2000. Don't let your babies grow up to be Dekes. *Seattle Times.* 19 July.

Anonymous. 1995. Female genital mutilation in Kenya. *Women's International Network News.* 44(29):A8.

Anonymous. 1997. Trial by fire at the Citadel. *People Weekly.* 46(27):160.

Anonymous. University faulted over hockey hazing probe Vt. Attorney General wants anti-hazing law. *Hec News.* 4 February 2000. http://www.edc.org/hec (4 February 2000).

Carter, D. Vermont judge orders some hazing records opened. *CampusSafety.org.* 16 December 1999. http://CampusSafety.org (16 December 1999).

Crane, M. "Hazing Research." 19 April 2000. Response to a survey. (19 April 2000).

Foxman, P. "Hazing Research." 23 May 2000. Response to a survey. (23 May 2000).

Foxman, P. Interviewed by author. 10 March 2000.

Foxman, P. Interviewed by author. 8 March 2000.

Gibeaut, J. 1997. Shield a prosecution sword. *ABA Journal.* 83:36–37.

Gose, B. 1997. Efforts to end fraternity hazing have largely failed, critics charge. *Chronicle of Higher Education.* 43(32):A37–A38.

Guernsey, L. 1997. Two women leave the Citadel, blaming the administration for hazing incidents. *Chronicle of Higher Education.* 43(20):A32.

Hoffer, R. 1999. Praising hazing. *Sports Illustrated.* 91(10):31.

Hoffman, A., Schuh, J., and Fenske, R. 1998. *Violence on Campus: Defining the Problems, Strategies for Action.* Gaithersburg, Maryland:

Aspen Publications.

Hoover, N. 1999. National Survey: Initiation rites and athletics for NCAA sports teams. Alfred University. 30 August.

Katz, J. 1995. Reconstructing masculinity in locker room: The Mentors in Violence Prevention Project. *Harvard Educational Review.* 65(2): 163–174.

Kelleher, S. 2000. Hell Week. *Seattle Times.* 16 July.

Kelleher, S. 2000. More "work parties" and "caves." *Seattle Times.* 16 July.

Kelleher, S. 2000. Times story prompts UW to change rules to rule out hazing. *Seattle Times.* 20 July.

Lively, K. 2000. University of Vermont cancels hockey season. *Chronicle of Higher Education.* 46(22):A56.

Maher, R. 1996. Female genital mutilation: The struggle to eradicate this rite of passage. *Human Rights.* 23(4):12–15.

McInally, D. 2000. Hazing. Interview by Chris Bollinger. 10 May.

McInally, D. "Hazing Research." 15 May 2000. Response to survey. (15 May 2000).

Mravic, M. 2000. Vileness in Vermont. *Sports Illustrated.* 92(4):34.

Mullen, E. Speaker: Hazing must stop everywhere. *Herald Masthead.* 2 April 1997. http://www.wmich.edu/herald/1997/apr/2/28 48.htm (25 October 1999).

Nuwer, H. 1990. *Broken pledges.* Marietta, Georgia: Longstreet Press, Inc.

Nuwer, H. 1999. Hazing-Separating rites from wrongs. *The American Legion Magazine.* 147(1).

Nuwer, H. 1999. *Wrongs of Passage.* Indiana.

Pino, N., and Meier, R. 1999. Gender differences in rape reporting. *Sex Roles: A Journal of Research.* 40(11/12):979–990.

Prichard, J. Felony charges dropped in deaths originally blamed on hazing. *Star-Telegram.* 11 January 1999. http://www/star-traveler.com/ news.doc/1047/1:BPAGE27/1:BPAGE270111 99.html (22 June 2000).

Reisberg, L. 1999. Court says U. of Nebraska had duty to protect pledge from hazing. *Chronicle of Higher Education.* 46(12):A55.

Reisberg, L. 2000. Coming to a campus near you. *Chronicle of Higher Education.* 46(32):A66–A67.

Schubert, R. 2000. UW aims to improve its cooperation with police. *Seattle Post–Intelligencer.* 18 July.

Siegal, D. 1994. *Campuses Respond to Violent Tragedy.* Phoenix: American Council on Education and The Oryx Press.

Silverman, S. 2000. Sorority members settle with victim in ISU hazing case. *The Pantagraph.* 15 June.

Smith, K. Interviewed by author. 8 March 2000.

Taylor, M. Despite hazing scandal, fans stand by UVM. *Boston Globe.* 2 January 2000. http://www.edu.org/hec (2 January 2000).

Welsh, S. 1995. A dangerous rite of passage. *World Press Review.* 42(10):39.

Whitaker, L., and Pollard, J. 1993. *Campus Violence: Kinds, Causes and Cures.* New York: The Haworth Press, Inc.

CHAPTER FOURTEEN
HOMICIDE AND NON-SEXUAL ASSAULT

Abel, D. UNH brawl raises new doubts about fraternities. *Boston Globe.* 20 March 2000. http://www.boston.com/dailyglobe2/080/met ro/UNH_brawl_raises_new_doubts_about_fr aternities+.shtml (20 March 2000).

Alvi, S., and Selbee, K. 1997. Dating status variations and woman abuse. *Violence Against Women.* 3(6):610–628.

Anderson, C. 1994. Investigation confirms murder's claims. *Science.* 265(5171):463.

Anonymous. 1996. Athletes on campuses charged with assault. *Chronicle of Higher Education.* 43(12):A8.

Anonymous. 1995. Authorities investigate why Harvard honor student stabbed her roommate to death and later hanged herself. *Jet.* 88(6):52–53.

Anonymous. 1998. Three injured during half-time band brawl between Southern University and Prairie View A&M. *Jet.* 94(20):51.

Anonymous. 1995. In Brief: Oakland U. student missing for 28 days is found dead. *Chronicle of Higher Education. 42*(8):A4.

Anonymous. 1997. Campus police kill man as he fatally stabs girlfriend at University of Michigan. *Jet. 92*(21):39–40.

Anonymous. 2000. Columbia woman killed in dorm boyfriend later dies on subway tracks. *The Record.* 6 February.

Anonymous. 1996. Death threat found at San Diego State. *Chronicle of Higher Education. 43*(15):A12.

Anonymous. 1997. Family allowed to sue over murdered student. *Chronicle of Higher Education. 43*(41):A10.

Anonymous. 1997. Former Hopkins student sentenced in slaying. *Chronicle of Higher Education. 43*(46):A6.

Anonymous. 1997. In Memoriam: Tamara Sonya Williams. *The Michigan Daily.* 23 September.

Anonymous. 1999. N.C. State player convicted in shooting. *Chronicle of Higher Education. 46*(17):A56.

Anonymous. Security on campus update #173. *Security on Campus.* 11 April 2000. http://campussafety.org (14 April 2000).

Anonymous. 1996. Student killed in shooting at Penn State. *Chronicle of Higher Education. 43*(5):A8.

Anonymous. 1999. Suspect in racial shootings had a troubled past. *Chronicle of Higher Education. 45*(45):A8.

Anonymous. 2000. Suspect in University student's death kills self. *Times Union.* 6 February.

Anonymous. 1998. Two Butte football players charged with murder. *Chronicle of Higher Education. 45*(13):A8.

Anonymous. 1997. Two killed on Michigan campus. *Black News Today.* 24 September.

Anonymous. 1998. Two Maryland men slain during college spring break festivities. *Jet. 93*(23):12.

Anonymous. 1998. Two security officers killed on the job. *Chronicle of Higher Education. 44*(20):A8.

Barrows, M. 2000. Arrest made in UCD assault: Suspect traced to L.A. home. *Sacramento Bee.* 9 April.

Bogel-Allbritten, R., and Allbritten, W. 1991. Courtship violence on campus: A nationwide

survey of student affairs professionals. *NASPA Journal. 28*(4):312–318.

Boone, B. How I could just kill a man. *Oregon Commentator Online.* http://darkwing.uoregon.edu/~ocomment/ocarchive/oc98_99/oc3_6.htmil (23 May 2000).

Burd, S. 1996. Murder of three professors at a thesis defense causes a stunned campus to ask, why? *Chronicle of Higher Education. 43*(2): A14–A15.

Came, B. 1992. Death in a classroom. *Maclean's. 105*(36):44–45.

Campbell, C. 2000. Violence at Georgetown. 30 July. *Washington Post.*

Cohen, J. 1997. Friend may know reason behind attack. *The Michigan Daily.* 25 September.

Dandeneau, C., and Fontaine, J. 1997. Violence in gay and lesbian domestic partnerships. *Sex Roles: A Journal of Research. 36*(5–6):431–432.

Desruisseaux, P. 2000. Student and companion killed in Costa Rica. *Chronicle of Higher Education. 46*(29):A58.

Elliott, P. 1996. Shattering illusions: Same-sex domestic violence. In Claire Renzetti (Ed.), *Violence in Gay and Lesbian Domestic Partnerships.*

Evans, P. 1992. *The Verbally Abusive Relationship.* Holbrook, MA: Bob Adams, Inc. Publishers.

Garnets, L., Herek, G., and Levy, B. 1992. Violence and victimization of lesbians and gay men. In *Hate Crimes.* Newbury Park: Sage Publications.

Geraghty, M. 1997. Hidden pregnancies and babies' deaths raise painful questions for colleges. *Chronicle of Higher Education. 44*(3): A49–A50.

Gleick,E. 1996. Three kids, one death. *Time. 148*(25):69–70.

Gonzales, M. Dorm students back in rooms. *The Greeley Daily Tribune.* 26 September 1996.

Goode, E. 2000. When women find love is fatal. *New York Times.* 15 February.

Gose, B. 2000. Court upholds right of a university to deny degree to student who killed another. *Chronicle of Higher Education. 46*(28):A52.

Hamberger, K. 1996. Intervention in gay male intimate violence requires coordinated efforts on multiple levels. In *Violence in Gay and Lesbian Domestic Partnerships.* New York: Harrington Park Press.

Haworth, K. 1997. Va. Wesleyan suspends 23 athletes after brawl. *Chronicle of Higher Education.* 43(26):A42.

Hepburn, S. 1997. Best friend shocked, hurt by violent death. *The Michigan Daily.* 24 September.

Hepburn, S. 1997. Report details Williams murder. *The Michigan Daily.* 25 September.

Hewitt,B., Harmes, J., Clark, C., Williams, K., and Sellinger, M. 2000. Their paradise lost. *People Weekly.* 53(13):173–177.

Hewitt, B., Longley, A., Brown, S., and Eftimiades, M. 1995. Death at Harvard. *People Weekly.* 43(23):40–43.

Howe, R. 1996. A fatal friendship. *People Weekly.* 46(1):65–71.

Hunnicutt, K. 1998. Introduction to women and violence on campus. In *Violence on Campus: Defining the Problems, Strategies for Action* Allan Hoffman, John Schuh, and Robert Fenske (Eds.), Gaithersburg, Maryland: Aspen Publishers.

Kaihla, P. 1992. Concordia's trials. *Maclean's.* 105(45):52–55.

Kosseff, J. 1997. Campus experts decry, abuse, offer assistance. *The Michigan Daily.* 24 September.

Landolt, M., and Dutton, D. 1997. Power and personality: An analysis of gay male intimate abuse. *Sex Roles: A Journal of Research.* 37(5–6):335–359.

Lively, K. 1997. Many murders on campuses involve neither students nor faculty members. *Chronicle of Higher Education.* 43(28):A46.

Mann, E. Columbia student stabbed to death. *WSN news.* 7 February 2000. http://www.nyu.edu/pubs/wsn/00/02/07/NcolumbiaStab.htm (8 February 2000).

Mann, E. 2000. In wake of Columbia U. killing, security changes not foreseen. *Washington Square News.* 10 February.

Marcus, D. 2000. Murder on campus: Can it be averted? *U.S. News and World Report.* 20 February.

Merrill, G. 1996. Ruling the exceptions: Same-sex battering and domestic violence theory. In *Violence in Gay and Lesbian Domestic Partnerships,* Claire Renzetti and Charles Miley (Eds.), New York: Harrington Park Press.

Murphy, C. 2000. Mother calls GU response to son's death ineffective. *The Washington Post.* 20 July.

Murphy, C. 2000. GU hears testimony in student's death. *Washington Post.* 23 July.

Plona, K. 1997. Murder alarms students, sparks parental fears. *The Michigan Daily.* 24 September.

Prose, F. 1997. Halfway heaven: Diary of a Harvard murder. *People Weekly.* 48(14):43–48.

Prosser, E. Shootings mar campuses nationwide. *The Digital Collegian.* 30 September 1996. http://www.collegian.psu.edu/archive/19996_jan-dec/1996-09-30d01-008.htm (30 May 2000).

Ray, A., and Gold, S. 1996. Gender roles, aggression, and alcohol use in dating relationships. *Journal of Sex Research.* 33:47–55.

Reilly, R. 1998. And the band fought on. *Sports Illustrated.* 89(14):112.

Renzetti, C. M., and Miley, C. H. (Eds.). 1996. *Violence in Gay and Lesbian Domestic Partnerships.* Bingham, NY: Harrington Park Press.

Rickgarn, R. 1989. Violence in residence halls: Campus domestic violence. In Jan Sherrill and Dorothy Siegel (Eds.), *Responding to Violence on Campus.* San Francisco: Jossey-Bass Inc.

Schefrin, N. 2000. Student found stabbed to death in Columbia U. dorm room. *Columbia Daily Spectator.* 7 February.

Schlesinger, L. Murder and sex murder: Psychopathology and psychodynamics. In *Lethal Violence: A Sourcebook on Fatal Domestic, Acquaintance and Stranger Violence.* London: CRC Press.

Shea, C. 1995. Harvard in shock after junior kills her roommate, then hangs herself, as students leave for summer. *Chronicle of Higher Education.* 41(39):A36.

Shook, N., Gerrity, D., Jurich, J., and Segrist, A. 2000. Courtship violence among college students: A comparison of verbally and physically abusive couples. *Journal of Family Violence.* 15(1):1–22.

Stronsnider, K. 1997. Virginia Tech player convicted of assault. *Chronicle of Higher Education.* 43(46):A45.

Thernstrom, M. 1997. *Halfway Heaven.* New York: Doubleday.

Vogt, A. Fraternities suspended due to fight.

Spokane.net. 10 March 2000. http://www.spokane.net:80/news-story-body.asp?Date=031000&ID=s753412&cat= (14 March 2000).

Walker, L. 1980. *Battered Woman.* New York: Harper Collins.

Wanat, T. 1996. Football players' attack on a fraternity house stuns U. of Rhode Island. *Chronicle of Higher Education. 43*(10):A44.

Wolff, A., and Stone, C. 1995. A college problem, too. *Sports Illustrated. 83*(7):16–18.

CHAPTER FIFTEEN
ARSON AND BOMBING

Anonymous. Arson blamed in dorm fire. *Log Cabin Democrat.* 19 September 1998. http://thecabin.net/stories/091998/new_arson.html (22 June 2000).

Anonymous. Authorities say fatal dorm fire a hazing prank. *The Topeka Capital-Journal.* 31 October 1998. http://cjonline.com/stories/103198/new_dormfires.shtml (22 June 2000).

Anonymous. Arson prevention for America's churches and synagogues. *National Arson Prevention Initiative Announcements.* 26 June 1996. http://www.fire-investigators.org/churches.htm (21 June 2000).

Anonymous. 1998. Benedict College victim of arson. *Chronicle of Higher Education. 44*(27):A11.

Anonymous. Bomb threats and physical security planning. *Security Resource Net.* http://nsi.org/Library/Terrorism/bombthreat.html (21 June 2000).

Anonymous. Common sense key to fighting dorm fires. *Herald Online.* 2 December 1999. http://herald.wku.edu/opinion/dormfire.html (22 June 2000).

Anonymous. 1999. Dorm fire survivor still hurting; memory problems more frustrating than his physical injuries. *Cincinnati Enquirer.* 26 August.

Anonymous. Dorm fire is legal rollercoaster. *Journal Sentinel Online.* 22 July 1999. http://www.jsonline.com/news/nat/ap/jul99/ap-dorm-fire072299.asp (22 June 2000).

Anonymous. 1998. Fatal fire at Murray State ruled arson. *Chronicle of Higher Education. 45*(6):A10.

Anonymous. 1997. Five fires hit U. of Miami in week; 1 ruled arson. *Chronicle of Higher Education. 43*(22):A8.

Anonymous. 1999. Eight students arrested for bombs on two campuses. *Chronicle of Higher Education. 45*(33):A14.

Anonymous. 2000. Ex-student's trial in dorm fire at Murray delayed until October. *Cincinnati Enquirer.* 1 February.

Anonymous. 1999. Five once charged in Murray dorm fire file suit alleging wrongful arrest. *Lexington Herald-Leader.* 27 October.

Anonymous. 1998. Five students charged in Murray State fire. *Chronicle of Higher Education. 45*(11):A12.

Anonymous. 1999. Four men convicted of prank calls. *The Tennessean.* 15 August.

Anonymous. 1999. Jeanne Clery disclosure of campus security policy and campus crime statistics act. *Federal Register. 59*(82).

Anonymous. 2000. Jury convicts Fla. hate-crime bomber. *UPI.* 23 June.

Anonymous. 2000. A look at campus crime. *The Chronicle of Higher Education. 46*(40):A49.

Anonymous. Man arrested in university bombings. *ABC News.* 1 October 1999. http://abcnews.go.com/sections/us/DailyNews/bombing991001.html (17 January 2000).

Anonymous. The Michael Minger Act. *Campus Safety.* http://campussafety.org/publicpolicy/laws/ky/minger/index.html (21 June 2000).

Anonymous. 1999. Murray State student charged in fire death. *Chronicle of Higher Education. 45*(42):A10.

Anonymous. Patton's sprinkler stance frustrates victim's mother. *The Courier-Journal.* 15 November 1998. http://www.courier-journal.com/localnews/1998/9811/15/19981115pattonsprinkler.html (22 June 2000).

Anonymous. 2000. Shock of FAMU bombings fade as suspects trail nears. *Florida Today.* 16 June.

Anonymous. 1996. Smoke-bomb prank leads to death. *Chronicle of Higher Education.* *43*(10):A9.

Anonymous. 1998. Student killed by homemade bomb. *Chronicle of Higher Education.* *45*(6):A12.

Anonymous. 1996. Student pleads guilty to April bomb threat. *Chronicle of Higher Education.* *43*(17):A9.

Anonymous. Target arson. *Fire Investigators.* http://www.fire-investigators.org/ aaw/ArsonFac.htm (21 June 2000).

Anonymous. 1995. Three arson fires cause more than $1 million in damage to Clark Atlanta University Buildings. *Jet.* *87*(22):22–24.

Anonymous. 1999. University improves safety at dorm where fatal fire set. *The Tennessean.* 22 August.

Anonymous. 1999. White man arrested in bombings at Florida A&M University. *Jet.* *96*(20):18.

Barker, A. 1994. *Arson: A Review of the Psychiatric Literature.* Oxford: Oxford University Press.

Bridges, T., and Martin, D. Little information emerges on Lombardi. *Tallahassee Democrat Online.* http://www.tdo.com/local/famu bomb/1002.loc.whoheis.htm (10 July 2000).

George, J. Students sympathetic toward fire suspects. *Kentucky Connect.* 11 January 1999. http://www.kentuckyconnect.com/herald-leader/news/011199/local/docs/11dormfire.ht m (22 June 2000).

Gerth, J. Fatal Murray fire prompts calls for changes. *The Courier-Journal.* 1 October 1998. http://www.courier-journal.com/local-news/1998/9810/01/19981001dormfire.html (22 June 2000).

Green, M. FAMU takes extra measures for safety. *Tallahassee Democrat Online.* http://www. tdo.com/local/famubomb/famuan/0927famu an.htm (10 July 2000).

Hefner, D. On FAMU campus: feelings of justice, safety and relief. *Tallahassee Democrat Online.* http://www.tdo.com/local/famu bomb/0624.loc.verdictreax.htm (10 July 2000).

Howell, L. 1996. Arsons and racism. *Christian Century.* *113*(24):772–774.

Kennish, J. Preparing for bomb threats. http://kennish.com/bombthreat (21 June 2000).

Levin, B. 1976. Psychological characteristics of fire setters. In National Fire Protection Association, *Arson: Some Problems and Solutions.* Boston: National Fire Protection Association Publications.

MacDonald, J., Shaughnessy, R., and Galvin, J. 1977. *Bombers and Firesetters.* Springfield: Charles C. Thomas.

MacDonald, J., Shaughnessy, R., and Galvin, J. 1977. Bombing and firesetting. In *Bombers and Firesetters.* Springfield: Charles C. Thomas.

MacDonald, J., Shaughnessy, R., and Galvin, J. 1977. Bombers and their mothers. In *Bombers and Firesetters.* Springfield: Charles C. Thomas.

MacDonald, J., Shaughnessy, R., and Galvin, J. 1977. Victims and targets. In *Bombers and Firesetters.* Springfield: Charles C. Thomas.

MacDonald, J., Shaughnessy, R., and Galvin, J. 1977. Bomb disposal. In *Bombers and Firesetters.* Springfield: Charles C. Thomas.

MacDonald, J., Shaughnessy, R., and Galvin, J. 1977. Bomb threats. In *Bombers and Firesetters.* Springfield: Charles C. Thomas.

MacDonald, J., Shaughnessy, R., and Galvin, J. 1977. Criminal investigation. In *Bombers and Firesetters.* Springfield: Charles C. Thomas.

Malone, J. 1999. Chandler can't punish prosecutor in dorm-fire case. *The Courier-Journal.* 12 February.

Pjankuch, T. 1999. Aid sought in FAMU bomb case, recording photo released; more violence threatened. *Florida Times-Union.* 30 September.

Pjankuch, T., and Pendleton, R. 1999. Arrest in FAMU bombs, citizens recognized man's photo, voice in the release recording. *The Florida Times-Union.* 2 October.

Poynter, C. Two agencies left out of arson probe. *The Courier-Journal.* 23 January 1999. http://www.courier-journal.com/local-news/1999/9901/23/990123murrayprobe.htm l (22 June 2000).

Poynter, C. Murray fire suspect recall night of pranks. *The Courier-Journal.* 8 November 1998. http://www.courier-journal.com/local-news/1998/9811/08/19981108dorm.html (22 June 2000).

Poynter, C. Students move off campus after fire. *The Courier-Journal.* 13 October 1998. http://www.courier-journal.com/local-news/1998/9810/13/19981013murr.html (22 June 2000).

Poynter, C., and Malone, J. Murray dormitory fire was arson, police say. *The Courier-Journal.* 23 September 1998. http://www.courier-journal.com/localnews/1998/9809/23/19980923murrayfire.html (22 June 2000).

Rainey, T. Recent death sparks fire safety education. *Daily Egyptian.* 2 October 1998. http://www.dailyegyptian.com/fall98/10-2-98/fire.html (22 June 2000).

Rosica, J. Bomber guilty on 6 counts. *Tallahassee Democrat Online.* http://www.tdo.com/local/famubomb/0624.loc.lombardi.htm (10 July 2000).

Rosica, J. Ex-friend describes Lombardi. *Tallahassee Democrat Online.* http://www.tdo.com/local/famubomb/0621.loc.lombardi.htm (10 July 2000).

Rosica, J. Transcripts have bomber planning alibi. *Tallahassee Democrat Online.* 2 July 2000.

http://www.tdo.com/local/famubomb/0703.loc.lombardi.htm (10 July 2000).

Rosica, J. Trial could go to jury today. *Tallahassee Democrat Online.* http://www.tdo.com/local/famubomb/0623.loc.lombardi.htm (10 July 2000).

Rosica, J. Witness: He hid book on bombs. *Tallahassee Democrat Online.* http://www.tdo.com/local/famubomb/0622.loc.lombardi.htm (10 July 2000).

University of Georgia. *How Fast it Burned.* Produced and directed by the University of Georgia. 22 minutes. University of Georgia, 1989.

Van Biema, D. 1993. Clues in the ashes. *Time.* *142*(20):58–60.

Vance, D. After fire, safety on minds of Murray State students. *World Wide Edition of The Kentucky Post.* 7 November 1998. http://www.kypost.com/news.murray110798.html (22 June 2000).

Wilson, R. 2000. Radical group takes credit for lab fire. *Chronicle of Higher Education.* *46*(23):A18.

NAME INDEX

SUBJECT INDEX

ABOUT THE AUTHORS

John Nicoletti, Ph.D.

Dr. John Nicoletti is the co-founder of Nicoletti-Flater Associates with his spouse Lottie Flater and has been a police psychologist in the Denver metro area for more than twenty-five years. Over the last ten years, the Nicoletti-Flater private practice has expanded into the field of violence and violence prevention. After years of working with national corporations and government agencies, including the U. S. Postal Service, Dr. Nicoletti has established himself as a national expert in workplace violence.

During the mid-nineties, he expanded his expertise to help schools trying to develop violence prevention programs. On April 20, 1999, he was on the front line. Forty-five minutes after the first shots rang at Columbine High School he was on the scene assisting at the Command Center. In the weeks and months that followed, Dr. Nicoletti aided the community in many ways by conducting numerous debriefings and counseling sessions for law enforcement personnel, SWAT, the bomb squad, victim assistants, and investigators.

Dr. Nicoletti has received many awards for his distinguished contributions to the field of psychology. Most notably, in 1996 the Colorado Psychological Association awarded him the E. Ellis Graham Award and in 1998 the American Psychological Association awarded him the Karl F. Heiser Presidential Award for advocacy on behalf of professional psychology. On September 29, 1999, Dr. Nicoletti was awarded a distinction from the House of Representatives of the Commonwealth of Pennsylvania for "... his vital and meaningful work in helping our country's citizens overcome the horror and tragedy of violence, and for his commitment to eradicating violence in schools and the workplace. . . ."

In the last few years, Dr. Nicoletti has brought this expertise to colleges struggling to protect their learning environments. He is a co-presenter of the P.A.S.S. Program (Personal Advantage Safety Seminar), an experiential psychological and non-strength-based self-defense training conducted on numerous college campuses for students, faculty, and staff. Dr. Nicoletti has presented workshops on preventing college violence to dozens of campuses across the nation. Recently he addressed the BACCHUS & GAMMA Peer Education Network Regional Conference in the spring of 1999, and the Colorado/Wyoming Counseling Center Conference in May 2000.

Dr. Nicoletti has published several books and manuals as well. In 1997, he co-authored *Violence Goes to Work,* a very well received prevention manual for employers. Dr. Nicoletti also co-wrote and published, *Violence Goes to School: Lessons Learned from Columbine.*

Dr. Nicoletti received his Ph.D. in Clinical Psychology from Colorado State University in 1972. He has completed specialized training from the FBI in such areas as criminal profiling and tracking, the analysis of threats and violence, and trauma intervention techniques. In addition to all the above-mentioned accomplishments, Dr. Nicoletti also conducts preemployment screening and on-site evaluations for employees working on Antarctica. He is a member of the Association of Threat Assessment Professionals and the International Association of the Chiefs of Police. Some of his speaking engagements include: The Federal Bureau of Investiga-tion, United Airlines, Johns Manville, Army Research Labs, Ratheon Polar Services, U.S. West, U.S. Department of Energy, U.S. Postal Service, Arapahoe Community College, Colorado/Wyoming Counseling Center Conference, Regis University, University of Colorado–Boulder, University of Denver, and University of Maine

Sally Spencer-Thomas, Psy.D.

Dr. Sally Spencer-Thomas received her doctorate in psychology from the University of Denver in 1995. Since then she has worked for both Regis University and Nicoletti-Flater Associates in the capacities of counselor and health promotion specialist. She is the state coordinator for the BACCHUS & GAMMA Peer Education Network and supervises Choices, the award-winning peer education program at Regis.

In prior work as an employee of the Denver Police Department, she served as a Victim Advocate, counseling families in crisis. Dr. Spencer-Thomas received specialized training in Posttraumatic Stress Disorder (PTSD) from the Boston VA Medical Center.

Dr. Spencer-Thomas is a counselor, peer education mentor, and affiliate faculty member at Regis University. Through collaborative efforts between Nicoletti-Flater Associates and Regis University, she has promoted effective programming on violence prevention for women on college campuses.

Chris Bollinger, M.S.

Chris Bollinger is the Director of Residence Life at Heidelberg College in Tiffin, Ohio. Prior to this position, Mr. Bollinger served as the Assistant Director of Residence Life at Regis University, an Area Coordinator at Allegheny College, a Residence Manager at the University of Charleston, and as a Resident Assistant at Regis University. He holds an M.S. degree in Human Resource Management and has had many years of experience working in Residence Life.

Throughout his positions, Chris has been committed to education. He has facilitated staff training sessions on sexual assault, diversity, conflict resolution, responding to harassment, how to make successful referrals, and crisis management and follow up. He also served as a judicial hearing officer and facilitated a judicially required program on alcohol education. As a front-line responder to crises, he learned to evaluate crisis situations, assemble a response team, and coordinate necessary follow up.